THE CIVILIZATION OF THE AMERICAN INDIAN SERIES

THE
MIAMI
INDIANS

UNIVERSITY OF OKLAHOMA PRESS : *Norman*

THE MIAMI INDIANS

By Bert Anson

INTERNATIONAL STANDARD BOOK NUMBER: 0–8061–0901–7

LIBRARY OF CONGRESS CATALOG CARD NUMBER: 74–108793

COPYRIGHT 1970 BY THE UNIVERSITY OF OKLAHOMA PRESS, PUBLISHING DIVISION OF THE UNIVERSITY. COMPOSED AND PRINTED AT NORMAN, OKLAHOMA, U.S.A., BY THE UNIVERSITY OF OKLAHOMA PRESS. FIRST EDITION.

To
William F. Hale and Forest D. Olds
who have given able and unselfish leadership
to the Miami Indians

Preface

The student of the American frontier quickly becomes aware of the constant conflict between the Indians and the frontiersmen, which helped to shape the destinies of both. White men displaced the red, but failed to eradicate or completely assimilate them; in the process, the whites seldom tried to understand their adversaries and therefore preserved few systematic observations of the Indians. Today's historian of the frontier can sympathize with the predicament of early observers to some extent, for he, too, lacks adequate resources for understanding the Amerindian peoples.

Special areas of study have been developed to satisfy man's curiosity about his forebears. Archaeology, anthropology, ethnohistory, linguistics, and other disciplines have secured and analyzed much information about the first Americans. Treatises on the Indians were begun with the first observations by Europeans and definitive histories of some of the more important tribes have been written, but accounts of many other tribes remain fragmentary. Tribal history emphasizes one group of people who formed a political entity. Only in such a record does the language of the American Indians reflect their conviction and attitude that from their own tribe sprang the "true men" and all others were strangers, that their folk heroes were giants while those of other tribes were pygmies.

The Miamis are one of that large number of tribes to whom many references have been made but for whom there is no cohesive historical account. One of the small group of tribes which comprise the Illinois division of the Algonquian linguistic family, the Miamis participated in many of the incidents involving Europeans and Indians in the Great Lakes region from 1658 to 1847. French, British, and American accounts of battles, intrigues, and travels in this region include scattered bits of information about the tribe, under its various names, but few of them are more than isolated glimpses. The Miamis, in spite of many distinctive attributes in their past, emerged as a pivotal tribe only during the French and British imperial wars, the Miami Confederacy wars of the eighteenth century, and the treaty-making period of the nineteenth century.

Although the Miami tribe has enjoyed moments of power and influence, it has also suffered bitter defeats. It has managed to preserve its identity for a century while divided into two segments and despite efforts to terminate its political existence. A resurgence of prestige and personal pride has accompanied its recent successes in the courts.

Although the name *Miami* has been widely adopted and is familiar to all Americans, there have been few efforts to assemble the available information about the tribe into a convenient whole. This book was undertaken to provide such a synthesis, spanning the years from the Miamis' entry into historical records to the present and emphasizing the few occasions when they played a major role in the American experience. These occurred when the Miamis lost the protection of larger surrounding tribes and faced alone the threats posed by the white man. Unfortunately, in order to accomplish this task it has been necessary at times for me to go far afield—to prepare the way, so to speak, for Miami participation in some events by first analyzing the causes of those events in some far-off place, such as London, Paris, or Washington. The history of the Miamis must therefore include periods in which they were passive instruments of changing forces over which they had no control.

Overemphasis can be avoided when the active and spectacular is accompanied by the passive and commonplace, when a particular incident is put into the context of contemporary historical events, which it seldom dominates. The chronicles of a people should also be placed in proper perspective with the external forces about them.

The history of an Indian tribe necessarily submerges the fascinating details of personal exploits, peculiar customs, or bizarre events, leaving the pleasures of depicting the drama of individual response to life's challenges to the historical novelist. A battle won or lost, an annuity debauch, a marriage or puberty ceremony, or those many events which are epochal in the lives of individuals may be of no significance to the tribal group. Only events, customs, and individual exploits which contributed to the continuity of the tribe can be given historical recognition. The Miamis recognized this fact when they perpetuated the memory of great men by bestowing their names upon talented young warriors who might emulate them.

Historical judgments, interpretations, and points of reference cannot be avoided, even if they are evident only in the material which is included or omitted. Nevertheless, a history is suspect if the author indulges in an emotional catharsis when writing of an Indian tribe: the contemporary words of Indians or white men may have a far greater impact than the contrived emotional involvement of a historical researcher.

To an unusual degree, I am indebted to those who have collected and published primary material dealing with French and British exploration and trade on the frontier. United States government documents, especially those of the Bureau of Indian Affairs, are indispensable. The encyclopedic works of Frederick W. Hodge and John R. Swanton published by the Bureau of American Ethnology provide guidance for the uniform spelling of Indian names, although I have arbitrarily adopted the most customarily used and simply spelled versions of Miami names.

Since Miami residence was largely confined to three limited

areas, there is a great body of local historical material which serves as flesh to the bones of this survey. It comes from many places: outstanding scholars are constantly revising the significant themes of American frontier history, thereby enlarging our knowledge of the Indian and his way of life; new studies of Amerindian civilizations are being published annually by university presses and others; and hitherto neglected but essential information is being assembled in the legal evidence compiled by law firms, the Indian Claims Commission, and the decisions of the United States Court of Claims. I have used all of these sources.

The Bureau of Indian Affairs, the Indiana State Historical Society Library, the Ball State University Library, the Indiana University Library, the Oklahoma State Historical Society Library, the Thomas Gilcrease Institute of American History and Art, and the library of the American Philosophical Society have been generous in their assistance to me. *Indiana Magazine of History* granted permission for the liberal use of material published therein.

The Miami chiefs at the time of this writing, William F. Hale and Forest D. Olds, have made accessible to me materials which they have collected after years of labor, as well as many interesting Miami tales which cannot be included in a tribal history.

I acknowledge with gratitude the generous grant-in-aid from the Eli Lilly Foundation which has helped to make this book possible.

My colleagues sympathized with the pangs so evident while this volume was in preparation, and student assistants rendered invaluable aid as they labored with unfamiliar Indian names. Above all, my assistant, Paul W. Wehr, took countless hours from his own research to eliminate errors in grammar, construction, and concept. After all these efforts, I alone am responsible for any errors or misinterpretations which may remain.

BERT ANSON

Muncie, Indiana
September, 1969

Contents

xiii

Illustrations

xv

Maps

xvii

THE
MIAMI
INDIANS

1
EARLY MIAMI LIFE

Jean Nicolet led the French penetration of the western Great Lakes area in 1634 and made the first European contact with many new but friendly tribes of the great Algonquian linguistic family. His explorations were limited, for after 1649 the Ottawa and Iroquoian Huron tribes of the west were subjected to relentless attacks by the Five Nations of the Iroquois, who gathered furs to sell to Dutch and English traders. Despite this distraction, the French expanded their trading posts and missions west of Lake Huron. They were also involved during the 1670's in a decade of warfare waged by their allies, the Chippewa, Ottawa, and Huron tribes, against the Sioux. These wars produced French soldiers who were remarkable explorers and frontier diplomats. Only a few years elapsed before these men and their Jesuit and Recollet missionary counterparts completed the explorations begun by Nicolet. In the process, they introduced many western native American tribes to the record of history.

One of these, a part of the Illinois division of the Algonquian family, finally became known as the Miamis.[1] The first European

[1] Frederick Webb Hodge (ed.), *Handbook of American Indians North of Mexico,* I, 852–55, lists eighty-three variations of Miami tribal names. I have changed the

to hear of them was Father Gabriel Dreuillettes, who was informed by the Chippewas in 1658 that a small tribe which they called *Oumamik,* or "people of the peninsula," had recently migrated to the tip of Green Bay. Later the same year when Dreuillettes was at the mouth of the Fox River, which debouches into the head of the bay, he reported no contact with the new group. However, he believed Pierre Radisson and Jean Baptiste Des Groseilliers had visited them about 1654.[2] Historian Jules Tailhan thought Nicolas Perrot might also have heard of the Miamis in 1654, but Tailhan believed they had recently moved to a village about sixty miles up the Fox River at the portage to the Wisconsin River.[3] Bacqueville de La Potherie, who served with Le Moyne d'Iberville against the Hudson's Bay Company and as a royal official in New France, disputed this and claimed the Oumamiks, together with two bands of Mascoutins and Kickapoos, remained near the mouth of the Fox until about 1668. The devastating invasions by Iroquois war parties had begun in 1649, and the village near Green Bay contained only displaced fragments of these three tribes. At least one Miami band fled across the Mississippi but returned east after encountering the Sioux. Other bands took temporary refuge near the mouth of the Illinois River, while some probably fled north of the Grand River in Michigan to avoid the Iroquois.[4]

French *Huron* to the Anglicized *Wyandot* in subsequent references, although the name properly applies to only one division of the tribe, which moved south after 1649. *Ibid.,* 584–91.

[2] "Relation of 1657–1658," in Reuben Gold Thwaites (ed.), *The Jesuit Relations and Allied Documents,* XLIV, 247. Dreuillettes did not reach the Oumamik village, but secured his estimate of 24,000 inhabitants from "two Frenchmen," probably Radisson and Groseilliers, and from Indian accounts. Thwaites refers to this *Relation* as anonymously authored but states that Dreuillettes is one of the missionaries who is quoted.

[3] Emma Helen Blair (ed.), *The Indian Tribes of the Upper Mississippi Valley and Region of the Great Lakes,* I, 321. Tailhan was librarian of the École de Ste Geneviève in Paris and for many years was an agent for Jesuit missions abroad. He edited and published Perrot's *Mémoire,* included in *ibid.,* I, 31–272, with Tailhan's Preface, 25–30.

[4] "History of the Savage Peoples Who Are Allies of New France," by Claude Charles Le Roy, Bacqueville de La Potherie, in *ibid.,* I, 273–372; II, 13–136, 316–17, 321.

Father Claude Allouez was sent to Green Bay in 1669 to found the mission which he named St. Francis Xavier, usually called La Baye. He may have known of a village at the Fox-Wisconsin portage only by word of mouth, but he began the recorded history of the Miami tribe in his report to Claude Dablon, father superior of the Jesuit order at Quebec.[5] When Perrot visited a palisaded village at the portage from the Fox River in 1671, he found distinct groups of the Mascoutins, Kickapoos, and Miamis, and Miami Chief Tetinchoua greeted him in ceremonies worthy of royalty.[6]

Father Jacques Marquette, who reached the village in 1673 as he progressed on his momentous journey with Louis Jolliet, expanded the scanty information about the Oumamiks. He was impressed by their appearance, intelligence, and habits which he called superior to those of their allies in the village, probably because they listened courteously to his sermons. Later, two Oumamik warriors served as his guides across the portage to the Wisconsin River.[7]

Dablon usually referred to all the tribes south and west of Lake Michigan to the Mississippi River as the Illinois Indians. This grouping, probably a form of convenience, actually was fairly accurate. Most of the tribes belonged to the Illinois branch of the central division of the Algonquian family and were closely related. Conjectures about them must substitute for certainties until about 1700. After that date, even though its tribal characteristics were gathered in piecemeal fashion, the tribe whose many names the French converted to *Miami* can be identified with reasonable accuracy.

[5] "Relation of 1669–70: On the Mission of Saint Francis Xavier on the 'Bay of Stinkards,' or rather 'of Stinking Waters'; from Father Allouez to the Reverend Father Superior," in Thwaites, *Jesuit Relations*, LIV, 207, 227–31. Allouez omitted a description of the Miamis at this time, since only a small group was in the village with the Mascoutins, one day's canoe voyage up the Fox River.

[6] "Memoir on the Manners, Customs, and Religion of the Savages of North America," by Nicolas Perrot, in Blair, *Indian Tribes*, I, 222–23, 231–72. "Adventures of Nicolas Perrot, by La Potharie, 1665–1670," in Louise Phelps Kellogg, *Early Narratives of the Northwest, 1634–1699*, 83–87.

[7] "The Mississippi Voyage of Jolliet and Marquette, 1673," with Introduction by Claude Dablon, in Kellogg, *Early Narratives*, 323–36.

The Miamis contributed to discord among the Illinois tribes. As early as 1683—they had allied themselves with the French—they established a large village in the vicinity of Fort St. Louis, near Starved Rock on the Illinois River, where Henri de Tonti had collected his Illinois allies and a band of Shawnee fugitives.[8] Most of the Miamis resisted the Iroquois, and tradition credits one war party with the annihilation of an Iroquois force near present-day Terre Haute on the Wabash River in 1690. Even so, a party of about one hundred warriors from a separated Miami band became allies of the Senecas and Onondagas, who raided Tonti's command the same year. La Potherie described the deviousness of at least one Miami village, which welcomed a Shawnee war party returning with Iroquois captives, but after the Shawnees had departed, the same village sent two ambassadors with an Iroquois army as far as Lake Ontario.[9]

By the last decade of the seventeenth century, Iroquois hegemony in the west began to lose its force, though Iroquois influence never disappeared. The efforts of Governor Louis de Buade, Comte de Frontenac, the costly attrition of their wars of conquest, and the stronger resistance of French-led and French-armed Indians caused the Iroquois to contract their activities after 1684. The warring tribes finally ended hostilities in a great conference held at Montreal in 1701 at which Chichikatalo was the Miami spokesman. The Five Nations permitted or sponsored resettlement of the area south of Lake Erie by bands from their own confederacy and by the Shawnee, Wyandot, and Delaware tribes. At the same time, the Illinois tribes which had retreated to the west and north began to

---

[8] Ibid., 219–20.

[9] "Memoir on La Salle's Discoveries, by Tonty, 1678–1690 (1693)," in *ibid.*, 305–309. De Courtemanche led the Miami war party against the Iroquois east of Lake Michigan. Pierre François Xavier de Charlevoix, *History and General Description of New France*, IV, 269–70. La Salle's western confederacy of Indians, formed by 1680 against the Iroquois, included the Miamis, but they became the least reliable tribe of the confederacy. Louise Phelps Kellogg, *The French Regime in Wisconsin and the Northwest*, 219, 234, 250. Tonti's name is sometimes spelled *Tonty*, but the former spelling will be used here.

penetrate or return to the present-day southern Michigan, Illinois, Indiana, and Ohio area.[10]

The Miamis led this eastward migratory movement, sponsored by their French allies. Their vanguard position was not wholly of their own choosing. The Miamis west of Lake Michigan were intruders and strangers, even though among their relatives and allies. Chippewa, Sioux, Sauk (Sac), and Fox wars made the area west of Lake Michigan an uncomfortable refuge. Moreover, the French needed the fur trade and the most productive trapping areas lay between the Great Lakes and the Ohio River. The Potawatomis and Kickapoos were also migrating eastward from the crowded Mississippi River borders; since the bands often moved together, the dispersed Indian tribes gradually resumed the entities they had formed before their flight from the Iroquois.

The Miamis probably had less to fear from the Iroquois than did their Illinois allies, but their eastward movement was slow and thus casts doubt on their later pretentions of long residence in the Wabash and Miami valleys. Marquette, Dablon, and La Salle gave the name *Miamis River* to the present St. Joseph River, which flows into Lake Michigan on the east, because of the Miami village found at its mouth in 1669. This was the tribe's eastern outpost when La Salle built Fort Miamis at the site during the winter of 1679–80. When the French erected St. Joseph Mission there, they also gave the river its present name. Between 1686 and 1693, another St. Joseph Mission and a fort were constructed at a bend in the river about sixty miles above its mouth. A village of Miamis and Potawatomis sprang up on the site, about four miles downstream from the crossing place of the Great Sauk Trail and now the loca-

<hr>

[10] Blair, *Indian Tribes*, I, 348–50; II, 132–36, 254–55. Francis Parkman, *Count Frontenac and New France Under Louis XIV*, 471–73. Mitchell's map of 1755 shows the western boundary of Iroquois influence extending from the Illinois River to Chicago, or "Quadoghe." Frank M. Setzler, speculates on the woodland origin of the Algonquians in "Archeological Perspectives in the Northern Mississippi Valley," in *Essays in Historical Anthropology of North America, Published in Honor of John R. Swanton,* in *Smithsonian Miscellaneous Collections,* Vol. 100, pp. 253–90.

tion of Niles, Michigan. This village remained the principal center for the Miamis for a quarter of a century.[11]

By 1690, another Miami village, probably of the Wea band of the tribe, was located where Chicago now stands. Sieur de Montet was commandant of the little garrison placed there, and Father Pierre François Pinet served its Mission of the Guardian Angel.[12] The following year, a Miami band accompanied Tonti to the straits between Lakes Huron and Erie and settled near the Ottawa villages. The Sieur de La Durantaye said in 1687 that the Miamis had once resided at the straits, and they were present when he traveled from the Illinois River to Fort Detroit and nearby Fort St. Joseph, then under the command of Daniel Greysolon, Sieur Dulhut.[13]

The Miamis were not naïve tools of French colonial policy; their migration was only partly one of cooperation. While it is not possible to identify all of the reasons for their temporary disenchantment with the French, the latter's policy of concentrating traders and soldiers at a few posts which the Indians were induced to visit began in 1696, bringing increasing numbers of Chippewa and Ottawa villages into the Detroit area. Antoine de La Mothe Cadillac, who founded Detroit in 1701, admired the Miamis, but, influenced by a Miami feud with the Ottawas which developed after Sioux attacks on the former, he sent an armed force to overawe them in 1707.[14] The tribe accepted the rebuke, and a party of Miamis was led by Jean Baptiste Bissot, Sieur de Vincennes, to aid Commandant Charles Renaud Dubuisson when Detroit was threatened by a Fox siege in 1712. The Miamis were not disposed to accept French domination without resistance, however, and the Detroit

[11] Kellogg, *French Regime,* 204. "Memoir on La Salle's Discoveries, by Tonty, 1678–1690 (1693)," in Kellogg, *Early Narratives,* 288, 299.

[12] "The Voyage of St. Cosme, 1698–1699," in Kellogg, *Early Narratives,* 346–47. Milo M. Quaife, *Chicago and the Old Northwest, 1676–1835,* 40–42.

[13] "Memoir on La Salle's Discoveries, by Tonty, 1678–1690 (1693)," in Kellogg, *Early Narratives,* 308–309.

[14] Bernard DeVoto, *The Course of Empire,* 153. Milo M. Quaife, *The Western Country in the 17th Century,* 69–71. Cadillac was appointed commandant in the west in 1794. He called the Miamis "fine people, humane and polite," but so prone to intratribal wars that they were in danger of extinction. Charlevoix, *History and General Description of New France,* V, 185–88, 202–203.

band soon drifted south to the headwaters of the Maumee River, once called the Miami of the Lakes.[15]

Meanwhile, the Wea band collected in villages on the middle Wabash between the mouths of the Tippecanoe and Vermilion rivers, and the Piankeshaw bands moved eastward to the banks of the lower Wabash. At the same time, the larger Potawatomi tribe began to displace the Miamis in the hunting grounds south of Lake Michigan and on the St. Joseph River.

The Miami bands reluctantly moved from the vicinity of the Great Lakes at about the same time the Shawnees and Delawares, distant relatives of the Miamis, were moving into the area east of the Scioto River. These eastern tribes, who soon allied themselves with the Miamis although they were still under the influence of the powerful Iroquois, brought with them samples of goods secured from English traders. Perhaps the first Miami contact with the English was made on the upper Great Lakes as early as 1685.[16]

There was also a rapid increase in the number of Chippewa, Potawatomi, and Ottawa villages in the Detroit area, crowding these hunting grounds. Although we cannot be certain, the Miamis may have occupied parts of the region east of the Wabash before the incursions of the Iroquois. It was fertile, and Miami villages quickly sprang up as far east as the Scioto River, so that by 1725, the Miamis were firmly established in the area which they soon called their historic homeland.

From French accounts of the Miamis before they reached the Maumee, about 1712, anthropologists and ethnohistorians have constructed a fairly satisfactory description of the tribe. The task of differentiating Indian tribes is not an easy one. It is especially complicated when they live near each other and acknowledge close relationships which even may indicate a common origin. Their

[15] Blair, *Indian Tribes,* II, 123–32. Pierre-Georges Roy, "Sieur de Vincennes Identified," *Indiana Historical Society Publications,* VII (1911), 45–68.

[16] Verner W. Crane, *The Southern Frontier, 1670–1732,* 62–63, tells of the efforts of Francis Nicholson, governor of Maryland and later of Virginia, to secure the aid of the colonies of New York and South Carolina in Great Lakes exploration and trade. Kellogg, *Early Narratives,* 230–31, 254–55, discusses Albany merchant Johannes Roseboom's expedition to Mackinac in 1685.

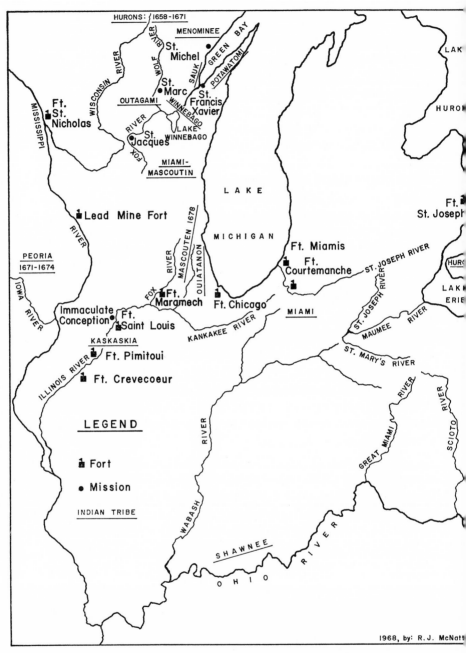

The West, 1650–1700. Adapted from Louise Phelps Kellogg, *The French Regime in Wisconsin and the Northwest*.

own accounts, linguistic connections, political organization, cultural habits, and especially their kinship systems all contain material basic to identification. Much of the information about the Miamis has been assembled from the observations of early French traders, explorers, and priests by W. Vernon Kinietz[17] and George Irving Quimby.[18] For information secured at a later date, we owe much to Henry Rowe Schoolcraft,[19] who wrote voluminously of the Chippewas and their Algonquian relatives. The incidental observations of treaty commissioners and works by such artists as George Winter or James Otto Lewis are descriptive of the Miamis only after a long period of contact with European culture.[20]

The Miamis had no legends or myths of previous migrations. Even Little Turtle's frequently repeated statement that "my Fathers kindled the first fire at Detroit; thence they extended their lines to the headwaters of the Scioto; thence to its mouth; thence down the Ohio to the mouth of the Wabash and thence to Chicago over Lake Michigan" may refer only to the period beginning about 1700.[21] Miami preference for the region nearer the Great Lakes after the menace of Iroquois war parties vanished in the Wabash Valley casts a reasonable doubt on their claim the tribe had formerly occupied the area between the Scioto and the Wabash.

Linguistic evidence can be used to support the tribe's claim to earlier occupation. The other Illinois tribes—Kaskaskias, Ca-

[17] W. Vernon Kinietz, *The Indians of the Western Great Lakes, 1615–1760*, 161–225. Charles A. Hanna, *The Wilderness Trail*, I, 127–28, 134; II, 87. DeVoto, *The Course of Empire*, 151–52.

[18] George Irving Quimby, *Indian Life in the Upper Great Lakes, 11,000 B.C. to A.D. 1800*, 133–139.

[19] Henry Rowe Schoolcraft, *Historical and Statistical Information Respecting the History, Condition, and Prospects of the Indian Tribes of the United States* was most useful in preparing this study. See also his *Personal Memoirs of a Residence of Thirty Years With the Indian Tribes on the American Frontiers.*

[20] *The Journal and Indian Paintings of George Winter, 1837–1839*, with Introduction by Howard H. Peckham. Plates XXIII to XXX show Miami individuals or scenes. R. Carlyle Buley, *The Old Northwest*, II, 580, compares the work of these two artists. Bernard DeVoto, *Across the Wide Missouri*, 399, is uncomplimentary toward Lewis' work.

[21] *American State Papers*, Class II, *Indian Affairs*, I, 562–82, contains Wayne's report on negotiations leading to the first Greene Ville treaty, including Little Turtle's speech.

hokias, Michigameas, Tamaroas, Moingwenas, and Peorias—used dialects almost identical to that of the Miamis.[22] However, other Algonquian tribes, such as the Menominees, Shawnees, and Delawares, have dialects which show many similar characteristics, the similarities being most obvious in words for such common terms as *mother, father, devil, brother, sister,* and *husband.*[23] The Nantikokes of Maryland used a related dialect, and Christopher Gist observed in 1751 that one of his Mohican guides, from New York Colony, was able to serve as his interpreter to the Miamis.[24]

Linguistic comparisons are unreliable, however, since there is no way to evaluate the degree of contact accretions. In the words of anthropologist Robert Wauchope:

> One does not go about it, however, by simply matching words that sound alike. Instead, one analyzes the basic language structure, its fundamental type, the nature of its idioms and its grammar, and the similarity in sound and meaning not only of whole words but also of parts of words, roots, and grammatical forms. A certain number of coincidental sound resemblances must be expected between any two languages, whether they are related or not.[25]

Such linguistic relationships hint of migrations and dispersions in previous centuries. The Walum Olum, or Red Score, of the Delawares seems to identify the Miamis with the *Wemiamik,* or "beaver people," the Delawares encountered during their eastern migration.[26] George E. Hyde ventures the opinion that the Miamis might even have been north of the Ohio River and made contact with the

---

[22] "An Account of the Manners and Customs of the Sauk and Fox Nations of Indian Tradition," by Thomas Forsyth, in Blair, *Indian Tribes,* II, 199–202. Forsyth, who traded in northern Indiana before he became Indian agent at Peoria, was well acquainted with the Miamis. He believed they had lived in the Wabash Valley before the Iroquois invasions.

[23] Schoolcraft, *Historical and Statistical Information,* Part II, Appendix A, 270–81. Constantin F. S. Volney, *A View of the Soil and Climate of the United States of America,* Appendix B, 352–401.

[24] Hanna, *The Wilderness Trail,* II, 274.

[25] Robert Wauchope, *Lost Tribes and Sunken Continents,* 113.

[26] *Walum Olum or Red Score,* 194.

Mississippian people, from whom they absorbed some ritualistic and complex political forms.[27]

The Miami political organization closely resembled those of the Sauk, Fox, Potawatomi, and Ottawa tribes. An understanding of Miami political and social forms depends upon a brief definition of terms. The tribe was a sovereign political entity with a supreme tribal council attended by delegates from all bands. The band was a division of the tribe, primarily, but not solely, based on geography. The bands lived in villages for subsistence purposes, usually in adjacent areas. When Indian bands contain only the members of a number of totemic clans, they are called *phratries*; the Wea and Piankeshaw bands closely approximated this type of grouping. The villages of a band sent delegates to meetings of the band council, which in turn sent delegates to the tribal council.

The social system of the Miamis was based upon a gens or patrilineal clan system. The gens or clan chiefs, as well as the village chiefs, of course, were important political figures. Quimby undoubtedly referred to the precontact period when he stated the Miamis actually had no chief of all their separated bands. Evidence from French sources indicates that in the 1740's they considered Le Pied Froid to be chief of all the Miamis, while Le Gris unquestionably led the entire tribe in the 1780's and 1790's.

There were six Miami bands at the time of the earliest French contacts: Atchatchakangouens, Kilatikas, Mengakonkias, Pepicokias (or Tepicons), Weas, and Piankeshaws. The first three became so intermingled in historic times that the names were discarded for the general term *Miami*.[28] The Weas and Piankeshaws, who probably absorbed the Pepicokias, were often mistaken for separate tribes. By 1818, they no longer sent delegates to the Miami council fires; in fact, they established their own tribal councils and

[27] George E. Hyde, *Indians of the Woodlands*, 57, interprets Perrot's observations on the rituals and power surrounding the Miami chief as demonstrating prior contact. Blair, *Indian Tribes*, I, 146n., 223.

[28] Hodge, *Handbook of American Indians*, I, 852–55. Their most important totemic clan was called the Crane by Perrot and Atchatchakangouen by Allouez. Blair, *Indian Tribes*, I, 270n.

each became a separate entity. Soon after, they formed a confederation with their relatives, the Peorias and Kaskaskias.[29] Individual members from all the bands who fled from American encroachment collected near the Wea country and established a temporary group known as the Eel River or Thorntown band. It partially reintegrated with the Miamis on the upper Wabash and Eel rivers in the early 1800's.

Most historians credit the band chiefs with equal power, and Hyde, using Perrot's observations, concluded they were treated as if they were of divine origin. In 1671, when Perrot placed a garrison which he named St. Jacques at the Miami village on the Fox River portage, he was received with honor by their tribal chief, Tetinchoua, whose authority seemed extraordinary to Perrot. The Frenchman said this village, which contained nearly twenty thousand people, had recently migrated east of the Mississippi after receiving news of peace with the Iroquois. Hyde concluded the Miamis had acquired a sun-king tradition from cultural contacts with either Mississippian mound builders or southwestern tribes, since all Miami chiefs wielded great power. This may have been the result of their admitted abilities, but it also seemed to rest upon Miami devotion to office. A unified tribal organization under one chief could not have maintained communication with all the bands while the tribe was widely dispersed at the time of its first European contacts. However, by 1750 the Miamis had both a civil, or principal, chief and a war chief for the entire tribe.

Tribal membership was customarily based on clan relationship; adoption of outsiders required sanction by the tribal council. The villages were large and contained families from most of the clans and band divisions of the tribe, since families frequently moved from one village to another, even those of other clans and bands. The village chief was elected by a village council composed of

[29] *Before the Indian Claims Commission: Findings of Fact*, decided March 26, 1954, in Docket 67 *et al., 2–626–28*, details the changes which occurred as the Weas separated from the Miamis and which are revealed in the Miami treaties of 1805, 1809, and 1818. Hodge, *Handbook of American Indians*, II, 925–26.

14

members from smaller councils of each band and clan. The village councils included the heads of all families in the clans; band councils included village and clan chiefs from a particular band. Obviously, any of these leaders might also be war chiefs.

By 1700, the grand council of the village, band, and clan chiefs was held at the village on the St. Joseph River; after about 1712, it was always held on the headwaters of the Maumee. During the eighteenth century, the Weas and Piankeshaws repeatedly refused to make any important political decisions until they had been approved by a tribal council at this place.[30] Although the name *Kiskanon* (or *Kekionga*) is applied to the tribal council village, there were at times as many as seven separate Miami villages within a few miles of the Maumee source, and the councils were not always held at the same one.

The tribal, band, or clan chieftainships were not hereditary. The title of war chief was bestowed only upon warriors who could lead a series of successful raids. A Miami seldom became a fully accepted warrior or adult before he was twenty-five or thirty years old, and the chiefs were those with the most ability—or fewest failures. The French explorer Louis Deliette, Tonti's nephew, described in great detail the Miami methods of warfare, from the ritualistic beginnings of a raid to the celebrations or mourning when the war party returned. His account shows Miami war customs differed little from those of other Algonquian tribes. There was one unusual note: Marquette regarded the Miamis as almost invariably successful warriors, a tribute to either their courage or their sagacity. The frequency and success of Miami raids, of course, determined the prestige of the war chiefs. During periods of extended warfare, the tribal war chief became the principal Miami figure at councils and treaty negotiations. A civil chief

---

[30] Howard H. Peckham, *Pontiac and the Indian Uprising*, 278–85. "Gamelin's Journal," enclosed in a letter from Governor Arthur St. Clair to Secretary of War Henry Knox, August 23, 1790, in William Henry Smith, *The St. Clair Papers*, II, 155–60. Croghan in 1763 and later Gamelin encountered Miami unity. The notable exceptions were La Demoiselle's rebellion and Chief Tobacco's devotion to George Rogers Clark. Kellogg, *French Regime*, 130, 185.

often addressed a council through a "speaker"; a war chief seldom did so, since his leadership was due to personal magnetism.[31]

Moravian missionary David Zeisberger described the duties of the civil or principal chief of the Delawares and the personal qualities of wisdom and restraint which the office demanded. His account aptly summarizes the requirements of the same office among the Miamis:

> A chief may not presume to rule over the people, as in that case he would immediately be forsaken by the whole tribe, and his counsellors would refuse to assist him. He must ingratiate himself with the people and stand by his counsellors. Hence, it is that the chiefs are generally friendly, gracious, hospitable, communicative, affable and their house is open to every Indian. Even strangers who come on business are put in the chiefs house and are accommodated with the best it affords. . . .
>
> It is the duty of the chief to maintain peace as long as possible. It is not in his power to begin war as long as the captains are averse to this. Without their consent he cannot accept a war belt. If it is received this is on condition that he will turn it over to the captains for consideration. The chief must endeavor to preserve peace to the utmost of his power. If the captains are unanimous in declaring war he is obliged, as it were, to deliver the care of his people for the time being into their hands, for they are the warriors.[32]

This description can be appreciated when we recall that small, independent war parties conducted raids whenever a village possessed a few young men who needed the experience and credentials of warriors. If the raid punished a traditional and distant enemy, such as the Chickasaws, the peace chief faced no diplomatic problem. However, an unsuccessful group which had been in the forest

---

31 "Memoir Concerning the Illinois Country," by Louis Deliette, in Theodore C. Pease and Raymond C. Werner (eds.), *Collections of the Illinois State Historical Library*, 23, French Series, I (1934), 302–395. Kinietz, *Indians of the Western Great Lakes*, 197–202, quotes Deliette's description of Illinois war parties. His translation of Antoine Denis Raudot's "Memoir Concerning the Different Indian Nations of North America" includes Letters 69, 70, and 71, dealing with hunting and war parties of the Illinois tribes, 404–408.

32 Archer Butler Hurlbert and William Nathaniel Schwarze (ed.), *David Zeisberger's History of the North American Indians*, 92–93, 98.

for months sometimes took the scalps of friendly tribesmen who crossed their path, and the principal chief was then required to exert every effort to prevent a general war with an allied tribe.

There is little agreement on the number or even the names of the Miami clans. Some were probably lost when they failed to rejoin the tribe after 1700. A member of the tribe said in 1969 that there once had been fifteen clans, but the Indiana Miamis utilized twelve names for a ceremony that year. Early French accounts generally name ten or even a smaller number. The usual symbols, signifying a common ancestry, were the crane, eagle, turtle, elk, wolf, loon, buzzard, panther, turkey, raccoon, duck, fox, bear, deer, acorn, and fish. In 1736, Michel M. Chauvignerie classified the Miamis as those Indians with the elk and crane totems; Ougatonous (Weas), the serpent; Peanquichas (Piankeshaws), the deer; and Petikokias (Pepicokias), the acorn totem. Frederick Webb Hodge lists two totems, the elk and crane, but says the turtle and bear symbols were sometimes used. He also cites ten gentes, or clans, of which the crane was the most important. The buzzard, acorn, elk, and raccoon symbols were omitted in a recent document.[33]

That clan identification was vital to the Miamis is illustrated by the fact that each clan group in a village had a chief. Clan chiefs were the most important members of the village council, and one of their number was elected civil chief. And, of course, clan leaders usually attended tribal councils.

Miami clan membership involved the kinship system, which was similar to that of the Sauks and Foxes. Marriage into one's own clan was forbidden. A child's lineage descended unilaterally in the male line from the mother's brother, but the child was always a member of its father's clan. The Miamis ignored generations. A mother's brothers and their male descendants (through males) were all "uncles," daughters of "uncles" were "mothers," and children of "mothers" were "brothers" and "sisters." Such a system

---

[33] Schoolcraft, *Historical and Statistical Information,* Part III, 555. Hodge, *Handbook of American Indians,* I, 854. Photostatic copy of Miami Charter No. 3003 in the Long House League of North American Indians, 1961, in my possession.

perpetuates the male family line of the mother and often indicates a sedentary society and a relatively abundant food supply. The system buttressed Miami village life by keeping children with their mothers.[34] As long as large villages contained several clans, it was possible for unmarried adults to secure partners from other clans while remaining in the same village. Smaller villages lost their male members—usually temporarily—as they sought wives from other clans in other villages.

In 1900, Gabriel Godfroy testified that the older Miamis sometimes employed the kinship system among themselves, although they had long used the white man's terms in public to avoid confusing their neighbors.[35] The Miami system was different from that of the Chippewas and Potawatomis, who differentiated between generations; its complexity explains the difficulties encountered in deciphering Miami genealogies.

The matrilineal-descent concept and its recognition of relationships that were actually remote is indicative of Miami aversion to incest or to marriages between even distant relatives. Such a restriction not only helped to preserve clan membership, but also supported the dignity and freedom of the Miami woman, who ruled the household. Both men and women were permitted extensive sexual freedom before marriage (which usually occurred during the late twenties), but marital fidelity was strictly enjoined thereafter. A couple's relatives were the prime movers in marriage negotiations. The Miamis practiced a limited degree of polygamy, and sisters of the wife were preferred as second wives. Divorce was nearly always by the wife—and frequent—and was accomplished when she removed her husband's possessions from the household. Divorce by the husband was rare, since it usually invoked retribution from her male relatives. Adultery by a wife was unusual in

[34] Quimby, *Indian Life,* 136.
[35] Photostatic copy of notes taken by attorney Elmer S. Morris in preparation of deposition of Gabriel Godfrey, Miami County, Indiana, in 1900 for Mitchell inheritance suit in Ottawa County, Oklahoma, Circuit Court. The copy was made by Forest D. Olds of Miami, Oklahoma, from the Elmer S. Morris papers in the Miami County (Indiana) Museum.

Miami society, but when it occurred, it was punished by nose clipping or ear cropping. Adultery by a husband went unpunished unless it became the grounds upon which his wife divorced him.[36] Although the Miami woman ruled her household, Father Pierre François Xavier de Charlevoix counted that authority a mixed blessing:

> The Nastiness alone of the Cabins, and the Stench which naturally arises from it, is a real Punishment to any one but a Savage. It is easy to judge how far both must go among People who never change their Linen or Clothes but when they drop to Pieces, and who take no Care to wash them. In summer they bathe every Day; but they rub themselves directly with Oil or Grease of a strong Scent. In winter they continue in their Filth, and in all Seasons one cannot enter their Cabins without almost being poisoned.
>
> All they eat is not only without any seasoning and commonly very insipid, but there reigns in their Meals a Slovenliness which exceeds all Description. What I have seen, and what I have heard, would frighten you. There are few Animals who do not feed cleaner. . . .[37]

The Miami cultural pattern varied widely from that of related tribes in only a few characteristics. Although most of Schoolcraft's observations concerning the Algonquian family apply to the Miamis and much of Kinietz's work dealing with the tribe is inferred from studies of the Illinois, the distinctive Miami tribal characteristics which differed from those developed by other groups were more significant than the similarities which existed.

The Miamis were first known to the English as the tattooed or naked Indians, and certainly the men of the tribe deserved such epithets. In spite of the severe weather encountered near the Great Lakes, they wore only skin shirts, leggings, and moccasins in winter; during the summer, a simple breechclout and moccasins enabled them to display the intricate tattooing which had been worked into the skin during the years in which they were growing

---

[36] Kinietz, *Indians of the Western Great Lakes*, 204–207.
[37] Pierre François Xavier de Charlevoix, *Letters to the Dutchess of Lesdiguieres; Giving an Account of a Voyage to Canada*, Letter XXVI, August 5, 1721, 244.

to adulthood. The descriptive terms were converted to various forms of the name *Twightwee*, which may have come from the English interpretation of the Miamis' word for themselves, "cry of the crane," but was probably derived from the Algonquian word *tawa*, meaning "naked."

Miami men wore utilitarian, roughly dressed, unornamented skins most of the time. Fringed, beaded, and quilled clothing was worn only for festive occasions. Women usually were lightly tattooed on the cheeks or chin. Described as "fully clothed" at all times, they wore skin clothing reaching to the knees; shawls, bonnets, and leggings were added when the weather was severe. The skins were carefully dressed, smoked, made pliant, and ornamented.[38] White men on the frontier never duplicated the Indians' skill at preparing skins, but even the finest of these were discarded by Miamis whenever they could secure European cloth.

Another significant characteristic of the Miamis was their possession of a soft white corn that was completely different from the flint corn of their neighbors. The fact that it was not to be found among other near-by tribes tends to support the hypothesis of earlier Miami contact with Indians in the Southwest, where many varieties of this grain had developed.[39] Corn was the staple item in the Miami diet, and its harvest was celebrated by a fall festival. It produced a superior soft flour, and its importance to the tribe partially explains why the Miamis finally left the St. Joseph River,

[38] Kinietz, *Indians of the Western Great Lakes,* 167–68. Martin Chartier, a trader who had once accompanied La Salle and Tonti, and a band of Shawnees were driven from the Illinois country by the Naked Indians (Wittowee or Twightwee) in 1692 and sought sanctuary in the English colonies. Chartier's examination before the Maryland Colonial Council gave to the English their first reliable information about the Miamis. He and his Indians settled in Maryland for a time. Hanna, *The Wilderness Trail,* I, 126–30, 134, cites *Maryland Colonial Proceedings,* III, 341–50, for this incident. Hodge, *Handbook of American Indians,* I, 853.

[39] Harold E. Driver, *Indians of North America,* 38–42. Kinietz, *Indians of the Western Great Lakes,* 171–72, cites Sabrevois, with an explanatory note on the development of corn by Volney Jones of the Ethnobotanical Laboratory of the University of Michigan. The best source is Jacques Charles Sabrevois de Bleury's "Memoir on the Savages of Canada as Far as the Mississippi River," in Reuben Gold Thwaites (ed.), *The French Regime in Wisconsin, 1634–1727,* in *Collections of the State Historical Society of Wisconsin,* XVI, 363–76.

with its unfailing sturgeon and a plentiful supply of buffalo near its meadows; why they deserted the fishing and travel routes of the Great Lakes; why they crossed a hundred miles of hunting and fishing in hundreds of lakes and swamps to settle in the fertile valleys of the Wabash and the three Miami rivers.

While corn was the basis of many facets of their culture, the Miamis also raised melons, squash, pumpkins, and beans and used the uncultured fruits and berries of the forests. They dried fruit and grain and stored these in their houses; corn was cached in underground pits for the winter. A reserve of five bushels of corn, safely stored and supplemented by other foods, was considered adequate provision for a family's winter and spring needs. Perrot claimed the Miamis preferred vegetables and grain foods to meat.

Summer was a time of stability, especially for tribes able to store enough food to escape the lean times of early spring which haunted those who depended upon uncultivated fruits and grains. Although Miami women cultivated the gardens and cooked the food, the men cleared the fields and helped to harvest the crops. During the winter hunts, too, the division of labor was based less on sex than on skills or physical ability. Men were able to pursue and carry game back to the camps, where women and children prepared the flesh and skins. If there were not enough women in camp, men helped in these tasks, which were not considered menial. Like all Algonquian tribes, the Miamis recognized various classes of people, based primarily on ability and lineage, but they did not develop a caste system.[40]

The Miamis were lighter in color than the other Illinois tribes but usually somewhat shorter. The men wore their hair short, except for long locks which dangled before and behind their ears. They were a warrior tribe and during their migrations had frequent conflicts with their allies. However, they usually settled major quarrels in long, peaceful councils—at which they excelled.[41] And the Miamis provide an excellent illustration for Harold E.

[40] Kinietz, *Indians of the Western Great Lakes*, 172–75.
[41] Kellogg, *Early Narratives*, 233–34. Volney, *View of the Soil*, 352–401.

Driver's statement that malnutrition and disease were two of the most important determinants of what anthropologists call "Indian modal personality patterns," which corresponds to historians' "national character constructs" of a tribe. Their self-assurance and dominant position among their neighbors can be traced in part to their stable and provident village life, based more on agriculture than on hunting.[42]

Annual harvests were celebrated with dancing, games, and music from drums, rattles, flutes, whistles, and notched sticks and bones. There was a second festival which was in many ways even more important: the occasion of the Miamis' return from their winter hunting grounds with furs and maple sugar. This marked the resumption of normal life in the villages, which had been partially deserted for months.

Sometimes the peace was shattered by unusual outbreaks. At least one European, Father Charlevoix in 1721, found life in a Miami village on the St. Joseph River near Lake Michigan far from idyllic:

> The Savages of these Parts are naturally Thieves, and think all good Prizes that they can catch. It is true, that if we soon discover that we have lost any Thing, it is sufficient to inform the Chief of it, and we are sure to recover it; but we must give the Chief more than the Value of the Thing, and he requires further some trifle for the Person that found it, and who is probably the Thief himself: I happened to be in this Case the Day after my Arrival, and they showed me no Favour. These Barbarians would sooner engage in a War than make the least Concessions in this Point. . . .
>
> Many Savages of the two Nations which are settled on this River, are just returned from the English Colonies, whither they went to sell their Peltry, and from whence they brought back a great deal of Brandy. It has been divided according to Custom; that is to say, every Day they distribute to a certain Number of Persons as much as is necessary for each to get drunk, and the whole was drank in eight

[42] Driver, *Indians of North America*, 521. However, George Winter said the Miamis were taller than the neighboring Potawatomis. *The Journal and Indian Paintings of George Winter*, Plate XXVII.

Days. They began to drink in the two Villages as soon as the Sun was set, and every Night the Country resounded with frightful Cries and Howlings. One would have said that a Flight of Devils had escaped from Hell, or that the two Villages were cutting one another's Throats. Two men were lamed; I met one of them who broke his Arm with a Fall, and I said to him, that certainly another Time he would be wiser: He replied, that this Accident was Nothing, that he should soon be cured, and that he would begin to drink again as soon as he had got a fresh stock of Brandy.[43]

The comforts afforded by a Miami village hastened the return of its members from scattered winter hunting camps, and this, in turn, lessened the fear of attack by enemy war parties. During April and May, the fields were planted; by June, the young boys and warriors could plan the raids which might elevate them to adult status. Marriages were contracted, boys and girls were instructed in the skills which their society required, and tribal games, dances, and music were displayed. Best of all, there might be visitors from other tribes to entertain. Barring that, delegations of chiefs might be required in far-off villages to discuss weighty matters, and whole families accompanied these parties.[44]

Miami religious practices and beliefs were all-pervading. As the time for birth of a child approached, the mother was placed in a separate cabin which faced her husband's. She remained there, under the care of several women, for about fifteen days after the child's birth; then she bathed and returned to her husband's cabin, in which a new fire had been laid. The child was bound to a cradle-board, upon which it spent most of its time until the age of two or three. By then, it had been given a name. Both sexes fasted at the onset of puberty. Girls retired from the village for some time; boys sought visions and dreams which might reveal their guardian spirits, but also became inured to fasting and fatigue. A name change might also occur at this time.

The Miami boy lived in a paradise of permissiveness. He learned

---

[43] Charlevoix, *Letters to the Dutchess*, 226, 228.
[44] Kinietz, *Indians of the Western Great Lakes*, 185–96, 202–207.

by emulation and through mistakes. Discipline or punishment was never physical. Because of the Miami kinship system, he was seldom out of sight of a fond adult relative who treasured him and admonished or helped him.[45] As a result, he approached manhood well versed in the skills and customs of the tribe and eager to gain full status as a warrior. His raids were preceded by elaborate ritualistic preparation. After each raid, appropriate ceremonies— mourning, torturing and burning of captives, adoption or enslavement of accepted prisoners—were properly observed. If his conduct on several raids proved acceptable, he was advanced to full warrior status and responsibility in the village council and became eligible to enter into a formal marriage contract. Most of the Miami customs were important to the welfare of the tribe, village, and clan and thus were attended with propitiatory rituals.[46]

The earliest observers seldom agree on the extent of Miami belief in spirits. However, some perspective can be gained by studying the mature Miami man's association with the grand medicine society, the Medawin (or Medewiwin). It is found, under various names, in all North American tribes. The Meda (or Meta) was a magician or priest who practiced the art of medical magic and prophecy through communion with the spirits. The supreme power for the Miamis was the sun, maker and master of life, while the Manito was the power for good and evil which existed in all things, animate or inanimate, including man. The Meda appealed to the Manito in inanimate objects in order to release its secret energies, which the practitioner then used for the purpose of propitiating or banishing malignant spirits wherever these might be found. The society, whose membership was voluntary and uninfluenced by lineage, had four degrees of membership, all determined by the proficiency of the member. Although its ceremonies were public, instruction in its rites was private.

A Meda was usually summoned when medical practitioners, or

<hr>

[45] *Ibid.*, 202–204. Quimby, *Indian Life*, 136.
[46] Kinietz, *Indians of the Western Great Lakes*, 196–202. Quaife, *Western Country*, 69–70.

shamans (called *Muskekewininee*), failed to cure an illness. The latter, considered inferior to the Medas, were restricted to the use of medicinal herbs and therapies considered less powerful than the spirit of the Manito. The Miamis understood and used such herbs extensively, and Kinietz cites a long list of barks, roots, and berries and their preparation for specific illnesses or injuries.

Also found among the Algonquians was the Jeesukewin class of priests, which lacked an organized society. The individual Jeesukeed, locked away in solitude, prophesied or predicted events. Like the Meda, he, too, appealed to the spirit of the Manito for power by exhibiting charms and fetishes from which the spirit's energies could emerge.[47]

Schoolcraft and Governor Lewis Cass of Michigan Territory witnessed a Medawin ceremony among the Miamis near Fort Wayne in 1821 while seeking confirmation of rumors that the Miamis had practiced cannibalism at recent Wabeno gatherings. Although they could never be sure, they suspected that the Wabeno meetings, a corruption of Medawin rites into midnight orgies designed to propitiate only malign spirits, had indeed sometimes used human victims.[48]

Artist George Winter summarized the white settlers' view of Miami spiritual life by saying the Miamis were superstitious while the Potawatomis were religious. The Roman Catholic church maintained closer relations with the Potawatomis than with the Miamis, however, and Winter's statement was made at a time when most Potawatomis were devout Catholics.[49] And of course the Miami belief that the spirit of Manito resided in both animate and inanimate objects could not be accepted by the whites. The Miamis conceived the soul to be a flying phantom, an image of the deceased

---

[47] Schoolcraft, *Historical and Statistical Information*, Part I, 358–68.

[48] The *Vincennes Indiana Centinel and Public Advertiser*, August 7, 1821, announced that Governor Lewis Cass, accompanied by Agent Schoolcraft, had departed from Vincennes in July on his circuitous trip from Detroit to the impending Chicago treaty session. It was while he was at Fort Wayne that Cass secured scraps of information on the Miami Wabeno rites.

[49] *The Journal and Indian Paintings of George Winter*, 48, Plate XXVII. Kinietz, *Indians of the Western Great Lakes*, 211–21.

individual, which journeyed to a world more agreeable than this one.[50] The dead were sincerely mourned, and prescribed mourning and burial rites were followed. Burial was usually by interment, with logs placed over the grave, but hollow-log and scaffold burials were sometimes used. All burial places were venerated. The differences in burial customs seem in no way related to rank in Miami society. They suggest that geographic location or convenience determined the type of burial.[51]

Significant changes affected the tribe during the chaotic period before 1700. Earlier they possessed Stone Age implements and a reasonably stable culture based on a favorable ecological adaptation, but when they entered the Wabash and Miami valleys, they brought with them iron tools and weapons. The introduction of these items by Europeans strongly influenced Miami culture. When their enemies obtained guns, knives, traps, and comfortable clothing, it was imperative that the Miamis acquire them, too, in order to survive. Once this economic relationship (mainly with the French) was established, it led to the Indian's nearly total dependence upon the white man for goods he could not do without. Since the furs of forest animals had to be used to secure European goods, the Miami can hardly be blamed for discarding his ritualistic relationships with these animals. Besides, the French traders were accompanied by missionaries who constantly attacked many of his long-accepted values and presented a new system of religion.

It is unrealistic to presume that changes in the Miamis' social values occurred only after contact with the whites or that the Miamis experienced periods in which there were no forces for change at work in their society. We can say with some assurance, however, that they possessed certain cultural patterns at the time of their first encounter with the French. Social and political changes occurred much earlier—when the Miamis acquired their soft white corn, when they were more closely united with other Algonquian

[50] Ake Hultkrantz, *Conceptions of the Soul Among North American Indians*, 76. *Indians of the Western Great Lakes*, 211–21.
[51] Kinietz, *Indians of the Western Great Lakes*, 207–21.

groups, when they migrated to new ecological situations—but our evaluation of them must be conjectural. These situations may have called for nothing more than leisurely adaptation; white contact, especially after 1700, required rapid adaptation.

By 1700, there were Frenchmen in all Miami villages. Whether missionaries, traders, or soldiers, they were audacious, virile young men from Canada, possessors of the white man's knowledge who were stimulated by the dangers and freedom of the frontier. These men and their descendants were well equipped to become leaders among the Indians and to initiate changes in tribal life.

2
THE FRENCH PERIOD
IN INDIANA, 1700-1763

The Miamis moved into the area bounded by the Ohio, Wabash, Maumee, and Great and Little Miami rivers at the beginning of the eighteenth century. Their first hundred years there constituted their Golden Age, followed by a half-century of decline and disintegration.

The eighteenth century saw a remarkable change in Miami political attitudes and practices. They developed a semi-agricultural culture, secured unshakable alliances with their neighbors, and maintained a firm union among the tribal bands. The new attitudes sprang from an evolving Miami conception of themselves as undisputed lords of the valley of the Wabash and Maumee rivers and were nourished by their successful efforts to preserve these lands.

The fertile valley provided an ideal ecological environment in which they could resume and develop the agricultural aspects of their community life. The woods and streams were filled with game and fish, and hunting and fishing were pleasant diversions instead of an arduous way of life. The woods produced maple sugar, fruits, berries, and nuts. It was a more hospitable environment for the Miami way of life than the prairies of Illinois or the pine forests near Lake Michigan. When the Miamis reached the Wabash-

Maumee Valley, they stubbornly resisted efforts by the French to induce them to return to the north and west. And the attraction of British trade goods drew them only as far east as the Great and Little Miami rivers. The region became, possibly for the second time, their "home from time immemorial."

Since geography had a profound influence on the culture and political policies of the Miamis, a cursory examination of the assets and liabilities the location of their new home afforded is in order. Although the French fort at Detroit was but little more than a hundred miles away, the land route was so nearly impassable because of swamps that the Miamis no longer found themselves at the doorstep of French authority. Ascending the Little St. Joseph River from the Maumee, the traveler encountered similar swamps. The longer water route began as a pleasant canoe trip down the Maumee, but became an unpredictable and hazardous encounter with fate once the traveler entered Lake Erie. Voyages from Kekionga to Detroit were not undertaken during periods of strong storms.

The Black Swamp lay south of the Maumee. It could be traversed only by canoe on the Auglaize River, which flows into the Maumee from the south, or crossed on foot during extremely dry or freezing weather. Because of these barriers, Kekionga was approached from the east only by way of the Maumee.

Kekionga was more accessible from the southeast. The St. Mary's River was the principal route of travel from its portages to the Auglaize or to the tributaries of the Great Miami. The two Miami rivers run parallel until both enter the Ohio, and tributaries of the two were easily portaged. Early French maps designated them as *Rivière de la Roche* and *Rivière Blanche* to avoid confusion with the *Oumee*, or Maumee, River of Lake Erie.

The Salamonie, the Mississinewa, and both forks of the White River of Indiana were short and easy portages from the Great Miami, as were the Auglaize and St. Mary's rivers. The first three led to the Wabash at widely separated points. They were canoe routes through swampy lands which were fine hunting areas. Thus

29

the Miamis' location made them both traders and expert but unenthusiastic canoemen.

East of the Little Miami River Valley, trails over rolling highlands led to the Sandusky and Scioto rivers, which became the new homelands of the Delawares and Shawnees. The swamps and highlands east of the Auglaize and Little Miami were natural barriers separating these hunting lands, and as Thomas Hutchins' map of 1764 shows, the Miamis had no villages beyond the Little Miami.

In the first half of the eighteenth century, there were no Indian villages between the Ohio and the headwaters of the White River of Indiana; the Miami tribe was too small to populate this glaciated region. The ancient earthworks of past Amerindian cultures had long been deserted, and the Mosopeleas, Osages, and other Siouan groups had migrated from the Ohio Valley. The later Shawnee migration was east of the Scioto River.[1] Equally important, this hundred miles of glacial ridges, plus the broad Ohio, furnished the Miamis some protection against raids by Muskhogean war parties from the south.

The most populous but vulnerable Miami villages were those on the lower and middle Wabash River. The Piankeshaw band, though intermingled with their Kaskaskia and Peoria relatives, were on the edge of the Illinois prairies and little more than a hundred miles from the Mississippi. Therefore, they were especially vulnerable to attacks by Chickasaw war parties and to the blandishments of Spanish traders from the west and English traders from the Cumberland Valley.[2]

The Weas, who occupied the middle Wabash Valley from the Eel, or L'Anguille, River south to the mouth of the Vermilion, had migrated from their Fort Chicago village and from west of Lake Michigan by the first quarter of the eighteenth century. About one thousand warriors lived in five villages on the *Oubache*; the

---

[1] Hyde, *Indians of the Woodlands*, 61. John R. Swanton, *The Indian Tribes of North America*, 298, "Southeastern North America." Hodge, *Handbook of American Indians*, I, 948; II, 156–58, 530–36, 577–79.

[2] Frances Krauskopf (ed.), "Ouiatanon Documents," *Indiana Historical Society Publications*, XVIII (1955), 2, 150, 152, 186–87, Crane, *The Southern Frontier*, 273–74.

French called four of them Ouiatanon, Petitiscotia, Les Gros, and Peanguichia. The last was evidently a Piankeshaw village intermingled with the Weas, since its name was customarily used by the French for the Piankeshaws. The Weas were concentrated below the mouth of the Tippecanoe River at the point which was most accessible to travelers from east, west, or north. It was the gateway to the western prairies and the Kickapoo, Mascoutin, Sauk, and Fox lands. The Tippecanoe was the usual route to the lake-and moraine hunting grounds of the Potawatomis, who carried their furs down that river or down the Eel to the Wabash.

Neighboring tribes were destined to exert important political influence on the Weas and Piankeshaws. The Sauks and Foxes lived on the Illinois River about 125 miles west of the Weas, while Kickapoo and Prairie Potawatomi, or Mascoutin, villages were located a few miles up the Vermilion. The hunter tribes retained habits which the Miami were abandoning at this time, including a contentiousness that made them seek any excuse for taking part in war. Consequently, the French soon learned the lower Wabash Miami bands were more prone to strife than their relatives at Kekionga.

Wea clothing and customs showed the French had caused few changes in these aspects of tribal life since their first contacts half a century earlier. The men still preferred scanty clothing, and the Wea was the only division of the Illinois which still used nose clipping to punish unfaithful wives. Even more surprising, the Wea villages were "extremely clean."[3]

The major bands had moved "recently" from the St. Joseph River of Lake Michigan to Kekionga, situated on the headwaters of the Maumee. The new tribal council center was therefore protected but not isolated. It was at a reassuring distance from both the French and the English and on the border between tribes allied to both European nations.

The upper Wabash and Eel rivers run parallel courses about fif-

---

[3] "A Memoir of the Indians Between Lake Erie and the Mississippi," written at Detroit in 1718, tells of Miami migrations in E. B. O'Callaghan (ed.), *Documents Relative to the Colonial History of the State of New York*, 885–92.

teen miles apart until they converge at present-day Logansport, Indiana. Potawatomi villages dotted the lake region north of the Eel, while the Miamis settled in the valley of the two rivers and on the tributaries flowing into the Wabash from the east—the most sheltered part of the Miami country. An eight-mile portage separated the Little Wabash from the St. Mary's near its confluence with the St. Joseph River of Indiana, which is the headwaters of the Maumee.

Because the Miamis were astride the best route between Canada and Louisiana, the French feared they would become involved in wars or alliances which would jeopardize the route and even threaten French destruction. But the Miamis had suffered attrition during their seventeenth-century wars, and the tribe's prestige—even its existence—depended upon its ability to adapt to events over which it had little control. Of these, the most important were the changing economic and political situations resulting from the imperial aspirations of France and England.

Cadillac said Miami political tactics in the seventeenth century courted eventual extinction.[4] Dreuillettes' first estimate of their population, 24,000, was based on fragmentary information, mainly because of his difficulty in distinguishing linguistic variations among the Illinois.[5] An estimate of 4,500 for the Miamis alone in 1695 was more realistic,[6] but this number may have included the Peorias. European diseases and Iroquois war parties took a heavy toll in the last half of the seventeenth century, although some Miamis may have remained with allies to whom they fled during the Iroquois holocaust. Captain Thomas Hutchins, with Colonel

---

[4] Thwaites, *French Regime*, I, 172–73. *Ibid.*, 211–13, reproduces Father Jean Mermet's letter of April 19, 1702, to Cadillac, warning the latter that twelve Miamis planned to go to the English to secure trade goods and that the tribe intrigued against the French. Governor Vaudreuil's conference with Indian envoys at Mackinac in 1703 seems to prove that the series of Indian clashes was generated by Miami conferences with English-allied Mohawks. *Ibid.*, 221–27. Krauskopf, "Ouiatanon Documents," 140–41.

[5] Hodge, *Handbook of American Indians*, II, 852–54.

[6] Kinietz, *Indians of the Western Great Lakes*, 164. Kinietz also produced a Miami location chart which is convenient. *Ibid.*, 165.

Henry Bouquet's 1764 expedition to the Muskingum River, calculated Miami warrior strength at 250 Piankeshaws, 350 Miamis, and 400 Weas, so that an estimate of about 2,000 Miamis at the close of the French period seems accurate.[7] They had been a scattered and migratory people for at least fifty years. They had been at war constantly—with enemies, friends, relatives—and had antagonized the French. In the eighteenth century, the Miamis reversed their quarrelsome attitude. Instead of intratribal schisms and irresponsible wars against their neighbors, they developed strong alliances and a diplomatic finesse which served them well.

In 1696, the French adopted a new Indian policy which benefited the Miamis politically. The so-called Concentration Policy was intended to limit the activities of the *coureurs de bois*, or unlicensed traders, who carried furs to English and Spanish markets, plying the Indians with whisky in order to obtain them. Father Charlevoix asserted that the Miamis at St. Joseph Mission had already been debauched by 1721.[8] However, the Concentration Policy necessitated long and therefore infrequent journeys to Detroit by the Miamis and thus deprived them of convenient access to the goods they required. There were no longer resident priests in the Miami villages, and missionary visits were rare. Although the Miamis lacked French goods, they escaped French political and religious control.

It is an error to use the terms "French tribes" or "English tribes" when recording the events of this period. Although the white men were able to present trading inducements, they could not enforce the loyalty of the Indians, who very properly followed their own self-interests. The Great Lakes region was, therefore, Indian country in every respect.

[7] William Henry Smith, *Historical Account of Bouquet's Expedition Against the Ohio Indians in 1764*, with Preface by Francis Parkman, 118, 125. Hanna, *The Wilderness Trail*, II, 362–67, gives excerpts from Hutchins' "Journal," from the original in the Bouquet Papers.

[8] Kellogg, *French Regime*, 260. Charlevoix, *Letters to the Dutchess*, 228. Thwaites, *French Regime*, I, 214–17, includes a synopsis of the evils of the fur trade written by Father de Carheil to the intendant of Canada, J. B. de Champigny, dated August 30, 1702.

Tribes not under close French observation were receptive to English traders or their Shawnee, Delaware, and Iroquois emissaries. The French soon became aware of the weakness in their trade system and in 1714 revised their former policy by constructing new posts and reoccupying those which had once been important.[9] The action fostered a closer relationship with the Miamis. Three of the most important posts—Forts Miamis, Ouiatanon, and Vincennes—were located in Miami territory on the closely guarded trade route to Louisiana. Various reports of traders and commandants at the posts supply much of the available information about the Miamis after 1714. Since most of these men were able individuals, they did much to shape the course of Miami history.

The man who began to arouse in the Miamis a broadened awareness of French Indian policy and their own role therein was Jean Baptiste Bissot, Sieur de Vincennes. He accompanied Henri de Tonti to the Mississippi in 1699, having been sent to the Miamis on the St. Joseph River by Governor Frontenac in 1696. In 1712, he led a Miami war party to relieve Detroit when it was besieged by the Foxes during the First Fox War, and about 1715, he accompanied the Miami migration to the headwaters of the Maumee. It was his responsibility to make certain the tribe used French goods; to keep the council and warriors from quarreling with the Ottawas, who served as middlemen in the fur trade; and to maintain the peace which Cadillac had secured between that tribe and the Miamis. Vincennes was also ordered to determine whether the Potawatomi hunters north of the Wabash wanted to deal with English traders and to use Miami warriors against them should they make the attempt.[10] By 1722, Fort St. Phillippe (later Fort Miamis) had been built at Kekionga. It is possible that Vincennes con-

---

[9] Thwaites, *French Regime,* I, 377–79, contains a part of Governor Vaudreuil's letter of October 30, 1718, to the French Council recounting his effort to pacify the Indian tribes, Kellogg, *French Regime,* 291–92.

[10] "Vincennes Identified," 45–68. Kellogg, *French Regime,* 280–82, briefly recounts the savage attack by the Foxes and the equally savage reprisals of the French and their allies during the winter of 1711–12. Thwaites, *French Regime,* 11, 15n.

structed it before his death in 1718 or 1719, yet it is neither certain nor verifiable who ordered its erection or when it was constructed.[11]

At first, the Wea villages were more important than those at the Maumee. François Picote de Belestre, sent to construct Fort Ouiatanon, expected it to be a temporary post, for the French still had hopes of persuading all of the Miami bands to return to the Fort Chicago and St. Joseph River areas. They also hoped to coax the Shawnees to settle on the Maumee and Wabash, thereby detaching that tribe from the Iroquois alliance. It was a practical plan, for the Great Lakes trade routes utilized the growing Mackinac fur depot, where the Miamis would be subordinate to the powerful Chippewa-Ottawa-Potawatomi, or "Three Fires," alliance. Best of all, however, the Miamis would be removed from their new proximity to the English-oriented tribes settling west of the Appalachians.[12] In 1718, Belestre was replaced by the younger Vincennes, François Marie Bissot, born about 1700, who had joined his father at Kekionga early that year and was destined to become the most important Frenchman among the Miami. Renaud Dubuisson then moved to the Maumee and assumed over-all command of the two little trading-post garrisons on the Wabash.[13]

The Miamis refused all inducements by the French to move north and west. They had undoubtedly learned that periodic wars were inevitable when they intermingled with the northern tribes. The French commandants followed their superiors' instructions in pushing the project, but it is doubtful whether they pressed their arguments very strongly since they understood, even if the French government did not, the tendency of the Miamis to create strife when they encountered northern tribes. The Frenchmen's position therefore resembled that of the Indian civil chiefs—they tried to persuade but were too wise to command.

[11] Krauskopf, "Ouiatanon Documents," 141–42.

[12] *Ibid.*

[13] Roy, "Vincennes Identified," 92. Krauskopf, "Ouiatanon Documents," 142. Thwaites, *French Regime*, 443, identifies the younger Vincennes as François Margane, a nephew of Jean Baptiste Bissot.

The Second Fox War, 1727–42, changed many French plans: it closed the Green Bay and Illinois routes to Louisiana, leaving the Wabash as the only safe one. The war not only alienated many of the western tribes, but made Miami loyalty a necessity, and it was just at this time that the French could place little reliance upon Miami friendship. At a conference of western chiefs at Montreal in 1731, Governor Charles de La Boische, Marquis de Beauharnois, tried to persuade the Miamis to withdraw to the Lake Michigan area. He also sought to gain permission from the tribe—especially the Wea band, together with the Wyandots—to allow scattered Shawnee bands in the Wabash Valley. Vincennes took the principal Miami chief of Kekionga and three Wea chiefs to the conference, but the Governor gained little support for his plan.[14]

Since the tribe's refusal to withdraw to the north left its lower Wabash bands exposed to attacks from the south, Vincennes was transferred to the jurisdiction of the Louisiana colonial government and ordered to build a fort on the lower Wabash in order to guard the Piankeshaws and to block Chickasaw access to the lower Ohio River. He began the fort in the winter of 1731–32. The next year, he said he needed at least thirty soldiers to defend his post and to overawe the Miamis and the neighboring Illinois. French efforts were unimpressive, inasmuch as Chickasaw raiders captured six French soldiers and continued to make the Mississippi River hazardous for all French flotillas.[15]

In 1736, Vincennes and the Illinois commandant Pierre d'Artaguiette, led a small force of French soldiers and Indian allies, including a strong band of Piankeshaws, down the Mississippi. They expected to drive the Chickasaws into a converging French force from Louisiana. The southern detachment was delayed, but the northern unit, refusing to wait, attacked and was defeated. Vincennes was captured and burned at the stake, and France lost its most capable emissary to the Miamis. His successors were

14 Hanna, *The Wilderness Trail,* I, 300–301.
15 Vincennes' letters of March 7 and 21, 1733, are in Roy, "Vincennes Identified," 92–94.

never able to exert comparable influence in the tribal councils or among Miami chiefs.[16]

The French policy of persuasion, equality, and brotherhood with the Indians must be qualified at this point. Although it may have been the one most congenial to the temperament of the French and most productive to their colonial plans, it was also the policy forced upon them by their limited resources and the manpower at their command in the vast continental interior. When necessary, they waged relentless warfare, especially against the Foxes. Yet a Vincennes or an Allouez served their basic purposes more efficiently than could more numerous forces.

However, a new penetration of the upper Ohio River region by British traders occurred at this time. Miami leaders, aware that their economic interests could be advanced by forcing the French and English traders to compete for furs the Indians gathered, created a political crisis for the French, who were at a disadvantage in the competition. Cadwallader Colden noted in 1724 that strouding, a cheap muslin and the principal cloth bought by the Indians, cost a British trader £10 in Albany but that French traders had to pay £25 for it at Montreal.[17] Evidence indicates that an Indian could secure the same quality of goods from an English trader for fewer pelts than from a Frenchman. Moreover, the Iroquois and their satellite tribes had been uniformly victorious in war, and potential Miami alliances with them were attractive because they served as middlemen for British goods. The Miamis no longer believed that European trade necessitated war or that they could be forced into trade alliances. Their partial French cultural adaptations did not include loyalties to a French government which interfered with any aspect of their own sovereignty.

[16] *Ibid.,* 99. Thwaites, *French Regime,* II, 259n. "Report of Richardville on D'Artaguietta's Expedition Against the Chickesaws," in Caroline and Eleanor Dunn (transs.), "Indiana's First War," *Indiana Historical Society Publications,* VIII (1924), 2, 74–143.

[17] Thwaites, *French Regime,* I, 258. "A Memorial Concerning the Fur Trade of the Province of New York," written by Cadwallader Colden in 1721, is the best source regarding the extent of English knowledge of the trade at that time. Cadwallader Colden, *The History of the Five Indian Nations of Canada,* II, 33–57.

The Miamis were finally persuaded that their earlier wars—even treacheries—against the Shawnees, Ottawas, the other Illinois tribes, and among themselves were fruitless. Separate hunting areas, tribal unity, and peaceful alliances produced larger quantities of furs and more general council meetings. Conferences like the one held by Governor Philippe de Rigaud, Marquis de Vaudreuil in 1703 convinced the Miamis that all Indians could profit during the white-inspired "Beaver Wars," in which various tribes sought control of pelt-producing regions. They were prepared to exploit these new viewpoints.

By the end of the first quarter of the eighteenth century, the upper Wabash Miamis were making efforts to improve their contacts with the eastern tribes. In 1727, they accepted a war belt against the English, sent to them by an eastern Delaware band and a band of Iroquois. The Delawares planned to retaliate against the British settlers because the colony of New Jersey had hanged one of their chiefs. Such temporary conflicts were routine matters on the frontier, however, and the Delawares and Iroquois were soon mollified. Nevertheless, the Miamis' participation in the affair was significant. While no large number of British traders had reached their country, it was essential that they ally themselves with the eastern tribes before such trade could develop. Therefore, any alliance with the Iroquois was worth while, even though they might be forced to oppose the British. Besides, if such a war failed, retribution would fall on the eastern tribes rather than the remote Miamis. Meanwhile, their young warriors could gain needed experience and glory while fighting with the Iroquois, called Six Nations with the addition of the Tuscarawas about 1715.

The plan to attack the settlers was revealed when a Pennsylvania trader, James Le Tort, who planned an expedition to the Miamis in 1728, was warned by his friend Mme. Montour that there would be warfare on the western frontier that summer. The doughty "Queen of the Iroquois" had lived for some time among the Miamis, and her sister, the wife of a chief, was still with the tribe. Le Tort reported the scheme and the Miamis' involvement, and Governor Patrick Gordon warned the Pennsylvania Council.[18] Governor Beauharnois of Canada was a farsighted man. He knew the Delawares and Iroquois would soon be reconciled with the British because their economic advantage as middlemen dictated such a political alliance. In 1733, Beauharnois sent the Sieur Desnoyelles to bring the Miamis to Kekionga for council as a step toward their removal to Lake Michigan and the Detroit area. Desnoyelles was more successful than had been anticipated, for only three bands refused to attend: Le Baril, at the mouth of the Little Miami, the most distant village; a band on the Kiepigon, or Tippecanoe, River; and the village near Turkey Lake, twenty miles north of the Eel River in the Potawatomi country.[19] Most of the Miamis returned to their villages after the meeting, but a few remained on the Maumee. All had been glad to assemble for a tribal council, but Desnoyelles' promises of French protection and more convenient trading posts were all too familiar, although the license system in use after 1714 was fairly successful at Kekionga and Ouiatanon.

Under the license system, a trader was permitted to take four canoeloads of goods to his post. He supplied his own canoemen and goods and conducted trade at the post. The government built a small fort and supplied a garrison to protect the trader. The licensee's contract was specific, and his accounts were carefully audited. Along with the commandant's reports, these were used to maintain constant supervision of Indian affairs. The Miamis were satisfied with the prices, quality, and quantity of goods supplied by the French—until they encountered better bargains.[20]

The Miami bands which remained at Kekionga lived in comparative tranquillity for nearly a generation. Half-isolated from excessive French military and religious interference and nearly in-

[18] Hanna, *The Wilderness Trail*, I, 94–95. A genealogy of the important Montour family is given in *ibid.*, 199–206.

[19] Thwaites, *French Regime*, II, 184–87. Hanna, *The Wilderness Trail*, I, 332.

[20] Theodore C. Pease and Ernestine Jenison (eds.), "Illinois on the Eve of the Seven Years War, 1747–1755," *Collections of the Illinois State Historical Library*, XXIX (1940), 23–31, reproduce the contract of Sieur Charly Saint-Ange for trade at the Miami post (Kekionga) from 1747 to 1750.

accessible to war parties from the southern tribes, they were at peace with all their neighbors. Even when friction developed, the French were able to smooth things out rather easily. One such outbreak was the "Wea War" of 1734, in which that band pillaged its own trading post. A force of 324 Frenchmen, Wyandots, and Ottawas was assembled at Detroit to put down the uprising, but when the group reached Kekionga to collect more warriors, it was told the peace pipe had been smoked by the trader and the warriors.[21] In another incident, the Kekionga Miamis nearly waged war on the Weas in 1740 when Wea Chief Le Peau Blanche killed a Miami warrior. The French commandant at Ouiatanon finally pacified the Miamis with gifts to "cover the body."[22]

One result of such conflicts was a renewed effort by the French to settle a Shawnee village among the Weas to serve as a counterbalance to the aggressive Illinois and Kickapoos on the Vermilion River. The Shawnee allies of the Iroquois were viewed by the western tribes with nearly the same respectful fear accorded the Six Nations. Attempts to separate the Shawnees from the English were made with the knowledge that British traders might follow them to the Weas. However, the proposal won favor from all of the tribes and the Shawnees gladly accepted their role and settled among the Weas in 1741.[23] As a result, the Kekionga bands had a more stable existence than those on the lower reaches of the Wabash and were more devoted to the French. Two other factors also contributed to the general peace: tribal councils were held at Kekionga, and the principal and war chiefs recognized by the French usually came from these divisions of the tribe.

The period of stability lasted about a generation. Not even the newly developed Miami unity could maintain continual harmony among the diverse bands. The Weas and Piankeshaws became restless over France's failure to counter Chickasaw raids effectively. They had frequent contacts with British and Spanish traders and

---

[21] Krauskopf, "Ouiatanon Documents," 146–47, 149.
[22] *Ibid.*, 149.
[23] Hanna, *The Wilderness Trail,* I, 300–302, 304.

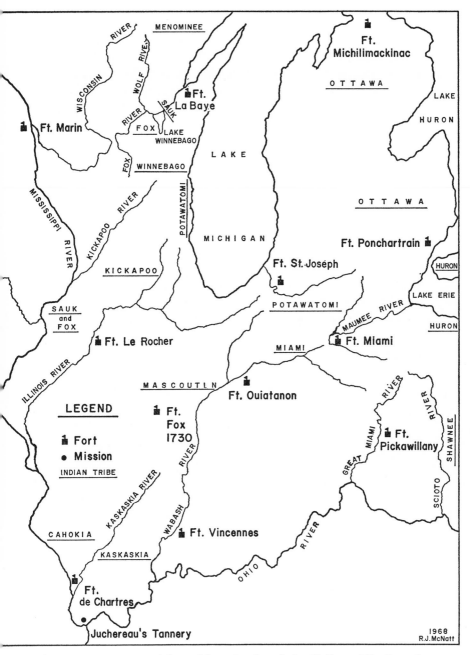

The West, 1700–1760. Adapted from Louise Phelps Kellogg, *The French Regime in Wisconsin and the Northwest.*

had been close to the Fox wars.[24] They carried some of their dissatisfactions to the Kekionga councils, but soon returned to the lower stretches of the Wabash. They still used the prairie hunting grounds and cherished their ties with the other Illinois tribes and their Kickapoo allies, who had been intermingled with them since about 1734. They were still the most populous divisions of the Miami tribe, but they resented their subordinate position at councils on the Maumee.

The most severe crisis in Miami unity began in 1747 as a small part of the French-British imperial struggle. It was in this contest for supremacy that the Miamis played, for the first time, a significant role in American history. The British naval blockade of Canada during King George's War in 1740–48 shut off the supply of trade goods with which France supported her Indian allies in the west. In contrast, the eastern tribes secured English goods, which were becoming cheaper and more abundant as the Industrial Revolution increased production in textile and iron factories. Such goods crossed the Appalachian Mountains in ever growing quantities on the pack horses of Pennsylvania and Virginia traders.

France tried to meet this situation by leasing its posts to individual traders, who profited from monopolies while serving as agents for Indian affairs. Sieur Charly Saint-Ange paid an annual fee of three thousand livres for a monopoly of all trade at Fort Miamis and on the White River (probably of Indiana) from 1747 to 1750. The arrangement required him to furnish the post commandant with lodging, firewood, an interpreter, transportation, and presents for the Miamis. The Miamis had no other source of supply for their necessities, no other market for their furs, and they could not possibly benefit from such a system because no matter what the goods cost, Saint-Ange was certain to make a profit.[25]

---

[24] "I relied to a great extent on the Miamis, the Ouiatanons and the Pianquichias [against the Fox] but mortality among them (from smallpox) may disturb my plans." Beauharnois to the French Minister, May 3, 1733, in Thwaites, *French Regime*, II, 175.

[25] Pease and Jenison, "Illinois on the Eve of the Seven Years War, 23–31.

Piankeshaw Chief La Demoiselle led a Miami rebellion against this system in 1747. He had kept his village in the Kekionga area after 1734, but now, dissatisfied with his relationship with the French and influenced by Wyandot Chief Nicolas, he moved it to a site just below the junction of Loramie Creek and the Great Miami River, at the beginning of one of the portages to the St. Mary's River. The new village, Pickawillany, was near the protection of the Delawares and Shawnees and was easily reached by British pack-horse trains or by canoe from the Ohio River. It became a magnet for English traders, who called its chief "Old Britain," the "Piankeshaw King," or the "Great King of the Miamis." Although he was not the principal chief of the Miamis, he was probably the Piankeshaw chief of the lower Wabash Valley band. The fact that he was a Piankeshaw did not exclude him from the chieftainship of the entire tribe, but the French, well informed concerning Miami affairs, called Le Pied Froid of Kekionga the principal chief and Le Gris of Tepicon village the war chief.[26]

La Demoiselle's action threatened a complete Miami break from the French after nearly a century of alliance; it also created a violent schism in the tribe. The Sieur Douville, commandant at Fort Miamis, took two Kekionga chiefs to Detroit in August, 1747, to explain the crisis. The chiefs told an alarming story: La Demoiselle had promised the Senecas to assassinate both Douville and Paul Joseph Le Moyne, Chevalier de Longueuil, the Detroit commandant. The latter immediately sent his most trusted officer, Ensign Joseph Guyon Dubuisson, the younger, to take command of Fort Miamis and hold it at all costs. It was a timely decision, for the Miamis had pillaged their trader's post during Douville's absence, but Dubuisson easily restored order.[27]

[26] Krauskopf, "Ouiatanon Documents," 214. Wilbur R. Jacobs, "Presents to Indians Along the Frontiers in the Old Northwest, 1748–63," *Indiana Magazine of History*, XLIV (September, 1948), 245–56. Peckham, *Pontiac*, 35. Hanna, *The Wilderness Trail*, II, 261–64, 281, 286, gives a coherent account of La Demoiselle's movements, including selections from Céleron's "Journal." Hanna, *The Wilderness Trail*, I, 146–48, says La Demoiselle left the Kekionga area in 1747 and established his new village "soon after." Thwaites, *French Regime*, II, 280 n., sketches Nicolas' career.
[27] Hanna, *The Wilderness Trail*, II, 259–60.

Governor of New France Roland Michel Barrin, Marquis de La Galissonière, wrote to his superiors in Paris in November, 1747, that La Demoiselle was the heart of the league of pro-English tribes in Ohio. A part of the Wyandot village at Detroit preceded the Miami defection when Chief Nicolas moved to a new site on Sandusky Bay. The majority of the Sandusky village soon moved to the Maumee to be nearer Detroit's protection, but a few Miami warriors joined Nicolas.[28]

These developments on the frontier were due to the activities of traders from Pennsylvania and Virginia, who continued their operations even after the European phase of King George's War ended. Chief among them were George Croghan of Pennsylvania and Christopher Gist of Virginia. They crossed the Appalachian ranges with pack-horse trains to continue their trade with the Western Iroquois, or Mingos, and the Delaware and Shawnee villages. Croghan established his base at Logstown, about fourteen miles below the junction of the Monongahela and Allegheny rivers, which together form the Ohio. Gist was the agent of the Ohio Company, established in 1748 to secure a royal charter for a speculative land grant west of the Appalachians.[29]

La Demoiselle asked the Iroquois to arrange a general council with the Pennsylvania commissioners in 1747, but their chiefs advised him to wait. On July 20, 1748, Commissioner Richard Peters, assisted by Andrew Montour, Conrad Weiser, and George Croghan, completed a treaty at Lancaster in which the English promised to send traders to the western tribes if the Indians would give effective protection to white pack trains. Although La Demoiselle did not attend, the treaty was made with three Miami chiefs from Pickawillany, a Seneca, two Oneidas, two Mohawks, and three Shawnees. The Miami chiefs were Aquenackqua, Navecqua, and Assesspansa (later called the "Young Piankeshaw

[28] *Ibid.*, 136, 259. Thwaites, *French Regime*, II, 481–85. The Governor said the Miamis had recently seized eight French traders at their Fort Miamis post.

[29] Kenneth P. Bailey, *The Ohio Company of Virginia and the Westward Movement, 1748–1792*, 18–19, 139–41. Albert T. Volweiler, *George Croghan and the Westward Movement*, 32–36.

King" and probably the son of La Demoiselle). The presence of Aquenackqua, an Eel River Miami and the father of the future war chief Little Turtle, is proof that not all the Miamis at Pickawillany were Piankeshaws, even at this early date. The Miami chiefs bolstered their importance in the eyes of the commissioner by announcing that twelve other Wabash and Illinois tribes were interested in joining the alliance.[30]

The Iroquois gave their consent to the alliance, and the Delawares were certain to join the Shawnees. English penetration of the west had been accomplished, but there remained the question of whether the other Miami bands would join the alliance. If they did so, it seemed certain that the Illinois tribes would follow them, and English trade and political influence would replace that of Louisiana and New France.

Le Comte's mixed band of Piankeshaws and Weas from near Ouiatanon joined their relatives at Pickawillany, and in spite of Le Pied Froid's pleadings, Chiefs Le Péan and Le Sac à Pétun also came with their villages from the Maumee. Finally, Le Pied Froid's village followed in 1750, leaving only the tribe's highest chief and his family at Kekionga. Pickawillany came near to assuming an importance superior to that of Kekionga, whose council fire lost its unifying effect.

Captain Charles D. Raymond, commandant at Fort Miamis in 1749 and 1750, was replaced by Louis Coulon de Villiers as the French sought to restrain the Miamis. In a letter which graphically depicts France's efforts to control her Indian allies, Raymond protested his removal and recounted his own successes:

> In 1749 The General Detached Him [Raymond] from the Command of That Garrison [Niagara] And Sent Him orders to go and take Command at the Miamis post where he stopped le pied froid, the Great Chief of the Miamis nation, and All of his Band who were about to

[30] Hanna, *The Wilderness Trail*, II, 137–39, 261–62. Volweiler, *George Croghan*, 64–66. The commissioners were told that the Miamis and their allies had one thousand warriors in twenty towns on the Wabash. Thwaites, *French Regime*, III, 58–60, quotes a letter from the commandant of the Illinois post warning Raymond of the ferment among the Illinois tribes.

abandon that post and Go over to The English. By his Continued efforts and watchfulness and The care he took to Maintain Spies among the Revolted Miamis and Their allies, he Discovered The Intrigues of a Conspiracy, Balked its plans and Frustrated their Execution. That Conspiracy had Been hatched by the pianguichias, The ouyatanons of the Band of le Comte, The Revolted Miamis, the Chaouanons and a number of Renegade yrocois who Had Withdrawn to the Belle Rivière and had Drawn into Their Plot the nations of the ylinois Country who were to act at the time Indicated to Them. The letter Written to Him on the Subject by Monsieur Benoist, the Commandant of the ylinois, he Sent to Monsieur de la jonquiere, who Stated that he had Forwarded It to Your Grace; a copy thereof is hereto annexed. By those negotiations he Won over The families of le péan and of le Sac à pétun, the leading ones among the Revolted Miamis. Their Return to the post brought back there The remainder of That nation and restored Harmony everywhere. He had Managed Matters on That Occasion and Had Reason to Hope for a successful Result When his unexpected and unseasonable recall, which surprised That Nation, caused them to Suddenly Change their attitude, and matters Became So unsatisfactory from that time, that they were in a Desperate condition and Without any Chance of Improvement. . . . [De Villiers] obtained no other result than seeing The Band of le pied froid leave the post of Miamis and Go over to the English, without being able to stop them; and there Remained with the Sieur de villiers at that post only le pied froid and his family, Making 3 or 4 Lodges. The families of le péan and of le Sac à pétun, who had just come to Miamis to join him [Raymond] would no longer Hear of Returning when they learned of his recall. Had he been Retained at that Post, They Would have come there and he Would have Availed himself of their Influence over the remainder of the Revolted Miamis to induce them to Return. The Band of le Pied froid, whom he would have Strengthened in their loyalty on their arrival, would not have left that post.

Despite the commandants' efforts, neither could stem the migration to the new town.[31]

Meanwhile, the French sent Pierre Joseph Céleron down the

[31] Hanna, *The Wilderness Trail*, II, 281–82. Krauskopf, "Ouiatanon Documents," 214–15. Raymond's letter of October 1, 1751, is in Thwaites, *French Regime*, III, 94–98.

Allegheny and Ohio rivers with a military force to overawe the Indians and drive out the British traders. He had little success. Even Le Baril's village of six cabins refused to leave its place at the mouth of the Little Miami to return to the Wabash. Céleron reached Pickawillany September 13, 1749, but failed to persuade La Demoiselle and his fifty or sixty warriors to withdraw. Céleron held a council at which only La Demoiselle and Le Baril received gifts, and this may have prompted one of the lesser chiefs, Le Péan, to complain to Raymond that

> the [Ouiatanons] had been faithful until the present, but they were disheartened by being poorly received by M. the general, who hardly looked at them and allowed them to leave without giving them anything more than a bagatelle. . . . [32]

Céleron then continued to Kekionga, where Le Pied Froid had remained, and to Detroit.[33]

In 1850, the French followed this failure with a plan to place forts on the trans-Appalachian routes in order to isolate the upper Ohio Valley tribes from British traders. It, too, failed when the Delawares and Iroquois refused to give them permission to fortify the Ohio River's source.[34]

Diplomacy had failed the French, and as Pickawillany grew to a trading center of at least four hundred warriors and dozens of English traders, hostilities became inevitable. It first took the form of French harassment and threats. Several English traders to the Ohio country were seized by the French in 1750, among them John Patten of Pennsylvania, who was captured near Kekionga and taken first to Detroit and then to Quebec and Paris. He was released in Paris and made his way to England, then back to the colony. Patten reported that Pickawillany was at that time a vil-

---

[32] Krauskopf, "Ouiatanon Documents," 215.

[33] Hanna, *The Wilderness Trail*, II, 262–63, 284–85. Thwaites, *French Regime*, III, 36–58, contains Céleron's "Journal" as translated from Pierre Margry, *Découvertes et Établissements des François dans l'ouest et dans le Sud de l'Amérique Septentrionale* (Paris, 1886), VI, 666–726.

[34] Randolph C. Downes, *Council Fires on the Upper Ohio,* 20, 43–44, 53, 58. Peckham, *Pontiac,* 37.

lage of about two hundred warriors.[35] Trader Hugh Crawford informed Governor James Hamilton of Pennsylvania that the Miamis were resisting every threat and inducement of the French to make them desert the English. The French circulated rumors at Fort de Chartres, on the Mississippi, that the Shawnees and Miamis planned to attack the Illinois tribes.

While George Croghan was at Logstown in November, 1750, he was told that La Demoiselle remained adamant and wished to move to the Ohio River.[36] He urged the Pennsylvania Assembly to fortify the upper Ohio, but the advice was not followed because of the colony's policy of economy—or parsimony. The upper Ohio tribes then asked for a British fort in their midst, but a year later they began to grasp the implications of the Ohio Company's plan to place settlements west of the mountains: the company had built Fort Cumberland in Maryland in 1750.[37]

Croghan went to Pickawillany with Gist in February, 1751, to negotiate a new treaty with the Indians. When he presented it to the Pennsylvania Assembly, he tried to impress that reluctant group by describing the western tribes as more powerful than the Iroquois. The colony repudiated the treaty, but the persistent trader realized English prestige depended upon support for his trading post at La Demoiselle's village. Unless this precaution were taken, the rapid English advance to the west could become a disastrous maneuver. Despite the assembly's lack of action, Croghan held a council with the Indians at Logstown in May. He told the tribesmen, including Miami delegates, that Pennsylvania had ratified the treaty negotiated three months earlier.[38]

Pierre Jacques de Taffanal, Marquis de La Jonquière, governor of New France until his death in early 1752, reviewed the situation

[35] Hanna, The Wilderness Trail, II, 268, reproduces portions of Patten's report. Howard W. Eavenson, Map Maker and Indian Traders, 5–8, 9–16, 118–25. Eavenson also contains accounts of Patten's capture and imprisonment in six appendices, 113–27.

[36] Hanna, The Wilderness Trail, II, 264–65, 267–68.

[37] Bailey, The Ohio Company, 139–41, 164–65.

[38] Hanna, The Wilderness Trail, II, 271–79, reproduces the Darlington edition of Gist's "Journal" of 1751. Hanna also explains Croghan's deception, 281. Volweiler, George Croghan, 74–75.

for the French minister of the Navy, Antoine Louis Rouillé, Comte de Joüy, in a report dated June 25, 1751. He accused Piankeshaw Chiefs La Mouche Noir and Le Peau Blanche of forming an alliance with La Demoiselle and said they were determined to join their bands to the latter's group. The Weas at Ouiatanon also were wavering, and both lower Wabash bands were in contact with Iroquois agents of the British. Jonquière feared that any tribes south of the Wabash were actually or potentially anti-French— a compliment to the energy of the British traders.[39]

On October 29, Jonquière summarized his efforts to combat the Miami menace. He had just failed for the third time to obliterate Pickawillany. On the first occasion, Céleron had collected a militia force, but after twenty days of consultation with Indian allies, he abandoned plans to attack.[40] A small force of Adirondack Indians next tried to reach Pickawillany, but they were turned back by the Ottawas.[41]

In his latest attempt, Jonquiére had ordered François Picote de Belestre to destroy Pickawillany, and an expedition of about fifty Nipissing Indians from Canada and a few warriors from other tribes departed from Detroit. Most of the Indians deserted at Sandusky after the Ottawas and Chippewas there threatened to attack the party if it harmed the Miamis. Belestre led his remnant to Pickawillany in spite of this, but found the village practically deserted; an Ottawa woman had hurried ahead to warn La Demoiselle of the approaching force. The Nipissings killed a man and woman to assuage their pride and were also accused by the Miamis of scalping a friendly Miami warrior near Kekionga on their return journey. Thomas Cresap heard practically the same

---

[39] Hanna, *The Wilderness Trail*, II, 153–55, quotes Jonquiere's letter. A portion of Captain Raymond's "Service Journal" is quoted in *ibid.*, 265. Thwaites, *French Regime*, III, 94–98, quotes Raymond's letter of October 1, 1751, in which he details his efforts to control the Miamis.

[40] Thomas Cresap's report on the affair was made to Lieutenant Governor Robert Dinwiddie of Virginia on November 20, 1751, and is reproduced in Hanna, *The Wilderness Trail*, II, 283–84. Jonquiere's letter is in *ibid.*, 283–84.

[41] Longueuil to the French Minister, April 21, 1752, in Thwaites, *French Regime*, III, 104–17. Hanna, *The Wilderness Trail*, II, 283–84.

account from La Demoiselle's son, except that the Miamis thought Belestre's warriors were Canadian Adirondack Indians. The Miamis soon retaliated against the expedition by scalping two French traders, and a full-scale war seemed inevitable.[42]

Charles Le Moyne, Baron de Longueuil, acting governor of New France, reported on the undeclared war in April, 1752. The Piankeshaws had taken five French scalps near the Vermilion River and La Demoiselle's warriors had secured two more near Kekionga, but the French had killed at least thirty Miami warriors. His own soldiers were too few to serve as garrisons and at the same time supply a field force. He was compelled to turn, therefore, to nearby tribes to secure scouts and auxiliaries, but the Miami system of alliances and relationships seemed to be an insurmountable obstacle to such a plan of action. Longueuil had good reason to regret the change from the days of Nicolas Perrot, when many tribes would have welcomed a war against the Miamis. Even though it had killed the two most loyal Miami chiefs, Le Gris and Le Pied Froid, the Governor's hopes rested upon the current smallpox epidemic. Such an outbreak destroyed the Indians' will and ability to wage war, and Longueuil thought it more effective than a military expedition.[43]

By 1752, Pickawillany had become an important trade center from which English traders traveled to the Indian villages of present-day Ohio and even to the Wabash River in Indiana. The Indians were more conscious of the post's strategic value than was Pennsylvania. Even the Iroquois, in a council held at Logstown in June, 1752, finally promised to let Virginia place settlements west of the mountains, but this concession to protect the little outpost came too late.[44]

[42] Hanna, *The Wilderness Trail*, I, 23–24, quotes Longueuil's report. See also *ibid.*, II, 285–88.

[43] Thwaites, *French Regime*, III, 104–17, gives the complete report.

[44] Bailey, *The Ohio Company*, 136–37. In 1752, the Iroquois again refused to permit the French to build forts along the Allegheny River. Photostatic copy of Item 1687, Detail of Indian Affairs, 1752–1754, prepared for Governor Hamilton, Pennsylvania, and used with permission of the Library of the American Philosophical Society, Philadelphia.

Although La Demoiselle and his followers behaved in a manner logically coherent and easily understood by Indian standards, the result was equally logical in terms of French and English imperial policies. The French finally turned to Indian auxiliaries not influenced by the Miami system of alliances to halt Miami migration and British trade expansion. Charles Langlade, a mixed-blood French-Indian trader on the western shore of Lake Michigan who was not even in the French Indian service, destroyed Pickawillany on June 21, 1752. He led two French aides and about 250 Nipissing Indians from the Mackinac area to Detroit, avoided detection by the villages along the Maumee River, and captured the town with no loss to his own party. Fourteen Indians, including La Demoiselle, and one white man were killed; five English traders were captured and their goods confiscated. Once more a remarkable French leader had overcome the greater resources of the British colonies.[45]

Whether La Demoiselle was boiled and eaten as a mark of esteem for his personal qualities or as a threat to the Miamis is immaterial; the destruction of Pickawillany was the kind of practical diplomacy which was most effective on the frontier. The British and their allies were confounded and made frantic gestures to recover their prestige. Trader Thomas Burney escaped the attack and carried the news to the Miamis' allies and to Pennsylvania. Croghan's partner, William Trent, with Burney and twenty Shawnees and Iroquois, reached Pickawillany in July. The village was deserted. Most of the Miamis had returned to Kekionga or the eastern tributaries of the Wabash, but the Young Piankeshaw King, or Assesspansa, and Turtle fled with a small group to the Shawnee villages. A council was held there, and La Demoiselle's widow was one of the speakers as the Delawares, Shawnees and Iroquois promised the Miamis they would be avenged.[46]

The "Pickawillany problem" had been solved, but Longueuil feared reprisals. When Michel Ange, Marquis Duquesne de Menne-

[45] Volweiler, *George Croghan*, 78–79. Thwaites, *French Regime*, III, 128–31, contains Governor Duquesne's entire report to the French minister.
[46] Bailey, *The Ohio Company*, 136–38; Captain William Trent's "Journal" is given in full in Hanna, *The Wilderness Trail*, II, 291–98.

ville, became governor of New France in August, 1752, he asked for a pension to reward Langlade, but the Detroit commandant reported the Miamis were becoming more dangerous. They had scalped two French soldiers near Kekionga, while the Piankeshaws had killed seven more in addition to one French citizen and three slaves.[47]

Decisive action by the British through the Pennsylvania or Virginia colonies, united with their Indian allies, could have brought on a border war in 1752, for the Miamis and their allies and relatives were ready for vengeance. But a smallpox epidemic undoubtedly created chaos in the tribe, and they had no hope of success against the French without substantial support.

Practical support did not materialize. Lieutenant Governor Robert Dinwiddie of Virginia sent only a letter of sympathy to the Miamis on the loss of their chief (La Demoiselle) in November, 1752.[48] On May 31, 1753, the Pennsylvania Assembly voted £200 for condolence presents to the Miamis and £600 for "necessities" to the other Ohio tribes. The fact that the Miamis were represented at a council held for the Iroquois and western tribes by Pennsylvania Commissioners Richard Peters, Isaac Norris, and Benjamin Franklin at Carlisle on October 23, proved they still hoped for British help against the French.

At Carlisle, the Indians showed their comprehension of the strategic situation and of their own needs. They now demanded three strong English trade centers west of the Appalachians and suppression of the whisky traffic. Since there was still no British imperial policy concerning Indian affairs and Pennsylvania was unwilling or unable to take this step alone, the council was fruitless. Even though the Ohio Company had built Fort Cumberland on the upper Potomac in 1750, this group of speculators now shrank from a direct confrontation with the French.[49]

[47] Hanna, *The Wilderness Trail*, II, 290–91, quotes portions of both reports.
[48] Bailey, *The Ohio Company*, 136–43. Volweiler, *George Croghan*, 81.
[49] Photostatic copy of the treaty signed with the Ohio Indians at Carlisle in October, 1753, used with permission of the American Philosophical Society, Philadelphia. Hanna, *The Wilderness Trail*, II, 307. Bailey, *The Ohio Company*, 164–65, 191–93.

The French were more enterprising. They constructed forts at Presque Isle on Lake Erie and Fort Le Boeuf on French Creek in 1753, then reached the Allegheny River with Fort Machault near the mouth of French Creek. When the British began to erect a fort at the Ohio Forks, the French immediately invested the area and built Fort Duquesne.[50]

The recalcitrant Miamis and the pro-British tribes became alarmed and demanded military aid. When this was not forthcoming, the disgusted Iroquois migrated back to their New York area, thus abandoning their support of the British and their influence among the western tribes.[51] The Miamis who returned to the Wabash-Maumee region now had no alternative but to accept French goods and traders with the best grace possible under the circumstances. French domination of the western tribes seemed complete, and those bands of the Miamis which had faithfully supported this alliance were reinforced by the warriors who had abandoned Pickawillany. For the first time, the Miami villages at Kekionga possessed more warriors than the lower Wabash villages.

There was no attempt to punish the rebels. That the Miamis could be induced to migrate—or, if offended, were capable of joining the eastern tribes or building a confederacy among the Illinois tribes—remained a definite threat to the French. If the hostility of the Foxes had proved costly to the French in men, trade, and alliances, the hostility of the Miamis could prove to be disastrous. The Miamis could form a very formidable Indian confederacy, since it would probably include the Shawnees and Delawares, along with the Illinois tribes. At the same time, the Miamis were well out of an enterprise which had seemed to offer promising trade advantages but had failed because the British colonies had vacillated. They were proud of the influence they had exerted. They now returned to the Wabash-Maumee Valley to resume their French contacts, certain they were a power which could not be ignored.

[50] Bailey, The Ohio Company, 174–93.
[51] Peckham, Pontiac, 38–39. Entry of May 21–24, 1751, in "Résumé of the Proceedings of the Ohio Company, October 24, 1743–May 24, 1751," in Lois Mulkearn (ed.), George Mercer Papers Relating to the Ohio Company of Virginia, 6.

The French had learned a valuable lesson from their past efforts to subdue or control Indian tribes by encouraging intertribal wars. In 1755, they initiated a new policy of peace and pacification among their allies. The Iroquois withdrawal to New York, plus British colonial timidity in 1752, cleared the way for later French rapport with the Shawnees, Delawares, Ottawas, and Wyandots. The new Miami *rapprochement* also helped in dealing with these tribes and restoring French supremacy in the Illinois confederacy.[52]

The last battles in the French and Indian War, 1754–63, were fought far to the east, but distance did not prevent western tribes from joining the French. Although their nearest neighbors, the Potawatomis, were active in the war, the Miamis apparently took little part in it, except for the 250 Miami warriors who accompanied Belestre in the 1755 French campaign launched from Fort Duquesne against General Edward Braddock.[53] The Miamis probably had no intention of fighting against either the Iroquois allies of the British or the French-allied Algonquian tribes about the Great Lakes. They were convinced they could not escape French control of their own trade, nor were they certain the British could secure control of the Ohio Valley trade. Their actions coincided with French necessities. The French did not need Miami warriors in the east; they needed a strong and loyal tribe on the Wabash route to Louisiana.

The events of 1752 left their imprint on the Miamis in other ways. The Kekionga band's influence was enhanced. The Wea and Piankeshaw bands once more consulted it and followed its councils, except at the time of George Rogers Clark's invasion a generation later. The lower bands had suffered severe losses of prestige and leaders at Pickawillany, and they now turned to Kekionga or to the Potawatomi, Kickapoo, and Illinois tribes for support more than ever before. Some of the deterioration in the habits of the Weas which Governor Henry Hamilton noted in 1779 resulted

52 Thwaites, *French Regime*, III, 163.
53 Kellogg, *French Regime*, 425.

from this loss in the band's morale. It was no longer the largest and most warlike Miami band, nor even the cleanest![54]

The Miami tribe experienced definite changes from 1700 to the close of French domination south of the Great Lakes in 1763. The most obvious was its decrease in size. From an estimated 4,500 persons when it began moving east, it shrank to about 1,750 in 1764. There had been no great attrition through war, but there were at least three smallpox epidemics—in 1715, 1733, and 1752. In fact, the disease appeared to be endemic by the last named year.[55]

The amalgamation of the Miamis' culture with that of the French had increased. Contact between the two had been limited before 1700. At first, only small contingents of French soldiers and traders, together with their employees, were permitted in the Miami villages—a feature of French policy. These residents were on uncertain ground with the Indians; their government supervised them with endless regulations, they did not have an active church among the villages, and virtual war existed for several years.

There was little intermarriage between the Miamis and French during the first thirty years in Indiana. Church records at Vincennes, begun April 21, 1749, indicate few marriages or baptisms of Indians took place, and we may be sure the Roman Catholic missionaries always recorded such events.[56]

French names recorded before 1750 reveal few which became important among the Miamis, with the notable exceptions of Godfroy and Richardville. Jacques Godfroy commanded the Wea post

[54] John D. Barnhart (ed.), *Henry Hamilton and George Rogers Clark in the American Revolution, With the Unpublished Journal of Lieut. Gov. Henry Hamilton*, 129, 131.

[55] Krauskopf, "Ouiatanon Documents," 222, cites the list of Thomas Hutchins, *The Papers of Sir William Johnson*, X, 545. Smith, *Historical Account*, Appendix II, 116–20, contains accounts by an English officer and various traders of the Miami villages.

[56] Jesuit Father Sebastian L. Meurin recorded a marriage on this date in the first entry of "Records of the Parish of St. Francis Xavier at Post Vincennes, Indiana," translated from the French by Edmond J. P. Schmitt in *Records of the American Catholic Historical Society of Philadelphia*, XII, 41–60, 193–211, 322–36.

in 1735 and Joseph Richardville in 1748, and both also served at other posts along the Wabash.[57] The Ouiatanon post housed about twenty French traders, as well as their employees and soldiers, from 1746 to 1754. This post was the most lucrative on the Wabash, but it was also the most susceptible to Indian intrigue. It did not become an attractive place for retired *voyageurs* and soldiers, as did Vincennes.

Father Joseph de Bonnecamps, who accompanied the Céleron expedition in 1749, said there were at that time eight "miserable huts" and twenty-two fever-ridden Frenchmen at Fort Miamis.[58] When John Patten was a prisoner there the following year, the French force consisted of a captain, an ensign, and about fifty men. Only nine or ten became permanent settlers at Kekionga.[59]

Post Vincennes, situated among the Piankeshaws, became a French community in the middle of the wilderness. By 1758, about seventy-five men and women had permanently settled there, among whom were "18 or 20 good inhabitants who raise their wheat, tobacco and corn."[60] It was a French outpost among the remnants of the Piankeshaws.

By 1760, the families of successful Miami hunters wore clothes made from European cloth at least part of the time. The women's household equipment was "modernized" with iron kettles, needles, thread, and steel knives. The men discarded their traditional war clubs for a few guns of inferior quality, steel knives, and iron hatchets. In order to conserve ammunition, the bow and arrow and the snare were reserved for hunting. Hunting and pelt preparation had increased in importance because furs supplied the currency for trade. However, the Miamis also had a prime source of revenue in the corn they supplied to traders, soldiers, and other tribes. They were able to see the value of their control of portages, and the one

[57] Krauskopf, "Ouiatanon Documents," 147, 184–85, 208–209.
[58] Bailey, *The Ohio Company*, 166, reproduces Bonnecamp's map of Céleron's expedition. Hanna, *The Wilderness Trail*, II, 262–64, quotes extensively from Céleron's "Journal."
[59] Hanna, *The Wilderness Trail*, II, 268.
[60] Paul C. Phillips, "Vincennes in Its Relation to the French Colonial Policy," *Indiana Magazine of History*, XVII (1921), 311–37.

between the Little Wabash and St. Mary's rivers became their most valued possession.

When they acquired axes, hoes, and knives, the Miamis used less time clearing land for new fields, building dugouts and boats, erecting cabins, and preparing meat. Their increased leisure was used for games, dances, and council meetings, which they craved. The traditional celebrations and practices of the Medewiwin and Jeesukewin societies occupied more of their time than ever before.

The most important change, however, was the growth of Miami political sophistication. The Miamis had learned that the land they occupied had more value because of its location than because of its fertility. They had learned much concerning the value of their furs, the ways of traders, and the rivalry between the French and British. Most of all, they had learned the value of alliances, of wise leadership, of unity, and especially of caution.

A new series of lessons began when Fort Niagara was captured in 1759 and French control of the west ended. Deputy Superintendent of Indian Affairs George Croghan held councils with the western tribes, including the Miamis, in 1758, 1759, and 1760. Major Robert Rogers occupied Detroit in 1760, and the first detachment he sent into the hinterland occupied Fort Miami in December of that year. Another period of historical change for the Miamis had been ushered in.

3
THE BRITISH PERIOD,
1760-1783

The era of British sovereignty introduced the Miamis to a new facet of European civilization: ownership of land in fee simple. The British imperial government assumed the "white man's burden" of Indian guardianship by proclaiming that title to Indian tribal land resided in the British Crown; the French had not presumed to make such a claim before transferring the territory to the British. The Treaty of Paris of 1763 made the Indians aware that European trade had been only a means by which the French and British penetrated their land in order to claim it—a high price for the tribes to pay for the trade goods which had become so necessary for their comfort or even survival. The Indian allies of these two nations had been mere tools of the policy when they fought in the earlier Beaver Wars. Under terms of the Proclamation of 1763, the British attempted to placate both their land-hungry colonists and their new Indian wards by creating an Indian reservation.

Only very slowly did the Indians comprehend that the latest war had been one of conquest in which their land had been the prize. They had failed to grasp the European's concept of land ownership and sovereignty. Briefly stated, the members of an Indian tribe held in common the privilege to "enjoy and use" a more or less well-defined area. They had given Frenchmen tenancy rights at certain sites, but no more, and insisted the British had acquired only those tenancy rights by their defeat of the French; any further claims in the Treaty of 1763 were invalid by Indian standards. The British point of view assumed the French were the actual owners of all territory ceded in the treaty; the French had gained sovereignty by the right of discovery and exploration but had lost it through British conquest. The Treaty of 1763 suddenly revealed to the Indians that this had also been the well-masked pretension of the French.[1]

The British concept of land ownership, from which American practices evolved, was itself chaotic. The doctrine of *res nullis*, in which absolute title to imperial lands resided in the Crown, came under attack, especially by land speculators. *Res nullis* denied Indians title to their land but recognized their right to hold, enjoy, and use it.[2]

Sir William Johnson became the resident agent of these policies. General Edward Braddock, commander-in-chief of the military forces in North America, sought to coordinate the actions of his Indian auxiliaries by commissioning Johnson "Superintendent of Indian Affairs North of the Ohio River" in 1755. The following year, the British Lords of Trade appointed Edmond Atkin to the same office for the southern tribes, but both men acted under the military command. The same body inquired of Governor Thomas Pownall of Pennsylvania about "the proper attitude which should be assumed toward the Indians" by the British government. Pownall explained that colonial governors had always directed colonial-Indian affairs, but suggested that all Indian affairs should be placed under Johnson.[3]

---

[1] Cyrus Thomas, Introduction, in Charles C. Royce (comp.), *Indian Land Cessions in the United States*, 527–33, reviews European policies of conquest and their emulation by the United States as given in the Supreme Court decision Johnson and Graham's lessee *vs.* McIntosh & Wheaton, p. 543 *et seq.*

[2] Francis S. Philbrick, *The Rise of the West, 1754–1830*, 23.

[3] Royce, *Indian Land Cessions*, 555. Lawrence Henry Gipson, *The British Empire Before the American Revolution*, IX, 41–54, 336–37. Volweiler, *George Croghan*, 115–20.

Johnson continued to operate under Braddock's commission during the war. He crowned his able direction and use of the Indians by his personal command of the force which captured Fort Niagara in 1759. This battle was the final engagement in the west; soon afterward, on August 7, the Delawares, Ottawas, and Shawnees sent a delegation of chiefs there to meet George Croghan, Johnson's chief deputy. In September, the Miamis and some other Ottawa chiefs reached Pittsburgh and made peace with the British.[4] The long war had found the French unable to supply the western tribes with goods. The Indians, who were always responsive to the realities of superior forces and cheaper goods, were willing to forget the futility and indecisiveness of the British colonial governments in 1752. The isolation of Detroit after the capture of Fort Niagara proved to them, quite as well as to the French command, that the war between France and Britain in the west was finished.

The Miami chiefs were present as about one thousand Indians gathered at the "good will conference" held by Croghan and Colonel Henry Bouquet at Pittsburgh in August, 1760, which signaled the beginning of British control west of the Appalachians.[5] Major Robert Rogers was sent to secure Detroit and to garrison the little forts and posts along the Ohio and about the Great Lakes. Rogers and Croghan reached Detroit November 29, 1760, and in December, Rogers sent a force under Ensign Robert Holmes to occupy Forts Miamis and Ouiatanon. However, Lieutenant Edward Jenkins did not occupy the latter until November, 1761, after the little garrison at Fort Miamis had been safely established.[6]

Croghan was always accompanied by Iroquois at his Indian councils because they were his most potent agents in securing al-

---

[4] Peckham, *Pontiac*, 54–56. Photostatic copy of the minutes of the September 3, 1759, conference at Pittsburgh, from a copy of William Trent's original documents in the Library of the American Philosophical Society, Philadelphia. Chief Masheconaghta, War Chief Mischgha, and seventeen Twightwee warriors were present.

[5] Volweiler, *George Croghan*, 114.

[6] Peckham, *Pontiac*, 65. Jenkins' letter of November 4, 1761, to Colonel Henry Bouquet at Detroit tells of his departure to his new command. *Michigan Pioneer and Historical Collections* (cited hereafter as *MPHC*), XIX, 118.

legiance from the western tribes. He climaxed his efforts to pacify them and obtain their cooperation in a grand council which convened at Detroit on September 9, 1761. Sir William Johnson attended this council in order to impress the Indians with Britain's benevolent purposes. The meeting was harmonious, and there appeared to be no serious obstacles to the transfer of tribal loyalties from France to Britain.[7]

Meanwhile, a definitive treaty of peace between the European powers was pending and the Lords of Trade faced the problem of governing the inhabitants of Britain's newly acquired territories. The British government and her colonies had previously ignored Indian possessory rights to their soil. On November 23, 1761, the Lords of Trade, with King George III present, had reported:

> . . . to enter into a detail of all causes of complaint which our Indian allies had against us . . . it will be sufficient for the present purpose to observe that the primary cause of that discontent which produced these fatal effects was the Cruelty and Injustice with which they [Indians] had been treated with respect to their hunting grounds, in open violation of those solemn compacts by which they had yielded to us the Dominion, but not the property of those lands.[8]

A month later, the Lords of Trade sent to the governors of the colonies instructions to observe the rights of the Indians and the terms of all treaties made previously or face the penalty of dismissal. This was followed by the appointment of Sir William Johnson and John Stuart as royal agents for Indian affairs. Their authority now rested with the Lords of Trade.[9]

Johnson's department included the northern colonies and the western territory north of the Ohio, in which he had been functioning since 1755. George Croghan at Fort Pitt was his chief deputy and agent to the western tribes. Croghan faced a difficult situation, for the Senecas, the westernmost Iroquois tribe and the most influ-

---

[7] Peckham, *Pontiac*, 77–78. Volweiler, *George Croghan*, 155–56.

[8] Royce, *Indian Land Cessions*, 554.

[9] *Ibid.*, 555–59. Philbrick, *The Rise of the West*, 1–33, contains a comprehensive summary of British policies in the west from 1763 to 1768.

ential among the Ohio and Indiana tribes, were already circulating a war belt.[10]

Various councils with the Indians from 1758 to 1761 had failed to solve immediate problems. Needed in the new area were garrisoned forts from which British authority could govern the French, Indians, and traders. British requests for suitable sites at first met with little Indian enthusiasm. A major source of irritation arose from British insistence that the Indians deliver up all white captives. Because of their adoption policies, the Indians resisted loss of their new white "relatives." The Indians' demand for trade to satisfy their needs was met to a limited extent in 1759. The license system hindered authorized trade, and because it could not be enforced, there sprang up an illegal trade which concentrated upon supplying the Indians with whisky. General Jeffery Amherst, commander-in-chief of British forces in North America after 1758, restricted the funds expended on presents provided at councils by the superintendents of Indian affairs. And the Indians demanded reassurance their lands would not be invaded by squatters, a task the British were totally incapable of performing.

The first stirring of Indian resistance came when the Senecas attempted to provoke an uprising in 1761; they had been restless since the British used Cherokee and Catawba scouts on the northern frontier in 1756 and 1757. The Delaware Prophet attempted to incite his tribe to resist the British in 1762. Likewise, some disaffected Frenchmen perpetuated a smoldering dissatisfaction among the habitants in the west. More gifted leadership was required to reconcile the Indians' very real grievances, and it was soon supplied by Ottawa Chief Pontiac. The Lords of Trade labored to meet the problems Britain had acquired with its new empire. The policies incorporated in the Proclamation of 1763, had they come earlier, might have prevented the outbreak of the Indian war known as Pontiac's Uprising if they could have been enforced.[11]

[10] Peckham, *Pontiac*, 74.
[11] In *ibid.*, 92–111, is a summation of the complex courses of Pontiac's disaffection

Croghan was aware that many French habitants and a large number of France's former Indian allies did not accept the verdict of military defeat. In 1762, reports from traders and from the commandant at Fort Ouiatanon indicated some French habitants were fomenting trouble on the Wabash. He sent his assistant, Ensign Thomas Hutchins, to investigate the western forts and tribes. Hutchins visited Forts Miamis and Ouiatanon in July, 1762. Because he found there had been a severe epidemic (probably smallpox) among the tribes near the latter post in the spring, he believed it would have enhanced British prestige if he had been able to distribute presents generously. However, General Amherst's policy limited largesse, a requirement in Indian diplomacy, and British relations suffered from a lack of generosity at Indian councils.[12]

The Indians, of course, were not immediately aware of British efforts to establish an orderly economic and political system of imperial government that would include their protection. The Proclamation Act of October 7, 1763, which was intended to be temporary, was based on sound principles reached in the recent inquiries of the Lords of Trade. However, once initiated, such acts may become self-perpetuating. The proclamation defined the western boundaries of the coastal colonial settlement, the Floridas, and Canada and reserved a vast expanse of territory between these areas and the Mississippi to the Crown. This was to be Indian territory, under the jurisdiction of imperial agents, in which the natives were not to be molested or disturbed by private purchases, treaties, surveys, or settlements.[13]

with the British. Volweiler, *George Croghan*, 129. Clarence Walworth Alvord, *The Mississippi Valley in British Politics*, I, 287–325, is a classic account of British-Indian relationships.

[12] In addition to the blow to their national pride, French traders, who lost their monopolistic control of Indian trade, feared the new competition with English traders. Hanna, *The Wilderness Trail*, II, 362–67. Smith, *Historical Account*, 125. Krauskopf, "Ouiatanon Documents," 222, includes Hutchins' estimate of Miami warriors, which included 230 "Mineami or Twightwea," 200 Ouiatanon, and 100 "Pyankishaw."

[13] Royce, *Indian Land Cessions*, 558–59, quotes the section of the Proclamation of 1763 dealing with the newly formulated Indian policy. Gipson, *British Empire*, IX, 41–54.

The imperial policies underlying the proclamation were developed primarily to ensure control of Indian affairs and secondarily to ensure an orderly disposal of Crown lands in the future. Indian trade policies, colonial boundaries, and western settlements soon influenced the colonial and imperial positions. Spheres of authority were soon disputed among the new Indian superintendents, the military authority establishment, and colonial governors.

The Crown's position was forecast in earlier decisions. Johnson's treaty for Pennsylvania with the eastern Delawares promised that colony would make no settlement west of the Susquehanna without the tribe's consent. In a proclamation issued in October, 1761, Colonel Henry Bouquet, commandant at Fort Pitt, extended this principle to include Maryland and Virginia and enforced it by removing settlers from the Monongahela River country. It soon became evident, however, that it was impossible to keep whites from the new Indian reservation, which had become an attractive refuge for undesirable colonial residents.[14]

Another change was made in 1763 when the colonial governors' authority in Indian affairs was given to the two Indian superintendents. In April, 1764, Johnson received his commission as "sole agent and superintendent of Indian Affairs for the Northern parts of North America."[15] In addition, since there was no provision for a government for the French habitants, they became the concern of the British military authority.

The former pro-French tribes did not wait to understand the new British policies. Despite periodic conflict with the French and occasional trade with the British, their cultural adaptations and loyalties had been established by a century of French contact. The worst shock to their self-esteem came with the realization that their French allies, despite years of declared brotherhood and equality, regarded them as captive nations by ceding the Indians' land to the British. Although the Great Lakes tribes were not strangers to subjugation, they felt they had not lost the late war to the British

14 Philbrick, *The Rise of the West*, 2–3.
15 Royce, *Indian Land Cessions*, 559.

and the French defeat therefore should not include them as a prize of war.

The Miamis' caution and respect for power prevented any hasty actions on the occasion of the Seneca protests in 1761. However, the various forms of discontent in combination brought on the uprising of 1763 by less cautious tribes and leaders. Irreconcilables among the French settlers, Indian fury at the parsimony of the British government, and colonial squatters' infiltration into the western valleys of the Appalachians gave impetus to the evangelical racism of the Delaware Prophet in 1762 and to the political promises of Ottawa Chief Pontiac in 1763.

Seneca intransigence did not wane, and the Miamis at Kekionga received a war belt from them in March, 1763. Ensign Robert Holmes, commandant at Fort Miamis, was told they refused to accept the belt and had no desire for war. He sent the war belt to Major Henry Gladwin, the Detroit commander, with the assurance the Miamis had repudiated any involvement in the affair.[16] Meanwhile, Pontiac was able to collect a large group of warriors, primarily from the Ottawa, Chippewa, and Potawatomi villages near Detroit. When he commenced his attack against its fort on May 15, other warriors proceeded to capture both Sandusky and Fort St. Joseph at Niles. With the war so near at hand, the Miamis could not escape involvement. Pontiac sent Jacques Godfroy and Mini Chesne, two Detroit traders and his most active French supporters, with a force of Indians to the Illinois tribes, and a Kekionga war party eagerly prepared to join them. When the Miamis realized the extent of Pontiac's early successes, they agreed to capture their own fort. On May 25, they took three British soldiers, even though the garrison had been alerted. Two days later, they waylaid Holmes and a sergeant by using a Miami girl to decoy them from the fort. The eleven soldiers remaining in the fort accepted terms of surrender; four were taken to Pontiac, while the other seven were either kept as prisoners or massacred.

---

[16] Peckham, *Pontiac*, 106. Wallace A. Brice, *History of Fort Wayne From the Earliest Known Accounts of This Point to the Present Period*, 60–61.

The Miami warriors then proceeded down the Wabash with Godfroy and Chesne in what had now become a military expedition. At Ouiatanon on June 1, the Weas helped them take the fort and capture Lieutenant Jenkins and twenty soldiers. The prisoners were taken to Fort de Chartres on the Mississippi, where the French had remained in command. There the captives could be used as evidence of Pontiac's success and held to serve as hostages in the event the British rallied from their first defeats.[17]

The latter possibility was obvious to the Miamis. When Pontiac failed to secure Detroit and Fort Pitt and many of his allies left the Detroit siege to go on their winter hunts, the Miamis sent a delegation of one hundred warriors to Detroit on October 8, 1763, to observe the situation. They were not deceived by Pontiac's claims. Since they were only observers, half the warriors returned home; those who remained declared they would follow the guidance and policy of the Wyandots. The Wyandots' influence was great in that they were accorded the right to speak first at any council, even in the presence of the Six Nations.[18] They were not as closely allied to the French as were the Chippewas and Ottawas, and the Miamis wisely relied on their advice at this time—a significant development in Miami policy. The anti-Pontiac factions of the Ottawas, Mississaugis, and Chippewas sent delegations into Detroit to confer with Major Gladwin on terms for making peace with the British, while many of Pontiac's French supporters quietly slipped away to the safety of the Wabash and Illinois country.

Pontiac lost his last hope for the united support of the Illinois tribes on October 30, 1763. Major Pierre Joseph Neyon de Villiers, who had not yet been replaced by the British as commandant at Fort de Chartres, sent letters to him urging peace and denying French aid would be given to continue the war. The same message

---

[17] Peckham, *Pontiac*, 158–61. Jenkins, Ouiatanon, to Gladwin, Detroit, June 1, 1763, in Clarence Walworth Alvord and Clarence Edwin Carter (eds.), *The Critical Period, 1763–1765*, 12–13. *MPHC*, XIX, 212–19.

[18] Peckham, *Pontiac*, 234. Louise Phelps Kellogg, *Frontier Advance on the Upper Ohio, 1778–1779*, 310–12, emphasizes the position of leadership which the Wyandots exerted among the Great Lakes tribes.

was also sent to the Wabash tribes and their French residents.[19] Pontiac retired to the island at the rapids of the Maumee, Roche de Bout, with his Ottawa and Wyandot followers and several French irreconcilables. However, the war was not yet over, for while the Detroit tribes made peace, the chief quietly set about rebuilding his alliances.

The English also prepared to recoup their losses and prestige. General Thomas Gage replaced Amherst as supreme commander and made plans for a general Indian council at Niagara. George Croghan hastily returned from England to reinforce Johnson's western policies, while military expeditions were planned to relieve Detroit and to punish the Ohio tribes which had supported Pontiac. Detroit was still in a state of intermittent siege in March, 1764, when Pontiac began a journey to restore the resolution of his allies.

Still admired by his Miami neighbors, Pontiac could not expect to continue the fight by removing it to the Wabash and to Illinois without their full support. The young Miami braves were easily inflamed: they had missed nearly all the excitement and glories of the war, except at the capture and pillage of Fort Miamis the previous year. A few small parties of warriors always slipped away at the call of any respected warrior (even those of other tribes) or familiar French traders. The Miami chiefs could not prevent this and no doubt had used the unfavorable reports brought home by these scattered warriors to persuade the tribal council to continue its semblance of neutrality.

Pontiac's first efforts to regain support were made at Kekionga. The Miamis still held some English prisoners, and they probably tortured and killed two of them at Pontiac's urging. He stirred the warlike spirit of the tribes as he moved through the Wea, Kickapoo, and Potawatomi villages on his way down the Wabash to Fort de Chartres. Although De Villiers advised him to make peace, the chief held a war council near the fort on April 17 with the nearby Illinois tribes. It left them belligerent and made the region unsafe

---

[19] Peckham, *Pontiac*, 236. De Villiers, Fort de Chartres, to Sieur Dabbadie, New Orleans, December 1, 1763, in Alvord and Carter, *The Critical Period*, 49–57.

for future British emissaries. He then began his return to the Maumee.[20]

During Pontiac's absence from Detroit, the pro-British Ottawa bands, the Wyandot warriors, and the Miami delegation of observers again met with Gladwin to sue for peace. At the same time, Pontiac's allies went to Albany to treat with Johnson for peace. Later that summer, Johnson held a conference at Niagara at which these two parties of warriors were the only ones who had participated in the attacks on the British.[21] Some Menominees, Sioux, Foxes, Sauks, Crees, and the villages of Ottawas and Chippewas who had resisted Pontiac's schemes were there in force.

When Pontiac returned from the Illinois country to his Maumee village, he attempted to continue the war with those of his allies who refused to make peace. The Shawnees and Delawares remained the most irreconcilable belligerents, but they were little influenced by Pontiac's leadership. They were committed, not to an Indian confederacy or the return of French rule, but to preserving their lands west of the Appalachians. The Miamis, living between their traditional relatives, the Illinois and lower Wabash tribes, and their allies, the Delawares and Shawnees, once more had recourse to the diplomacy of expediency as they awaited results of the English counteroffensive in the summer of 1764. It appears the Miamis were not yet ready to sustain Pontiac or to accept his leadership in a nascent concept of Indian hegemony.

After Johnson's Niagara council, the British began their offensive in August by dispatching Colonel John Bradstreet from Niagara toward Detroit with twelve hundred men. Lulled into a false sense of security by the Delawares and Shawnees about their own and Pontiac's intentions, Bradstreet, on August 26, sent Captain Thomas Morris without a military escort to accept the submission of the hostile warriors.

Morris' party illustrates the contending forces in the war. It was composed of the pro-British Ottawa chief Atawang, a Chippe-

[20] Peckham, *Pontiac,* 244–45.
[21] *Ibid.,* 252–54.

wa chief, and a force of Oneida warriors under Chief Thomas King. Jacques Godfroy and Mini Chesne, arrested at Detroit but released and taken east to serve as guides for Bradstreet, were ordered to escort Morris to Pontiac's village. A Delaware and Shawnee delegation had carried war belts up the Maumee to Kekionga a few days before, and Pontiac, supported by six hundred warriors, was at first hostile toward the British. However, Atawang and Thomas King reminded Pontiac of Johnson and his Iroquois, and he soon became more conciliatory. Morris sent Atawang to Detroit to warn Bradstreet, while Pontiac added his nephew, Atawang's son, and the visiting Miami chief Naranea to Morris' detachment to ensure its safe journey up the Maumee to Kekionga.

The detachment arrived there September 7, and Morris waited while his allies tried to pacify the Miamis. When he entered the village, Morris was made a prisoner, but Le Gris, at that time a war chief, made sure the tribe did not commit itself too deeply. Two minor leaders, the son of Chat Blanc and Vis en l'Air, hid Morris to prevent his being tortured, while François Godfroy and St. Vincent, French traders in the village, along with Atawang's son and Naranea, calmed the crowd of impulsive warriors. The Swan, or La Cygne, another chief, favored hospitable treatment of Morris because the British held his children as hostages at Detroit. Morris' account of his capture and release is quite graphic:

Continued our march. Got into easy water, & arrived at the meadow near the Miamis Fort pretty early in the day, having had nothing to eat. Met at the bottom of the meadow by almost the whole village, who had brought spears, bows & arrows, & tomahawks to dispatch me; but I had the good fortune to stay in the canoe when the rest went ashore, tho' ignorant of their intention. Arrived at the fort. The chiefs assembled, passed me by when they presented the pipe of friendship, led by Indians to the village on the other side of the water & told me to stay in the fort with the French, tho' care had been taken before my arrival to forbid the French to let me into their houses, & some strips of wampum which the French had spoken upon to spare my life had been refused. We wondered at this treatment, as we expected that I should

69

be civilly received. This change of temper was owing to the Shawnee & Delaware, fifteen of them having come there with fourteen belts & six strings of wampum in the name of their nations & of that of the Senecas who had declared that they would perish to a man before they would make peace with the English. Seven were returned to their villages, five were gone to Wyant, & three had gone the morning I arrived (a most fortunate circumstance for me, for they were determined to kill me) to St. Joseph. The Shawanese & Delawares begged of the Miamis either to put us to death, (the Indians & myself) or to tie us & send us prisoners to their village, or at least to make us return. They loaded the English with reproaches, as monstrous as false, such as the malice of savages only, could invent, and added that while the sun should shine they would be at enmity with us. The Kicapous who happened to be at the Miamis village on their way home were so affected with the speeches of the Shawanese & Delawares that they declared they would dispatch me at their village, if the Miamis should let me pass. The Shawanese & Delawares concluded their speeches with saying, when they presented the last belt, "this is the last belt we shall send you, till we send you the hatchet, which will be about the end of the next month." (October) Doubtless their design is to amuse Col. Bradstreet with fair language, to cut off his army at Sandoski when least expected, & then to send their hatchet to the nations. A hellish plan, but not a foolish one: & well worthy of so detestable a race of mortals.

To return to myself. I was left in the fort, & two warriors, (the son of Chat blanc, (white cat) & vis en l'air) (Face in the Air) with tomahawks seized me, one by each arm & dragged me along to the water side where I imagined they intended to put me into a canoe, but they pulled me into the water. I concluded their whim was to drown me & then scalp me; I soon found my mistake, the river being fordable, they led me on till we came very near their village, & there they stopt me & stript me; they could not get off my shirt, & in rage & despair I tore it off myself. Then they bound my arms with my sash & drove me before them to a cabin where was a bench on which they made me sit. I was led by the Cabin where were my faithful & valliant Indians who never put out their heads to look at me, the whole village was in an uproar. Godefroi prevailed on St. Vincent, who had followed me to the water side but had turned back, to come along with him, and encouraged Pontiac's nephew & the little Chief's [Atawang] son to take

70

my part. St. Vincent brought the great belt & Pondiac's nephew spoke. Namamis [Naranea] seemed to encourage Godefroi to support me. Godefroi told the Cygne (the Swan) that his children were at Detroit, & that if they killed me, he could not tell what might befall them. He spoke likewise to the Cygne's son (a young fellow who afterwards came often to visit us & said he had a desire to go to Detroit but that he was afraid) who whispered (to) his father & the father came and untied me. The son of Chat blanc upon my speaking, got up & tied me by the neck to a post; when young Pacanne (king of the village, but yet a minor) rode up and untied me saying "I give that man his life. If you want meat, go to Detroit or upon the lake, and you'll find enough; what business have you with this man, who is come to speak to us?" When Pondiac's nephew had done speaking, Vis en l'air said "Since it is so, I give it up." An Indian then presented me his pipe, & I was dismissed by being pushed rudely away. I made what haste I could to a canoe & got to the fort, having received on my way a smart cut of a switch from an Indian on horseback. Mr. Levi & some soldiers who are prisoners came to see me. I was never left alone as the villians who stript & tied me were always lurking about to find an opportunity to stab me. Lay in L'Esperance's house.[22]

One decisive act by Pacanne saved Morris. On examination, the effort was probably made only after the villages had been satisfied by a few days of warlike excitement. Pontiac, Thomas King, and Jacques Godfroy were convinced their efforts had saved Morris, but Pacanne and other Miami chiefs had probably made the decision to preserve his life from the first. The hostile Miami demonstration certainly speeded Morris on his way to the safety of Detroit.

The many villages situated at the head of the Maumee River and collectively known as Kekionga employed a method of treating with the contending forces which had the outward appearance of political disunity but was in fact a calculated attempt by the Mi-

[22] Quoted from "Thomas Morris' Diary," published in *The Old Fort News*, I, (February, 1941), a publication of the Allen County-Fort Wayne Historical Society (Indiana), with Introduction by Howard H. Peckham. "Journal of Captain Thomas Morris, of His Majesty's XVII Regiment of Infantry; Detroit, September 25, 1764" is in Reuben Gold Thwaites (ed.), *Early Western Travels, 1748–1846*, I, 301–28.

amis to discern the stronger party and align themselves with it. It was not surprising, therefore, to find the group at Detroit following Wyandot leadership in making overtures for peace while the Kekionga villages were hostile to the British and Naranea was both ally and critical observer of Pontiac. The method revealed itself even more strikingly when the villages welcomed the Shawnee and Delaware war delegation and next day also welcomed Morris' pro-British escort of Ottawas, Chippewas, and Senecas.

Bradstreet held a council at Detroit September 5–7 at which Naranea was the unofficial representative of the Miamis.[23] Despite the council's peaceful intentions, without the presence of Pontiac at its deliberations, nothing of any importance or lasting value could be accomplished. Besides, the Delawares and Shawnees remained on the war path.

The course of all peace negotiations with these tribes depended on the expedition of Bouquet, which left Fort Pitt October 1. He subdued the Muskingum Delaware villages and took hostages in order to force the chiefs to treat with Johnson, recovered two hundred white captives and secured a promise for the release of a hundred more, and forced the Delawares and Shawnees to send a delegation to the Wabash tribes to testify that their earlier reports in September had grossly exaggerated British defeats.[24] This removed the Indian barrier to British advance to the western Great Lakes and the Mississippi, effectively neutralized the Miamis, and cost Pontiac all chance of support along the Wabash.

Bouquet's use of force illustrated his ingenious grasp of Indian psychology, yet the effects of his expedition were not immediately comprehended by Pontiac or by Pontiac's Indian opponents. The chief retired to his Maumee village for the winter of 1764–65, still confident he could secure support from Indians on the southern

---

[23] Peckham, *Pontiac,* 261. John Montressor, in Bradstreet's force at Sandusky, wrote: "Declined an attack on the Miamis Village, they producing their chiefs for Peace, the whole agreeing to meet us in Council for the purpose at Detroit. Their Chiefs embarked onboard our Fleet." Photostatic copy of the original letter in the Library of the American Philosophical Society, Philadelphia.

[24] Peckham, *Pontiac,* 262–64. Gipson, *British Empire,* IX, 123–26.

Mississippi, where intractable habitants were still numerous, unite them with those of the northwest, and so resume his campaign against the British. He sent a letter to Le Gris, urging him to close the Wabash route to travel by any pro-British habitants who might be active. Even General Gage believed Pontiac could still dictate to the Wabash and Illinois tribes.[25]

Bouquet and Gage correctly assessed the animosity of the distant tribes in the Illinois country, but failed to appreciate the sophistication of the Miamis. The winter of 1764–65 was noteworthy for agitation on the frontier, and this tribe of realists listened to the pleadings and threats of all groups. A halfblood Shawnee named Kaski and Illinois Chief Lavacher went to New Orleans to seek help from the French governor but received none. They returned to Fort de Chartres to lead the opposition to overtures from Lieutenant John Ross for British control at a council on April 4, 1765. Pontiac arrived April 8 and at first opposed Lieutenant Alexander Fraser, who was sent from Fort Pitt by Gage and Johnson to prepare the way for a council with George Croghan. Chippewa, Potawatomi, Mascoutin, and Kickapoo warriors remained intractable, and for the first time, Pontiac began to doubt his French, Delaware, and Shawnee support. He protected Fraser while the council waited for Croghan.[26]

Deputy Superintendent Croghan, detained at Fort Pitt by a spring council with five hundred warriors, finally started down the Ohio with a delegation of allies and former enemy warriors on May 15. On June 8 at Shawneetown, Illinois, about eighty Kick-

[25] "A Court of Inquiry Held by Order of Lieutenant Colonel Campbell, Detroit, March 16, 1765," in James Sullivan *et al.* (comps.), *The Papers of Sir William Johnson,* IV, 676–80, cites Jean Baptiste Beaubien's testimony that the letter was written by St. Vincent, a French trader who aided Pontiac, to a Miami chief, probably Le Gris. This was the chief called *Le Petit Gris,* or The Dappled Fawn, during the 1770's but later known as Crippled Ankles. He was chief of one of the St. Joseph River villages at Kekionga, and his influence equaled that of Little Turtle and Pacanne until about 1795. See Henry Hay's "Journal," edited by Milo M. Quaife, first published in *Proceedings of the Wisconsin Historical Society* and reprinted, with Quaife's "Fort Wayne in 1790," in *Indiana Historical Society Publications,* VII (1921), 7, 208–61.

[26] Peckham, *Pontiac,* 267–77. Alvord and Carter, *The Critical Period,* 515–16, contains Fraser's report to Gage.

apoos and Mascoutins attacked the camp, killed two whites and three Shawnees, and captured Croghan and the remainder of his party. The captors were aghast at finding they had attacked Delaware, Shawnee, and Seneca warriors, for they believed retribution was inevitable. After the angry Indians were released, they proceeded to Fort de Chartres to make formal protests; the white men were marched to Vincennes. The disheartened warriors received little comfort from the Piankeshaws at that post and marched the prisoners up the Wabash to their own village near Ouiatanon. Their Wea neighbors there were furious at the insult given the eastern tribes, and on June 30, when the Kickapoo and Mascoutin chiefs returned from Fort de Chartres, they released the Croghan party. Most of these Wabash chiefs were former friends of Croghan; they had traded with him at Pickawillany and were familiar with the tactics of Shawnee and Iroquois war parties.

Croghan held a council at Ouiatanon at which his captors sought his protection from Shawnee revenge and begged for the British to garrison their frontier forts once again. A Miami chief from the upper Wabash came to the council and offered his own band's submission to the British. Three weeks later, Pontiac sent word to Croghan that he was returning from Kaskaskia, accompanied by Croghan's Indian delegation. Upon Pontiac's arrival, Croghan held a longer and more formal council at Ouiatanon. For the first time, Pontiac promised to end his resistance and to meet Sir William Johnson.

On July 23, 1765, a party headed by Croghan and Pontiac started up the Wabash to Detroit. Croghan collected the white prisoners held in the Miami and Ottawa villages on the way and reached his destination August 17.[27] Bradstreet, already there assembling the Great Lakes malcontents of 1763 and 1764 for a council, immediately treated with the Wabash tribes. The latter submitted to the British, but not without insisting upon recognition of a permanent

[27] Clarence Walworth Alvord and Clarence Edwin Carter (eds.), *The New Regime, 1765–1767*, 1–22, contains Croghan's "Journal" to Gage on the Fort Pitt negotiations; Thwaites, *Early Western Travels*, I, 126–67, contains Croghan's "Journal" of his 1765 trip to the west.

Indian boundary.[28] When the provisions of the proclamation were fully explained, they were surprised and relieved that it embodied nearly all of their demands:

> ... whereas it is just and reasonable, and essential to our interest and the security of our colonies, that the several nations or tribes of Indians with whom we are connected, and who live under our protection, should not be molested or disturbed in the possession of such parts of our dominions and territories as, not having been ceded to, or purchased by us, are reserved to them, or any of them, as their hunting grounds; .... [29]

The proposed meeting between Pontiac and Johnson finally took place in July, 1766, in a council at Fort Ontario, situated at the mouth of the Onondaga River. It is important to note that while nearly all the western tribes and the Iroquois met Superintendent Johnson, the Miamis, by evading the conference, hoped to escape punishment for their part in the uprising. Their duplicity was exposed by an Onondaga chief who announced that his tribe had recently received a belt from the Miamis warning them to beware of the animosity of the other western tribes.

The Miamis might have found themselves in an intolerable position with this disclosure. Should Pontiac return the belt, as he quickly volunteered to do, they would have to explain not only their deceit toward him but also their willingness to sacrifice the accord they had established with their western relatives and allies in a maneuver to gain friendship with the Iroquois. They were fortunate that Pontiac presumed to dictate policy for all western tribes —a presumption which Johnson quickly used for his own purposes and which caused the Ottawa chief to become the focal point of quarrels among his defeated allies. The rivalry removed Pontiac's power to punish the Miamis.[30]

[28] Volweiler, *George Croghan*, 182–88. Croghan prepared two "Journals" of this expedition. That emphasizing his Indian negotiations has been reprinted many times, including Carter and Alvord, *The New Regime*, 43–44, and Gipson, *British Empire*, IX, 117–23.
[29] Royce, *Indian Land Cessions*, 558.
[30] Peckham, *Pontiac*, 288–97.

Croghan was active in 1766. After conferences with tribesmen at Fort Pitt, he moved down the Ohio to a conference with the Ohio Indians at the mouth of the Scioto River. He then sent warriors from these tribes to the Wabash and Illinois regions to counteract the dissatisfaction there, especially among the French. Croghan followed later and on August 25 met about one thousand warriors from twenty-two "northern and western" tribes, including the Miami bands at Fort de Chartres. The Indians were co-operative, but Croghan mistrusted the French who had moved to Spanish territory.[31] A year earlier, he had said of Kekionga's French occupants:

> The Indian Village Consists of about 40 to 50 Cabins besides nine or ten French Houses a Runaway Colony from De Troit during the Late Indian War, they were concerned in it and Being affraid of Punishment came to this Post where ever since they have Spirited up the Indians against the English. All the French residing here are a lazy indolent People fond of Breeding Mischief and Spiriting up the Indians against the English and Should by no Means be suffered to remain here. . . .[32]

His opinion of the traders remained unchanged.

Unchastened by their narrow escape from punishment for their duplicity with the Onondagas and unmindful of their promises to Croghan, the Miamis continued to circulate war belts. In fall of 1766, a Wea band chief, The Goose, who had accompanied Croghan up the Wabash in 1765, and a party of Miami warriors brought Pontiac two war belts: one from French officers west of the Mississippi in Spanish territory and the other from the Arkansas tribe. Pontiac refused the bait and sent his nephew to warn the Detroit commander that other belts might be circulating on the frontier.[33]

Pontiac's Uprising had not quelled Indian unrest on the frontier. The chief still represented an uncertain quantity, especially to the

---

[31] Croghan, Fort de Chartres, to Johnson, September 10, 1766; Croghan, Fort Pitt, to Gage, January 16, 1767, in Alvord and Carter, *The New Regime*, 373–77, 487–95. Captain H. Gordon's "Journal" of this expedition is in *ibid.*, 290–310.

[32] Alvord and Carter, *The New Regime*, 36.

[33] Peckham, *Pontiac*, 232, 245, 267–68.

Delawares and Shawnees, who in the summer of 1767 resumed their resistance to squatter encroachments on the Ohio, and to the pro-French Illinois Indians, who hoped he could be persuaded to continue his anti-British activities. The Ohio tribes had already discovered that the British promise of protection for their hunting grounds did not deter squatters. Although his nephew led at least one successful foray against the Ohio River settlers, Pontiac himself became a bulwark in British efforts to prevent a general uprising.[34] His peace-keeping efforts alienated some of his former followers and failed to gain the trust of pro-British factions in their tribes.

The change from warrior to conciliator brought outcries of betrayal. It would be duplicated by other chiefs in the future, notably Little Turtle of the Miamis. Pontiac's assassination in 1769 by a Peoria Indian brought many charges of English implication but only a few acts of vengeance. Other events relegated his death to the position of a minor incident. The entire Pontiac episode demonstrated the weaknesses inherent in any confederations which the western tribes might establish. The major flaw was the refusal of any one tribe to accept a subordinate position in an alliance with others.

Even though some bands were more loyal to their French ties than others and even though at least 125 French families, castigated by Johnson in 1765 as the "worst sort" of settlers,[35] continued to live in the tribe's villages, the Miamis quickly adjusted to British control of their area. They were still far enough away from the Appalachian frontier to escape the immediate pressures which the colonial frontiersmen were now exerting on the Delawares and Shawnees. With British governmental control in the west centered at Detroit, the tribe was also far enough from that fort to maintain its fiction of sovereignty.

Sir William Johnson, expecting trouble to recur among Pontiac's former adherents in the west, sent his deputy, Croghan, to Detroit

[34] *Ibid.*, 301.
[35] Charles Elihu Slocum, *History of the Maumee River Basin*, 120.

and Mackinac in the fall of 1767. Croghan's prestige was expected to prevent any minor uprising. He learned the Miamis and Illinois had been invited to a great council with the Senecas and Shawnees at Old Shawneetown near the mouth of the Scioto but was assured that only intertribal conflicts were to be considered. Actually, the Indians' real concern was how to deal with the white settlers of the Appalachians. Alexis Loranger *dit* Maisonville, the veteran Ouiatanon trader, said the Miamis were disappointed over British failure to provide trade but would take no action of any kind unless assisted by the Shawnees and Delawares. Andrew the Huron, one of Croghan's agents on the Wabash, confirmed this report but added that the Miamis were prepared to be friendly with the British if trading posts were placed among them.[36]

Croghan held a council at Fort Pitt on April 26, 1768—a preliminary to the important Treaty of Fort Stanwix, negotiated later the same year. The pact marked a change in authority for Indian trade affairs, although the royal superintendencies were retained. The new North American policy came about when the Lords of Trade created a department for American affairs in 1768. Its first secretary of state, Lord Hillsborough, in effect placed the regulation of Indian affairs according to the provisions of the Proclamation of 1763 on the shoulders of the colonial governors.[37]

The Treaty of Fort Stanwix, signed November 6, together with the Treaty of Hard Labor, made with the Cherokees the same year, was recognition that the Proclamation of 1763 had failed to restrain settlers, traders, and speculators.[38] However, Sir William Johnson and others who negotiated the treaties were the very land speculators the new policy was designed to control. The treaty in effect moved the eastern boundary of the Indian reservation west to the Ohio River in order to legalize the land titles of the thirty thousand

[36] Howard H. Peckham (ed.), *George Croghan's Journal of His Trip to Detroit in 1767*, 17–22, 25–33, 37.

[37] Philbrick, *The Rise of the West*, 20–21.

[38] *Ibid.*, 25–33. "Sir William Johnson," *Dictionary of American Biography*, I, 124–28. Walter H. Mohr, *Federal Indian Relations, 1774–1778*, 9. Louis De Vorsey, Jr., *The Indian Boundary in the Southern Colonies, 1763–1775*, is the most reliable recent work dealing with the Fort Stanwix treaty cession.

settlers already established west of the first proclamation line. The combination of colonial and British speculators in the western land companies had been successful, therefore, in exerting sufficient pressure on the British Parliament to invalidate the proclamation.

By the Fort Stanwix treaty, the Iroquois ceded the land they claimed between the Appalachian Divide and the Ohio River. But the Shawnees objected to cession of the land, which was their principal hunting grounds, because they had never acknowledged Iroquois conquest or overlordship. Thus when white surveyors moved into the Monongahela and Kanawha valleys, they found the Shawnees determined to defend their claims. Moreover, the Shawnees had never observed the submission made to Colonel Bouquet in 1764. They now attacked the settlers from Virginia and Pennsylvania.[39]

Even though the Fort Stanwix and Hard Labor treaties had removed official Indian claim to many square miles of territory, they failed to satiate the frontiersman's desire for land. The inexorable wave of squatters again pushed into Indian lands north of the new line; General Gage's proclamations of 1772 and 1773 were directed at their removal. Some squatters may have entered Indian lands at the instigation of speculators who, about 1773, seized the opportunities offered by the Camden-Yorke Opinion, handed down in the Mogul case of 1757. This ruling, which stated a purchaser could secure legal title to land from its native owners without royal consent, would have removed from the Crown and colonial governors much of their control of Indian affairs.

The Crown's position as primary landowner was restated in the Land Act of February, 1774. The next month, General Frederick Haldimand reissued the pertinent provisions of the Proclamation of 1763 and declared void all land purchases in violation of these provisions. The Quebec Act of June 2, 1774, reasserted the Crown's supremacy and denied application of the Camden-Yorke Opinion to the Indian reservation. Settlers and land speculators conse-

[39] James Alton James, *The Life of George Rogers Clark*, 7, describes the reaction of the Ohio and Indiana Indians to the Treaty of Fort Stanwix of 1768.

quently turned to the colonial governments for methods of securing title to western lands.[40]

Lord Hillsborough's policy assigned protection of the frontier to the colonies, and Gage withdrew the Fort Pitt garrison in 1771. Inevitably, border atrocities increased and Lord Dunmore's War broke out in 1774. Johnson tried to prevent it by having his agents, Croghan and Alexander McKee, meet at Fort Pitt in May, 1774, with representatives from both the Virginia and Pennsylvania colonies and delegations from every western tribe except the Shawnees.[41] Although the Indian delegates seemed to favor peace, small bands of warriors from the Miamis, as well as other tribes, joined Shawnee war parties in raids along the upper Ohio River.

The war reached its climax at Point Pleasant, situated at the mouth of the Kanawha River, where, on October 10, Cornstalk and his Shawnee warriors were defeated by the frontier militia, commanded by Colonel Andrew Lewis. Another force under Governor Dunmore of Virginia marched on the Shawnees' Scioto River towns. At a council held at Camp Charlotte on the Scioto, the Shawnees and their allies agreed to resign all claims to the land south and east of the Ohio in compliance with the terms of the Treaty of Fort Stanwix.[42] The Shawnee concession was a victory for frontier squatters and land speculators, but it would cost them dearly in the future. For forty years, the western tribes clung to the Ohio River demarcation concept, and a series of savage wars was fought in an effort to force the whites to observe it.

The Wabash tribes saw a new and frightening white threat at work in the negotiations conducted at Fort Stanwix and Camp Charlotte. Until now, they had experienced only the diplomacy of the Beaver Wars, and even Pontiac's Uprising appeared to them

---

[40] Philbrick, *The Rise of the West*, 42–44. Hillsborough to Johnson, May 13, 1769, in Clarence Walworth Alvord and Clarence Edwin Carter (eds.), *Trade and Politics, 1767–1769*, 540–41.

[41] James, *George Rogers Clark*, 12, 16–17.

[42] Reuben Gold Thwaites and Louise Phelps Kellogg (eds.), *Documentary History of Dunmore's War, 1774*, xxiii. Volweiler, *George Croghan*, 301–305. James, *George Rogers Clark*, 12, 16–17, says some Miamis fought in Lord Dunmore's War.

primarily a war of French *versus* British trade interests. The Miamis learned from the Ohio Indians who had been ejected from Atlantic Coast colonies that the frontiersmen posed a threat to their own land and existence. Even imperial and colonial Indian agents were unable to protect their Indian charges from colonial practices or to combat the voracious land hunger of squatters and speculators.

The Miami warriors who took part in Lord Dunmore's War withdrew to the Wabash-Maumee river area, but the Shawnees persisted in their attacks on white frontiersmen. They had new provocations after 1774: Detroit and Fort Pitt became headquarters for the diplomatic tug-of-war between British and colonial traders and agents.

There is abundant evidence of sincerity in official government attempts to neutralize the Indian tribes during the early stages of the American Revolution, or at least to minimize Indian involvement. Councils at Detroit and Fort Pitt were frequent and Miami delegations attended most of them, but they did not attend the 1776 grand council at Fort Pitt at which American Indian Agent George Morgan secured promises of neutrality from most of the frontier tribes. There is no way to determine the extent of Miami involvement in the infrequent war parties sent out from 1774 to 1777.

The American Congress recognized the importance of potential military forces on the frontier by creating three Indian departments on July 12, 1775, and placing the tribes north of the Ohio in the Middle Department.[43] Efforts were made at first to keep the Indians quiet, but the impossibility of neutralizing these tribes, with their warrior cultures, forced abandonment of the policy in 1777.

Meanwhile, the British hoped to govern the western frontier from four posts in charge of lieutenant governors. Edward Abbott,

[43] Mohr, *Federal Indian Relations*, 31–33, 47. Benjamin Franklin, James Wilson, and Thomas Walker were named commissioners for the Middle Department. Richard Butler was its first continental agent to the Indians. He was succeeded by George Morgan. Lawrence F. Schmeckebier, *The Office of Indian Affairs*, 12.

newly appointed to the post at Vincennes, recognized the inade-
quacy of the British plan and quickly returned to Detroit. Upon
the shoulders of Henry Hamilton, appointed to the Detroit post,
fell the principal burden and responsibilities for conducting Indian
affairs in the west.[44]

Detroit was the focal point for British activity among the Indians, and Congress considered using Indian auxiliaries in a campaign against that fort. However, campaigns on the Atlantic Coast
prevented General George Washington from sending reliable troops
to the frontier. Besides, the American militia, always an uncertain
military quantity unless led by gifted commanders and steadied by
disciplined troops, was not ready for the task.

Occasional Indian raids on Kentucky, usually by way of the
Detroit-Maumee-Miami River route through Miami country,
helped to promote exaggerated and mutual distrust on the use of
the Indian auxiliaries. George Morgan later estimated that the total
Indian military potential in the northwest at this time was eight
thousand warriors, of whom only eight hundred were Miamis. The
estimate could not have been accurate, since it included only four
hundred warriors from the larger but less well-known Potawatomi
tribe.[45]

Captain James Wood and Simon Girty were sent among the Ohio
tribes to announce the first American conference. Although royal
agents had already preceded them to enlist auxiliaries for the British forces at Montreal, British influence had been weakened by
George Croghan's retirement from the Indian service in 1772 and
the death of Sir William Johnson in 1774. The Americans, by holding conferences with the Indians at Fort Pitt and Albany, hoped
above all to keep the Iroquois neutral. They were willing to make
nearly any promise or threat to the other tribes to help accomplish
this end. They also wanted to ascertain the possibilities of mounting a western attack on Detroit and Fort Niagara to support the

[44] John B. Dillon, *A History of Indiana*, 110. Clarence Walworth Alvord, *The
Illinois Country, 1673–1818*, 312–13.
[45] James, *George Rogers Clark*, 31. Morgan's information on the tribes west of
Lake Huron was evidently incomplete.

Montreal-Quebec expeditions of Generals Richard Montgomery and Benedict Arnold.[46]

The initial goal of Iroquois neutrality was gained, but the Iroquois objected to an armed expedition through their country. The American plan for offensive action on the frontier was an example of grandiose scheming without adequate resources. In April, 1776, Colonel George Morgan, an able and experienced Indian trader, was named Indian agent for the American Middle Department to succeed Richard Butler. Morgan sent William Wilson into the Ohio country with White Eyes, a pro-American Delaware chief, to invite the tribes to a council. After visiting a Wyandot village near Detroit, the two conferred with Henry Hamilton at the fort. Hamilton was inhospitable; he accused them of treason to the king, but because of his own precarious position, he did not detain them. He soon began plans for a confederacy of the northwestern tribes to attack the American frontier.[47] But in spite of the plans for military campaigns, Shawnee war parties, and an occasional raid into Kentucky by the Wabash Indians, the frontier remained comparatively undisturbed until 1777.

Although Holston and Watauga settlements sustained severe attacks from southern Indians, Fort Pitt and the Allegheny frontier endured nothing more than rumors of Indian raids in late 1776. Commissioners of the Continental Congress and Virginia met the Iroquois and western tribes during the fall of 1776 at Fort Pitt, but the Miamis did not attend. After the chiefs promised neutrality in the war, twelve of them were persuaded to go to Philadelphia for presentation to Congress. This accord was fortunate, for the American defense of the frontier on the Ohio had been reduced to only three forts. One hundred militiamen were stationed at Fort Pitt, an equal number at Fort Randolph on the Big Kanawha, and twenty-

---

[46] Mohr, *Federal Indian Relations,* 35–42, 54. Colonel John Campbell, superintendent of Indian affairs at Quebec at this time, had about fifty agents cooperating with the British military post commanders. Butler's and Morgan's headquarters was at Fort Pitt. Apparently, no Miamis attended the American conference. Thwaites and Kellogg, *Documentary History,* xxiii–xxiv.

[47] James, *George Rogers Clark,* 45.

five at Wheeling, or Fort Henry.[48] This was the last period of frontier peace for nearly twenty years.

Henry Hamilton was active during 1776. At Detroit on June 17, he held a major Indian council which was attended by all of the tribes in the region, including the Miamis. Encouraged by their response, he became convinced he could send at least a thousand warriors against the Americans. The Miamis were among the tribes receptive to his proposal to attack the American settlers. Charles Beaubien, the influential French trader at Kekionga who served Hamilton as interpreter to the Miamis, had already established an enviable reputation as a warrior in Shawnee raids on Kentucky.

Hamilton's plans to send warriors against the American frontier were approved by Governor Guy Carleton in 1777 after the latter received orders to use Indian auxiliaries, both in the west and with Colonel Barry St. Leger's invasion of New York.[49] Hamilton had dispatched fifteen war parties from Detroit by July, 1777, and the "bloody year" in Kentucky was in full progress. American hopes of constructing Indian alliances to counter this were shattered when frontier militiamen murdered the friendly Shawnee chief Cornstalk while he was a hostage.

The desperate border warfare of 1777 brought to the fore the most important frontier leader of the American Revolution, George Rogers Clark, and Clark brought the American Revolution to the Miamis. Clark, with previous experience in Lord Dunmore's War and now a major in the Kentucky militia, undertook the task of protecting the exposed settlements.

By 1778, the American effort began to appear hopeless, and the

48 Reuben Gold Thwaites and Louise Phelps Kellogg (eds.), *The Revolution on the Upper Ohio, 1775–1777, 216–17*. Mohr, *Federal Indian Relations,* 34–35. James, *George Rogers Clark,* 49–50.

49 Reuben Gold Thwaites and Louise Phelps Kellogg (eds.), *Frontier Defense on the Upper Ohio, 1777–1778,* 7–13. This is an extract from Hamilton's official report of his conference. It was captured by Clark at Vincennes. Barnhart, *Hamilton and Clark* 32, 64. Hamilton tried to specify the fighting tactics of the Indians at this council, prohibiting the killing of women and children. Carlton first objected to Hamilton's use of Indian war parties. Hamilton's "Journal" and autobiography are in the Houghton Library (Rare Books and Manuscripts of Harvard University), of the Harvard Library.

danger and high cost of loyalty to a losing cause were great enough to make deserters of many men, including Simon Girty and Alexander McKee. Eventually, thirteen hundred frontier settlers were enlisted by the British, and Girty's and McKee's Indian war parties dealt severely damaging blows to the Americans.[50] General Edward Hand, commander of Fort Pitt, attempted to recoup American prestige by attacking Detroit and Sandusky in February, but his efforts produced only the frustrating "Squaw Campaign." Disappointed, he asked to be relieved of his command.

Upon assuming command, General Lachlan McIntosh faced the threat of attack by nearly two thousand warriors. Determined to attack Detroit and Oswego in a rash movement, he distributed presents valued at $10,000 among friendly bands of Delawares to secure permission for his army to cross their lands. McIntosh then initiated the American policy of building a chain of forts which could serve as a supply line and as a barrier between Indians and white settlers. As he marched westward, his force paused to build Fort McIntosh at the mouth of Beaver Creek. It stopped again on the Tuscarawas River to build Fort Laurens, but the problems of expiring enlistments and scanty supplies ended the expedition at this point.[51]

While attention was focused upon events on the upper Ohio, Clark had planned in secrecy. As early as April, 1777, he became convinced that the "Illinois country," the region west of the Miami River, was the most vulnerable spot in the British defense of Canada. He expected Hamilton to concentrate his forces against the American threat from Fort Pitt, and he was well aware that the British had never succeeded in establishing firm control of the Illinois country. He hoped to secure support from French and Indians who had opposed British occupation scarcely a decade earlier, force Hamilton to defend a new area south and west of Detroit, and overawe the tribes whose scalping parties plagued

[50] Mohr, *Federal Indian Relations*, 63–70, says 68 families left Fort Pitt to join the Loyalists in the early years of the Revolution and that Hugh Kelly and James Fleming had raised 1,300 Loyalist troops on the frontier by 1781.
[51] James, *George Rogers Clark*, 54–56, 58–62, 65–66.

Kentucky. He sent two spies to Kaskaskia to learn the strength of pro-British sentiment in the country. They found little support for the British among the approximately one thousand white people, six hundred Negro slaves and four hundred "poor Indian warriors" in the area. Clark considered the report favorable for his plan and traveled over the eastern mountains in early winter to confer with Governor Patrick Henry of Virginia.[52]

Through the good offices of Thomas Jefferson, George Wythe, and George Mason, Clark secured Henry's support and that of the Virginia government. He was promoted to lieutenant colonel and promised three hundred acres of land for each of his men. After much difficulty in securing sufficient volunteers, he began to descend the Monongahela River on May 2, 1778, with 150 men and reached the Falls of the Ohio twenty-five days later. With a force swelled in Kentucky to about 175 men, he captured Kaskaskia and its commander, Philippe de Rastel de Rocheblave, on July 4. Clark then sent Father Pierre Gibault and Dr. Jean Laffont to Vincennes to ascertain whether that village was loyal to the British. On being reassured Vincennes was politically passive, he dispatched Captain Leonard Helm to occupy Fort Sackville, which Helm did in July.

To solidify his position, Clark maneuvered brilliantly to secure the support of Indians, French settlers, and, especially, the Spanish at St. Louis. Miami warriors attended his five-week Cahokia council in August and September. Tribes from the Great Lakes to the Mississippi and Ohio rivers also attended. He succeeded in temporarily neutralizing the most distant tribes, secured alliances with the nearest, and profoundly impressed all of them. The Piankeshaw chief Tobacco, whose support was vital to the control of Vincennes and the lower Wabash, became his most important ally.[53]

News of Clark's success reached Hamilton at Detroit on August 7 as he waited for the expected American attack from the east. Al-

[52] *Ibid.*, 69, 112.
[53] *Ibid.*, 115–30. Clark was surrounded by thousands of warriors, but he placed a few of the most belligerent chiefs in irons and so impressed the council that ten or twelve tribes entered an alliance with him.

though he had little fear of an immediate attack from Clark's forces, he understood the fickle (or practical) loyalty of the Indians. Although Clark did not stop all war parties directed at the Kentucky frontier, he was able to neutralize a large number of uncommitted tribes and even to secure some warriors as auxiliaries to be used against Canada.

Hamilton departed from Detroit on October 7 with 161 men, including 33 regulars; 128 volunteer militia, of whom 14 were officers of the Indian Department; and 70 Chippewa, Ottawa, and Potawatomi auxiliaries. Although his trip over the Maumee-Wabash route would be a difficult one, his chief concern was the attitude of the tribes along it. He may have heard, as David Zeisberger reported, that Kekionga had first taken his war belt in 1777 but then discarded it after the Miamis had counseled with the Weas and Kickapoos. On the Maumee, Hamilton met a French trader to the Weas and was told the false news that Clark had already moved up the Wabash and captured the villages at Ouiatanon. But Hamilton's most important test came on October 24 when he arrived at the Maumee's headwaters, where Pacanne and Le Gris presided over the most important Miami bands. The Lieutenant Governor wrote in his journal:

24th. . . . We proceeded about 8 o'clock, had put ashore at the plain near the Miamis Village, where Young men of that nation saluted as usual with several discharges of small arms, Our Savages returned the compliment, after which was a kind of mock battle with blank powder. . . . Assembled the chiefs of all the Nations present, informed them of the cause of my coming, and thanked all present for their cheerful and quiet behavior—told them they were to have an Ox to each nation tomorrow, but no rum— . . . . The Miamis at this Village had been told by Celoron, that the Rebels were at Ouiattonon, which alarm'd them so much, that several hid their Stores in the woods—The Gros Loup is my authority— . . . . visited the Chiefs of the Miamis in their Village—The Petit Gris, and Gros Loup made me a present of 3 large basketts of Young corn, dried pumpion, and Kidney beans, saying that such coarse fare might serve for my cattle if I could not eat it myself but that they thought I would not scorn their present tho so inconsiderable as it was presented with sincere goodwill— .... The War Belts were then produced, when taking up my own and that of Major Hay, I sung the War Song, in which I was followed by the Deputy agent, the chiefs, and principal warriors of the different nations—Most of them complained, that I did not wet the Grindstone with Rum, and that they had great difficulty in sharpening their father's Axe.[54]

Although the young warriors frequently joined war parties, the tribal council had not yet given support to the British. Hamilton's reception proved much different from that given Thomas Morris fourteen years earlier. Hamilton's impressive response to Clark's attack persuaded a Kekionga war party to join the expedition and so ensure a friendly reception in the Miami villages at the mouth of the Eel River. Hamilton describes the warriors' preparations:

This night the Indians sung to their Nattes as the French call them—These are Budgets which contain little figures of different kinds, some as Amulets, some as household Gods, these when they go to war they paint with vermillion—Their Priests who are usually their doctors are provided with an apparatus very different from our quacks, this is usually carried in the budget and consists of the heads, bones or skins of certain animals, preserved Birds in the feather, Snakes skins, Bows and arrows contrived with springs to bundle up with the other valuable effects, Wolves teeth Panthers claws, Eagles talons & ca—The Juglers have these at hand for whenever, by drenches steam baths or emetics they have procured any relief from [for] one of their patients, they feign to have drawn a Bears tooth or Birds claw out of the part affected which when they produced to the sick man his imagination seldom fails to take part with the Doctors skill and perfect the cure—[55]

When the British force reached the Wea villages, several chiefs who had attended Clark's council at Cahokia and Chief Little Face with a band of Wea warriors joined the party. Hamilton needed them, for he next met the Piankeshaws, Clark's strongest sup-

---

[54] James, *George Rogers Clark*, 131–44. Barnhart, *Hamilton and Clark*, 111–18, 130–42. Thwaites and Kellogg, *Frontier Defense*, 102, cite Zeisberger's letter of September 23, 1777, to General Edward Hand at Fort Pitt.
[55] Barnhart, *Hamilton and Clark*, 127.

porters, and the Kickapoos below the Vermilion River, who were always of uncertain temper.

Major Jehu Hay of the Detroit militia, sent to Vincennes to spy on the American situation, rejoined Hamilton at Fort Ouiatanon. Learning from him that Clark had left Vincennes unguarded, Hamilton proceeded there December 17, 1778. After the French inhabitants renewed their oaths of allegiance to Britain, Hamilton and ninety of his soldiers manned Fort Sackville. The remainder of his troops returned to Detroit and his Indian allies to their villages.[56] While the garrison was thus lightly manned, Clark recaptured the village and fort on February 24, 1779, and Miami enthusiasm for the British cause evaporated as rapidly as it had been aroused.[57]

Clark's success did not halt Indian attacks on the frontier by any means. Nevertheless, he removed a large number of warriors from the British sphere of influence and made an attack on Detroit a possibility. And thousands of immigrants moved into Kentucky, believing it was now safe from Indian raids.[58]

The frontier commanders had high hopes they could attack Detroit. While he awaited Kentucky and Virginia troops, Clark sent emissaries to the Weas and Miamis to secure their permission to ascend the Wabash. The Piankeshaws were firm supporters of Clark, but the other Miami bands delayed their final commitment until after the American campaign was abandoned when militia reinforcements did not arrive.[59] Meanwhile, the new Detroit lieutenant governor, Major Arent S. De Peyster, spent the summer in defensive preparations instead of mounting attacks on Fort Pitt or Vincennes.

Events in the summer of 1779 were disastrous for British-Indian alliances. Only the Sioux and Menominees were considered

---

[56] *Ibid.*, 133–77. James, *George Rogers Clark*, 133–36.

[57] James, *George Rogers Clark*, 137–44. Louise Phelps Kellogg, *The British Regime in Wisconsin and the Old Northwest*, 173.

[58] James, *George Rogers Clark*, 171, 177–78. John D. Barnhart, *Valley of Democracy*, 30–31.

[59] *Ibid.*, 171–72, 276.

dependable allies; even Charles Langlade at Milwaukee and Alexander McKee at Michilimackinac could not hold their Indian auxiliaries together for expeditions into the Wabash country. In addition to the threat of an invasion by Clark, the heretofore invincible Iroquois were humbled in New York, and the possibility of French or Spanish expeditions on the Mississippi River against the British alarmed the Indians.

Clark sent copies of the French-American alliance of February 6, 1778, to the Wabash tribes while he endeavored to conceal from them the insurmountable difficulties his proposed offensives faced. He failed when the Indians destroyed Colonel David Rogers' party of seventy men near Cincinnati and captured Clark's dispatches, which revealed his military weaknesses.

British prestige among the Indians was revived by American failure to improve on Clark's initial successes. By the spring of 1780, the British could again contemplate reconquest of the Illinois country. To restore his alliances, De Peyster distributed presents valued at £84,000 at Indian councils. Plans were made to send Langlade down the Illinois River against the new Spanish enemy and Kaskaskia, another party down the Wabash against Vincennes, and a third to harass Clark at the Falls of the Ohio.[60] Small war parties renewed their attacks on Kentucky, where the tide of immigration made victims more available.

The expedition against St. Louis was beaten off by the Spanish as Clark hastened to prepare Kaskaskia's defenses. Colonel Henry Bird set out from Detroit with 150 whites and 1,000 Indians to attack the Falls of the Ohio during Clark's absence. Bird, who moved by way of the Maumee and Miami rivers, was diverted to the Licking River settlements, where he captured two stations. Clark quickly returned from Kaskaskia to Kentucky, raised a force, and crossed the Ohio on August 1. The Shawnees burned Old Chillicothe on the Little Miami River upon his approach. Clark en-

---

[60] Louise Phelps Kellogg (ed.), *Frontier Retreat on the Upper Ohio, 1779–1781*, 17–18. The documents of participants in the action are in *ibid.*, 79–94, 104. General Haldimand's report to General Henry Clinton is in *ibid.*, 122–23.

countered a large force of warriors at strongly fortified Piqua on the Mad River near present-day Springfield, Ohio, and destroyed the food supplies of both Indian towns. His prompt reprisal against the Ohio tribes ended raids on Kentucky from the north for the rest of the year.[61]

British fear of direct French intervention in the west finally materialized in 1780. That year, Augustine Mottin de La Balme, who had come to America in 1776, entered the western country. He reached Vincennes in July and was cordially received by the habitants as a Frenchman and emissary of Congress. He raised a force of eighty French and Indian horsemen at Vincennes and Kaskaskia in October and set out, ostensibly to conquer Detroit. He moved up the Wabash, and four days after leaving the Wea villages, he attacked Kekionga and destroyed it. La Balme then retreated to a camp on the Aboite River ten miles southwest of Kekionga. The Miamis of the village had evaded him, and two French traders, Peter Lafontaine and Charles Beaubien, helped the Eel River chief Little Turtle collect neighboring warriors. That night, the French force was obliterated. The action ended tenuous French hopes of planting an armed force in the area north of the Ohio. It also served to bring the most important war chief produced by the Miamis to the attention of history: Little Turtle was to be a major force in frontier war and diplomacy for the next thirty years.[62]

Much of the American prestige secured by Clark's first attacks in the west was lost in 1781. Other than the reduction of the Delaware villages at Coshocton on the Tuscarawas River near the Muskingum by Colonel Daniel Brodhead in the spring, the frontier

[61] James, *George Rogers Clark*, 249–52, explains Clark's defensive measures. His attack north of the Ohio River was important to the Miamis because they had given a Delaware band permission to occupy the west branch of the White River about 1770, and the eight villages there were closely allied to Kekionga. Hodge, *Handbook of American Indians*, I, 385–87.

[62] James, *George Rogers Clark*, 213–15. Brice, *History of Fort Wayne*, 103–105. Clarence Walworth Alvord, *Kaskaskia Records, 1778–1790*, 162n., 168, 186–88, contains correspondence concerning La Balme. Major Arant S. De Peyster, Detroit, to General H. Watson Powell, November 13, 1780, in *MPHC*, XIX, 581, believed La Balme was a prisoner even then on his way to Detroit.

was placed on the defensive by threatened or actual Indian attacks. Clark again proposed to attack Detroit via the Wabash route in order to immobilize the majority of the hostile Indians who received supplies and instructions from there. Because he received no support from Virginia authorities or Kentucky settlers, his plan was not carried out.

Although the Revolutionary War ended in the east in 1782, only Clark's maneuvering prevented a debacle on the frontier. He made ostentatious preparations for offensive movements across the Ohio River and circulated proclamations of Cornwallis' defeat and British troop withdrawals from the seaboard. British authorities in Canada countered Clark's propaganda with more presents to the Indians at treaty councils, especially one at Detroit in February which included all their wavering allies. This brought renewed Indian attacks on the frontier settlements in the spring. The warfare reached a new point of ferocity with the massacre of the Christian Delaware Indians at Gnadenhutten by a force of Pennsylvania frontiersmen under Colonel David Williamson. The Indians countered by destroying Colonel William Crawford's force near the upper Sandusky towns in June, 1782.[63]

Clark began to gather militiamen at the mouth of Licking River to attack the Shawnee towns in Ohio after a large force of Indians under Alexander McKee raided Kentucky settlements at Bryant's Station and Blue Licks in August. In November, Clark led his force of one thousand mounted men against Chillicothe, then destroyed Piqua, the Shawnee stronghold at the mouth of Loramie Creek on the Great Miami. He dispersed the enemy, burned five Shawnee towns, and posed a threat to Detroit.[64] The effects on Indian morale were salutary from the American point of view.

The official announcement in April, 1783, of the signing of a preliminary peace treaty halted American plans for constructing new frontier forts and garrisoning old ones. A new era began, one in which the Indian tribes of the northwest assumed even greater

[63] James, *George Rogers Clark*, 264–68.
[64] *Ibid.*, 277–78.

importance. It was at this time that the Miami lands emerged as a sanctuary for Indians who resisted American attempts at pacification and occupation north of the Ohio River.

British control of former French regions north of the Ohio from 1759 to 1783 was vital to the Miamis. However, the imperial policies, if not their performance, embodied in the Proclamation of 1763 and the Quebec Act of 1774, although approved by the Miamis, failed to dominate the tribe's actions. The British also failed to secure stability on the frontier, to meet the trading needs of the tribe, and to exclude white settlers. The Treaty of Fort Stanwix, which had set the Ohio River as the boundary of white expansion, became the Indians' *quid pro quo* in future councils and treaties.

The Miamis had been rent by the opposing appeals of the Americans and British at opposite ends of the Wabash. Because of the American alliance and threats to the Piankeshaws and the Weas on the lower Wabash and because of British control of the Kekionga region, tribal councils had failed to unify Miami policies. It remained to be seen whether the Miamis, under these conditions, could reconstruct a united front in opposition to American settlement north of the Ohio. In order to counter such a breakdown in their intratribal relations and thwart American and British efforts, the Miamis attempted to make their Kekionga councils increasingly important to tribal unity. They realized their fate was irrevocably bound to their eastern allies, the Wyandots, Shawnees, and Delawares, but the latter two tribes were even less cohesive than themselves.

Miami strength lay in the wisdom which some of the chiefs were to contribute to the deliberations of more powerful tribes. The Wabash-Maumee Valley, not the Ohio country, was the Indian-American-Canadian frontier line of confrontation. While its inhabitants were subject to British and American demands for loyalty, it did afford the Indian tribes the last area from which they could defend the Ohio River line and await an inevitable trial of strength with American settlers. The young Miami warriors had gained experience in the many raids and battles they fought under white and Indian commanders, and the use of modern weapons completed their education in disciplined frontier warfare. The tribe's manpower was never endangered and its losses were negligible.

The Miamis made positive contributions to the Indian cause. Little Turtle gained stature as a war chief at a time when few Indian leaders escaped defeat. Pacanne and Le Gris gained respect as subtle chiefs and councilors. In the minds of American frontiersmen, the concept of a giant "Miami Confederacy" formed and expanded.

The tribe had gradually accepted British imperial policies, which gave them agents and traders while attempting to exclude white settlers. They had also learned that white men were unpredictable but necessary allies. Nor was it unusual for the Miamis to reproach British agents for the treaty which had assumed an unacknowledged pretention of sovereignty over their lands. No matter with whom the Indians were to ally themselves, be it the British or the Americans, they were destined to lose and be forced to accept the role of conquered nations.

The Indians were aware that colonial immigrants were pressing on their frontiers and that no white government had yet successfully protected them from this menace. Nevertheless, they accepted the basic terms of the Fort Stanwix treaty as their final concession and prepared to defend it. As the British sought to retain control of the Old Northwest, this fact was of paramount importance to an understanding of the forthcoming British-Indian alliance. Miami policies and attitudes thus became decisive when the Americans began to assert control of the territory northwest of the Ohio.

4
THE MIAMI CONFEDERACY

Another Treaty of Paris, this time the one signed in 1783 which ended the American Revolution, became the instrument by which Miami lands once again were transferred to a former enemy. The new American confederation gained a vast area between the Appalachian Mountains and the Mississippi River and inherited with it the same Indian problems the French and English had failed to solve. In fact, the problems had grown more complex. During the century of contact with Europeans, the native Americans had lost much of the credulity which permitted the French and English to manipulate them in war or trading schemes. They had absorbed and profited from many facets of European culture, even though they were struck down by epidemics of new diseases carried by the white men.

By this process the Miamis had become sophisticated diplomats and traders and, above all, more efficient fighting men. Their chiefs and warriors had taken part in nearly every war or council between the whites and Indians since the 1740's. With its limited number of warriors, occupying the only region from which an Indian military offensive could be launched, the tribe emerged as a bulwark of Indian resistance against white expansion north of the Ohio

95

River during the decade after the Treaty of Paris. The Miamis were now the easternmost tribe whose traditional lands were intact, and they had by this time developed a clearer understanding, not only of the strategic value in the location of their lands, but also of the American concept of land ownership. When Miami resistance collapsed in 1795, the last hope for a permanent line of demarcation between Indians and whites east of the Mississippi River vanished.

The Miami resistance of this period at first seems out of character. However, the tribe had gained a wealth of experience in the previous quarter-century and had lost little of its numerical strength or its status with allied tribes. The Miamis were now well acquainted with the white man's policies on the frontier. When an Indian orator announced that white men's ways puzzled him, he referred to the *why*, not the *what* and *how*; a dead and scalped white settler's mouth filled with dirt by his attackers was not a senseless object, but a logical response by some warrior to the white man's desire for land. As the Miamis became leaders in the Indian frontier line of defense, they abandoned their former role as calculated opportunists and united in uncompromising resistance to white encroachment.

The position was not easy to assume. It violated much of the tribe's hard-won attitude of protective diplomacy. After Pontiac's Uprising, the Miamis became reconciled to British governmental policies because these left the tribe practically undisturbed as French and English traders moved freely along the Wabash and British officials tried to keep colonial settlers east of the Ohio while enforcing comparative peace among the tribes. The decade between 1765 and 1775 later seemed to the Miamis to have been the flowering of a Golden Age. It was, in fact, their last period of tribal unity and tranquillity, if not of power. The Miamis recognized the difficulties the British government experienced in attempting to prevent the frontiersmen from bursting into their lands and disrupting what had come to be a settled way of tribal life. Lord Dunmore's War and the settlement of Kentucky and Tennessee showed

96

the force of white expansion toward the Ohio, and the tribe had no illusions about the policies of the new country which claimed jurisdiction over them in 1783.

When the Treaty of Paris of 1783 disposed of the western tribes' lands without their consent, the Indians first turned on the British living among them. An efficient Canadian Indian Service continued to operate among the tribes south of the Great Lakes to protect the interests and safety of Canadian fur traders placed in jeopardy of Indian retaliation. Indian resistance to American settlement promptly increased. At a council held at Sandusky in August, 1783, with thirty-five tribes, Canadian support was assured to the Indians, who in turn overwhelmingly agreed to oppose American settlement north of the Ohio. To secure unity among themselves, the Indians once again revived the idea of common tribal ownership of those lands.[1]

The United States attempted to continue the old British policies established after 1763, partly because most Americans assigned to Indian affairs had gained their experience in the field as agents of the British governments, but also because this was the system most familiar to the Indians.[2] The Continental Congress had assumed direction of Indian affairs by an act of July 12, 1775, and a committee divided its functions between three departments. In practice, the agents and superintendents reported to the Congressional Board of War, as well as to the Congress, and final decisions ultimately went to the country's commander-in-chief, General George Washington.

On May 1, 1783, Congress sent a resolution to Secretary of War Benjamin Lincoln requesting him to inform the Indian tribes the war had ended. This Lincoln did, but without first informing the acting commissioner for the Northern Department, General Philip Schuyler.[3] Ephraim Douglas, trader and Indian agent, carried

---

[1] Downes, *Council Fires*, 283.
[2] Royce, *Indian Land Cessions*, 533. Schmeckebier, *Office of Indian Affairs*, 3–5. *American State Papers*, Class II, *Indian Affairs*, II, 8.
[3] Slocum, *History of the Maumee River Basin*, 149. Schmeckebier, *Office of Indian Affairs*, 12. Mohr, *Federal Indian Relations*, 32.

Lincoln's message but was unable to convene the western tribes at a single council. He blamed the British officers who still held the forts south of the Great Lakes for his failure. Meanwhile, Major De Peyster held a grand council at Detroit on July 6 in an effort to placate his disgruntled allies. The Miamis responded to De Peyster's invitation, but not to Douglas'. This was unusual. It indicated the depth of their growing hostility against the Americans, for the tribe normally attended councils of both friends and foes.[4]

Congress again attempted to follow former British imperial policies when on September 22, 1783, it passed an act designed to restrain squatters from invading Indian lands. On October 22, it proposed to develop this plan by establishing a demarcation line between the settlers and the Indians. Commissioners were appointed March 4, 1784, to negotiate treaties with the Indians.[5] The treaty policy made an auspicious beginning with the Iroquois at Fort Stanwix on October 22: they relinquished all claims to land north and west of the Ohio River and to leadership among the western tribes.[6]

These tribes were torn by indecision at first. A party of Shawnees captured trader John Leith during the summer, and he was held prisoner at the Delaware town on the headwaters of the Great Miami, where a grand council of tribes was held in October. Although the Indians still appeared undecided on their policies, Leith reported that Shawnee, Mingo, and Cherokee warriors and white renegades were the most warlike, whereas the Wyandots and Delawares were the least inclined to active resistance. The Wea chiefs, the only speakers for the Wabash tribes at the council, supported the belligerents. The major Kekionga chiefs did not commit themselves at the council, which illustrates once more their careful deliberation in all momentous decisions.[7]

---

[4] Slocum, *History of the Maumee River Basin*, 149–52.

[5] James, *George Rogers Clark*, 306–308.

[6] *Ibid.*, 308. Royce, *Indian Land Cessions*, 648–49.

[7] Kellogg, *British Regime*, 209. "The Examination of John Leith" is the Appendix of Smith, *The St. Clair Papers*, II, 632–33.

The Miamis could not have behaved otherwise. They were too near their Delaware, Wyandot, and Shawnee allies to jeopardize their rapport with these divided tribes and too conscious of the need for unity to risk alienating any of their bands on the lower Wabash. During the last years of the Revolution, several bands of Delawares had aided the Americans. To prevent a continued division of the important Delaware tribe, the Kekionga chiefs dared commit no injudicious acts or make imprudent speeches which would foster pro-American sentiment.

Congress tried to demonstrate its good faith to the Indians by adhering to the Treaty of Fort Stanwix and the boundary line it established between settlers and Indians. In the summer of 1785, Colonel Josiah Harmar sent Ensign John Armstrong with a detachment of the newly organized frontier Regular Army north of the Ohio River to remove squatters from Indian lands. Harmar established headquarters at the mouth of the Muskingum River and named the new post Fort Harmar. The Colonel was charged with maintaining peace on the frontier from Franklin, at the mouth of French Creek, to the new fort, but he was unable to prevent either squatter settlement or Indian raids across the Ohio with a force which numbered less than six hundred men in 1785 and only eight hundred by 1788.[8]

A congressional commission led by George Rogers Clark went to Fort McIntosh to meet the western tribes and on January 21, 1785, secured a treaty with some Wyandot, Delaware, Ottawa, and Chippewa chiefs. The Treaty of Fort McIntosh was unusual in that it confirmed to these tribes lands in most of the northern half of Ohio from the Cuyahoga River to the Maumee. The chiefs gave up all claims to lands south, east, and west of the boundary. The treaty failed to secure lasting accord, however, because the four tribes were not fully represented at the negotiations, their delegates acted contrary to the 1783 Sandusky council, and the Miamis and Shawnees were not parties to the agreement. The American

[8] Gayle Thornbrough (ed.), *Outpost on the Wabash, 1787–1791,* 13. Kellogg, *British Regime,* 206–207.

position, a radical departure, was evolved from the proposal of October 15, 1783. The "grant" was bestowed and the tribes' lands limited in an avowal that title was American to "give, not to receive."[9]

Commissioners Clark, Richard Butler and Samuel H. Parsons tried to rectify this weakness with a council at Fort Finney, located at the mouth of the Great Miami, on January 31, 1786. The commissioners first sent Samuel Montgomery and three other messengers to invite all the western tribes. The Delawares and Wyandots finally appeared after sending word of the meeting to the British at Detroit. The American envoys reached "Miamitown" September 13, 1785, but the leading chiefs were absent and the unfriendly Miami warriors stole their horses, which were returned only after the Americans "bought" them back. Montgomery asked the Miamis to carry word of the council to the lower Wabash tribes, but they refused. The emissaries quickly left, but within a few miles their horses were stolen again, this time at one of the little villages springing up near Kekionga.[10]

In the end, only the Shawnees signed the treaty. They repudiated British sovereignty, accepted the supremacy of the United States, and disclaimed all ownership to land south and east of a line running from the Fort McIntosh line to the Wabash near Ouiatanon. The treaty won approval from the Shawnee chiefs at the council only because of dissension in the tribe, Harmar's removal of squatters on their lands, and the commissioners' open display of force. As expected, the rapport was only temporary.[11]

Because of increasing border hostilities, neither of the 1786

[9] Charles J. Kappler (ed.), *Indian Affairs: Laws and Treaties*, II, 4–5. The ordinance is in W. C. Ford *et al.* (eds.), *Journals of the Continental Congress, 1774–1789*, XXV, 681–93.

[10] David I. Bushnell (ed.), "Journal of Samuel Montgomery," *Mississippi Valley Historical Review*, II, (1915), 261–73. Montgomery blamed part of the disorderly Miami behavior on the absence of the principal chiefs, "Pedigue" at Detroit and Pacanne at Vincennes. His plight might have been serious had his Wyandot guides not protected him.

[11] Kappler, *Indian Affairs*, II, 12–13. Harmar found 600 white families in the Muskingum area and 1,500 squatters between the Scioto and Miami rivers. James, *George Rogers Clark*, 331.

treaties was carried into effect, but they eventually served as bases for terms of the Treaty of Greene Ville. More important, because by 1786 the Miami tribe was the only one on the Ohio frontier which had been unwilling to meet the Americans in council and had refused to make a treaty with the commissioners, it emerged as the natural leader of the confederation movement.

The antagonists' positions were clear. The member tribes had factions which refused to accept any treaty, while those chiefs who agreed to negotiations lost their importance. British troops still occupied the forts south of the Great Lakes, and Canadian Indian agents and traders operated freely north of the Ohio. American squatters were endangered as they moved into the newly ceded land north of the Ohio and south of the Fort McIntosh line, following or even preceding surveyors who attempted to run their lines according to the provisions of the Land Ordinance of 1785. The squatters succeeded in provoking Indian attacks.

American agents to the Indians were at first overaggressive, few in number, and poorly financed. Congress improved the situation by passing a new ordinance to regulate Indian affairs, reducing the number of Indian departments from three to two, each with a superintendent responsible to the secretary of war. Richard Butler headed the Northern Department. Trade and residence in the Indian country were barred to noncitizens, travel there was restricted to persons with permits, and traders were required to secure licenses. More important, there was no effort to impose American law in the Indian country.[12]

In spite of these well-meaning policies, the frontier was once again engulfed by hostilities. Although Indian attacks against American settlers, both north and south, were at first uncoordinated, Shawnee and Miami raiding parties often were augmented by warriors from other tribes.

Vincennes, of course, was the village most vulnerable to attack. It had no civil government which could direct its defenses, but its 900 French and 400 Americans in 1786 numbered among them

[12] Schmeckebier, *Office of Indian Affairs*, 16.

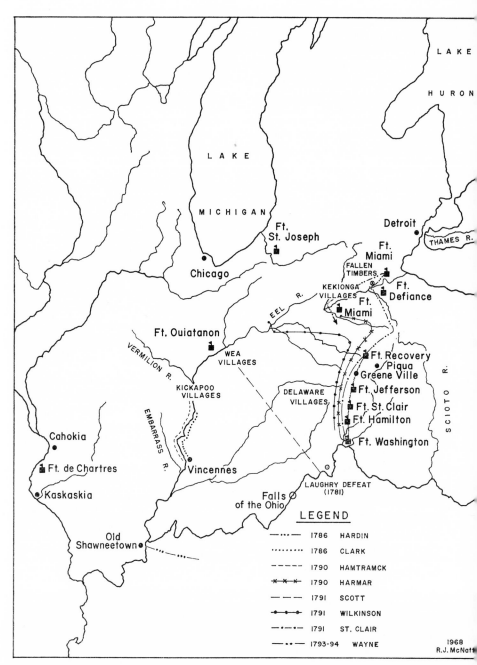

LAKE HURON

LAKE MICHIGAN

Ft. St. Joseph

Detroit

THAMES R.

Ft. Miami

FALLEN TIMBERS

Chicago

KEKIONGA VILLAGES

Ft. Defiance

Ft. Miami

EEL R.

Ft. Ouiatanon

VERMILION R.

WEA VILLAGES

Ft. Recovery

Piqua

Greene Ville

KICKAPOO VILLAGES

DELAWARE VILLAGES

Ft. Jefferson

SCIOTO R.

EMBARRASS R.

Ft. St. Clair

Ft. Hamilton

Cahokia

Ft. Washington

Ft. de Chartres

Vincennes

Kaskaskia

LAUGHRY DEFEAT (1781)

Falls of the Ohio

Old Shawneetown

LEGEND

----···	1786	HARDIN
········	1786	CLARK
------	1790	HAMTRAMCK
✕✕✕	1790	HARMAR
---	1791	SCOTT
—•—•—	1791	WILKINSON
—·—·—	1791	ST. CLAIR
—··—	1793-94	WAYNE

1968
R.J. McNatt

American campaigns against the Miami Confederacy, 1783–1794.

some of the most enterprising yet lawless men on the frontier. The travail of Vincennes began in the summer of 1786 when an expedition of Kentuckians led by John Hardin attacked an Indian village near Old Shawneetown on the Ohio River below its junction with the Wabash. The Wabash Indians immediately raised a party of 450 warriors and moved down the river to attack the Americans at Vincennes. The French inhabitants, led by Jean Marie Phillipe Le Gras, François Bosseron, Jean Baptiste Vaudry, Pierre and Antoine Gamelin, and other prominent Frenchmen, fearing an Indian siege in which all Vincennes would be the target, persuaded the Indians to leave after they had fired a few shots.[13] John Small and Moses Henry, prominent Americans at Vincennes, noted the passage of 26 war parties through Vincennes that summer. One was an Eel River Miami party which brought both scalps and prisoners from Kentucky.[14]

Vincennes joined Kentucky settlers in seeking relief by appealing for aid to George Rogers Clark. He sought to accomplish this by striking the Indians' villages with some twelve hundred militiamen. Three days' march above Vincennes, however, some of his men mutinied and Clark retreated. He placed a small garrison in a blockhouse at Vincennes and secured a promise from the lower Wabash Indian chiefs that they would meet him in a council the following spring.[15]

Although the first attack on Vincennes was perpetrated by the lower Wabash Miamis and their Illinois neighbors, it necessarily caused the Miami bands on the upper Wabash to become concerned. Fortunately, the tribe was led at this time by gifted chiefs. Le Gris was principal chief and Little Turtle war chief, but the most intriguing Miami leader was Pacanne.

This chief, whose village was on the St. Joseph River, was often away and left his nephew, young Jean Baptiste Richardville, as

---

[13] Thornbrough, *Outpost on the Wabash,* 14, 23n., 24n.
[14] Leonard C. Helderman, "Danger on the Wabash: Vincennes Letters of 1786," *Indiana Magazine of History,* XXXIV, 4 (December, 1938), 455–67, edits six letters from the John Filson Collection.
[15] Thornbrough, *Outpost on the Wabash,* 14–16.

spokesman during his absence. Pacanne took a small part of his band, including warriors, women, and children, to the lower Wabash in 1785 and remained there nearly two years. He was able to observe American and French actions while constantly consulting with the Piankeshaws and Weas, who had been fractious in the past and were prone to follow Kickapoo or Mascoutin leadership, which was usually warlike. Pacanne frequently returned to the Maumee or Detroit, and his presence on the lower Wabash indicated the tribal council was kept informed of the plans of the separated Miami bands. Both Le Gris and Pacanne were called principal chief by contemporaries, but evidence favors the supremacy of Le Gris because of Pacanne's absence from the Maumee much of the time. Pacanne also claimed to be opposed to the belligerent majority of the Kekionga Miamis.[16]

In spite of the minor role usually played by the Miamis' principal chief during a war, Le Gris continued to exert great influence in his own tribe and with the nearby Miami Confederacy villages. Antoine Gamelin praised him, and Henry Hay believed he exerted a decisive influence in conferences with Delaware and Shawnee chiefs and Canadian Indian agents on the Maumee and was the equal of Joseph Brant and other respected leaders of the Indian Confederacy.[17]

In time of war, the Miami war chief overshadowed all others. Attacks on enemies were generally carried out by small numbers of warriors, such as Little Turtle's party of fifteen which ravished the settlements around Fort Washington in 1789. Little Turtle's victory over La Balme and his successful forays against the Ameri-

[16] Thornbrough, *Outpost on the Wabash*, 47, 108. Pacanne had rescued Thomas Morris in 1768. Hanna, *The Wilderness Trail*, II, 362–67. Barnhart, *Hamilton and Clark*, 45, calls him the head chief of the Miamis. Pacanne to Commissioners, Vincennes, September 25, 1785, Draper MSSIM123, William Clark Papers, Draper Manuscript Collection, microfilm copy in Ball State University Library.

[17] Le Gris, or Crippled Ankles, was Nakakwanga. The spelling is *Nawuakounande* in a speech of 1773 and *Nahgohquangoh* in the Treaty of Greene Ville. Antoine Gamelin referred to him as the "Great chief of the Miamis." Quaife, "Fort Wayne in 1790," 293–361. Hay's "Journal" was originally published in *Proceedings of the Wisconsin Historical Society* in 1914 under the title "A Narrative Life on the Old Frontier." Gamelin's "Journal" is reprinted in Smith, *The St. Clair Papers*, II, 155–60.

cans made him the greatest war chief of his tribe. By 1790, he had earned election to supreme command of the united war parties of the Miami Confederacy.[18]

By 1786, the Indians' successful summer campaigns had halted implementation of the treaties and agreements made during the previous twelve months. More important, the raids made easier the consolidation of resistance to the United States into the powerful Miami Confederacy. A grand council was held at Sandusky in November and December, at which time Joseph Brant, the Mohawk chief, lost his dominating influence in the confederacy. The council's purpose was to strengthen the tribes' resolution to preserve the Ohio River boundary, and toward this end, the confederacy established its headquarters on the Maumee near the trading post of Alexander McKee, who became the guiding spirit of Canadian support.

The Miamis' name was given to the confederacy partly because the Americans were ignorant of the tribe's size, holding as they did exaggerated ideas of its warrior strength. There was some justification for using "Miami Confederacy," however, for the name signified the Miami-Maumee River frontier. The Miami lands became the outpost—the last frontier—of Indian resistance. The region had attracted remnants of some eastern Miami bands and discontented and recalcitrant factions from other tribes, which swelled the number of villages and warriors. Miami determination to resist the Americans made the Wabash-Maumee lands and people important in fact as well as speculation. The Wabash and Maumee

---

18 Little Turtle's exploits in peace and war have received more attention than the Miami tribe and all of its other members. Brice, *History of Fort Wayne,* 201 n., gives the basic facts generally used by biographers. Little Turtle, a war chief who was also the tribe's "speaker" at councils and treaty negotiations, can be understood only through a study of those speeches. His most important orations were those made at Greene Ville in 1795. Wayne's report in *American State Papers,* Class II, *Indian Affairs,* I, 562–83. Calvin M. Young, *Little Turtle (Meshekinnoquah), the Great Chief of the Miami Indian Nation,* is more accurate on the facts of Miami history and the exploits of William Wells than on the career of the Chief. See pp. 179–202. S. F. Kaler and R. H. Maring, *History of Whitley County, Indiana,* 80, cite their interview with Kilsoquah and her son in which they categorically asserted the Chief was not part Mohican but was instead one-fourth French.

rivers, protected by the Indiana "wetlands," the glaciated lake region, and the Black Swamp of northwestern Ohio, formed a barrier behind which the confederacy operated unhindered. Its scalping parties hit American settlements and retreated to the safety of the Miami country.

The Miami Confederacy was a formidable combination. It included seven Canadian tribes, segments of the western Iroquois, and the tribes between the Great Lakes and the Ohio River. It was established while the thirteen former colonies, now the newborn United States, were struggling to their feet and while the British imperial structure was susceptible to the importunities of Canada.[19]

American response to the Miami Confederacy was directed by a new government organization and new agents. The "Ordinance for the Government of the Territory of the United States Northwest of the River Ohio" was enacted by Congress July 13, 1787. Arthur St. Clair of Pennsylvania was appointed governor, with ex officio duties as superintendent of Indian affairs in the territory. He was responsible to Henry Knox, secretary of war, in his duties as superintendent.

Knox ordered Colonel Harmar to station a garrison of his small army at Vincennes in the summer of 1787 to replace Clark's unauthorized force. Harmar occupied Vincennes, negotiated for an Indian council in July, and crossed to the Kaskaskia-Cahokia region to bolster sagging American prestige. His guide and hunter on the expedition was Pacanne, who was eventually placed in American "employ" as an emissary of the United States. Harmar returned to Vincennes and met about 120 Piankeshaws and Weas at a council in early September.[20]

Major John Francis Hamtramck, who was placed in command

[19] Kellogg, *British Regime,* 209–11. Hamtramck, Vincennes, to Harmar at the Muskingum, January 1, 1788, tells of Brant's activity on the Maumee River. See Thornbrough, *Outpost on the Wabash,* 58–63. The "Speech of the United Indian Nations" at the Sandusky Council reached Congress after being delayed six months by the Shawnees. Paul W. Wehr, "Treaty of Fort Finney, 1786: Prelude to the Indian Wars," unpublished M.A. thesis, Miami University, Oxford, Ohio, 1958.

[20] Harmar at the mouth of the Muskingum to Secretary of War Knox, November 24, 1787, in Thornbrough, *Outpost on the Wabash,* 46–57.

of the garrison when Harmar returned to the Ohio River forts, organized a local government, conferred with visiting parties of Indians, tried to restrain the American inhabitants from provocative acts, and operated an espionage system. During the summer of 1788, his supply trains were attacked, and his interpreter, Jean Baptiste Constant, the Wea trader, reported that five or six scalps were brought daily to Kekionga and one prisoner was burned while he was visiting there.[21] War parties against the Kentucky settlements were in the field at all times.

Hamtramck's diplomatic efforts were nullified in August, 1788, when a party of sixty Kentuckians, led by Patrick Brown, crossed the Ohio on the west side of the Wabash and marched to the Embarras River. They attacked an Indian village a few miles from Vincennes, killed nine men, and took twenty horses. Hamtramck refused to aid them, but could not confiscate their booty or drive them out of the village with his small force. He was aghast when he learned the village was that of Pacanne and the Piankeshaw chief La Demoiselle and that the victims included the father-in-law of the former and a man named Montour from the Mingo tribe. The attack came while Pacanne was on the Maumee to secure for Hamtramck news of the summer Indian council at McKee's trading post. His band withdrew to the Terre Haute area to wait for him; La Demoiselle and most of the Piankeshaws and Kickapoos near Vincennes moved to Kaskaskia. After the attack, Hamtramck and Vincennes' French leaders convened all the Indians they could gather to assure them that Brown's party would be punished. However, Hamtramck was powerless to control any of the Kentuckians who remained in Vincennes. When Pacanne returned, he quietly rejoined his band and returned to Kekionga without reporting to Hamtramck. This was indeed an ominous sign.[22]

21 Hamtramck, Vincennes, to Harmar, Fort Harmar, August 12, 1788, in *ibid.*, 105–108. This letter also informed Harmar that Pacanne had gone to McKee's post to secure for the Americans information about a council which would be held at that place during the summer.

22 Hamtramck, Vincennes, to Harmar, Fort Harmar, August 31, 1788, in *ibid.*, 114–20. F. Clever Bald, "Colonel John Francis Hamtramck," *Indiana Magazine of*

From his territorial capital at Marietta, Governor St. Clair made unsuccessful overtures for a council during the summer of 1788. However, that winter he did entice questionable representatives from the Potawatomi, Delaware, Wyandot, Ottawa, Chippewa, and Sauk tribes to Fort Harmar; they signed two treaties on January 9, 1789. The first confirmed the terms of the treaty made at Fort Stanwix in 1784 by which the Iroquois relinquished their claims to the land west of the Ohio River. The second reaffirmed the terms of the Fort McIntosh treaty of 1785.[23]

One of the apparently minor provisions of the Fort McIntosh and Fort Finney treaties now began to assume more significance to both Indians and Americans. Article 5 of the first McIntosh treaty stated:

> If any citizen of the United States, or other person, not being an Indian, shall attempt to settle on any of the lands allotted to the Wyandot and Delaware Indians in this treaty, . . . such persons shall forfeit the protection of the United States, and the Indians may punish him as they please.

Article 7 of the Fort Finney treaty included the same provision, and it was reaffirmed in Article 7 of the two Fort Harmar treaties. The latter also provided that Indians who committed crimes against citizens of the United States, presumably while on former Indian lands, were to be delivered to the United States for trial and punishment. The Indians acceded to this as a just measure which balanced the privilege of enforcing Indian laws on American citizens on Indian lands. The commissioners would have been ignorant indeed had they expected Indians to punish American intruders on Indian lands without arousing popular frontier protest.[24]

History, XLIV, 4 (December, 1948), 355–56, is an excellent study of Hamtramck's career at Vincennes.

[23] The two treaties, with the signatures of the Indian chiefs, are in Dillon, *History of Indiana,* 602–609. Harmar's explanation of the treaties is in Harmar, Fort Harmar, to Hamtramck, Vincennes, February 15, 1789, in Thornbrough, *Outpost on the Wabash,* 150–55.

[24] Secretary of War Timothy Pickering said that by 1795, the United States had ceased to demand that Indian murderers of whites be brought in by their tribes, since

The Fort Harmar treaties renewed the American attempt to quiet the Indian claims to southern Ohio so that area could be surveyed and sold to white settlers. Had the treaties been accepted by the Miami Confederacy, they would have weakened its central purpose: to preserve the Ohio River boundary, which was already breached by two American settlements. The Fort Harmar treaties tacitly recognized that the Wabash Valley tribes posed a separate problem which would require future treaties. In spite of American attempts to placate the Ohio tribes, these treaties could not prevent the oncoming war and were never put into effect. It remained for the Treaty of Greene Ville to complete their purposes.

In the fall of 1789, the Potawatomis from the village on the St. Joseph River sent a war party to Major Hamtramck offering to fight against the Miamis if they were given ammunition and supplies. The commandant knew there was a latent antipathy between the two tribes and that a Potawatomi chief had been killed by a Miami some years before. Hamtramck feared this to be a ruse and neither accepted nor rejected it. As St. Clair said of the Fort Harmar treaties, the object was to divide the tribes, but no Indian-American alliance was dependable at this time. His caution was justified, for the same Potawatomi band then proceeded to raid the Kentucky settlements. While they were retreating to the Ohio, a body of militia overtook them and killed the chief with whom Hamtramck had negotiated.[25]

The combination of spring planting and the Indians' inevitable consultations on the terms of the new Fort Harmar treaties provided a brief lull on the frontier in early 1789. Rumors went unchecked; usually they predicated a grand council of the tribes on the Maumee.

It was not long until the lower Wabash tribes renewed their raids on Kentucky and the Vincennes area. That summer, the war parties

the United States had become unable to punish its own citizens for murdering Indians. Wilcomb E. Washburn (ed.), *The Indian and the White Man,* 354.

[25] Hamtramck, Vincennes, to Harmar, Fort Harmar, March 28, 1789, in Thornbrough, *Outpost on the Wabash,* 157–63. St. Clair explained that the Indians were divided and it was possible to create war between them. *American State Papers,* Class II, *Indian Affairs,* I, 10.

began to steal or destroy the settlers' cattle. Hamtramck noted that even French and English traders were killed, but Negro slaves were safe because of their value.[26] In August, John Hardin led another Kentucky force in an attack on a Shawnee village in the Wea area; twelve Indians were killed. Again the Vincennes commandant was powerless to stop or punish the raiders.[27]

Such raids were understandable, but St. Clair, who still hoped for a general peace, understood it could not be secured until he was able to protect the Indians as well as the whites. The lower Wabash tribes frequently offered to make peace and often protested their friendship, but their war parties operated continuously. Even a band of about eighty Wea warriors with whom Hamtramck secured an alliance in February, 1790, was untrustworthy. The only Indians who refused to make any concessions to the United States were the Kekionga Miamis. Hamtramck complained that no news had filtered through from that heavily guarded enemy area for fifteen months.[28]

A British subject visited Miamitown, near Kekionga and provided a most informative report on Kekionga and the Miami Confederacy chiefs. Henry Hay, son of Major Jehu Hay (captured by Clark at Vincennes in 1779), visited the little village in the winter of 1789–90. He was convivial as well as perceptive, and his British antecedents made him a welcome guest and afforded him opportunities to observe the inhabitants which no American could have gained. He noted that seven villages about the Maumee's headwaters were nearly deserted when the Indians were in their winter camps a few miles away. Miamitown was then occupied by French and British traders, who entertained Hay in their homes. He clearly identified both the individual white people and the Indian

[26] Hamtramck, Vincennes, to Major John P. Wyllys, Fort Harmar, May 27, 1789, in Thornbrough, *Outpost on the Wabash,* 169–71. Emma Lou Thornbrough, *The Negro in Indiana Before 1900,* 1–16, cites several Miamis who owned slaves, including Little Turtle.

[27] Hamtramck, Vincennes, to Harmar, Fort Harmar, July 29, 1789, and August 14, 1789, in Thornbrough, *Outpost on the Wabash,* 178–83, 183–85.

[28] Harmar to Hamtramck, January 13, 1790; Hamtramck to Harmar, March 17, 1790, in *ibid.,* 213–16, 220–27.

Courtesy Grant County (Indiana) Historical Society
Jean Baptiste Richardville. From a lithograph by J. O. Lewis.

François Godfroy. From a lithograph by J. O. Lewis.

chiefs who frequently visited the town to trade their peltries or to confer with war parties returning from Kentucky. Hay developed a feeling of admiration for the personal qualities of Le Gris, whom he considered the principal, or civil, chief of the tribe. He spent much time with Jean Baptiste Richardville and often breakfasted with Le Gris. He saw war parties return with scalps and occasional prisoners, met Little Turtle and two Shawnee war chiefs, Blue Jacket and Captain Johnnie.

In another near-by village at this time was a Delaware band which threatened to move to Spanish Missouri because the Miamis refused to give them land for permanent settlement. Le Gris was in constant communication with the other Miami bands through messages from Little Face and other Wea chiefs of the villages near the mouth of the Tippecanoe River and with The Soldier, chief at the Eel River towns near present-day Logansport. The Detroit commandant, Major Patrick Murray, still issued passes to traders to the Wabash country, and men such as Hay kept him supplied with information. According to Hay, in early March the principal Shawnee chief, The Wolf, came to Miamitown and asked for a meeting of the traders at which he informed them the scattered Shawnee bands were going to concentrate at a village on the Maumee. The traders were pleased because the plan would help protect them from future attacks by the Americans.

By 1790, intermarriage between the Miamis and the French was common, and Hay commented upon many of them. Richardville was the most important mixed blood, but Peter Lafontaine, Antoine Rivarre, and many others had married into the tribe and Hay found this mixed society no bar to rank in the social life of Miamitown. He was kept awake the night of March 22 by festivities at the Miami village across the river from Miamitown. The village war totem had been out on the warpath since the preceding fall and was being returned to its resting place in the trophy house with all the ceremonies due it.[29]

[29] Quaife, "Fort Wayne in 1790." The Delawares on the White River of Indiana after 1770 were not considered owners of the region by the Miamis. One band of Delawares moved to Missouri in 1789 with Spanish permission. Hay's reference

111

While Hay's account of the Miami villages indicated the Indians' confidence in the ultimate success of their newfound unity, the United States prepared to attack their homeland in order to disrupt them. St. Clair made a final effort to secure a general treaty with the confederated tribes in 1790. His "peace message" was sent to Hamtramck, who, on March 16, 1790, dispatched Pierre Gamelin up the Wabash with it. The Indians at the Vermilion River refused to permit Pierre to go beyond that point, so, on April 5, Antoine Gamelin undertook the important mission. The latter held councils with Wea, Shawnee, and Potawatomi warriors, and all told him they would be guided by the Kekionga band. He was then permitted to proceed to Kekionga, where he met the Indians of many tribes in regular councils and in private talks with warrior chiefs. The Miamis refused to make any decision on St. Clair's proposal until they had conferred with the British at Detroit. Antoine describes the events:

The 23d April, I arrived at the Miami town; the next day, I got to the Miami nation, the Chaouanon [Shawnees], and Delawares, all assembled. . . . In a private discourse with the great chief, he told me not to mind what the Chaouanons would tell me, having a bad heart, and being perturbators of all the nations. He said the Miamis had a bad name, on account of mischief done on the River Ohio, but he told me it was not occasioned by his young men, but by the Chaouanons, his young men going out only for to hunt.

The 25th of April, Blue Jacket, chief warrior of the Chaouanons, invited me to go to his home, and told me: "My friend, by the name and consent of the Chaouanons and Delawares, I will speak to you. . . . We can not give an answer without hearing from our father, at Detroit, and we are determined to give you back the two branches of wampum to send you to Detroit to see and hear the chief." . . . The 26th of April, . . . I went to the great chief of the Miamis, called Le Gris; his chief warrior [Little Turtle] was present. I told him how I had been served by the Chaouanons; he answered me, that he had heard

---

indicates that another Delaware village, dissatisfied with living in Miami country, considered joining the first emigrants. Hodge, *Handbook of American Indians*, I, 385.

of it; that the said nations behaved contrary to his intentions. He desired me not to mind those strangers, and that he would soon give me a positive answer; "we must send your speeches to all our neighbors, and to the Lake nations; we can not give a definitive answer without consulting the commandant of Detroit." . . . he was well pleased with the speeches, and said [them] to be worthy of attention, and should be communicated to all their confederates, having resolved among them-[selves] not to do anything without an unanimous consent. . . . The same day, Blue Jacket, chief of the Chaouanons, invited me to his house for supper, and, before the other chiefs, told me that, after another deliberation, they thought [it] necessary that I should go myself to Detroit, to see the commandant, who would get all his children assembled to hear my speech. I told them I would not answer them in the night—that I was not ashamed to speak before the sun.

The 29th of April, I got them all assembled. I told them that I was not to go to Detroit; that the speeches were directed to the nations of the river Wabash and the Miami, and that, to prove the sincerity of the speech and the heart of Governor St. Clair, I have willingly given a copy of the speeches, to be shown to the commandant of Detroit; that his Excellency will be glad to hear that his speeches have been sent to Detroit, and, according to a letter wrote by the commandant of Detroit to the Miamis, Chaouanons, and Delawares, mentioning to you too to be peaceable with the Americans. . . . Blue Jacket got up and said to me: "My friend, we are well pleased with what you say; our intention is not to force you to go to Detroit; it is only a proposal, thinking it for the best. Our answer is the same as the Miamis. . . ." Le Gris, chief of the Miamis, asked me, in a private discourse, what chiefs had made a treaty with the Americans at Muskingum. I answered him, that their names were mentioned in the treaty. He told me that he had heard of it some time ago, but they are not chiefs, neither delegates, who made that treaty; they are only young men, who, without authority and instruction from their chiefs, have concluded that treaty, which will not be approved. They went to that treaty clandestinely, and they intend to make mention of it in the next council to be held.[30]

---

[30] Thornbrough, *Outpost on the Wabash*, 224 n., identifies the members of the important Gamelin family. Smith, *The St. Clair Papers*, II, 155–60, contains Gamelin's "Journal."

The most futile American effort to separate the Wabash tribes from the Miami Confederacy occurred in May, 1790. Thomas Proctor was sent to the Iroquois in New York in the hope that a party of those influential warriors would accompany him to the Wabash. At the same time, the Iroquois were asked to furnish St. Clair a band of warriors if the confederacy refused to end its resistance. The Iroquois did not like the proposal, and Proctor's party was not sent to the Wabash.[31]

Having correctly concluded that he could not win the Northwest through diplomacy, St. Clair decided to take the offensive after reading Antoine Gamelin's report. The summer was one of American military preparations, and the governor's headquarters were moved to Fort Washington, now Cincinnati.

Confidence and security marked the Miami Confederacy's councils on the Maumee, while insecurity, dissatisfaction, and habitual deprivation comprised the normal state of affairs for residents of Vincennes and other American outposts.

Colonel Josiah Harmar projected a major attack against Kekionga by way of the Miami Valley, and in order to secure its success, he ordered Hamtramck to make a diversionary attack up the Wabash. Hamtramck marched September 22 with 330 men. The Kentucky militiamen went as far as the Vermilion towns, which the Indians abandoned on their approach. When Hamtramck ordered an advance into the Wea and Kickapoo country farther up the river, the militia refused to move because it was on half-rations. Nevertheless, his mission accomplished its purpose. The 600 Wabash warriors waiting to ambush him above the Vermilion were unable to return to Kekionga to meet Harmar's main thrust.[32]

Since the Americans usually attacked Indian towns in the fall of the year, the confederacy was prepared to remove its noncombatants to safety in the swamp country toward the Elkhart River north of the Maumee by pack horse and on human backs while the war-

---

[31] Downes, *Council Fires,* 317. Smith, *St. Clair Papers,* II, 216–17.
[32] Hamtramck, Vincennes, to Harmar, Fort Washington, November 2, 1790, and November 28, 1790, in Thornbrough, *Outpost on the Wabash,* 259–64, 266–67.

riors awaited American attacks. So it was that when Harmar's army reached the Maumee source, it found the villages deserted.

Harmar marched from Fort Washington on September 30 with 1,453 men, including 320 Regular Army soldiers. They advanced up the Little Miami, crossed the Great Miami near Piqua, then moved up Loramie Creek to the portage to the St. Mary's and descended that river to the Maumee. They reached the Miami villages October 17 but found them abandoned.

On October 19, Colonel John Hardin and 300 men, scouting the surrounding country for Indians, were unfortunate enough to find Little Turtle and 400 warriors. The ensuing struggle saw the militia mauled and driven back into Harmar's main force. The army then spent the next day destroying five Indian villages, including the Delaware and Shawnee towns mentioned by Henry Hay.

On October 21, Harmar decided it was useless to build a fort whose garrison could not be supported with either men or supplies and ordered a retreat to Fort Washington. The next day, however, Hardin persuaded him that if a force of 400 men returned to Kekionga immediately, it would wreak havoc on the unsuspecting Indians as they returned to their villages. Major John P. Wyllys was detached that night to execute an early-morning ambush, which Harmar expected would restore prestige to the Americans and instill some fear in the hearts of the Indians. This hope was smashed as 340 troops chased small groups of warriors through the brush.

Meanwhile, Little Turtle, with a large force of well-disciplined warriors reinforced by Ottawas and Iroquois, saw that Wyllys' force of 60 regulars was unsupported and seized the opportunity to destroy it. Harmar was able to countermarch only 30 men to his detachment's relief. After the straggling soldiers rejoined Harmar's main force, the Colonel declined all further suggestions by Hardin to renew the attack against Kekionga and retreated to Fort Washington.

Harmar sustained the loss of 183 Americans killed and 31 wounded in the campaign, which he believed had destroyed about 20,000

115

bushels of corn, a large amount of vegetables, and more then 100 wigwams and cabins. The destruction was hard on the Indians, but the campaign failed in its purpose. A court of inquiry was held in 1791 to examine Harmar's conduct during the campaign. He was exonerated.[33]

The Indians' losses were about equal to those of the Americans and the destruction of their villages just before winter weather set in was a serious matter, but their morale was high. They had expected attack, had removed their women and children and much of their food supplies, and had repulsed an invading army. The real significance of the campaign was the renewed confidence of the Indians that they could meet the Americans in battle and expect a successful conclusion. Little Turtle had led the Miami warriors to victory in a major engagement; the center of the Indian Confederacy again was a safe refuge for the bands which had moved their villages to the Maumee area. Once again the frontier militia had proved unwilling or unable to meet well-led Indian warriors. The Indians felt they had won the war to preserve their Ohio River line.

President Washington reacted promptly to the American loss. He considered the site of the Miami villages to be the military key to the frontier, a point at which a strong permanent base must be secured at all cost. In March, 1791, Secretary of War Henry Knox ordered St. Clair to place a garrison there while General Charles Scott of Kentucky created a diversion by attacking the middle Wabash towns. The same month, Congress proposed expansion of the frontier Regular Army to three thousand men. Instead of acceding to Indian demands that the Americans withdraw to the Ohio, Knox for the first time proposed a Wabash-Maumee line of demar-

---

[33] Harmar, Fort Washington, to Hamtramck, Vincennes, November 29, 1790, in *ibid.*, 268–69. Dillon, *History of Indiana*, 245–54, includes excerpts from the reports of Captain John Armstrong and Harmar. It remains the best account of Harmar's expedition. On the retreat, Harmar threatened to turn his artillery on any group of men or officers who left the ranks during march or engagement. See *American State Papers*, Class V, *Military Affairs*, I, 20–30, for the work of the court of inquiry into Harmar's conduct.

cation between Indians and whites instead of the Fort Harmar line.[34]

Scott led about 800 mounted Kentucky militiamen across the Ohio near the mouth of the Kentucky River on May 23, 1791. He campaigned during the season when the Indians planted their crops and amused themselves, a time seldom used for military expeditions by the Americans, who were accustomed to attack after the harvest. Scott marched directly through hilly southern Indiana to reach the Wea towns by June 1. While his main force destroyed growing crops and other food supplies, Colonel John Hardin burned a nearby Kickapoo village and Colonel James Wilkinson burned Kethtipecanunk, a Miami village eighteen miles up the river. Without the loss of a single soldier, Scott killed 32 warriors and took 58 prisoners; he released the incapacitated and returned to the Falls of the Ohio. It was the most effective and creditable showing by an American force since Clark's campaigns of 1778–79.[35]

St. Clair had counted on the unexpectedness of Scott's attack. His spies informed him that the chiefs of the confederacy were concentrating their villages on the Maumee behind the Black Swamp barrier. This, however, exposed their distant flank on the lower Wabash. Then St. Clair caught his opponents off guard with a second expedition—again against the middle Wabash towns.

On August 1, Colonel Wilkinson led five hundred mounted troops from Fort Washington. He feinted an attack on Kekionga by moving north to the portage between the Great Miami and St. Mary's rivers, where he turned and drove for his objective. Wilkinson burned Kenpacomaqua, The Soldier's Miami village six miles above the mouth of the Eel River, then moved down the Wabash to a Kickapoo village and the Wea villages (which had been rebuilt after Scott's attack) and destroyed them all. He also captured the family of Wea Chief Little Face. The Kentucky militia performed well for Wilkinson and he planned to march against the major

[34] Dillon, *History of Indiana*, 259–60.
[35] J. W. Whickcar, "General Charles Scott and His March to Ouiatanon," *Indiana Magazine of History*, XXI, 1 (March, 1925), 90–99. Kellogg, *British Regime*, 214. Scott's "Report" is in Dillon, *History of Indiana*, 262–67.

Kickapoo villages west of Ouiatanon, but the absence of good trails and the fatigue of his men and horses caused him to take Scott's return route to the Falls of the Ohio.[36]

Scott's and Wilkinson's successes proved that any attack on the Piankeshaws, Weas, or Kickapoos on the lower or middle Wabash demanded good timing and careful preparations, as well as solid leadership. Assistance from the Potawatomis to the north could reach these villages within one and one-half days, and warriors from the Kekionga area were scarcely farther. So, to be successful, American raids had to be prepared in secret. The troops had to be marched for days without meeting war parties and finally hope to find northern-village warriors far away on another expedition. Then their only escape was a five-day march to the Ohio before they could feel safe from pursuit.

Although the disorganized mutiny of Hamtramck's men became a lucky and fortunate event in that it saved them from a fatal ambush, both Scott and Wilkinson profited from good planning and surprise. The latter tactics were designed only to destroy the Indians' food supplies and thereby keep scalping parties from leaving their villages. American commissioners could hope to negotiate peace only while the war parties were inactive, and if these tactics failed, a costly major offensive to destroy the warriors of the confederacy was the alternative.

The American campaigns during the summers of 1790 and 1791 were designed to keep the Miami Confederacy off balance, disrupt its traditional summer activities, and harass its allies so they would consent to meet St. Clair in a general council. They had a contrary effect. The Miamis and Shawnees became more resolute, the tribes north and west of the Maumee were alarmed, and the British at Niagara, Detroit, Mackinac, and other posts supported the preparations for an imminent American attack. Little Turtle; Blue Jack-

---

[36] Governor St. Clair's instructions to Wilkinson are in his orders of July 31, 1791. Smith, *The St. Clair Papers,* II, 227–29. Wilkinson's report is in *ibid.,* 233–39, and in Dillon, *History of Indiana,* 267–71.

et, the Shawnee war chief; and Buckongahelas, the Delaware chief, with the help of Alexander McKee, Matthew Elliot, and other British Indian agents and traders who infested every Indian village, exhorted the Indians to remain steadfast in their confederacy.

St. Clair and Richard Butler, his second in command, collected an army of regulars and militia at Fort Washington. The frontier forts were nearly denuded of troops, and capable officers, such as Hamtramck, were attached to St. Clair's army. His adjutant, Ebenezer Denny, wrote on November 8, 1791:

The prediction of [defeat by] General Harmar before the army set out on the campaign was founded upon his experience and particular knowledge of things. He saw with what material the bulk of the army was composed; men collected from the streets and prisons of the cities, hurried out into the enemy's country, and with the officers commanding them totally unacquainted with the business in which they were engaged, it was utterly impossible they could be otherwise [than defeated]. Besides, not any one department was sufficiently prepared; both quarter-master and contractors extremely deficient. It was a matter of astonishment to him [General Harmar] that the commanding general [St. Clair] who was acknowledged to be perfectly competent, should think of hazarding with such people and under such circumstances, his reputation and life, and the lives of so many others, knowing too, as both did, the enemy with whom he was going to contend; an enemy brought up from infancy to war, and perhaps superior to an equal number of the best men that could be taken against them. It is a truth, I had hopes that the noise and show which the army made on their march might possibly deter the enemy from attempting a serious and general attack. It was unfortunate that both the general officers were, and had been disabled by sickness; in such situation it is possible that some essential matters might be overlooked. The Adjutant-General Colonel Winthrop Sargent, an old Revolutionary officer, was, however, constantly on the alert; he took upon himself the burden of everything, and a very serious and troublesome task he had. But one most important object was wanting, can't say neglected, but more might have been done toward obtaining it; this was a knowledge of the collected force and situation of the enemy; of this we were perfectly ignorant.[37]

The army began its slow march toward Kekionga in early September, 1791. Fort Hamilton was constructed twenty-five miles up the Great Miami on September 17. Twenty miles upstream, a stockade fortification named Fort St. Clair was built. Fort Jefferson was then constructed about the same distance farther north, about six miles south of what is now Greenville, Ohio.

Progress was slow. Desertions and sickness reduced the force to about fourteen hundred able-bodied men. The Indians under Little Turtle hovered around them, picked off stragglers, and captured supplies. St. Clair reached the headwaters of the Wabash near present Fort Recovery on November 3 after advancing his army about ninety miles since September 7. Thinking he was about fifteen miles from either Kekionga or the Indians' main encampment, he lightly fortified his camp, planning to attack the Indians the following morning.

The Indians seized the chance to demoralize the militia by means of a dawn attack. Their retreat engulfed the reserve battalions. Whenever the soldiers thrust at any point, the warriors gave way, then struck the weakened American lines. After Butler and a large number of officers had been killed and their artillery captured, the demoralized army began a retreat which did not end until it reached Fort Jefferson, where Hamtramck had returned after pursuing a large number of deserters with a regiment of St. Clair's best troops. The losses would have been greater had the Indians not abandoned their pursuit after about four miles in order to seize the booty. Nevertheless, American casualties were appalling: 39 officers killed, 22 wounded; 593 men killed or missing, 242 wounded. The large number of camp followers also suffered heavy casualties, and the army's supplies and equipment were lost.

When the battle developed, the combatants were about equal in

---

[37] *American State Papers, Military Affairs,* I, 36–39. This excerpt is from "The Military Journal of Ebenezer Denny," also included in Slocum, *History of the Maumee River Basin,* 171–73.

number. The Indians probably lost no more than 150 warriors, and even today the battle remains a classic example of the calamity which sometimes resulted when well-led and experienced Indian warriors opposed poorly led and trained soldiers.[38]

St. Clair's defeat was disastrous to American prestige, but other circumstances prevented the Indians from taking full advantage of the opportunity to clear the country north of the Ohio River. Lord Dorchester, governor-general of Canada, met a grand council of the tribes at Quebec during the summer of 1791 to reaffirm Canadian support for a neutral Indian state, and both he and the Indians expected the recent victory would force Americans to the inevitable conclusion that the area could not be conquered. It was a fatal miscalculation by both Dorchester and the Miami Confederacy.[39] A new British secretary of state for foreign affairs was prepared to advise the Indians to accept any reasonable compromise solution, although he remained adamant on continued British possession of the posts south of the Great Lakes.

As Britain's home government became more distracted by the shifts in alliances during the French conflict in Europe, Lieutenant-Governor John Graves Simcoe, who replaced Dorchester by becoming the first governor of Upper Canada, wanted neither a compromise nor a neutral Indian state. Acting upon his own initiative, he worked for a conclusive decision in the Ohio country. The Indians thus found themselves in a war of attrition supported by allies who gave them much more vocal support than physical aid. They were opposed by what seemed to them endless numbers of Americans who were now led by a first-rate military commander, General Anthony Wayne.[40]

[38] Smith, *The St. Clair Papers*, II, 262–67, includes the Governor's report to Knox. Another detailed account of the expedition is in Brice, *History of Fort Wayne*, 131–42. The most vivid descriptions of battles during this period are those of Theodore Roosevelt, *The Winning of the West* (New Library Edition), Vol. III, Part 1.

[39] Philbrick, *The Rise of the West*, 152–55. Lord Dorchester's speech to the Indians is in *MPHC*, XXIV, 309–13.

[40] Downes, *Council Fires*, 329–30. Kellogg, *British Regime*, 214–16. Lieutenant Colonel J. G. Simcoe, Niagara, to Lord Dorchester, August 20, 1792, in *MPHC*, XXIV, 459–66.

Wayne did not want to attack the confederacy before making another effort to bring the Indians to council. Colonel James Wilkinson, now commanding Fort Washington, sent two messengers to Kekionga with "speeches" in April, 1792; both were captured and killed by the Miamis before they reached their destination.[41] Secretary of War Knox then sent veteran trader Peter Pond to the western posts. Pond was soon convinced the Indians' determination and unity could be broken only by war.[42]

The United States finally capitalized upon the relations which George Rogers Clark had developed with the lower Wabash tribes and the fact that these tribes were not an integral part of the Miami Confederacy. In the fall of 1792, Commissioner Rufus Putnam negotiated a treaty with nine of them, including the Piankeshaws, Weas, and a part of the Eel River band. This would have been a better deterrent to their raids than the military attacks of earlier years, but the agreement was not ratified by Congress, which wanted a definitive treaty for the entire northwest frontier.[43]

The Indian confederates went from the Quebec meeting with Dorchester to a council on the Auglaize River in 1792 and apparently reached a firm understanding on the Ohio River boundary. They then agreed to meet American commissioners the next year. In April, 1793, President George Washington sent Benjamin Lincoln of Massachusetts, Beverly Randolph of Virginia, and Timothy Pickering of Pennsylvania to meet Colonel Simcoe at Fort Niagara. They were instructed to secure the Indians' approval of recent American treaty cessions, especially those made at Fort Harmar and the Great Miami. However, they also had secret instructions to withdraw American control from all the areas north of the Ohio River except the grants already made to the Ohio Company, Symmes Purchase, and Clark's Grant. This was the United States' first admission that the Indian policies of the ordinance of October

---

[41] Dillon, *History of Indiana*, 293–95.
[42] Kellogg, *British Regime*, 217.
[43] Dillon, *History of Indiana*, 293–95. Colonel Alexander McKee, Maumee Rapids, to Simcoe, July 26, 1794, said the wavering lower Wabash tribes had come to the council to rejoin the confederacy. *MPHC*, XXIV, 696–98.

15, 1783, were no longer feasible; it summarily refused to accede to Britain's demands to retain forts on American soil.

The commissioners conferred with Simcoe until June, when Joseph Brant brought a delegation of chiefs from the Indian Confederacy council fire at Maumee Rapids. Said Brant: "Brothers: The people you see here are sent to represent the Indian nations who own the lands north of the Ohio, as their common property, and who are all of one mind–one heart." The commissioners assured him that General Wayne, who replaced St. Clair at Fort Washington, had been ordered to immobilize his troops until their talks were completed, but sent word to Secretary of War Knox that Indian rumors of Wayne's military road-building activities were jeopardizing the council.

A major conference was arranged, to be held at the mouth of the Detroit River. The Americans arrived there July 21 and continued to treat with the Indians until August 23. Cat's Eyes, the Shawnee; Sawaghdawunk; the Wyandot; and Simon Girty presented the Indians' arguments. They declared that recent American purchases were made, not from the tribes, but from venal or corrupted individual chiefs. They said this was the position taken by the tribes gathering at Maumee Rapids and that only the 1768 Fort Stanwix boundary was acceptable.

The commissioners asserted that the Treaty of Fort Stanwix was made with the British, who had given the Americans new land west to the Great Lakes only a decade before. The Fort Harmar and Great Miami treaties were made with the Americans, they said, and many of the Indians who had signed them were at this very council. The commissioners admitted they could not remove the settlers already north of the Ohio. The finally made their secret and final concessions and offered to pay another—larger—sum for previous land cessions. The Indians' right to the soil was acknowledged in a statement which became a basic part of U.S. Indian policy:

As he [the King] had not purchased the country of you, of course he could not give it away. He only relinquished, to the United States, his claim to it. That claim was founded on a right, acquired by treaty with other white nations, to exclude them from purchasing, or settling in, any part of your country; and it is this right which the king granted to the United States. Before that grant, the king alone had a right to purchase of the Indian nations, any of the lands between the great lakes, the Ohio, and the Mississippi. . . . Brothers; We now concede this great point. We, by the express authority of the President of the United States, acknowledge the property, or right of soil, of the great country above described, to be in the Indian nations, so long as they desire to occupy the same. We only claim particular tracts in it, as before mentioned, and the general right granted by the king, as above stated, and which is well known to the English and Americans, and called the right of pre-emption, or the right of purchasing of the Indian nations disposed to sell their lands, to the exclusion of all other white people whatever . . . .

The chiefs responded at length and concluded with irrefutable logic:

If the white people, as you say, made a treaty that none of them but the king should purchase of us, and that he has given that right to the United States, it is an affair which concerns you and him, and not us. We have never parted with such a power.

The chiefs asserted that only peace treaties were intended at Fort McIntosh, Fort Stanwix, and the Miami River and that they did not realize they were ceding land. This explanation was scarcely a credible one, but their next point was worthy of their astuteness. They asked the United States to take the money intended for the Indians and use it to alleviate the distress of the poor white squatters. They then declared no further council was necessary, for they would meet the Americans again only to establish a permanent boundary at the Ohio River.[44]

The commissioners had not appeared before the confederacy's

[44] *American State Papers*, Class II, *Indian Affairs*, I, 340–61, contains the commissioners' "Report," from which Dillon quotes extensively, 301–29. Joseph Brant, Niagara, to Joseph Chew, Secretary of Indian Affairs, declared the Miamis and Shawnees were the uncompromising members of the confederacy. *MPHC*, XXIX, 614.

tribal council; only Indian deputations had crossed to Elliott's Trading Post to meet them. The tribes had met constantly for a month, sending their messages intermittently. There were Miami chiefs in all of the deputations, but none spoke or was named. The Indians' policy was being forged on the Maumee, not in conferences with the commissioners.[45]

It finally became obvious that a final solution could be reached only through military means. From this time on, white emissaries were no longer protected by flags of peace, and only one means of communication remained open to opponents. This was through the Delawares, who had villages supporting both peace and war. The tribe still retained great prestige among both whites and Indians, and its warriors were welcome in any army camp or village.

General Wayne spent 1792 and 1793 in the frustrating process of training and equipping an army. In the fall of 1793, after the failure of the peace commissioners, he moved up the Great Miami to a site beyond Fort Jefferson. Here, in November, he built Fort Greene Ville as his winter camp. Progress was slow because warriors constantly harassed stragglers and supply trains. One of the latter was destroyed near Fort St. Clair by a band, led by Little Turtle, which killed Lieutenant Lowry and fourteen men.[46] The following month, Wayne sent Colonel Wilkinson to build Fort Recovery and to bury the grisly reminders of St. Clair's defeat at that site.

The British made preparations to meet Wayne's advance. The Indians were encouraged to resist by Lord Dorchester in a council held at Quebec in February, 1794. He followed up by instructing Simcoe to build a new British fort, called Miami, on the Maumee near Elliott's Trading Post.[47]

Wayne marched north from Fort Greene Ville on July 28 with an army officered by a large number of untrained searchers for

[45] Dwight L. Smith (ed.) "William Wells and the Indian Council of 1793," *Indiana Magazine of History*, LVI (1960), 3, 215–26, includes Wells's deposition to Wayne on Indian unity.
[46] Benson J. Lossing, *The Pictorial Field-Book of the War of 1812*, 51–62.
[47] Lossing, *Pictorial Field-Book*, 52. Philbrick, *The Rise of the West*, 156. *MPHC*, XXIV, 642–43.

political and military glory. The best and worst individuals on the frontier were in Wayne's command, and he had no inclination to sacrifice his mission because of misguided subordinates. He planned to erect and garrison a line of forts, a new military frontier into the heart of the confederacy.

One of Wayne's most valuable units was the group of Choctaw and Cherokee scouts under Chief Hummingbird. These inveterate enemies of the northern tribes were the General's insurance against surprise—and he had need of them. Hostile Indians surrounded his army, and every party detached from the main force was in danger of annihilation.

Another of Wayne's scouts was William Wells, who had been captured in Kentucky by a Miami war party in 1774 when he was eight years old. Adopted by Little Turtle, he eventually married the Chief's daughter. Wells fought with the Miamis in their victories over Hardin, Harmar, and St. Clair; however, he came to regret his part in the warfare against the Americans. With Little Turtle's approval, he left his wife and children among the Miamis and joined Wayne's army, where he soon commanded a force of scouts. His action was acclaimed by the whites and approved by the Miamis. Wells's knowledge of the terrain, the various tribes, and the individual leaders of the confederacy was more extensive and reliable than information from any other source.[48]

Wayne repeatedly made overtures for a council, but all efforts failed. Since he was deep in Indian country and was becoming more firmly established with strong fortifications behind him, Little Turtle was forced to make an attempt to dislodge him quickly. The Chief's warriors were poorly supplied and could be kept in the field only for brief periods because they were needed in their villages.

Little Turtle made his major thrust June 30, 1794, when his forces were well rested and free from winter hunting and spring planting duties. More than 1,000 warriors attacked an escort party

---

[48] Much has been written concerning Wells's career. Bert J. Griswold (ed.), *Fort Wayne, Gateway of the West, 1802–1813,* 19, cites the most reliable sources of information. Dillon, *History of Indiana,* 310, describes Wayne's Indian scouts.

126

of fewer than 150 soldiers outside Fort Recovery. The troops reached the safety of the fort after losing 25 men and more than 200 horses.[49] The attacks continued, but Little Turtle's best-planned efforts proved insufficient to disrupt Wayne's defenses, although the General's supply lines were harassed constantly.

On July 22, General Charles Scott and 1,600 mounted Kentucky militiamen joined Wayne's regulars, and the slow march to the Maumee was continued. Fort Adams was built on the St. Mary's River a short distance beyond Fort Recovery, and on August 8, the army reached the mouth of the Auglaize, where Fort Defiance was built near Blue Jacket's deserted Shawnee villages. The fort was located about fifty miles above the new British Fort Miami, constructed by order of Governor Dorchester to give the Indians a supply depot closer than Detroit.[50] Wrote Lieutenant John Boyer of the Fort Defiance area:

This place far excels in beauty any in the western country, and believed equalled by none in the Atlantic States. Here are vegetables of every kind in abundance, and we have marched four or five miles in corn fields down the Oglaize [Auglaize] and there are not less than one thousand acres of corn (Zea mays) round the town. The land in general of the fir nature.

This country appears well adapted for the enjoyment of industrious people, who cannot avoid living in as great luxury as in any other place throughout the states, nature having lent a most bountiful hand in the arrangement of the position, that a man can send the produce to market in his own boat. The land level and river navigable, not more than sixty miles from the lake [Erie].

[49] *American State Papers,* Class II, *Indian Affairs,* II, 487.
[50] Dwight L. Smith (ed.), "From Greene Ville to Fallen Timbers: A Journal of the Wayne Campaign," *Indiana Historical Society Publications,* XVI (1952), 3, with an Introduction by the editor, is an excellent study of Wayne's campaign. The "Journal" was written by an unidentified officer who constantly criticized Wayne while magnifying General Wilkinson's services. Reginald C. McGrene (ed.), "William Clark's Journal of General Wayne's Campaign," *Mississippi Valley Historical Review,* I. (1914), 418–44, is less biased. The Anthony Wayne Papers are in the Historical Society of Pennsylvania Library. The "Diary" of Lieutenant John Boyer (or Bowyer) has been published several times, including Slocum, *History of the Maumee River Basin,* 189–206. Wayne's "Report" to Knox is in *ibid.,* 208–11.

The British have built a large garrison (fort) about fifty miles from this place, and our spies inform us that the enemy are encamped about two miles above it by the river. . . .[51]

Still hoping for some sort of peace, compromise, or capitulation, Wayne sent a speech to the confederated tribes on August 13. The chiefs promised to deliberate on its contents for ten days, which to them was a reasonable time for momentous discussions. They demanded that Wayne remain at Fort Defiance while the council took place, but he refused this, crossed to the north bank of the Maumee, and advanced toward the British fort at Maumee Rapids. On August 19, he began to build a temporary "Fort Deposit" on the north bank of the Maumee within sight of Fort Miami.

The allies held a council August 18, and it was a fateful one for the Miamis. Although Little Turtle had been the most successful war chief of the confederacy for five years and of the Miamis for fifteen, he tried to prevent a battle at this time. He knew the harassing tactics of the preceding two years had not weakened Wayne's forces and believed the confederacy had lost much of the momentum it had gained, after Harmar's and St. Clair's defeats, in the futile attack on Fort Recovery. The long summer saw Wayne's army encamped in the middle of the finest and most indispensable corn fields of America. Wayne had persisted while a large part of his opponents had dispersed to harvest the crops of their villages in present-day Indiana, Michigan, and Ohio. His presence within a few miles of Fort Miami, the British center of support to the Miami Confederacy, created severe problems for the British Indian Service. This fort on American soil could not be defended against American troops. Like a spy, it could not be admitted to exist, and Campbell's force of 450 troops lost their freedom to aid the Indians as Wayne approached.

Little Turtle had not been able to develop tactics which could disrupt the well-led and disciplined American army, and he feared that Wayne could not be defeated. When he supported a negotiated

[51] Slocum, *History of the Maumee River Basin,* 192, excerpted from the "Diary" of Lieutenant Boyer.

peace, he was accused of cowardice in a stormy council meeting. The wise Miami said:

> We have beaten the enemy twice under different commanders. We cannot expect the same good fortune to attend us always. The Americans are now led by a chief who never sleeps. The night and the days are alike to him, and during all the time that he has been marching on our villages, notwithstanding the watchfulness of our young men, we have never been able to surprise him. Think well of it. There is something [that] whispers [to] me, [that] it would be prudent to listen to his offers of peace.[52]

When he failed to convince his allies, Little Turtle gracefully abdicated his position of honor as commander-in-chief to Blue Jacket of the Shawnees and led only his own Miami warriors.

The Indians attacked Wayne's advancing columns on August 20, 1794. The terrain was favorable for an ambush, but the Indian army was not as well led as it had been in its earlier triumphs. The ravines, brush, and trees were dense on the banks of the Maumee, and the name given to the battle, Fallen Timbers, was well chosen. The Americans fell back from the first shock of the attack, but rallied and drove the warriors away in an hour. Only about half of Wayne's forces came under fire, and he had little chance to use his mounted troops because of the terrain. The Indians, when routed, withdrew toward the British fort. Theodore Roosevelt described the conflict with his usual felicity:

> At the same time the first line of the infantry charged with equal impetuosity and success. The Indians delivered one volley and were then roused from their hiding-places with the bayonet; as they fled they were shot down, and if they attempted to halt they were at once assailed and again driven with the bayonet. They could make no stand at all, and the battle was won with ease. So complete was the success that only the first line of regulars was able to take part in the fighting; the second line, and Scott's horse-riflemen, on the left, in spite of their exertions, were unable to reach the battle-field until the Indians were driven from it; "there not being a sufficiency of the enemy for the

52 Brice, *History of Fort Wayne,* 148.

Legion to play on," wrote Clark. The entire action lasted under forty minutes.[53]

Instead of attacking Fort Miami, Wayne destroyed the Indians' camps and corn fields, including the stores of Alexander McKee and other Canadians, for fifty miles along the Maumee. The British commander not only failed to help the Indians in their distress, but also refused to give them refuge in the fort when they pleaded for it.

There have been various estimates of the total forces engaged, but the most reliable seems to be that of Antoine Lasselle, captured from Captain Caldwell's Rangers, who said there were 175 Miamis among a total of 1,500 to 2,000 well-armed warriors and 70 white volunteers under Captain Caldwell. Wayne, who believed more than 900 of his troops were under fire, suffered light losses: 33 killed, 100 wounded. The Indian losses may have been double that number.[54]

The battle was a fiasco, and it cost the confederacy the bargaining position it had held since 1790. The Indian warriors congregated near the Canadian Indian agents and helplessly watched Wayne defy the British soldiers at Fort Miami. Once more the belligerent chiefs failed to comprehend that Lord Dorchester and Colonel Simcoe were servants of the British Crown, which was even then completing a new treaty with the United States, or that Major Campbell at Fort Miami was not empowered to give them military aid. Their councils were bitter, and many warriors returned to their villages, especially if they faced the imminent Canadian winter. The chiefs who favored continued resistance set their warriors upon Wayne's supply lines. Even those were soon placed on the defensive as the general began to plant permanent garrisons in the heartland of the Indian Confederacy. Meanwhile, winter and famine were added to the Indians' defeat and dissension.

From the day of the battle to the beginning of treaty negotiations, the frontier was in turmoil. Deserters and spies were busy;

[53] Roosevelt, *Winning of the West*, Vol. III, Part 1, 215.
[54] Slocum, *History of Maumee River Basin*, 212–17.

Wayne's forces lost men and supplies to straggling war parties, and prisoners were continually taken by both sides. Wayne also kept spies circulating in the Indian country, observing the indecisive councils of the still formidable army below Fort Miami, as well as the actions of Major William Campbell. While the tribes from Canada and the northern Great Lakes could withdraw and excuse their failures and shortcomings, the Miamis could do neither.

After resting his army at Fort Defiance, Wayne began to cut a road along the north side of the Maumee River toward its source at Kekionga. When he reached there on September 17, he found nearly five hundred acres of cleared farm land—testimony of Indian determination to build an expanded center for the confederacy. On the east side of the St. Mary's River about two miles above its junction with the St. Joseph and midway between the former's ford and the northwest trail to Lake Michigan, Wayne built a fort named for himself. Major Hamtramck assumed command of it upon the General's return to Fort Greene Ville.[55] From this point, Wayne could receive reinforcements from Fort Washington or could return to attack the Indians in the Maumee area. Only after the fort had been constructed did he begin preliminary negotiations for a new treaty.[56]

The Indians thoroughly enjoyed long-drawn negotiations and diplomatic bargaining, and this fact was never better illustrated than during the nine months preceding the final Greene Ville treaty of August 10, 1795. Because the Miamis had prepared for three years to meet an American invasion, they kept their women, children, and supplies north of the Eel and Wabash rivers. As a result, only a few old Miamis came to the forts that winter to receive food, even though the 1794 harvest of the vast corn fields along the Maumee had been destroyed. Because some bands were inde-

[55] Wayne, Miami Villages [Fort Wayne] to Knox, October 17, 1794, tells of his plans for numerous garrisons. *American State Papers,* Class II, *Indian Affairs,* I, 548.

[56] Wayne made his preliminary proclamation for the ensuing treaty of February 22, 1795, without first notifying Governor St. Clair. Smith, *The St. Clair Papers,* II, 343–44n. Secretary of War Timothy Pickering's instructions of April 8, 1795, to Wayne for the impending treaty negotiations are quoted in Washburn, *The Indian and the White Man,* 343–53.

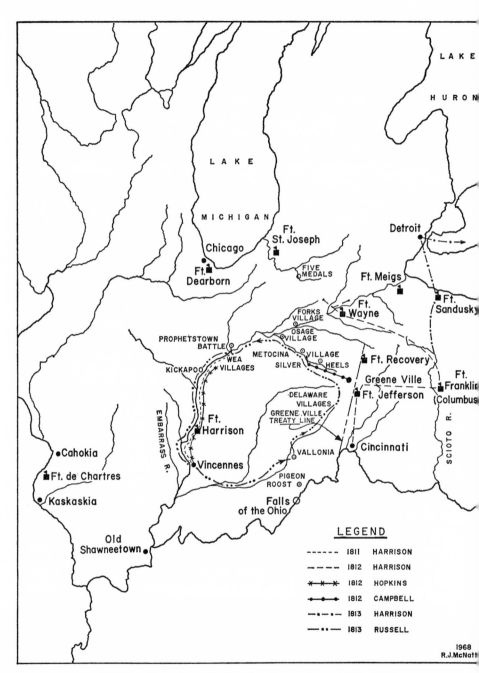

LAKE

HURON

LAKE

MICHIGAN

Ft.
St. Joseph

Detroit

Chicago

Ft.
Dearborn

FIVE
MEDALS

Ft. Meigs

Ft.
Sandusky

FORKS
VILLAGE

Ft.
Wayne

OSAGE
VILLAGE

PROPHETSTOWN
BATTLE

METOCINA
WEA
VILLAGES

VILLAGE

SILVER

HEELS

Ft. Recovery

KICKAPOO

Greene Ville

Ft.
Franklin
(Columbus)

DELAWARE
VILLAGES

Ft. Jefferson

Ft.
Harrison

GREENE VILLE
TREATY LINE

SCIOTO R.

Cahokia

VALLONIA

Cincinnati

Ft. de Chartres

Vincennes

EMBARRASS R.

PIGEON
ROOST

Kaskaskia

Falls
of the Ohio

Old
Shawneetown

LEGEND

	1811	HARRISON
- - - -	1812	HARRISON
✱—✱—✱	1812	HOPKINS
•—•—•	1812	CAMPBELL
—•—•—	1813	HARRISON
—••—	1813	RUSSELL

1968
R.J.McNatt

Eighteenth-century Indian treaty cessions, 1768–1795.

cisive and others still wanted war, the spring councils became lengthy affairs as the Indians tried to form a unified policy.

In spite of American overtures for a general council or treaty, such decisions were never made hastily by the Indians. At first, the Miamis, Delawares, and Shawnees seemed opposed to meeting Wayne. The General used such well-known traders as Antoine and Jacques Lasselle and former Miami captives William Wells and Christopher Miller to persuade them of American strength and good faith. In early December, Hamtramck thought the Miamis were still guided by Alexander McKee, but later the same month he reported that two "war chiefs" came to the fort and promised that the tribe, still in the lake region north of Kekionga, would soon pass through on its way to Greene Ville. It was not until Little Turtle, Pacanne, Blue Jacket, and Buckongahelas had first met with Simcoe and McKee at Detroit—to complain of a lack of winter provisions—that they subsequently arranged for a council the following summer. Jean Baptiste Richardville, who had returned from the lower Maumee, promised to move his village to the Salamonie River as a token of his faith in American promises.

Since it was March, 1795, before Hamtramck could report that Le Gris, persuaded by Jacques Lasselle, had finally agreed to surrender, the Miamis were the last tribe to reach the treaty grounds. Hamtramck spent four days with Le Gris and found him a "sensible old fellow" with a thorough knowledge of the past war's causes.[57]

Secretary of War Timothy Pickering realistically instructed Wayne to secure the area south and east of the Fort McIntosh line; to find the "true owners" of the Indian lands, since some tribes claimed areas which were not their own; and, when he found overlapping claims, to work out a system of payment which would satisfy all claimants. Pickering wished to destroy Mohawk Chief Joseph Brant's concept of joint tribal ownership of Indian lands, and fixed tribal boundaries would accomplish this, besides meeting the ap-

---

[57] Slocum, *History of the Maumee River Basin,* 222–24, reproduces twelve letters written by Hamtramck during the winter of 1794–95 to report on affairs at the new Fort Wayne to his commander at Greene Ville.

proval of the Miamis and other western tribes whose lands were intact. Since the Indians had begun to realize that their interests were common, Wayne was ordered to secure all of the treaty provisions in one document, with a full representation of all chiefs from all the tribes. He was also instructed to obtain reservations for military and trading posts along the full length of the Wabash and Maumee rivers.[58]

Wayne wisely concentrated his demands on the contention that the land desired by the United States had already been purchased, or taken, in earlier treaties and the Indian tribes had been paid; that the land claims of some tribes were disputed by others; and that the sites he wanted had been granted to the French or British in the past. He reaffirmed the Indians' ownership of the land and the United States' exclusive right to buy it—a return to the policy toward Indian land ownership first issued by the British in 1763 and adopted by the Americans in September, 1783. The policy was altered in October, 1783, and again in the secret instructions of the treaty commissioners in 1793, but was restored in Pickering's instructions.

When Wayne persisted in his demands for American posts where the Miamis had once given sites to French or British authorities, there was little the chiefs could do except acquiesce. The military posts and American traders were not their greatest fear; that was the nearer approach of American settlers. The defeated confederacy lost its major objective—the Ohio River boundary—and the rival claims for control of certain areas divided the tribes at the treaty session.

The Indians probably expected Wayne to demand a new treaty line, but he did not. Instead, he insisted on the approximate line of the first Fort McIntosh treaty and of the three treaties which followed it. Five of the additional parcels he was ordered to secure were in Miami territory, and the tribe was willing to release these if, in return, it was given traders. Even the military posts were not innovations. However, Wayne could now ignore the concept

[58] Washburn, *The Indian and the White Man,* 343–53.

of an Indian boundary at the Ohio or British pretentions to rights on American soil south of the Great Lakes.

The diverse views of the Indians soon became apparent. Tarhe (The Crane) spoke first for the Wyandots, as was customary, and also represented the Delawares. He approved the terms of the Fort Harmar treaty and inserted the new concept that the lands belonged equally to all of the Indian tribes. The spokesman for the Three Fires (Chippewas, Ottawas, and Potawatomis) agreed to be bound by the same treaty but claimed their nations had land rights in the Ohio cession, for which they received no payment after 1789.

Little Turtle was the Miami spokesman, and his arguments were informed and impressive. This was not the customary role of a war chief, but Little Turtle was a fine orator and a logical statesman. He spoke ten times in all; several of his speeches were made for the Weas, Piankeshaws, Kickapoos, and Kaskaskias. The Miami chief disputed the territorial claims of the Delaware "grandfathers" and Wyandot "uncles" while completely ignoring any claims of the tribes from the west and north. He was obviously well versed in the history of tribal movements from 1700 to 1740. He said all of the tribes had recognized Miami ownership of the lands from Detroit to the Scioto River and from the Ohio and Wabash to Chicago.

Wayne countered the Miami argument by pointing out that the other tribes had also made some claims to parts of these lands with the French and British. He insisted that the United States had already paid twice for the lands south of the Fort Harmar boundary and would pay again, but he especially wanted to secure the sites which the Miamis had given to the French and British. There was some haggling about the location of these disputed tracts because it was obvious the Miamis were afraid that a trading post or military base at Fort Wayne soon would become a focal point for American settlement.

One of the issues became clearer when Tarhe suggested the United States should fix boundary lines between the tribes. Wayne was too experienced to fall into this trap. Any decision he could make in the matter would be the basis for future grievances which

135

could unite the Indians against the United States or initiate new intertribal wars.

The Kaskaskias, Weas, and Kickapoos selected Little Turtle to speak for their interests, and he did so—twice. The first time, he expressed his desire to support his Delaware and Wyandot allies, claiming the Fort Harmar line on the west took from those tribes some of their best hunting grounds and should end at the mouth of the Great Miami rather than touch the Ohio opposite the Kentucky River. It also would convince the Miamis' eastern allies of their desire for amity and reaffirm Miami unity concerning the problems which might plague the lower Wabash bands if settlers were excluded from the Whitewater Valley. He appropriately called the Maumee headwaters region the "glorious gate that all had to pass" in order to emphasize its importance to the lower Wabash tribes. His second speech came near the end of the negotiations when he spoke for the Wea chief Little Beaver to accept the conditions of the treaty.

Wayne's final speeches contained conciliatory promises, as well as answers to the Miamis' objections. He again reminded their allies that other nations had claims to parts of the land the Miamis claimed; that both French and English forts, as well as trading posts, had once stood at Fort Wayne and Chicago; and that most of the Miami allies seemed satisfied with the treaty terms. But he reduced the area he had requested for a garrison at Fort Wayne and promised to license only traders who were acceptable to the various villages. He also gave firm commitments to the Indians concerning the protection of French settlers among them. Nevertheless, the Miamis were not united behind their war chief. Only Little Turtle, Le Gris, Richardville, Cochkepoghtoh, The Soldier, White Loon, Little Beaver, Little Fox, and Francis eventually signed the treaty; Pacanne, Metocina, and many others did not, in spite of Wayne's efforts to get all of the chiefs to concur.

In the final treaty terms, a modified Fort McIntosh line was approved and the Americans were given passage rights along the established routes of travel. Clark's Virginia military grant of

136

150,000 acres across the Ohio from Louisville and a two-square-mile tract on the Little Wabash at the portage to the Maumee were new cessions, together with fourteen other sites at strategic points south of the Great Lakes. The Indians could feel that they had completed a very advantageous recovery from a war in which they had been demoralized by the defeat at Fallen Timbers and had been deserted by their Canadian allies. Despite this, it was a humiliating end to the most important attempt to establish an Indian state east of the Mississippi River.[59]

The Miamis were awarded an annuity of $1,000 in trade goods and the Wea, Piankeshaw, and Eel River bands were given $500 each. Seventy-three Miami and Eel River warriors and twelve Weas and Piankeshaws attended the negotiations. Little Turtle, at least, was now certain that the Indians had come under American rule and that the Miamis' only recourse was rapid adjustment to it. The tribe had seen the effects on Wea and Piankeshaw bands located near French, English, and American posts, but it was not prepared for a new phase of Indian-white contact: it had not yet encountered annuities and their effects on the Indians.

Lewis Cass, making a political speech at Fort Wayne in 1843, rejoiced at the elimination of the Indians from that rich area. Nevertheless, his description of the horrors of frontier warfare was not exaggerated.[60] The Waubenos flourished, and cannibalism was practiced on some occasions. White losses were greater than at any other time of Indian warfare, both on the battlefield and in village torture orgies, and retaliation against friendly Indians was often brutal and thoughtless. It was during this conflict, rather than the American Revolution or the War of 1812, that the western pioneers met the most powerful and sustained opposition the Indians could organize.

[59] Wayne's "Report" on the treaty negotiations is in *American State Papers*, Class II, *Indian Affairs*, I, 562–82. The Treaty of Greene Ville is in Kappler, *Indian Affairs*, Vol. II, 30–34. The most detailed study of the treaty is in Dwight L. Smith "Indian Land Cessions in the Old Northwest, 1795–1809," unpublished Ph.D. dissertation, Indiana University, 1948. Little Turtle's speech of July 22 is in *American State Papers*, Class II, *Indian Affairs*, I, 370–71.

[60] Brice, *History of Fort Wayne*, 122–23 n.

The concentration of Indians along the Maumee was possible because they increased their agricultural efforts. The large population restricted hunting activities, and agriculture, especially the production of corn, was the basis of village life. Wayne noted:

> The very extensive and highly cultivated fields and gardens show the work of many hands. The margin of those beautiful rivers, the Miami of the Lakes (pronounced Maumee) and Au Glaize, appear like one continued village for a number of miles both above and below this place; nor have I ever before beheld such immense fields of corn in any part of America from Canada to Florida.[61]

For a time it seemed the Miami Confederacy could develop into a stable political unit resembling the Six Nations of the Iroquois. The Indians' morale was high as they repulsed the Americans, and their warlike society flourished. The corn fields along the Maumee refuted the idea that Indians were indolent and improvident. An Indian state had nearly been created, one which might have duplicated the successes achieved in Indian Territory (Oklahoma) a century later.

The Wayne campaign should not be used as the terminal date of Miami national existence. Although it ended the Miamis' brief period of reliance upon war to solve their problems with the whites, they now turned to other tactics—and with marked success. They adopted much of the white viewpoint on land ownership, compromised when necessary, and fought tenaciously to preserve their homeland at treaty councils.

[61] Wayne, Fort Defiance, to Secretary of War, August 14, 1794, in *American State Papers,* Class II, *Indian Affairs,* I, 490–91.

5
THE FIRST TREATIES AND THE WAR OF 1812

The Treaty of Greene Ville inaugurated a new era of apparent peace on the frontier. The older Miami chiefs, such as Little Turtle, Le Gris, and Pacanne, were determined to abide by the terms of the treaty and did so in spite of the slowly rising tide of dissatisfaction in a few bands led by younger warriors. At first, even the rapid tide of white immigration into southern Ohio did little to disturb the Wabash tribes. Their only contact was with their favorite traders, and if any chiefs journeyed to Detroit or Canada for their favorite recreation, a council, they were little disturbed by Canadian overtures.

The Americans expanded their use of the "white father" device with their former opponents. It began with journeys to the national capital and Atlantic Seaboard cities during which they were shown the lavish aspects of American culture. They were indulged with interviews and attentions from important men, given medals and other gifts, and treated as visiting royalty. Not to be lost on the visiting chiefs was a view of American numerical strength, which usually convinced them that further war was futile. Such diplomatic treatment of Indian leaders was calculated to preserve their influence among their people. On his first journey to Philadelphia in

139

1797, for example, Little Turtle was lionized and his portrait was painted by Gilbert Stuart.[1]

The first—and probably the most important—cause for change within the tribe during this period was the deterioration of the Miami warrior society. It had supplied the goals which males found it necessary to achieve before they could assume a responsible role in the tribal society as a whole. The method of attaining them was grounded upon centuries of use, and it was impossible to provide substitutes within a few years. The Miamis were unable to change their warrior culture, but were equally unable to sustain its vigor. Since times were peaceful, it was no longer feasible to send a neophyte on the necessary expedition against the Potawatomis, the Muskhogean tribes, or the white settlements. And the chiefs' relations with the Americans were so changed they now sent offenders to the white men's forts for punishment.

In time, the cultural lag contributed to Tecumseh's call for rebellion to maintain the Indians' cultural *status quo*. The great Shawnee's appeal was for Indian unity in this cause, but the concept was contrary to the thinking of the Miami chiefs, who intended to honor their treaty commitments and who understood that their tribe must make some cultural adaptations. Tecumseh's brother, The Prophet, used a more potent argument: a complete return to Indian culture.[2]

The record of Miami habits and customs was enriched at this time by the observations of an intelligent and sympathetic observer, Count Constantin F. S. Volney, who spent the years 1795 to 1798 visiting among various Indian tribes of the United States. His most acute conclusions were reached from his interviews with Little Turtle.

Although Volney did not believe in the "noble savage in a state of nature," Little Turtle's personal qualities so impressed him that he came to admire the chief greatly. The Frenchman first encoun-

[1] Hodge, *Handbook of American Indians*, I, 771, reproduces a copy of this slightly less than complimentary portrait, which makes the chief appear old and less than robust. Contemporaries said he was tall, muscular, and saturnine.
[2] *Ibid.*, II, 714, 729–30.

tered the remnants of the Weas and Piankeshaws at Vincennes in 1797. He pitied them but was disgusted by their appearance and habits. He failed to reach the Fort Wayne and Detroit areas, but in the winter of 1798–99, he visited with William Wells and Little Turtle while they were in Philadelphia.

After a dozen conferences, Volney decided Wells was the only white man in America who was capable of giving intelligent aid to a researcher in the nuances of any Indian language. Together they compiled a Miami vocabulary which has been copied many times and which is probably less corrupted by accretions than the later efforts of William Thornton or those of Indian Agent Charles N. Hand, which were reproduced by Henry Rowe Schoolcraft.

Volney's report on the great chief and his tribe far outweighs the observations of later men. This was due largely to Wells, who had lived with the Miamis a quarter-century. In Wells's words:

. . . All your [Indians'] pleasures consist of eating and drinking, and these are not always to be had, and hunting. The utmost flight of ambition is to be a great warrior, of some repute among five or six hundred men. . . . The Indian never requires the service of another: to serve or obey in his eyes, is an ignominy reserved only for women. . . . Were Little Turtle to return home and die tomorrow, all his presents, clothes, hats, trinkets, would be scrambled for by his countrymen, and nothing go to his wife or children. Such is the custom of his tribe, and of many others: while living, each enjoys his arms, trinkets, and other moveables, but when dead, not even his knife or pipe falls to his children. They have no notion whatever of property in land *or houses*.

A life, thus hard, is constantly in danger. The changes to which his life is constantly exposed, are the chief subject of an Indian's thoughts. It is a frail vessel, momently liable to be broken by a thousand accidents. Death becomes so familiar to him, that he regards it with indifference: when inevitable, he resigns himself to it, or braves it with alacrity. Hence it is that he is attached to nothing but his weapons, or perhaps some associate, whose aid is useful to his safety. He regards his children as any other animal regards its young. He fondles and caresses them while present, but he leaves them without reluctance, and goes to hunt or to fight without thinking of them more. They may shift for themselves, and live or die; no matter, since death must, sooner or later, be their lot. Suicide is common among them: they kill themselves when tired of life, or thwarted in love, or in rage, when provoked without the means of vengeance. They live almost wholly to the present, they give little or no remembrance to the past, and hope nothing for the future. In health, they gambol, laugh, and sing; sick or weary, they lie down, smoke or sleep: but as they seldom possess the means or opportunity of food or repose, they can found on this no claims to liberty or happiness.[3]

In spite of Wells's pessimism and apparent lack of sympathy with some Miami customs, it is obvious that he hoped to convert his Indian friends to white men's habits so that they might survive when he said:

Yet the Indians of the Wabash, the Miamis, Putewatamies, etc., are better than they were a few generations ago. Longer intervals of peace, which they owe to the decline of the Six Nations, have allowed them to raise some corn and potatoes, and even cabbages and turnips. Their captives have planted peach and apple trees, and taught them to breed poultry, pigs and even cows: in short, they are as much improved as the Creeks and Chactaws.[4]

Volney decided Little Turtle was a wiser man and better versed on the effects of early education than Jean Jacques Rousseau. The decision was not a difficult one for Volney to make because he despised Rousseau's theories, but his refutation is impressive:

Here we have an Indian, who, in spite of the prejudices of his education, of prejudices sanctioned by the ancient and universal habits and opinions of his countrymen, had had penetration enough to discover the essential basis of the social state in the cultivation of the earth, and in landed property: for there can be no regular cultivation without a stable right of property.[5]

[3] Volney, *View of the Soil*, 356. The Reverend John Heckewelder's "Miami Vocabulary" was taken from Volney. William Thornton's "Vocabulary" was secured from Little Turtle and Wells in 1802 for President Jefferson. The originals are in the American Philosophical Society Library, Philadelphia; copies in my possession were used with the Society's permission.
[4] Volney, *View of the Soil*, 360, 373–74, 381.
[5] *Ibid.*, 385.

A mat-covered wigwam of the type used by the Sauks, Foxes, and Miamis.

A Miami chief at the Mississinewa Treaty, 1826. From a lithograph by
J. O. Lewis.

Peace prevailed on the frontier for nearly a generation. European events first supported it but ultimately destroyed it. The Napoleonic Wars occupied the attention of the British Empire, whose frequent clashes with the neutral United States left it unable to support the Canadian fur companies' efforts to regain control south of the Great Lakes. Even so, American trade restrictions were ignored north of the Wabash, where the routes for the transport of furs and trade goods were still controlled by the Canadian fur companies and still centered at Mackinac and Montreal. The Indian villages had traders of their own choice and so could secure their necessities by selling furs. A complicated series of events and changing policies which can be generalized as "the course of change" slowly altered the situation, and by 1809 another frontier Indian war was imminent.

In 1786, a congressional ordinance forbade travel or residence in Indian territory by non-American citizens, and trade licenses for travel there were issued only by the superintendent of Indian affairs.[6] In brief, the Indians' title to their lands was recognized and the federal government assumed responsibility for protecting them from trespassers, while the Indians retained the right to eject those trespassers not certified to them by the federal government. When the Northwest Ordinance of 1787 made the territorial governor the superintendent of Indian affairs in his territory, Governor St. Clair built forts to protect both Indians and white settlers.[7]

Article 1, Section 8, Clause 3 of the U.S. Constitution of 1789 placed the power to regulate Indian affairs in the hands of Congress, which in turn placed their administration in the hands of the War Department. The secretary of war, Henry Knox, had been in control of Indian affairs for years and, next to George Washington, was the man most conversant with these problems after 1775. The new government announced its basic policies through him in

[6] Reginald Horsman, "Western War Aims, 1811–1812," *Indiana Magazine of History*, LIII, 1 (March, 1957), 3–4, 12–13, defends the commercial causes of the War of 1812. His comprehensive work is *The Causes of the War of 1812.*

[7] Schmeckebier, *Office of Indian Affairs*, 16–19. The first "Intercourse With the Indians Act" was passed July 22, 1790.

1791, including, as a new feature, the formation of a "government factory system" to trade with the Indians in competition with the private traders, who were still primarily Canadians.[8] Soldiers at army posts, federal agents, the many government factors, and the licensed traders of this period constitute, therefore, important forces in Miami history.

Great things were expected of the factory system. It proposed to furnish trade goods and purchase Indian products at prices designed to restrain or eliminate traders and abolish the practice of using whisky in the bargaining process. One of the factories was established at Fort Wayne in 1802 and operated until it was burned by the Indians in 1812. Stationed there was a federal factor, or factory manager, who often promoted policies contrary to those of the Indian agent or the commandant of the fort. In practice, the system often supplied inferior goods, sometimes at costs equal to those of the private traders. The American trading companies, especially those of Detroit, fought it, and the concentration of John Jacob Astor's activities in the Northwest after 1808 turned this private-federal competition into a bitter battle. Astor's New York position at first required his cooperation with Montreal merchants, but on April 6, 1808, he formed the American Fur Company to utilize the terms of the non-intercourse and non-importation acts passed in 1802. He combined briefly with the Michilimackinac Company and the North West Company in the Southwest Fur Company in 1811, with the conditions of the agreement dependent upon the eventual destruction of the government factory system.[9]

The soldiers at frontier posts, including Fort Wayne, exerted less influence upon the Miamis than did the traders. The nature of their service limited contacts with the Indians; their duties and the Indians' infrequent visits to the forts prevented fraternization.

[8] Francis Paul Prucha, *American Indian Policy in the Formative Years,* 1–25.
[9] Ora Brooks Peake, *A History of the United States Indian Factory System, 1795–1822,* is the most recent study of this early extension of federal economic policy. Kenneth Wiggins Porter, *John Jacob Astor,* remains the comprehensive study of the American Fur Company.

Commanding officers and sutlers were exceptions to this generalization. The commandant of a typical post was usually intimate with individual Indians and privy to their attitudes, for such knowledge was essential to the execution of his duties. The careers of French and British officers—Vincennes, Caldwell, and Richardville, for example—illustrated officer participation in Indian affairs, even to the extent of marrying into the tribes.[10] The civilian sutlers' task of supplying military posts brought them into contact with Indians and often led to conflicts or alliances with licensed traders or federal factors.[11]

Of the traders among the Miamis before the War of 1812, many were of French descent and some were of French and Indian extraction. Nearly all had dealt with the Indians for many years, and all were equally at home in any village from Vincennes to Detroit. Those who had displeased the Indians during Pontiac's Uprising or the reign of the Miami Confederacy departed for the safety of the Mississippi River area. A few English traders had entered the Miami sphere, but most of them, such as the Abbott family of Vincennes and Detroit, seldom resided in Miami villages or hunting camps; they employed resident French traders.[12]

It was during the interwar period that French-Miami marriages became quite important to the tribe. Such traders as the Gamelins, Bourie, Bosseron, the Lasselles, Joseph Baron, Lafontaine, Aveline, Beaubien, Cicott, and Rivarre played leading roles in Indian-white relations. One reason for this—but one that is difficult to substantiate—was the successful effort by both Canadian and American authorities to use them as a means of controlling or influencing the Miamis' political position. Because it was a time of unreliable loyalties, many traders were members of the Indian service of both

[10] Bert Anson, "The Fur Traders of Northern Indiana, 1796–1850," unpublished Ph.D. dissertation, Indiana University, 1953, 28, 33–40, 45–49, 68–70.

[11] William Burnett to Porter, Gerard, and Ogilvy, Detroit, August 24, 1798, in Henry H. Hurlbut, *Chicago Antiquities*, 66–67. Burnett traded at present-day Benton Harbor.

[12] Charles B. Lasselle, "The Old Indian Traders in Indiana," *Indiana Magazine of History*, II (1906), 6, lists the licensed traders of 1801–1802.

Canada and the United States. Of these, John Kinzie was probably the most active political agent among the Miamis.[13]

William Henry Harrison, governor of newly formed Indiana Territory, was instructed to secure land cessions from the Indians as rapidly as possible. Because there was little land open to white settlement in the region, he proceeded to act with great energy. At a council held at Vincennes on September 17, 1802, to prepare for a treaty at Fort Wayne, the Wea, Eel River, Piankeshaw, Kaskaskia, and Kickapoo chiefs selected Little Turtle and Richardville as their spokesmen, together with Potawatomi Chief Winnemac. Harrison reported in detail to Secretary of War Henry Dearborn and explain the Indian strategy which delayed the treaty. He was convinced that Wells and Little Turtle controlled only the Eel River and a few Potawatomi chiefs. "Nine tenths of the tribe [Miamis] who acknowledged Richardville and Peccan for their chiefs (but who are really governed by an artful fellow called the Owl and Long Beard ...) utterly abhor both Wells and the Turtle," he wrote. The Governor deplored Miami claims to control of both the Piankeshaw and Delaware lands on the Wabash and White rivers and blamed Owl for delaying the council. Although Harrison was correct in believing Wells was popular with only a few of the Potawatomis, his principal error was in mistaking Richardville's rank and influence.[14]

At the Treaty of Fort Wayne on June 7, 1803, nine tribes ceded land surrounding Vincennes in Indiana and Illinois. No one tribe dominated this treaty. The Kaskaskias and Piankeshaws, who had the best claims, had been reduced to feeble groups and had moved from the immediate area before 1794. But the Delawares and

[13] Anson, "The Fur Traders," 30–40. Harrison, Vincennes, to Secretary of War Henry Dearborn, February 23, 1802, in Logan Esarey (ed.), *Messages and Letters of William Henry Harrison,* I, 37–39.

[14] Governor Harrison, Vincennes, to Secretary of War Henry Dearborn, March 3, 1803, in Esarey, *Messages and Letters,* I, 76–84. The Owl was Ozandiah, one of several chiefs of that name, which was frequently adopted by chiefs of the Mississinewa group of Miamis. Harrison explained the relationship of the Miami bands to each other in this letter. The land ceded is Tract 26 on Plate XIX, Royce, *Indian Land Cessions.*

Shawnees were signatories to the final treaty. That document gave the United States title to the area around the new territorial capital and preserved the French land titles. Actually, it was an extension of the limits of the vaguely defined Vincennes tract ceded in 1795 at Greene Ville. The only payment which the tribes received for an area approximately 1,500,000 acres was an annual distribution of 159 bushels of salt.[15]

Harrison next negotiated a series of treaties in August, 1803, with the Eel River, Wyandot, Piankeshaw, Kaskaskia, and Kickapoo tribes. Through these, he secured several small tracts on which the government could locate "houses of entertainment" on the road between Vincennes, Kaskaskia, and Clarksville. The tracts, never surveyed, were later retroceded.[16]

In the Vincennes treaty of August 18, 1804, the Delawares living on the west branch of the White River ceded the land between the Wabash and Ohio rivers and south of a line running between the Falls of the Ohio and Vincennes. The Delaware claim to this area had been conceded by the Miamis at a separate council of the two tribes at Fort Wayne the preceding June. On August 27, the Piankeshaws acknowledged the Delaware claim to a share of the title in the grant.[17]

On August 21, 1805, a treaty was negotiated with the other Miami bands at Grouseland, Harrison's mansion at Vincennes. The Kekiongas, Eel River Miamis, and Weas, along with the Delawares and Potawatomis, ceded the land north of Clark's Grant. The tract lay southeast of a line which began at the northeast corner of the 1803 Vincennes cession and ran northeast to intersect the Greene Ville line fifty miles north of the Ohio River near Brookville, Indiana Territory. The most important feature of the treaty was the

[15] *Stat. L., VII, 74.* Kappler, *Indian Affairs,* II, 47–48. Royce, *Indian Land Cessions,* 662–65, Plate XIX. Negotiations for the treaty are in *American State Papers,* Class II, *Indian Affairs,* II, 688.

[16] Royce, *Indian Land Cessions,* 664–65. *American State Papers,* Class II, *Indian Affairs,* II, 687.

[17] Kappler, *Indian Affairs,* II, 58–60. Royce, *Indian Land Cessions,* 664–69. The cession is the eastern segment of Tract 49 on Plate XIX, Royce. Harrison's negotiations are in *American State Papers,* Class II, *Indian Affairs,* II, 696–97.

disavowal by the Miami bands from the upper Wabash of their admission of any Delaware title. They now asserted the Delawares had been only tenants at will, without rights to the soil. However, admitting the Piankeshaws had given the eastern part of the tract to the Delawares in the 1760's, they finally acceded to the terms of the Piankeshaw treaty with the United States. Henceforth, the three upper Miami bands refused to acknowledge any other joint owners south of the Wabash and north of the tracts already ceded, thus becoming the sole conveyors of the 1805 grant. The band at Kekionga received an additional permanent annuity of $600 and the Wea and Eel River bands equal annuities of $250.[18]

Meanwhile, Harrison secured treaty cessions from the Piankeshaws and Kaskaskias on the west side of the Wabash and a huge area from the Sac and Fox tribes on both sides of the Mississippi River. By 1805, he had obtained about 46,000 square miles of Indian land and had excluded to the Indiana tribes access to the Ohio River from its source to the mouth of the Wabash.[19]

Obviously, Harrison was a master at Indian councils. It seems that the Miami chiefs, especially Little Turtle and Pacanne, were unwilling to use warfare to preserve areas which were not in their own immediate homeland and for which they had little need. Unable to defeat them by the logic such as Wayne used at Greene Ville, Harrison profited by exploiting the joint title of ownership which neighboring tribes held with the Miamis just north of the Ohio River.

It is difficult to offer any explanation for the Miamis' consent to these cessions other than that the tribe's cohesion was disintegrating. The Kekionga Miamis could no longer rally and lead the Weas and Piankeshaws, much less their Delaware or Shawnee allies, to a common cause as they had done in the past. The Greene

---

[18] Royce, *Indian Land Cessions,* 668–69. This is Tract 56 on Royce's map of Indiana. Kappler, *Indian Affairs,* II, 58–60.

[19] Annie Heloise Abel, *The History of Events Resulting in Indian Consolidation West of the Mississippi River,* I, 267–398, summarizes Harrison's treaty-making policies. The Piankeshaw treaty of December 30, 1805, is in Royce, *Indian Land Cessions,* 672–73.

Ville treaty had destroyed their faith in their more powerful allies, and their relatives were rapidly disappearing. Moreover, the weakened warrior society, after ten years of peaceful trade, daily contact with American agents, factors, and traders, plus a growing number of French and English marriage alliances, developed tribesmen who accepted the survival philosophy of the French settlers. Without warfare, there was no glory, and the fur trade and the little annuities substituted a life of greater dependency which some learned to accept.

The last-named factor, an intangible one, has received much credit for the Miamis' quiescence. But the lethargy was more a result of their laudable effort to observe the pledges they had first made at Greene Ville than a consequence of the degenerating effects of whisky. There is no doubt that honoring treaty pledges was as important to Little Turtle as it was unimportant to Richardville. The whole history of the Miamis supports the hypothesis that no treaty was sufficiently objectionable to merit their resistance—unless it posed an immediate threat to their existence. They did not yet see the Harrison treaties in this ominous light.

Meanwhile, opponents of Harrison's agreements generated one of the most important of all Indian resistance efforts. The young Shawnee warrior Tecumseh, a member of Black Hoof's band at Wapackoneta on the Auglaize River, gradually assumed leadership of those who objected to Harrison's extensive purchases. Tecumseh's plans for unified Indian resistance were given emotional overtones by his brother, The Shawnee Prophet. International diplomatic intrigues which preceded the War of 1812 encouraged the two leaders and presented them with the opportunity to implement their ideas.

Tecumseh's efforts were probably magnified in the imagination of the settlers in central and western Ohio. The Americans provoked the Indians by settling beyond the Greene Ville treaty line, by preventing them from hunting in the ceded territory, and by refusing to permit their ejection of unauthorized white trespassers. However, Black Hoof and the Delaware chief Anderson, or Kok-

149

towhanund, whose village was on the White River, were able to keep dissatisfaction among their tribesmen at a minimum. Consequently, the Shawnee brothers, with a small group of followers from several tribes, were forced to leave their own village sometime after 1801.[20]

Tecumseh traveled to tribal councils from the Great Lakes to the Gulf of Mexico to spread his message that the land belonged in common to all the tribes. He succeeded in securing control of the little Delaware village at present Muncie, Indiana, where The Prophet's message of Indian cultural purity and asceticism brought pilgrims from far and near. The Delawares at first welcomed The Prophet's band of Shawnees, Potawatomis, and a few Delawares, but they were soon disillusioned. An old chief who had signed the treaty of 1804, his nephew, and another, a Christian convert, were burned at the stake in 1806 at the climax of one of The Prophet's exhortations.

Governor Harrison sent a warning message to the Delawares, while the neighboring villages, led by Chief Anderson, protested against the rebels' act.[21] The unwelcome visitors then moved to a new site, which was carefully selected for its strategic position. The Prophet's town was on Burnett's Creek near the junction of the Wabash and Tippecanoe rivers—at the crossroads of travel for tribes. Here, prospective allies and surreptitious delegations could reach Tecumseh and The Prophet. More important, however, the chiefs could observe or intercept messengers who traveled to Fort Wayne and Detroit for the governor at Vincennes.

The Miamis now became Tecumseh's greatest obstacle. Although a few young Miami warriors joined the malcontents at the village, whose strength quickly overawed the Wea and Piankeshaw bands in the neighborhood, Little Turtle, Pacanne, and other chiefs were

[20] Esarey, *Messages and Letters*, I, 459–69, details Tecumseh's visit to Harrison at Vincennes in August, 1810, in which the Chief presented his grievances. Charles N. Thompson, *Sons of the Wilderness: John and William Conner*, 45–46. Jacob Piatt Dunn, *True Indian Stories, With Glossary of Indiana Indian Names*, 59–71.

[21] Dillon, *History of Indiana*, 424–26. Harrison's "Speech to the Delawares, Sometime in 1806," sent to counteract The Prophet's action, is in Esarey, *Messages and Letters*, I, 182–84. Thompson, *Sons of the Wilderness*, 45–46.

determined to observe the treaties they had signed. Moreover, Tecumseh's premise of common Indian land ownership violated the basis of Miami power and prestige. While the Miamis had accepted fugitive bands from the Delawares, Shawnees, and other tribes, they had no intention of forfeiting actual control of the upper Wabash areas. They had already lost part of their importance with the decline of the Piankeshaw and Wea bands on the lower Wabash, and without control of the Wabash-Maumee area, they would become a small and insignificant tribe indeed.

By now, the factory system and Indian agents among the Miamis had assumed greater significance. The agents' importance, probably distorted, is magnified by the fact that their reports to federal authorities contain much of the available information about the tribe and its activities at that time. On his second trip to Washington in 1802, Little Turtle pleaded for control of the liquor traffic, instruction in metal craftsmanship, and federal supervision of trade and annuity activities. His appeal so impressed Thomas Jefferson that the President appointed William Wells Indian subagent and John Johnston of Piqua manager of a new government factory at Fort Wayne. Jefferson probably encouraged the Quakers to send Philip Dennis and two others in 1804 to start an agricultural training farm along the Wabash River near the present boundary of Wabash and Huntington counties. The project failed in one year, as did William Kirk's effort to continue the farm the following year.[22]

Johnston and Wells were supposed to cooperate in political and commercial affairs involving the government and the Miamis, but they failed to do so. Their differences originated over the disposition of the Shawnee villages close to the Greene Ville line. Wells proposed to move the Shawnees back from the line, while Johnston supported their treaty-guaranteed right to protection from white encroachment.

Meanwhile, Johnston attributed his factory problems at Fort

[22] Gayle Thornbrough (ed.), *Letterbook of the Indian Agency at Fort Wayne, 1809–1815*, 10–13. Joseph A. Parsons, Jr., "Civilizing the Indians in the Old Northwest," *Indiana Magazine of History*, LVI, 3 (September, 1960), 207–12, details the failures of Dennis and Kirk.

Wayne to the five Canadians who were licensed to trade at that post. He blamed Wells for the failure of the Quaker farms, accused him of practicing intrigue and deception, of lack of principle, and of devotion to his own personal gain. Wells was censured severely by the War Department in 1807 and, in effect, placed under Johnston's orders.[23] Harrison admitted that Wells and Little Turtle had probably tried to thwart his efforts in the Treaty of Vincennes in 1804 and at Grouseland in 1805. Even though Harrison considered Wells indispensable, the secretary of war discharged him in early 1809 and appointed Johnston the Miami subagent to replace him.[24] Johnston thus held both governmental offices in Fort Wayne.

Despite Harrison's distrust of the Miamis, which tended to undercut the position of the old chiefs, they were able to maintain a traditional authority stronger than that exercised by chiefs in other tribes. The Governor also distrusted many of the citizens and traders of the territory, especially at Detroit, who held county or militia appointments from him and who also held secret commissions in the Canadian Indian service. Harrison's mistrust was understandable, for the frontier was an area of divided loyalties and espionage.[25]

Wells's discharge could have been unfortunate for peace on the frontier. The rejected agent was in no mood to restrain the Miami warriors should they pledge themselves to Tecumseh. An immediate outbreak that summer, when the many bands were in Fort Wayne to receive their annuities, could have brought dreadful con-

[23] Leonard U. Hill, *John Johnston and the Indians in the Land of the Three Miamis,* is exhaustive but biased in Johnston's favor. Prucha, *American Indian Policy,* 261, 275–76, analyzes the problems of the Indian service.

[24] Thornbrough, *Letterbook,* 15–21, summarizes Harrison's attitude toward Wells. Harrison's most vehement letter about his agent is in Esarey, *Messages and Letters,* I, 76–84. Harrison tried to negotiate separately with the Weas and Piankeshaws in order to facilitate his treaties and blamed Wells and Little Turtle for their efforts to make him treat with a united Miami tribe.

[25] William Wesley Wollen *et al.* (eds.), "Executive Journal of Indiana Territory, 1800–1816," in *Indiana Historical Society Publications,* III (1900), 3, 118–19. Anson, "The Fur Traders," 35–36. Wells, Fort Wayne, to Harrison, August 20, 1807, blamed Richardville, Owl, and Pacanne for dividing the tribe by holding at the Kickapoo towns a council which excluded the pro-American Miami chiefs. Esarey, *Messages and Letters,* I, 239–43.

sequences. Instead, the payment was uneventful. Of the $4,050 in annuities distributed by Harrison and Johnston, the Kekionga villages received $1,600 and the Eel River bands $150 under terms of the recent treaty. Because the payment was made in comparative peace, Harrison decided to make his next attempt to secure a new Miami land cession at Fort Wayne the same year.[26]

For the next three years, Wells remained an enigma in Wabash Indian diplomacy. No longer an agent, he still was an influential man, and the correspondence of all those who wrote of him must be used with caution if his part in the decisions of Miami councils are to be understood.

Harrison was confident his earlier treaties were acceptable to the Indians. After several exchanges with The Prophet, he finally discounted the potential strength of any confederation which Tecumseh could assemble. Harrison met with the Kekionga and Eel River Miamis, the Potawatomis, and the Delawares on September 30, 1809, at Fort Wayne. The Indians showed remarkable understanding of their own ill-defined territorial claims. The major tracts ceded, noncontiguous, are numbered 71, 72, and 73 on Charles C. Royce's map. They included the upper Whitewater River Valley and completed American control of the lower Wabash. In addition, the Miamis conceded that the Delawares shared ownership with them in the White River Basin—in spite of their claim in 1805 of sole ownership—and must consent to any Miami sale of Tract 72. Wea consent was required before Tract 71 could be ceded; Kickapoo consent was required before the little tract numbered 73 could be ceded. In a clause of the treaty, which the Indians approved later that year, the United States retroceded to the Wea band the Ouiatanon tracts, which had never been surveyed or occupied. Additional permanent annuities were given the Miamis: $700 to the Kekiongas, $400 to the Weas, and $350 to the Eel River band.[27]

[26] Harrison, Vincennes, to Secretary of War Dearborn, May 16, 1809, in Esarey, *Messages and Letters,* I, 346, 356–57. He was authorized on July 15, 1809, to make the new treaty attempt that fall.

[27] Harrison, Fort Wayne, to Secretary of War William Eustis, October 3, 1809, in

It should be emphasized that in the 1809 treaty the Kekiongas clarified their boundaries. They disposed of areas which the main body had shared with other tribes and other Miami bands by removing all other claims to the land they retained. It was a shrewd move. But the cessions, which aroused a storm of protest among their neighbors, became Tecumseh's best argument with other tribes. Even the Miami villages had dissidents who charged that the Kekionga cessions brought white settlers too close to them. In the annual distribution of 1810, the Mississinewa villages refused their annuities to show their displeasure with the treaty, and a few more Miami warriors moved to Prophetstown.[28]

Tecumseh's charges that the Americans used bribery and distributed whisky at the treaty negotiations are well supported; the old charges that tractable chiefs were persuaded to sign Harrison's treaties are not. Miami chiefs could little ignore the Miami council's debates or its decisions. The 1809 treaty was the tribe's repudiation of the swelling sentiment in other tribes for Tecumseh's land policies. It was a reiteration of the position which the Miamis had taken at the Treaty of Greene Ville.

Harrison secured title to nearly three million acres in his 1809 treaties. The Prophet visited him in the summer of 1809 and disclaimed any connection with British interests, but when Tecumseh proceeded to Vincennes in 1810, he vowed he would resist any effort to survey the new cessions in order to prepare them for white settlement. Rumors magnified every case of Indian depredation during 1810, and Harrison began to change his opinion of the strength of Tecumseh's confederation. He relied on the reports of Vincennes traders along the Wabash. John Conner was influential among the

---

Thornbrough, *Letterbook,* 66–69. Kappler, *Indian Affairs,* II, 73–75. Royce, *Indian Land Cessions,* 676–79. This purchase abrogated an earlier 1808 treaty in which a band of Brothertown Delaware Indians of New York had purchased from the Miamis a tract of land on the White River. John Candee Dean (ed.), "The Journal of Thomas Dean," *Indiana Historical Society Publications,* VI (1918), 2, 38. Harrison's journal of the negotiations is in Esarey, *Messages and Letters,* I, 239–43.

[28] Thornbrough, *Letterbook,* 90 n.

Delawares, and Joseph Baron was probably the most accurate agent in reporting news from the Miami villages. However, Harrison still did not trust Wells or most of the traders at Fort Wayne, such as John Kinzie, because their commercial ties lay with Detroit and Montreal. Since Harrison had gained firsthand knowledge of Miami political influence during his service in Wayne's campaign fifteen years earlier, it may also be true that he feared they were secretly supporting the Tecumseh movement and thus exaggerated the tribe's importance.[29]

The Governor heard many alarming reports from the frontier. These emphasized the presence of Canadian agents among the Indians, the warlike speeches given at Fort Malden, and Tecumseh's plans to unite the Indian tribes for an assault on western American settlements from the Great Lakes to Florida. Every event on the frontier was reported to the Governor by friendly Indians or traders or by individuals striving to maintain a favorable position with both sides. They undoubtedly included some Miamis and their traders.

The importance of the Miamis in 1810 is indicated by Harrison's re-evaluation of Wells's influence. He now believed Wells was in a position to influence Little Turtle, thus making the Miamis a pivotal tribe to both Harrison and Tecumseh. If the Miamis remained neutral, then Prophetstown was isolated and Tecumseh's stand against the cession of Miami land in 1809 lost much of its appeal to other tribes. Although a few of their warriors moved to Prophetstown, the Miamis had little desire to start a war which would inevitably be fought in their own villages, and Little Turtle and Pacanne continued to support the terms of the previous treaties. The tribe tried to reach a decision at a council on the Mississinewa that summer. Lapousier, the Wea chief, told Harrison the Miamis required him to attend the council. Upon his return, he reported

<hr>

[29] Robert B. McAfee, *History of the Late War in the Western Country*, 23–25. Lossing, *Pictorial Field-Book*, 191–93. Harrison's usual messengers to the Indians were William Prince, John Conner, Joseph Baron, Walter Wilson, Dubois, and Brouillette. Anson, "The Fur Traders," 35–36, 43–44. Dillon, *History of Indiana*, 442–47.

the tribe was still equally divided in its support for Tecumseh and the United States.[30]

At Tecumseh's council with Harrison at Vincennes on August 15, 1810, the chief rejected the Governor's advice and threats and promised that his confederacy of Shawnee, Wyandot, Kickapoo, Ottawa, Winnebago, and Potawatomi warriors would resist any survey or occupation of the newly ceded lands. The Prophet seized the boatload of annuity salt sent up the Wabash in early 1811, and Harrison prepared for war.[31]

Tecumseh again visited Vincennes in July, 1811, rejected an offer to visit Washington, and refused to stop his efforts to establish an Indian confederacy.[32] When Tecumseh visited the southeastern and Mississippi River tribes, Harrison prepared to march an army up the Wabash. He first sent messages to the tribes in the territory demanding that they send him all persons involved in the increasing number of murders of white settlers and demanding from the Miamis a complete disavowal of any alliance with the Prophet.

Lapousier, supported by Pacanne, Le Gris, Negro Legs, Osage, and Stone Eater, replied to Harrison's message:

. . . Father Your speech has overtaken us at this place, we have heard it, but it has not scared us, we are not afraid of what you say. We are now going on to that country which has been frequently visited by Tecumseh and we shall be able to know in the course of our journey whether he has told us lyes or not; that all the Indians were of the same opinion that he is; but when we return we shall be able to tell you whether what Tecumseh has told us to be true or not.

Father we the Miamis are not a people that is passionate, we are not so easily made angry as it is supposed you are. Our hearts is heavy as the earth, and our minds are not easily irritated. We don't tell people we are angry with them for light causes; we are afraid if we did fly in a passion for no cause we should make ourselves contemptible to others.

---

[30] Esarey, *Messages and Letters,* I, 470–71, 528–42, reproduces a number of petitions and reports on the growing severity of Indian depredations.

[31] Harrison to Secretary of War Eustis, August 22, 1810, in *ibid.,* 459–69, encloses Tecumseh's speeches at the council.

[32] Harrison to Secretary of War Eustis, August 6, 1811, *ibid.,* 542–46.

... We have told you we should not get angry for light causes. We have our eyes on our lands on the Wabash with a strong determination to defend our rights, let them be invaded from what quarter they may; that when our best interest is invaded, we defend them to a man, and be made mad but once. Father now consider your children the Miamies, what they have said to you. You have now offered the war club to us, you have laid it at our feet, and told us we might pick it up if we chose. We have refused to do so, and we hope this circumstance will prove to you that we are people of good hearts. . . .[33]

Silver Heels of the Mississinewa Delaware band then repudiated The Prophet and his doctrine. A Potawatomi chief reaffirmed his tribe's friendship with the Miamis, and Little Turtle, supported by White Loon, spoke twice:

... The transactions that took place between the white people and Indians at Greenville is yet fresh in our minds; at that place we told each other that we would in future be friends, doing all the good to each other and raise our children in peace and quietness. These are yet the sentiments of your children the Miamies.

Father you have told us you would draw a line, that your children should stand on one side and the Prophet on the other. We the Miamis wish to be considered the same people that we were at the Treaty of Greenville, holding fast to that treaty that united us the Miamies and Potawattimies. . . .

... Father I must again repeat you say you will draw a line between your children and the Prophet we are not pleased at this because we think you have no right to doubt our friendship towards you. . . .[34]

The Miamis then further demanded that the Delaware chiefs clarify their tribe's position. When the Delawares failed to meet this demand because they were unable to dissuade The Prophet from his plans, their chiefs went to Harrison for protection from Tecumseh. The Miami chiefs, not knowing the Delaware position, which left them unsupported, hurried down the Wabash to attempt to placate the Governor.

[33] *Ibid.*, 571–82, includes Harrison to Eustis, September 13, 1811, and his messages to the Indians with their replies. This excerpt is from *ibid.*, 577–79.
[34] *Ibid.*, 581–82.

When Harrison was certain the Delawares and Miamis would not support The Prophet, he immediately implemented his year-long preparations to attack Prophetstown. He marched from Vincennes in October, 1811, with eight hundred men, including a regiment of regular troops, built Fort Harrison at present-day Terre Haute, and sent twenty-nine Miami warriors from his Indian scouts to try to persuade The Prophet not to resist. The Miami scouts failed to mollify The Prophet. When they returned via the south bank of the Wabash, they failed to make contact with Harrison's force on the north side. Since the Miami party did not return, the Governor feared The Prophet had converted them to his cause. This misadventure helped Harrison decide on a firm course as he advanced toward the village on November 6.[35]

In the battle fought at Prophetstown the following morning, both sides sustained approximately equal losses, but the Americans won the field as the Indians dispersed the next day. Harrison's Miami scouts did not return in time for the fight, but were close enough to hear the battle in the distance. This demonstration of white aggressiveness restored much of the waning prestige of Little Turtle, Pacanne, Metocina, Osage, and other old Miami chiefs who had opposed Tecumseh. And it certainly disproved The Prophet's declarations that his followers could not be harmed.[36]

Peace came to the Wabash temporarily when Harrison returned to Vincennes and The Prophet retired for sanctuary to a village among the Miamis on the Mississinewa. Agent Johnston conducted the annual payment at Fort Wayne on November 22, 1811, and Indians who had been at the battle universally blamed The Prophet for their own misconduct. Johnston wisely absolved the culprits while lauding the neutral and pro-American chiefs.[37] Harrison, who

[35] Harrison to Eustis, October 13, 1811, *ibid.*, 591–603. Brice, *History of Fort Wayne*, 195.

[36] Harrison's reports of November 7, 8, and 18, 1811, to Secretary of War Eustis are in Esarey, *Messages and Letters*, I, 608–13, 614–32. Captain Josiah Snelling reported to Harrison that Wea Miami Chief Little Eyes and a war party were within hearing of the battle and visited the scene the next day. *Ibid.*, 643–46. Dillon, *History of Indiana*, 557–71.

[37] Thornbrough, *Letterbook*, 97–98n. Johnston's letter to the secretary of war

believed that the Shawnee chiefs, especially Black Hoof, could now counteract the influence of Tecumseh, still distrusted the loyalty of the Miamis and Potawatomis, as well as Little Turtle's power to restrain those tribes. The distrust was constantly strengthened by the enmity between Wells and Johnston and by Harrison's anxiety over the control of the Wabash-Maumee route to Detroit.

There was news that Tecumseh was still hostile, and when the new agent, Benjamin F. Stickney, arrived, he was accompanied by reinforcements for the garrison. Tecumseh was at Fort Wayne with a small bodyguard, but both he and The Prophet refused to attend the council which Stickney called in April with the Wyandot, Potawatomi, Eel River, and Miami chiefs. At the meeting, Charley, or Kitunga, the Eel River chief, declared the Miamis intended to observe the Treaty of Greene Ville but opposed sending a deputation to Washington.

The following month, the Miamis, Potawatomis, Winnebagos, Kickapoos, Ottawas, Wyandots, and Shawnees held a council on the Mississinewa River. The Wyandot chief chided the Wabash Indians and declared his tribe and the British wanted no more bloodshed. Tecumseh blamed the Potawatomis for the frontier clashes because they sold land not belonging to them; the Potawatomi chiefs agreed some of their young men were guilty. The Delawares said they were not interested in accusations but wanted peace, while the Miamis asserted they had not broken the peace and hoped the northern tribes would not permit their warriors to break it. Most of the Indians then reassembled at Fort Wayne for two days to report to the agent. They convinced Stickney that British intentions were peaceful, but Wells disagreed and said the new agent was being misled.

Tecumseh, after further travels, returned to Fort Wayne in July. He cast all pretense aside and told Stickney he was on his way to Fort Malden for powder and lead. Other chiefs told Wells that

is quoted in Hill, *John Johnston*, 55–56. Johnston said no Miami or Eel River warriors were among The Prophet's warriors at Tippecanoe. This was supported in Matthew Elliott, Amherstburg, to Colonel Isaac Brock, January 12, 1812, in Esarey, *Messages and Letters*, I, 616–18, giving the British view of Harrison's campaign.

seh intended to recruit a force of Chippewas to settle on
abash to reinforce him, although the Miamis had previously
ed that tribe permission to immigrate.[38] Harrison knew the
at Shawnee could attract some support and asked permission
to lead another expedition among the warriors in any village on
the frontier. Secretary of War William Eustis wisely refused the
request because he felt such a move would irrevocably drive the
Miamis and northern tribes into a British alignment.[39]

The United States declared war against Britain on June 18, 1812,
and the northwest frontier became a major theater of military operations. The Indians faced their familiar alternatives: alliance
with the British, who had deserted them in the past, or aid to the
United States, which implacably encroached upon their lands. A
third alternative, neutrality, did not exist. Although Harrison in
1814 castigated the Miamis to the secretary of war as a "poor,
miserable, drunken set, diminishing every year. Becoming too lazy
to hunt, they feel the advantages of their annuities," in 1812 he
was anxious for control of the strategic Wabash-Maumee portage
and frustrated by the equivocal maneuvers of the crafty Miami
chiefs. Albeit he distrusted their loyalty, he was forced to use Owl
and Stone Eater as his mediators to the Potawatomi and Kickapoo
chiefs, who offered to make peace. From them he also learned additional details of his battle at Prophetstown.[40]

At this critical juncture, Little Turtle died and the Miamis lost
the war chief who had been able to direct their destinies for forty
years. Little Turtle had signed every Miami treaty from 1795 to
1809 and had been the speaker for all of the Miami bands at most
of them. His policies and influence had been attacked repeatedly

[38] Agent Benjamin Stickney, Fort Wayne, to Governor Harrison, Vincennes, April
18 and 19, 1812, and enclosures, in Thornbrough, *Letterbook*, 102–10. Stickney to
Governor William Hull, Detroit, June 20, 1812, in *ibid.*, 140–43. Esarey, *Messages
and Letters, I*, 683–85, includes Harrison's conference with Owl. Wells's report of
the speeches is in *ibid.*, II, 48–53.

[39] McAfee, *History of the Late War*, 51.

[40] Harrison to Secretary of War Eustis, December 24 and 28, 1811, in Esarey,
Messages and Letters, I, 683–85, 686–92. Harrison is quoted from *ibid.*, II, 636–41.
McAfee, *History of the Late War*, 53–58.

in his own councils, but the Indian defeat at Prophetstown had restored his prestige. Tecumseh's confederation was blocked by the uncompromising resistance of Little Turtle, and continued Miami neutrality depended on his successors: Pacanne, who was old, and Richardville, François Godfroy, and other young chiefs who were less predictable leaders and might be misled by The Prophet and a few of his supporters (the latter had moved to the Mississinewa for the protection of the Miami villages).

In the middle of July, the Shawnee Prophet came to Fort Wayne with about one hundred of his followers, of whom a majority were warlike Winnebagos and Kickapoos. Double that number of Indians from other tribes were already there. When warriors spent the summer traveling to villages and forts, it was a sure sign that plans and counterplans were in the making. Nevertheless, Stickney and Johnston were made optimistic by the peaceful speeches of The Prophet. Wells, who was reappointed subagent to the Miamis in 1811, was better informed and told Harrison that The Prophet was more than ever the emissary of Tecumseh. Ironically, Harrison now scolded Stickney for his gullibility while dealing with clever Indian diplomats.[41]

The declaration of war, General William Hull's occupation of Detroit in preparation for an invasion of Canada, and the menace of The Prophet (once again stationed on the Tippecanoe River while Tecumseh moved freely among the various Indian tribes) combined to make the first part of the summer a time of nervous tension and gloomy foreboding for Indians and Americans alike. Captain Josiah Snelling, commandant at Fort Harrison, and his successor, Captain Zachary Taylor, found that even the decimated Weas under Chiefs Little Eyes and Lapousier were attracted by the prospects of war. Negro Legs, the Kekionga chief among them, was unable to counteract the war fever aroused by the Winnebago, Kickapoo, and Potawatomi warriors near by. William Wells also

[41] Stickney, Fort Wayne, to John Johnston, July 20, 1812, in Thornbrough, *Letterbook*, 165–69. Stickney's letters contained several naïve judgments, which were severely criticized by Harrison. The agent's reply to these in *ibid.*, 169–72, indicates the insubordination endured by territorial governors.

sent word to Taylor that a large force of Indians was assembling to attack Vincennes and Fort Harrison and that he could no longer keep Lapousier and Stone Eater from following The Prophet, whose earlier plans to retire to the west of Lake Michigan had been changed.[42]

Governor Harrison's frantic efforts to reinforce the western frontier were rewarded August 22, when he was commissioned a general of the United States Army, and on August 25, when Kentucky commissioned him to command its militia, as well as those of Indiana and Illinois. Harrison planned to build a chain of forts along the Illinois River to Chicago, to strengthen Fort Wayne by sending a regiment there, and to reinforce Hull at Detroit. Even in early August, Harrison believed the only way to secure the Wabash was to send a mounted force from the east to hit the Tippecanoe area before the Miamis could become alarmed, thereby ending their indecision once and for all.[43]

Johnston called on the neighboring tribes to meet August 15 in a council at Piqua, the center of his new Shawnee agency. Only the Wyandots and Shawnees, who had given General Hull permission to march his army to Detroit through their lands, attended. They seemed to be solid supporters of the American cause,[44] although the Miamis had reluctantly prepared to go to the council.

Before the Miamis started, Wells received orders from Hull to go to Fort Dearborn with instructions for Captain Nathaniel Heald to evacuate the fort. He collected a party of thirty or more Miami warriors and hurried to Chicago, where he found a large force of Winnebago and Potawatomi warriors assembled. Heald decided to abandon the post, in spite of protests by Wells and traders in the town, and as they marched from the fort on August 15, his

[42] Josiah Snelling, Fort Harrison, to Harrison, April 12, 1812; Harrison to Secretary of War Eustis, July 8, 1812; William Wells, Fort Wayne, to Harrison, July 29, 1812, in Esarey, *Messages and Letters,* II, 37–38, 67–70, 76–78.

[43] Harrison, Lexington, Kentucky, to Secretary of War Eustis, August 12, 1812, in *ibid.,* 84–88.

[44] McAfee, *History of the Late War,* 64, 67. Johnston prepared for a grand council to be held at Piqua in August, 1812; Harrison's temporary headquarters were moved to the frontier post the same month. Lossing, *Pictorial Field-Book,* 323, 324 n.

little party was overwhelmed by hostile warriors. Thirty-eight soldiers, two women, and twelve children were killed and twenty-eight taken prisoner. Only a few Americans escaped—through the stratagems of individual Indian friends. Wells, who had been warned by friendly Potawatomi chiefs that their warriors were determined to kill him, was butchered as he tried to defend the group. Two chiefs, Winnemac and Waubausee, tried to save him, but to no avail. Some accounts say his band of Miami warriors joined in the massacre after he was killed, which is possible, for the scene was one to intoxicate any warrior. One account, however, says the Miamis withdrew as soon as Wells was killed and promised to avenge him. Even though they threatened retribution, the Miamis' prestige had been injured because their warriors had been unable to protect Wells, their leader.[45]

Harrison made a tardy atonement for his past condemnations of Wells ("Poor Wells has also perished in endeavouring to save Capt. Heald with his company."), but did not recall his mistaken idea that Wells had more influence among the Potawatomis than the Miamis or that he had once claimed the Potawatomis were steadfast friends of the Americans.[46]

By August 16, 1812, the Miami delegation to Piqua had proceeded only one day's march when it received word of the fall of the American forts, as well as news of the Fort Dearborn massacre. The Miamis returned to Fort Wayne immediately to reconsider their position. It was now altered by the prospect of an enhanced position for Tecumseh among the Indian tribes, plus the fact that, unlike the situation in 1794, the British were now able

[45] Quafe, *Chicago and the Old Northwest*, 211–13, remains the most reliable account of the massacre. Thornbrough, *Letterbook*, 172–73 n, summarizes events on the Indian frontier during August and September. W. K. Jordan, Fort Wayne, to his wife, October 12, 1812, in Esarey, *Messages and Letters*, II, 165–67, recounts the experiences of a soldier sent to Fort Dearborn with Wells and his Miamis. White Loon saved his life, and Hunter escaped in time to serve through the siege of Fort Wayne.

[46] Harrison, Cincinnati, to Secretary of War Eustis, August 28, 1812, in Esarey, *Messages and Letters*, II, 98–101. At the close of his campaign in 1813, Harrison said: "The Miamis and Potawatimies deserve no mercy. . . . They have been (particularly the latter) our most cruel and inveterate enemies." *Ibid.*, 574.

to enter the frontier campaigns in a formal state of war.[47] Later that month, they held a council with their Indian allies at St. Joseph, near Mackinac, in which plans were made for simultaneous attacks on American posts about the Great Lakes, including the raids soon to be made on Forts Wayne and Harrison. The latter were to be supported by a British force assembled at Fort Malden under the command of Colonel A. C. Muir.[48]

News of the Fort Dearborn disaster created panic on the American frontier. The Fort Wayne commandant, Captain James Rhea, wrote to Johnston, who was at Piqua, on August 19:

> ... my dear friend do all you can to give us Some Assistance—from the best information I can get they [the Indians] are determinded on this place. . . . and every thing appears to be goin against us—for God sake Call on Gov. Meigs for to Assist us in Sending More Men. . . .[49]

He informed Johnston the women and children of the fort were being sent to Piqua for safety. Despite the urgency, when Antoine Bondie, a trader, brought word from Potawatomi Chief Metea that the warriors who attacked Fort Dearborn had begun to infest the forests about Fort Wayne, Rhea was reluctant to send a dispatch to Harrison. He was persuaded to send word to Meigs via Stickney, who sent a similar message to Harrison, who was then at Cincinnati.

Harrison was recruiting volunteers and inspecting the frontier forts when he received word of the fall of Fort Dearborn and Detroit on August 28. He immediately marched to Piqua, where he dispatched Colonel John Allen and 900 men to reinforce a body of Ohio militia which had been sent to reinforce Fort Wayne but which had stopped at Girtystown (St. Mary's). The fort was completely isolated by September 1, and Allen, too, halted at Girtystown until he could obtain information about the warriors who barred his path. He sent Logan, his principal Shawnee scout, to

---

[47] McAfee, *History of the Late War*, 127.
[48] Tanpoint Pothier to Sir George Prevost, September 8, 1812, in *MPHC*, XV, 141–44. Colonel A. C. Muir, on Maumee River, to Colonel Proctor, September 30, 1812, is the best account of the action of this force. *Ibid.*, 151–54.
[49] Thornbrough, *Letterbook*, 172–73 n.

determine the enemy's strength. Logan managed to slip through the Indians' camps, reassured the garrison that aid was near, and returned to Girtystown, where Allen again decided to wait for reinforcements. Fortunately for Rhea, the Indians mounted no concentrated attack and the garrison was able to maintain itself until September 10, when Harrison and his main force arrived and lifted the siege. Rhea was arrested, charged with drunkenness and incompetency, and forced to resign.[50]

The Miamis evidently had no desire to take part in an action which would bring Harrison's army into their own country. Perhaps they tried to avoid this by discouraging the Indians from making a full attack on Fort Wayne. Instead, a small band of their warriors went down the Wabash to take part in an attack against Fort Harrison on September 4 and 5. Captain Taylor barely saved the fort in a desperate struggle against the combined Winnebago, Shawnee, Kickapoo, Potawatomi, and Miami force.[51] A plausible explanation of the action can be made on the basis of the Miamis' habits: they were willing to wage war, but not on their friends and relatives in the villages about Fort Wayne.

When he arrived at Piqua, Harrison immediately sent detachments against neighboring villages which could have furnished warriors for the attack on Fort Wayne and which had in fact sent war parties as far south as the little settlement of Pigeon Roost near the Ohio River. Colonel James Simeral burned Little Turtle's village on the Eel River northwest of Fort Wayne, sparing only the chief's property, which he was ordered to protect. Colonel John Payne burned the Miami village at the Wabash forks and all others

---

[50] Brice, *History of Fort Wayne,* 212–23, is an account full of the individual exploits of the defenders. When Charley and other chiefs hastened to deny any Miami part in the siege, Harrison sent five to Piqua as hostages, claiming Chapine had led Miami warriors against the fort. Esarey, *Messages and Letters,* II, 149–51, 173–78. Harrison's report to the secretary of war is in *ibid.,* 143–47; his charges against Rhea, *ibid.,* 149–51.

[51] Zachary Taylor, Fort Harrison, to Harrison, Piqua, September 10, 1812, in Esarey, *Messages and Letters,* II, 124–28, contains the commandant's report of the attack. Lossing, *Pictorial Field-Book,* 317, says some friendly Miamis alerted Taylor before the attack.

for several miles below, while Colonel Samuel Wells destroyed the Potawatomi village of Chief Five Medals on the Elkhart River.[52] Harrison was determined to prevent the formation of another Indian confederacy on the Wabash-Maumee (which could interfere with his projected attack on Detroit and Canada) by destroying any and all villages that could furnish supplies and warriors to the British or to the large tribes about the Great Lakes who were allied with them.

A conference of American officers at Fort Wayne decided the Miamis should be treated as a hostile tribe. The attacks, for which the Miamis were unprepared, caused many of them to change their neutral position, and they sent nine war messages to the Delawares on the White River. One of the last two messages arrived on October 1—the same day the Miamis sent another peace delegation to Harrison at Girtystown.

The Miamis were now hopelessly split in their policies. While Richardville fled to the safety of Canada, the majority congregated on the Mississinewa. A delegation followed the American army to St. Mary's to make their peace with Harrison, but the general did not see them then. He hurried to Piqua, where he received news he had been appointed commander of the northwestern army to replace Hull. Immediately, he began preparations to march to the Maumee on his way to recover Detroit.

Before he left Fort Wayne, Harrison sent General James Winchester down the Maumee to collect supplies of Indian corn. Winchester was harassed by Indians before he got to Fort Defiance, and Harrison soon received dispatches saying Winchester faced two thousand Indians and a detachment of British regulars. Harrison led reinforcements to Defiance, but Colonel Muir's force was ordered to retreat when it found the Indians had not secured Fort Wayne.

Harrison then returned to St. Mary's to find the Miami chiefs still awaiting him. The first delegation, consisting of a French

---

[52] Harrison, Piqua, to Secretary Eustis, September 21, 1812, in Esarey, *Messages and Letters,* II, 143–47. McAfee, *History of the Late War,* 145–48.

trader named Longley, Stone Eater, and Little Thunder, had been augmented by the addition of Owl, Charley, Little Turtle's son, and others. Harrison was unyielding and demanded they send five chiefs, whom he named, to be kept in custody as hostages. The General's harshness was explained in a letter:

> The facts which we can prove upon them are the assistance given by Chappim one of their principal war Chiefs in the siege of Fort Wayne. One of these warriors participating in the murders committed in Clark County, Indiana, (Pigeon Roost) and a scalp exhibited (taken by him) in the town of Mississinaway, a Declaration made to the Delawares of their having taken up the tomahawk against the U. States and I may add their refusal to attend the council at Piqua. . . . There is great reason to believe that the Weas assisted in the late attack upon fort Harrison and Mr. [John] Johnsons thinks his brother was killed by a Miami. I have no doubt that some of the Chiefs have done everything in their power to prevent the young men from going to war with us, and as little that the great bulk of the tribe were decidedly hostile. The revolution in their disposition towards us was very sudden. The Declaration of hostility to us which I have spoken of above that was made to the Delawares was followed in two days by a message entreating the mediation of the Delawares in their favor. In the intermediate time our Army had appeared at Fort Wayne their Villages and provision destroyed and their utter extirpation threatened. . . . I will merely observe they can do us considerable injury if they are driven off and unite with the hostile bands which are collecting towards the southern extremity of Lake Michigan.[53]

Following the successful defense of Fort Wayne, General Samuel Hopkins was ordered to clear the lower Wabash. The first expedition left Fort Harrison on October 14, but Hopkins' army of volunteers mutinied and he retired to Vincennes. He collected a new army, left Fort Harrison in early November with 1,250 men, and burned the deserted Wea villages. He fought off an ambush,

---

[53] Harrison, Franklinton, to Secretary Eustis, October 13, 1812, in Esarey, *Messages and Letters,* II, 173–78, contains the excerpt quoted here. Harrison, Franklinton, to Eustis, October 26, 1812, *ibid.,* 189. McAfee, *History of the Late War,* 151–57.

but when he failed to bring the Indian warriors to bay, he retired to Fort Harrison.[54]

Meanwhile, the Miamis on the Mississinewa seemed to deserve Harrison's distrust. The five hostages whom the delegation to St. Mary's had promised to send did not arrive. Harrison countered this development by dispatching a trusted trader, William Conner, who was welcome in their councils, to watch the Mississinewa Miamis. Conner found them nearly unanimously opposed to the Americans because the latter, who showed little fortitude when facing the British at Detroit, tried to recoup some of their lost military prestige in the Wabash-Maumee Valley.[55] Although the more belligerent Miami warriors had participated in the summer and fall campaigns and at least a few went to Detroit or joined Tecumseh, those who remained on the Mississinewa had no intention of taking up arms, at least at this time. Wrote Harrison:

> Relieved from the fears exited by the late invasion of their country, the Indians from the Upper part of the Illinois river to the South of Lake Michigan will direct all their efforts against Fort Wayne. . . . Mississineway will be their rendevous. . . . From that place they can by their runners ascertain the period at which every Convoy may set out from St. Mary's and with certainty intercept it. . . .[56]

In the previous war against the United States, the Miamis had dispersed into the northern lake areas when their villages were threatened. Their congregation on the Mississinewa was a serious political and military error, unless it indicated their determination to remain neutral. If they had planned to join the British in 1812, it seems probable that they would have placed their villages on the Eel, or even the Elkhart, where they could have retreated to

[54] Dillon, *History of Indiana,* 496–500, 501–505. "The Expeditions of Major-General Samuel Hopkins up the Wabash, 1812," *Indiana Magazine of History,* XLIII, 4 (December, 1947), 393–402, tells of the second and successful invasion attempt.

[55] John Johnston, Piqua, to Harrison, Franklinton, Ohio, October 23, 1812, in Esarey, *Messages and Letters,* II, 186–87. Thompson, *Sons of the Wilderness,* 71–72.

[56] Harrison, Franklinton, to Secretary Eustis, November 15, 1812, in Esarey, *Messages and Letters,* II, 210–16.

Potawatomi or Chippewa sanctuaries. The Miamis failed to appreciate the fact that in wartime they could not be neutral. If they had decided to be noncombatants, they should have moved east or north from the war zone. Although Richardville moved to the safety of Detroit, most of the tribe's chiefs believed they had more to fear from Tecumseh's followers than from the United States and felt they were safe on the Mississinewa.

Harrison was fearful of an unknown but exaggerated number of warriors of uncertain temper on the flanks of Fort Wayne. He correctly estimated the danger from the tribes north and west of the Wabash River and thought Osage Town, near the mouth of the Mississinewa, could become their rallying point. After Hopkins' failure to secure the middle Wabash, this was a reasonable prediction, but it seems certain the Mississinewa villages had become the shelter for noncombatants, including the pro-American Delawares. The Miami chief Metocina had kept his band out of conflicts for years, and the list of other pro-American chiefs was a long one.

Harrison's soundest reason for attacking the villages was the fear of leaving a potential enemy force in his rear when he moved against Detroit the following year. He therefore ordered Lieutenant Colonel John B. Campbell and six hundred men from Franklinton, Ohio, to destroy Osage Town and all the intervening Miami villages on the Mississinewa, together with their winter provisions. William Conner served as guide and scout. Harrison also ordered Campbell to protect Richardville and his sons, as well as White Loon, Old Godfroy, Pacanne, and Silver Heels, the Delaware, because all of these chiefs were either pro-American or neutral.

The little army reached Silver Heel's village December 17. Although Campbell could have infiltrated the village without detection because of the severe weather, he attacked instead. Eight warriors were killed and as many escaped, while forty-two men, women, and children were made prisoner. Every one of them was of the Delaware tribe, which was allied with the United States. The troops destroyed all winter provisions, which proved a serious error because their own army had few supplies. Campbell then moved down the river and burned two more villages, including Metocina's at the mouth of Jocinah Creek, where the Miamis fought bravely from behind their breastworks.

Finally, Campbell retreated to encamp on the river near Silver Heels's village. He was attacked before daybreak on December 18 by the aroused Indians, led by François Godfroy (usually written "Francis" by this time), Joseph Richardville, and Little Thunder. Campbell lost 10 men killed and 48 wounded in the attack, which the Miamis pressed hotly. He was convinced he could not reach his major objective, Osage Town. Burdened with prisoners and wounded, hampered by bad weather, and believing Tecumseh and a large force of warriors to be close at hand, he retreated as rapidly as his troops could travel. Actually, his retreat was harassed by fewer than 200 Miami warriors, but his decision to withdraw was the correct one to make for 303 of his men, unfit for duty because of frostbite and wounds, were later carried into Greenville by a rescue party.[57]

While Campbell's campaign was justifiable on military grounds, it proved to be an unfortunate act. The Miamis never accepted its necessity, contending they had withdrawn from the theater of war to remain neutral. Earlier defeats were accepted as the fortunes of war, whereas the Mississinewa attack seemed to them an unprovoked destruction of neutral and defenseless villages filled with noncombatants—an early Sand Creek Massacre.

When Colonel Richard M. Johnson, future vice president of the United States, proposed a more ambitious expedition through the Indian country from Fort Wayne to Lake Michigan and the Illinois River, Harrison opposed his plan. The General described the winter habits of the Indians:

---

[57] Harrison, Franklinton, to Colonel John B. Campbell, November 25, 1812; Campbell, Mississinewa River, to Harrison, December 18, 1812; Campbell, Greene Ville, to Harrison, December 25, 1812, in Esarey, *Messages and Letters,* II, 228–31, 248–49, 253–65, give Harrison's orders and Campbell's preliminary and final reports of the expedition. Murray Holiday, "The Battle of the Mississinewa, 1812," a pamphlet of the Grant County (Indiana) Historical Society, is an excellent account of Campbell's expedition.

I am sorry not to be able to agree with my friend, Colonel Johnson, upon the propriety of the contemplated mounted expedition. An expedition of this kind directed against a particular town will probably succeed. The Indian towns cannot be surprised in succession, as they give the alarm from one to the other with more rapidity than our troops can move. In the months of February, March and April, the towns are all abandoned. The men are hunting, and the women and children, particularly to the north of the Wabash, are scattered about making sugar. The corn is in that season universally hid in small parcels in the earth, and could not be found. There are no considerable villages in that direction. Those that are there are composed of bark huts which the Indians do not care for, and which during the winter are entirely empty. The detachment might pass through the whole extent of country to be escoured, without seeing an Indian, except at the first town they struck, and it is more than probable that they would find it empty. But the expedition is impracticable to the extent proposed. The horses, if not the men, would perish. The horses that are now to to be found, are not like those of the early settlers, and such as the Indians and traders now have. They have been accustomed to corn, and must have it. Colonel Campbell went but 70 or 80 miles from the frontiers, and the greater part of his horses could scarcely be brought in. Such an expedition in the summer and fall would be highly advantageous, because the Indians are then at their towns, and their corn can be destroyed. An attack upon a particular town in the winter, when the inhabitants are at it as we know they are at Mississineway, and which is so near as to enable the detachment to reach it without killing their horses, is not only practicable, but if there is snow on the ground is perhaps the most favorable.[58]

The series of losses which Harrison inflicted on the Indians in Indiana and Ohio caused many bands to retreat to Detroit and Michigan. However, they carried a defeatist sentiment to the northern tribes, such as the Chippewas, and led them to second thoughts of British ability to protect their allies south of the Great Lakes.

---

[58] Lossing, *Pictorial Field-Book,* 494–95. James Monroe, Acting Secretary of War, to Harrison, December 26, 1812, in Esarey, *Messages and Letters,* II, 265–69. Harrison, Franklinton, to Monroe, January 6, 1813, in *ibid.,* 299–307, discusses his campaign plans and contains the quoted passage.

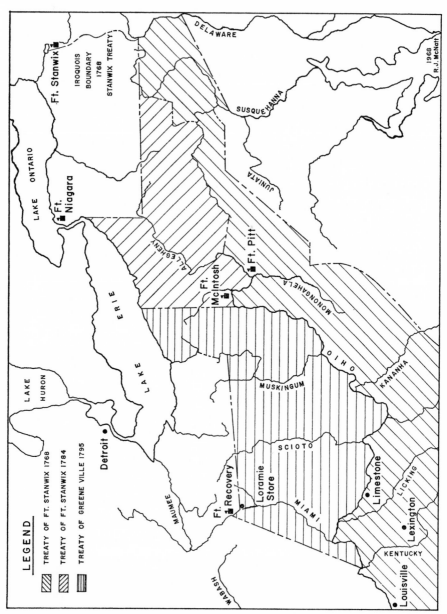

American campaigns into Miami lands, 1811–1813.

Anti-American sentiment rose in the spring of 1813 when Harrison's forces suffered a series of losses in Michigan Territory.[59] The General countered with a council of his allies at his Franklinton headquarters, near present-day Columbus, in June. He persuaded the Delawares, Shawnees, Senecas, and part of the Wyandots to remain pro-American, and for the first time he began to use Indian auxiliary forces from these tribes.

Before starting his major offensive to recover Detroit, Harrison sent Colonel William Russell to make sure his Wabash flank was secure. Russell marched from Vallonia, Indiana, to the Delaware towns on the White River and destroyed all of the Mississinewa villages, including those which had been rebuilt since Campbell's invasion. He followed the Wabash and made sure no Indian forces were gathered near by. His six hundred troops encountered no opposition on their month-long march to Vincennes, and Harrison was reassured.[60]

Planning to move against Detroit by water, Harrison embarked his army at Fort Meigs on September 24, 1813. Although he had 260 Wyandots, Senecas, and Shawnees under Black Hoof, no Miami warriors joined the expedition. A few Miamis, however, remained with Tecumseh, who had finally collected a force of 2,500 Indians.

The British army retreated from Detroit on September 27, but before Harrison began his pursuit, he secured an armistice with the neighboring tribes. On October 5, the British made their stand on the Thames River, and in the ensuing battle, they were defeated and Tecumseh killed.[61] After the American triumph, the tribes gathered at Detroit, admitted their error in believing British promises of victory, and offered to give at least token military aid to the victors. Seven tribes, led by the Chippewas and Ottawas and including the Kekionga, Wea, and Eel River Miamis, agreed to

[59] Lossing, *Pictorial Field-Book,* 477–78, 486–89, 545.
[60] Colonel William Russell, Vincennes, to Governor Thomas Posey, July 25, 1813, in Esarey, *Messages and Letters,* II, 497–99.
[61] Harrison, Detroit, to Secretary Armstrong, October 9, 1813, in *ibid.,* 558–65, is the official report of the battle. Lossing, *Pictorial Field-Book,* 545–57.

send their prisoners to Fort Wayne and to leave hostages with the Americans.[62]

Harrison's army, weakened by the departure of a large number of Kentucky and Ohio militiamen whose terms of enlistment had expired, was forced to occupy a defensive position until 1814 while the frontier war continued on the eastern Great Lakes. Fortunately, the final acts of the war occurred in Europe, and for all practical purposes, the campaigns in the Northwest ended in 1813, although there were a few engagements at the northern forts on the upper Great Lakes.

Harrison resigned his command May 11, 1814, after securing the Indians' promise to attend a general council at Greenville in July. With Lewis Cass, newly appointed governor of Michigan Territory, he completed a council at Greenville on July 22. About four thousand Indians, who had fought on both sides in the conflict, attended. Among them were the Miamis, the Eel River bands, the Weas, and portions of the Potawatomi, Ottawa, and Kickapoo tribes. The warriors again agreed to join the American forces if hostilities were resumed, but the Treaty of Ghent ended the war on December 24, 1814, and made this unnecessary.

Charley, the Eel River Miami chief, and Pacanne spoke for the Miamis at Greenville. They very properly objected to assuming any guilt for the actions of a few Miami warriors who fought against the Americans. Cass and Harrison refused to accept this and accused the tribe of duplicity, which they contended could be atoned only by the Miamis' agreeing to fight against the British. Only two Miami subchiefs refused to sign the treaty with 113 chiefs of other tribes.[63] The number itself was significant, for American commissioners, no longer relying upon a few chiefs' ability to control dissident warriors, secured the signatures of nearly every fam-

[62] Harrison, Detroit, to Secretary of War Armstrong, October 10, 1813, in Esarey, *Messages and Letters*, II, 573–75. The terms of the armistice are in *ibid.*, 577–79. Pacanne, Osage, and Wankema signed for the "Miamis," Kitunga (Charley) for the Eel River band, and Newa Shosa (Stone Eater) and Papahonga (Lapousier) for the Weas. Jean Baptiste Richardville signed with the Potawatomi chiefs.

[63] Kappler, *Indian Affairs*, I, 76. The "Council Journal" of Commissioners Harrison and Lewis Cass is in *American State Papers*, Class II, *Indian Affairs*, II, 828–36.

ily head to the terms of the treaty. Harrison obviously wanted to prevent another uprising.

The Miamis had made mistakes during the war, the primary one being their claim of neutrality, from which they hoped to achieve some measure of safety through either British or American protection. They were trapped in a position in which they were eventually regarded as a threat by Harrison. Another mistake was their failure to understand the significance to themselves of their buffer tribes' (the Wyandots, Shawnees, and Delawares) loyalty to the Americans. Without these and unwilling to accept the alternative—a retreat to the Potawatomi, Kickapoo, and Winnebago country—they exposed their lands to American forces.

Had they lived, Little Turtle or Wells might have persuaded the Miamis to accept an American alliance as the best of the alternatives which faced them. Even though they accepted Harrison's accusation at Greenville—that they had been guilty of sending war messages to the Delawares in 1812 when he destroyed their villages near Fort Wayne—they believed Campbell's raid on their towns after they had rejected Tecumseh's overtures and had assumed a noncombatant position were unjustified. Harrison had distrusted the tribe's motives for twenty years; he was now determined to secure their submission in 1814.

The second Greenville council marked the end of Miami military power and influence on the frontier. This was accomplished less by the agreements made at the council than by inexorable events of American expansion westward and by changes within the tribe. Harold E. Driver correctly considers that the very heart of Indian culture was its warlike orientation. Any loss of the warrior function of the males led to inevitable disintegration of Indian society, while no other way of life was yet accepted as a substitute.[64] Various Indian agents to the Miamis, and even Little Turtle, had made many attempts to direct the tribe to the white man's rural culture. The aid given by Quakers through Philip Dennis and William Kirk from 1804 to 1808 was a noteworthy effort. Nonetheless, it

[64] Driver, *Indians of North America*, 370–73.

was only one attempt and it accomplished little toward the goal of developing self-sustaining agricultural laborers among the Miamis. At the same time, their occupation with the fur trade made it possible for Miami warriors to retain some semblance of their former life, with its warrior code, but without any possibility of warfare.

After the war, a new generation of chiefs was elevated to office. The tribe needed brilliant leadership, for although it was no longer on the military frontier, it was now confronted with a more disruptive situation: the white civilian frontier.

6
THE TREATY YEARS, 1814-1840

The final years of Miami residence in Indiana are those best known to history. The new settlers who visited the Miamis' villages and witnessed their annuity payments not only became personally acquainted with them, but also contributed to stereotyping them in local Indiana history and folklore. Consequently, the result is a distorted and often ludicrous mass of information, neither flattering to the Indians nor often creditable to their white neighbors. This is unfortunate because this period of partial emigration to the west was the most complex, crucial, and interesting period in the tribe's long history, replete as it was with disintegration of political unity and cultural stability.

The War of 1812 ended the threat of British pretentions to regain the territory northwest of the Ohio River or to control its natives and its fur trade. The Wabash-Maumee ceased to be the frontier barrier behind which unknown numbers of tribes blocked American expansion. More important, since the Miamis could no longer formulate cohesive resistance among their allies and lead them in border warfare, they ceased to be a military or diplomatic threat.

After the war, the Miamis were significant only because of their acknowledged ownership of a large area of land which was vitally

177

important to white expansion. They were revealed as a small tribe from which a few bands were even then seceding and whose more numerous neighbors, especially the Delawares and Shawnees, were even more helpless before the waves of white immigration. The greatest tribute to Miami adaptability and acumen must be the admission that in such circumstances they were able to maintain some of their political and cultural unity and identity and to secure from their white conquerors an unusual amount of financial security, as well as some degree of harmonious rapport. In 1814, the Miamis were not only required to admit military defeat, but were also forced to seek replacements for their principal leaders, Little Turtle and Pacanne, who had died.

Pacanne died soon after signing his last treaty in 1814. His successor was his nephew, Jean Baptiste Richardville, or Peshewah (The Wildcat), whose mother, Tacumwah, had exerted great influence in the tribe for many years.[1] No war chief could match Little Turtle's stature after the War of 1812. Several warriors had distinguished themselves during the preceding decade, but the office had become an anachronism. Shapoconah, or Deaf Man, who died in 1833, had some claim to the office, but it was an empty honor and as he grew old, he retired to a Mississinewa farm. Francis Godfroy, or Palonzwah, was elected his successor about 1830, but his influence was due to his wealth, personal qualities, and rapport with Richardville rather than to the prestige of his office.[2] Although their tactics eventually caused many of the problems which have been peculiar to the tribe, both Richardville and Godfroy were masters at meeting the land cession and emigration demands of the federal government. The means they used to exert their authority were different from those of Pied Froid, Le Gris, Little Turtle, or Pacanne; without intermittent wars and without Indian alliances,

[1] Brice, *History of Fort Wayne,* 314–15n., furnishes the most familiar story of Richardville's election in an account originally told by the Chief to Allen Hamilton. *John Tipton Papers,* I, 323n.

[2] *John Tipton Papers,* I, 446–47n. Godfroy's exploits during the Battle of the Mississinewa secured his election in 1830 to succeed Shapoconah, or Deaf Man, who was inactive for years before his death. *The Journal and Indian Paintings of George Winter,* 162.

these new chiefs encountered new problems and were forced to adopt new tactics to cope with them.

The customary and often repeated summary of this period can be given briefly: the helpless Miamis were morally debauched at the annual payments, degraded socially by their intolerant exclusion from the civilization which supplanted them, and rendered politically unstable by treaty agreements with the federal government which were to be effective "in perpetuity" but which usually lasted less than ten years. Finally, they were driven west after every possible financial recourse had been extorted from them. In short, the stereotyped judgment was that a naïve and ignorant people was destroyed by every conceivable means, both ethical and unethical.[3]

The process by which all this was accomplished was much more complex, less one sided, and vastly more significant than this simple indictment. Obviously, the second Greenville council made only a temporary agreement; the Indians' postwar penance was performed at the Treaty of St. Mary's, Ohio, in 1818. An American land grab, it went far beyond the five previous Miami treaties in its scope and implications, and all subsequent Miami agreements were designed to complete its purposes. The federal commissioners were Governor Lewis Cass of Michigan Territory and Governor Jonathan Jennings and Judge Benjamin Parke, both of Indiana. The Miami and Wea bands, plus the Wyandots, Senecas, Shawnees, Ottawas, Delawares, and Potawatomis, participated in the talks. The central third of Indiana, a portion of northwestern Ohio, and fractions of Michigan and Illinois were ceded in treaties completed between September 7 and October 6. Although a treaty with the Delawares on October 3 included that tribe's agreement to emigrate to the west by 1821, the most important of all the treaties was that made with the Miamis on October 6.

[3] John B. Dillon, "The National Decline of the Miami Indians," *Indiana Historical Society Publications,* I (1897), 4, 121–43, is the most factual but eloquent indictment of American treatment of the Miamis. It was delivered first as a lecture in 1848. George Dewey Harmon, *Sixty Years of Indian Affairs,* 181, quotes the devastating charges made by the Senate Committee on Indian Affairs to the Thirty-third Congress.

The Miami negotiations reflected the schism of the Wea and Piankeshaw bands: they ceded all but one small reservation on the Wabash in separate treaties on January 9 and October 2, 1818. The villages on the Wabash near Logansport, which had served as the connecting link between the Weas and the upper Wabash bands, now became more closely allied to the villages about Fort Wayne. Although the Miamis on the Mississinewa remained an integral part of the tribe, their previous history had been distinctive and they had become the conservative element in tribal councils. They were composed for the most part of descendents from the eastern villages on the Great and Little Miami rivers of Ohio and had been somewhat secluded from contacts with the traders on the Wabash. They had made fewer marriage alliances with traders and had been in close contact with Delaware, Wyandot, and Shawnee bands for a century. These contacts, added to their anger at the invasions by Campbell and Russell, made this portion of the tribe conservative in the sense that they avoided involvements with whites as much as possible. They remained semi-isolated, which the Wabash villagers were unable to do.

More significant, the Miamis relinquished all of Tract 99 on Royce's map of Indiana, with the exception of six reservations, while 21 tracts totaling 49 sections, or 31,460 acres, were granted to Miami individuals. The Miamis ceded the major part of their tribal lands, which prepared the way for American occupation of the central third of Indiana. The reservations included the tribe's historic sites along the Wabash and its tributaries, which were still occupied, and its traditional winter grounds south of the Wabash River. The Big Miami Reserve and the Thorntown Reserve became the last areas of tribal community ownership. Because the nature of Indian tribal land ownership prohibited any one Indian the right to sole ownership of a portion of those lands and necessitated the consent of the tribal council before land could be alienated, the commissioners, in order to make alienation less difficult, established village land ownership.

The individual land grants illustrate the degree to which the

Miamis had intermarried with the whites. Creating individual reservations, which at first went only to Miamis of mixed ancestry, was a tribal concession to the "white land hunger" of such persons. The grants, or "Indian patents," could not be transferred without the approval of the President of the United States. The fourth and final departure from tribal ownership was made in Richardville's favor. The new chief received seven sections of land with fee simple patent or title, the symbol of freedom of the American landholder.

For its share of this cession of approximately 7,036,000 acres of land, the tribe was promised a perpetual annuity of $15,000, 160 bushels of salt, two water mills, and the services of a blacksmith and a gunsmith. These terms became the bases for future claims by the Miamis that the federal government failed to honor its fiduciary responsibilities to an Indian tribe which was its ward.

Of the land which the federal government had formerly acknowledged belonged solely to the Miamis, only reservations on the Maumee, St. Mary's, Wabash, and Mississinewa rivers remained in their possession. The commissioners were satisfied that the central third of Indiana was large enough to satisfy the needs of the land-hungry settlers, while the Miamis were forced to be content with a large annuity and a temporary respite from the threat of a forced emigration to the west.[4]

Although the St. Mary's treaty was a decisive factor in Miami history, less obvious events made contributions to these years of change. Among them was the withdrawal of federal troops from Fort Wayne in 1819. The fort had been burned during the siege of 1812 and was not rebuilt. The government factory had also burned, and although the system was not abolished until 1822,

---

[4] Kappler, *Indian Affairs*, II, 119–21. Royce, *Indian Land Cessions*, 688–89, 692–95. In 1954, the Indian Claims Commission decided the Miamis held undisputed title to 4,291,500 acres of the land ceded in Tract 99 in Royce, plus a half-interest with the Delawares in 3,859,000 acres, and the Weas had undisputed title to 815,000 acres. The six reservations were in ten plats numbered 142, 196, 197, 198, 251, 252, 253, 254, 256, and 258 on Royce's map. *Appeal No. 2–58*, U.S. Court of Claims, decided July 13, 1959.

private fur-company traders flourished at Fort Wayne without opposition after 1816.

The most insidious effects upon the tribe resulted from the government's placing the Indian agency at Fort Wayne. Annuity money replaced furs as the basis of Indian trade there. The payments were large, and the little village, which contained only fourteen white families in 1814, soon eclipsed Piqua, Greenville, and St. Mary's, Ohio, as the center of trade. The change in commerce began with the treaty signed at the foot of the Maumee Rapids on September 29, 1817, by which the federal government acquired the land between the Maumee and St. Mary's rivers from the Wyandots, Ottawas, and four other northwestern Ohio tribes. Trade increased after the St. Mary's treaties the following year. Fort Wayne became a major payment center where thousands of Indians received silver dollar and half-dollar coins, rather than questionable paper money, and where traders of all kinds gathered to separate the Indians from their money.[5]

The annual payment meetings were almost universally condemned by Indians and whites alike. After a few days of riotous behavior at Fort Wayne, the village tried to forget the events that had occurred. The debauching of the Indians can be traced in reports of drunkenness and murders, which certainly involved the Miami women more than ever.

The payments became the worst possible form of contact between the races. After a trip to Chicago, where he witnessed the Treaty of 1833, a huge gathering of thousands of Indians, traders, and spectators, Charles Joseph Latrobe wrote a description of Indian and white activities which was circulated nationally. John B. Dillon's essay "The National Decline of the Miami Indians" is based on this theme, as are several of Charles Cist's articles in *The Cincinnati Miscellany* and Jacob Burnett's articles in his *Notes on the*

[5] Dillon, "The National Decline," 137–40, cites Agent Benjamin F. Stickney's pungent and perceptive observations on the Fort Wayne post. John Tipton characterized the worst of the irregular traders—"the low vulgar clowns that infest groceries and Indian payments are unsafe company for young men"—in a letter to his son, Spear, in *John Tipton Papers,* II, 789. Royce, *Indian Land Cessions,* 684–89.

Early Settlement of the Northwestern Territory.[6] The payment system shattered the stereotype of the idealized or romanticized "savage but noble warrior" and gave impetus to the exponents of a "separation" system of some form which would remove the Indians from contact with the whites, preferably in an autonomous state west of the Mississippi River. During the 1820's and 1830's, the annual payments gave emotional color to every aspect of Indian affairs.

Because of national publicity, the Miamis for a time became the focal point for the conflicting views of men who sought a final solution to the Indian question. By 1818, they were the northeasternmost tribal unit confronting white expansion because the eastern tribes had been exterminated, absorbed into white communities, retired into cultural enclaves, or removed beyond the western frontier. Most Indians recognized that white habits and customs were often harmful to themselves. However, after a century and a half, the Miamis had no intention of abandoning whatever material benefits they had received from the white man. The Indian agents at Fort Wayne; the traders, who were in constant contact with the villages; and the white settlers, now discovered by hunting parties on every creek or river, became constant influences on Miami life through almost daily contacts.

The Miami lands were placed in the jurisdiction of the governor of Michigan Territory because Detroit was more accessible than Indiana's capital and because the governor of the new state of Indiana was not a federal official. Lewis Cass served as governor

[6] Isaac McCoy, *History of the Baptist Indian Missions*, gives the best eyewitness accounts of Fort Wayne from 1818 to 1821. By 1819, McCoy concluded that the Miamis could no longer be saved if they remained in Indiana. Peter LaFontaine told Thomas S. Teas in 1821 that nearly thirty Miamis were killed at the recent payment. Thomas Scattergood Teas, "Journal of a Tour to Fort Wayne and the Adjacent Country in 1821," in Harlow Lindley, *Indiana As Seen by Early Travelers*, 246–55. Charles Joseph Latrobe, *The Rambler in North America, 1832–1833*, II, contains descriptions of the Chicago treaties of 1833. Charles Cist, *The Cincinnati Miscellany*, also includes ten "Recollections" by John Johnston, trader and Indian agent at Fort Wayne and Perrysburg, Ohio. Jacob Burnett, *Notes on the Early Settlement of the Northwestern Territory*, 383–93. Quaife, *Chicago and the Old Northwest*, 348–67, is a factual account of the Chicago treaty which contrasts with emotional observations.

183

of Michigan Territory and superintendent of Indian affairs in the Northwest Territory from 1813 to 1831. It was a time of reorganization in federal Indian affairs, and Cass, with William Clark, superintendent of Indian affairs at St. Louis, played an important part in formulating policies. Cass and Clark have been called the most capable and successful of all Indian superintendents.

An act of 1818 provided that all agents be nominated by the President, with approval by the Senate. In 1824, the Bureau of Indian Affairs was established, and in 1832, the office of commissioner was created at the head of the bureau. Through these changes, Indian affairs remained, as before, under the direction of the secretary of war, an office which Cass held from 1831 to 1836. An act of June 30, 1834, specifically authorized certain superintendencies and agencies and was the basic statement of federal policy until the end of the treaty system in 1871.[7]

Cass was a federal commissioner at the Miami treaties in 1814, 1818, and 1826 and appointed the commissioners who negotiated the treaty of 1834. The Governor, whose interest in the anthropological and linguistic characteristics of the Indians had been aroused earlier, visited Fort Wayne in 1822 to study the Miamis and sent C. C. Trowbridge there in 1824 and 1825 to gather more information about the tribe. Consequently, his interest in the Indians went far beyond treaty making and the acquisition of land and contributed firsthand information to future scholars.[8]

[7] Schmeckebier, *Office of Indian Affairs*, 27–28. Francis Paul Prucha, "Lewis Cass and American Indian Policy," a Wayne State University publication for the Detroit Historical Society, 1967.

[8] W. Vernon Kinietz (ed.), *Meearmeear Traditions, by C. C. Trowbridge*, was compiled from information given by Richardville and Le Gros. The editor relies on earlier accounts from the French in his later studies of the Miamis. Cass's most important contribution to anthropology was *Inquiries Respecting the History, Traditions, Languages, Manners, Customs, Religion, etc., of the Indians Living Within the United States*. Robert W. Unger, "Lewis Cass: Indian Superintendent of the Michigan Territory, 1813–1831," unpublished Ph.D. dissertation, Ball State University, 1967, is an excellent study of Cass's work with the Indians. Much of Clark's policy is in Clark, St. Louis, to Secretary of War Barbour, December 6, 1825, and March 1, 1826, in U.S. Bureau of Indian Affairs, Letters Received, 1824–1881, St. Louis Superintendency, Microcopy K70, Part 2 (cited hereafter as Microcopy K70, followed by part number). His mature conclusions are in "Report of the Secretary of the Interior," *House Executive Documents*, 13 Cong., 5 sess., II, 134–40.

Benjamin F. Stickney was appointed agent at Fort Wayne in 1812 and served intermittently until 1821. A keen and satiric observer, he is best remembered for his tongue-in-cheek advice to Secretary of War William H. Crawford.

> . . . it is much cheaper reducing them by meat and bread than by the force of army. And from the observations I have had the opportunity of making, that 3 or 4 months full feeding on meat and bread, even without ardent spirits, will bring on disease and in 6 or 8 months great mortality. And could it be considered a proper mode of warfare I believe more indians might be killed with the expence of $100,000 in this way: than one million expended in the support of armies to go against them. . . . [9]

A congressional act combined the agencies at Piqua and Fort Wayne under John Johnston in 1818. Cass decided the duties at the latter village required a subagent, and Dr. William Turner, William Wells's son-in-law, was appointed—against the wishes of the Governor. Turner was removed for "unsatisfactory conduct" in 1820 and was succeeded by John Hays. Stickney served at the subagency during Hays's absence in 1820, but the new agent's health deteriorated under the rigors of the Fort Wayne climate and the strain of the duties of his position. The latter expanded after the treaties of 1818 with the increase in the number of Indian traders, primarily from the American Fur Company, and Hays resigned in 1823.[10]

The most important figure in the Indian affairs of Indiana for many years was John Tipton, who succeeded Hays at Fort Wayne. Because his comprehension of the obstacles facing the traders and settlers was modified by an understanding of the Indians' problems, he showed sympathy to and exerted great influences among both the tribes and the settlers. Tipton did not attempt the impossible,

[9] Benjamin F. Stickney, Fort Wayne, to Secretary of War William H. Crawford, October 1, 1815, in *American State Papers*, Class II, *Indian Affairs*, II, 84–86. Stickney also discussed the inherent conflicts between agents and military commandants in a letter published in Thornbrough, *Letterbook*, 230–41.

[10] Nellie A. Robertson, "John Hays and the Fort Wayne Indian Agency," *Indiana Magazine of History*, XXXIX, 3 (September, 1933), 221–36.

yet he protected the Indians to the best of his abilities. His influence among them was not confined to rapport with the chiefs; he was equally aware of the lot of the less important members of the tribe. Tipton moved the agency to Logansport in 1828 in order to limit white traders' access at annuity time. The site, at the mouth of the Eel River, was well suited to the purpose, being more accessible to the Potawatomi and the Mississinewa villages than Fort Wayne.[11]

The relocation of the agency ended Fort Wayne's importance to the tribe. The Miami on the Eel, Little Wabash, and Mississinewa soon swelled Osage Town, where Godfroy's store had a monopoly, and Fort Wayne traders moved to the new villages of Peru, Wabash, and Huntington.[12]

The white men among the Miamis were of all types, but contrary to popular belief, the regular traders licensed to travel among the villages were usually benefactors to the tribe. The Indians understood and depended upon them and requested specific men for their villages. While individual traders differed, many of them married into the tribe, sent their children to the best schools available, and later, with their families, emigrated west with the Indians. Some men of means financed traders who lived in the winter hunting camps, but were themselves prepared to turn their activities to other fields as fur-bearing animals and the Indians became minor sources of income.

The most questionable traders were those who made surreptitious sales to the Indians. They included men who were willing to sell anything to the Indians for money; the staple article, of course, was whisky. Most settlers had a supply, made when their corn crop was converted into marketable spirits, and the Indians knew it. Such traders, unlicensed, were barred from the payment grounds, but they haunted the Indians' trails. Soldiers, agents, and county sheriffs could not eradicate their activities.[13]

[11] Paul Wallace Gates, "Introduction, *John Tipton Papers,* I, 3–53.
[12] *Ibid.,* 19–22.
[13] Lasselle, "Old Indian Traders," 1–13. Anson, "The Fur Traders," 62–70, 77–85.

The "degradation" of the Miamis was usually misunderstood and depended upon each observer's interpretation of the word. To some, Chief Richardville's half-French ancestry was a mark of distinction, but to others it held the opposite meaning. The lithographic portraits J. O. Lewis made at the Miami treaty of 1826 show that his subjects had adopted white dress to varying degrees. To some observers, this is an indication of degeneracy; to others, of advancement. To still other people, the decline in the number of individuals of unmixed Miami ancestry was the surest sign the tribe was doomed, while a few thought improvement in the tribe was in direct proportion to the number of people of mixed ancestry. Were the Richardville and Godfroy families, who had adopted white customs and habits, degenerated or enlightened? Assimilation and acculturation are gradual processes, and even the white people who had frequent contact with the Miamis differed in their opinions on the subject. Many Indians who adopted white dress and customs became the cause of growing disunity between various Miami bands. Allen Hamilton, former subagent to the tribe, testified in 1854:

> To the question, "Was their right to receive their annuities ever disputed by any portion of the tribe?" the deponent gave the answer, "I heard some of the chiefs making an objection to their receiving it; but not on account of their not being Miamis, but because they did not live among the tribe, and that they dressed like whites; . . ."[14]

The Miamis, living under a changing and contradictory code, acted in ways which provide ample illustration that tribal morale was nearly destroyed. The Miamis' contact with the whites had existed on the basis of Indian superiority, or at least equality, for a century and a quarter; now they were rejected and made to feel they were to hold an inferior status. In their own land, they had

---

[14] "Letter From the Secretary of the Interior," *House Executive Document 23*, 49 Cong., 1 sess., IV, 3–17, includes a report from the commissioner of Indian affairs containing affidavits from Meshingomesia and other Miamis in 1855 that the Miamis felt adoption of "white" clothing and customs marked abandonment or desertion of the tribe. This attitude was demonstrated decisively at the 1834 treaty. *Ibid.*, 9.

ceased to be sovereigns and had become undesirables facing certain exile.

Stickney's prediction of Miami dissolution is not at all cynical when individual cases are studied. Old Peter Lafontaine told Thomas Scattergood Teas in 1821 that thirty Miamis had been killed in drunken brawls during the preceding month.[15] One of Fort Wayne's most famous early trials was that of Big Leg, or Neweling-wa, for the murder of his female slave. The community was accustomed to such events at the early payments, but his action took place in a quieter time in 1830. Allen County officials assumed jurisdiction in the case, tried the chief, and sentenced him to hang. He was pardoned by the governor, emigrated to Kansas in 1846, and later served as principal chief of the tribe in the west.[16] Nathaniel West, federal commissioner to investigate claims against the Miamis in 1838, said about sixty Miamis died in drunken brawls during 1838 alone.[17] Jane Slocum, younger daughter of Frances Slocum and Deaf Man, was widowed three times before she was twenty-five. Her grief was slight, for all had been "bad" Indians who could not resist the lure of whisky.[18]

The problem became even more complex when more treaties, with larger payments, were made; when Indian customs and activities became even more curtailed; and when thousands of whites began moving into the Wabash country each year. The treaties were the significant factor. Since they were products of the council, the chiefs, especially Richardville, became more important than ever, and their treaty arrangements seemed to highlight each downward step in the tribe's career.

Richardville was not a warrior, though he may have fought in

---

[15] Teas, "Journal of a Tour," 246–55.

[16] Brice, *History of Fort Wayne,* 300–302. Big Leg did not grasp the idea of execution by hanging, and his friends demonstrated the process by hanging a dog outside the jail where he could see it. He immediately demanded that he be shot instead.

[17] "Report of the Commissioner of Indian Affairs made November 25, 1838," *Senate Document I,* 25 Cong., 3 sess., I, 447. "Report of the Secretary of War," *Senate Document 164,* 26 Cong., 1 sess., IV, 2–10.

[18] Otho Winger, *The Lost Sister Among the Miamis,* 66.

raids and battles while a young man. He was a gifted politician and businessman who reached maturity while Le Gris, Pacanne, and Little Turtle led a strong nation; yet he had been trained in French and Canadian intrigue, especially by his mother.[19] As principal chief, he was the guardian of and spokesman for the tribe, a position buttressed by federal policy, which always based its relationships with the Indians upon the ability of the headmen of a tribe to control its members.

Sometime before 1818, Richardville abandoned white dress and became all Miami Indian. Some of his contemporaries thought it to be a superficial expedient to hold the loyalty of his tribe; others believed his grief over Indian conduct at treaty negotiations and annuity distributions and the decline of Miami power made his change sincere. Richardville attempted to educate his sons and grandsons at the Choctaw Academy in Kentucky, but none of the chief's sons seemed to possess the attributes of leadership needed by the tribe, although Isaac McCoy had a high regard for the oldest, Joseph Richardville.[20] Even though the Chief eventually ceased to use the English and French languages and wear white clothing, he retained the admiration of opponents for his business acumen. Despite his use of his office as chief to secure wealth—and he was reputedly the richest man in Indiana before his death—it is con-

[19] Tacumwah is usually described as a sister of Little Turtle, but she lived in the village of Pacanne, earlier described as the new chief's "uncle" (see Chapter 1 concerning the confusing kinship system of the tribe). Her first husband was Joseph Richardville, a trader who later lived in Canada, where his son, Jean Baptiste, occasionally visited him. Tacumwah then married Charles Beaubien, the most important trader at Kekionga and the operator of the portage. Josetta Beaubien Roubidoux was the only child of this marriage. After Beaubien's death, Tacumwah operated the St. Mary's-Little Wabash portage. She apparently exerted much influence on Miami policy for years. *John Tipton Papers,* I, 323n.

[20] The Choctaw Academy, sponsored by Richard M. Johnson, operated from 1825 to 1843. Its curriculum flattered the young Indian aristocrats but promoted occasional disciplinary infractions. In 1839, Richardville objected when his grandson, Lewis Cass, the child of Le Blonde Richardville, was placed in a vocational course. Shelley D. Rouse, "Colonel Dick Johnson's Choctaw Academy: A Forgotten Educational Experiment," *Ohio Archaeological and Historical Publications,* XXV (1916), 88–117. Gates, Introduction, *John Tipton Papers,* I, 22–44, shows the efforts made by white traders to keep the Miamis in Indiana until the tribe's resources were exploited.

ceivable that the Miamis would have been completely destroyed had they been led by a less astute man.

Francis Godfroy's career was similar to Richardville's. He fought in the War of 1812 and was later war chief, but he was primarily a merchant and the spokesman for the villages about the mouth of the Mississinewa River. The two chiefs acted in concert and thus were able to control the actions of the village chiefs who occasionally opposed them.[21]

The forces operating upon the Miamis after the Treaty of St. Mary's in 1818 can be summarized briefly. As the penalty for their real or imagined part in the late war, the Miamis ceded a large area of land to the federal government. They retained one large reserve and many smaller ones which might have been sufficient for individuals to continue some semblance of their former way of life were it not that each band was separated from all others. By collecting in groups, the villagers were also unable to disperse among the white settlers and achieve assimilation.

The Miamis tried to observe the terms of the treaty of 1818. They fished, farmed, and hunted, encouraged in the last, of course, by the fur traders. Some found the annual payments made even these activities unnecessary. These Miamis, discovering that they could secure credit with some traders, saw their charge accounts with these men grow large. They spent their annuities in debauches and needed credit to purchase necessities for the ensuing year. Both Richardville and Godfroy operated their own trading posts in an effort to exert some control over the credit system. Richardville finally moved his store and the tribal council house to the Forks of the Wabash and secured the land around the site so that he could limit trade to men of whom he approved.

The influx of settlers speeded demands for Miami emigration. Memorials to the state assembly urging such action contain some sincere concern for the welfare of the Indians, but they were about equally motivated by racial and cultural bigotry and by plans to

[21] Tipton to Governor Lewis Cass, October 6, 1829, and to Secretary of War J. H. Eaton, February 15, 1830, in *John Tipton Papers,* II, 209–10, 250–51.

secure Miami lands. Richardville, having long fought for delay and concessions, finally conceded in 1838 that the tribe would consider the idea of emigration and in 1840 decided that while some individuals of his tribe could retain some land in the state, others would have to emigrate, with the hope they could survive when removed from white contact.

Indiana's population of approximately 65,000 in 1816 rose to 147,000 in 1820 and 343,000 in 1830. These settlers demanded transportation routes over which to move their products to market, so federal support was sought for a highway from the Ohio River through the new state capital, Indianapolis, north to Lake Michigan. The frontiersmen looked to the day when the navigable portions of the Wabash and Maumee were connected. In later treaties, the Indians were persuaded to donate land for both routes (actually, the federal government secured the cession and donated the land in the name of the Miami tribe). All Miami treaties after 1818 ostensibly were made to secure land for transportation routes required by the influx of settlers.

The Weas ceded their reservation on the Wabash at the mouth of Sugar Creek on August 11, 1820, finally completing their separation from the Miami tribe. The next year, the Potawatomis, Ottawas, and Chippewas ceded the eastern half of a narrow strip across the northern boundary of Indiana. More important to the Miamis, the Potawatomis also sold their lands adjacent to the Wabash and Maumee rivers, a wedge-shaped tract extending from the Tippecanoe River east to the state of Ohio. It was the area into which the Potawatomis had filtered during the previous century but in which there were still a few scattered Miami villages.[22]

The 1826 negotiations were held at the mouth of the Mississinewa River, where the Miamis concluded their own treaty on October 23. It was made primarily to protect their villages north of

[22] *Stat. L., VII, 209.* The Weas ceded Indiana Tract 114 on Royce's map. Royce, *Indian Land Cessions,* 700–701; 716–17. The Weas then moved, with the Piankeshaws, to Illinois and Missouri and in 1832 to a reservation in Kansas. Both bands joined the new United Peoria and Kaskaskia tribe in 1854, then moved to the new Quapaw Agency in northeastern Indian Territory in 1868.

the Wabash and to alienate any claims they still retained to the area ceded by the Potawatomis. It also affirmed the tribe's satisfaction with the terms by which it had ceded its land in the Treaty of St. Mary's. The latter clause seems somewhat futile in view of the suits the Miamis have taken to the Indian Claims Commission since 1946.

The new treaty created three reservations at existing Miami villages north of Eel River. These were surrounded by land still held by the Potawatomis. Two village reservations were created between the Wabash and Eel rivers in the area acquired by the federal government. One other reservation at the Forks of the Wabash was north of that river. There were 92 sections, or 59,880 acres, in all. The Miamis also reserved for or made individual grants to twenty persons, nearly all of mixed ancestry, of 13,280 acres, or more than 19 sections of land, to be held by Indian title. These were located both north and south of the Wabash.

Although some semblance of tribal possession in common was fostered by the individual village reservations, they were in reality a new challenge to that concept. These enclaves were reduced in area and limited the Miamis' access from one village to another. Moreover, the old concept of tribal ownership was destroyed when the Miamis finally approved individual land ownership, even though Indian title was granted to only a few fullblood members of the tribe.

The prolonged treaty sessions, for no Indian wished to see these occasions made brief, saw the federal government give $31,040.53 in goods and supplies, and $26,259.47 in trade was promised for the next summer. An annuity of $35,000, with $10,000 to be paid in goods, was designated for 1827 and another of $30,000, of which $5,000 was in goods, for 1828, after which a permanent annuity of $25,000 was offered; the latter annuity superseded those of the earlier treaties. The usual minor items were promised to the chiefs as an inducement to sign the treaty: wagons and oxen to eight chiefs; houses not to exceed $600 in cost to nine chiefs; hogs, cattle, iron, steel, tobacco, and eight summer laborers to the village bands. An additional annuity of $2,000 was set aside for education and the care of the aged and infirm.

The Miami treaty accomplished its immediate purpose of securing lands essential for the development of new internal improvements in Indiana. It also confined the Miamis to scattered and reduced areas and seemed to prove that annuity funds were inexhaustible and that individual Indian debts could always be settled at a future treaty. It was an expensive treaty, but its cost was defended by Commissioners Cass, Tipton, and James B. Ray on the grounds they could not have secured the Potawatomi cession without the aid and approval of the Miamis.[23]

Two years later, when the Potawatomis ceded the land lying east of the proposed Lake Michigan road from Logansport to South Bend, the Miamis were finally surrounded by whites. This isolation was somewhat alleviated by the return of the Thorntown or Eel River band to the Wabash from Ten Mile Reserve, which they had received per Article 2 in the treaty of October 6, 1818. The band retroceded this reservation to the United States in August, 1828, and returned to the villages on the Five Mile Reserve at the mouth of the Eel River.[24]

Meanwhile, Richardville, who continued to reside on the St. Mary's River, began to develop the reservation at the Forks of the Wabash as the focal point of the tribe. He transferred the tribal councilhouse to the site in 1831 in order to isolate it from traders, except those the Miamis trusted, and from greedy white settlers. Even so, the impoverished whites became envious. Miami chiefs, whom they saw as the wealthy aristocrats of the frontier, and the villages' warriors, whom they saw with little need to learn the white man's life of toil because of the frequent treaty and annuity monies,

---

[23] Kappler, *Indian Affairs*, II, 199–201. Royce, *Indian Land Cessions*, 716–17. The six reservations are numbered 192, 193, 194, 195, 199, and 255 on the Indiana Detail map; the individual grants are not delineated. The Treaty Commissioners, Camped on the Wabash, to Secretary of War James Barbour, October 23, 1826, in *John Tipton Papers*, I, 598–606.

[24] Royce, *Indian Land Cessions*, 720–21. *Stat. L., VII, 307.*

aroused the settlers' financial envy and reinforced their racial antipathy.

By now, at least some of the Miamis had decided to emigrate to the west. In 1830, Tipton dissuaded two chiefs who wanted to lead a party of nearly a hundred west of the Missouri River. The agent sensibly counseled against a hasty exodus. He knew that such a party could scarcely survive without assistance and that reports of their hardships would deter the remainder of their tribe from emigration.[25]

The Mississinewa treaty of 1826 gave the Miamis only a temporary respite. Three events soon increased demands for migration by all tribes east of the Mississippi River. The first and most important was the Federal Removal Act of 1830; the second was the spectacular success of eastern canals, which led to plans for construction of a canal along the Wabash-Maumee between Huntington and Fort Wayne; the third was the anti-Indian hysteria which accompanied the Black Hawk incident in 1832.

The threat of forcible emigration had been implied in all early Indian treaties, even though most included the government's promise to preserve current tribal boundaries. The Delaware migration from Indiana in 1821 was the first instance of such a removal to fulfill a treaty provision. The Federal Removal Act of 1830, however, made Indian emigration a federal policy. There is no doubt that official policies toward the Indians were based on good intentions. Misguided, uninformed, and destructive as they were, they were not aimed at the destruction of the Indian people. Federal policies fluctuated from the goals of complete assimilation and acculturation to the opposite extreme of complete isolation through the creation of a separate Indian state. On the level of personal contact, attitudes toward the Indians ranged from the saintly practices of Isaac McCoy or Father Claude Allouez to the "dead Indian" concept of Colonel John M. Chivington. The 1830 act was an official admission that federal paternalism could not succeed while

[25] Tipton, Logansport, to Secretary of War John H. Eaton, September 13, 1830, in *John Tipton Papers*, II, 338.

the two races remained together. After 1830, every tribe went to treaty councils aware that it might be forced to agree to migrate to the west.[26]

The Wabash project depended upon the construction of a canal from the Maumee across the swampy portage to the Little Wabash and down that stream past its junction with the Wabash to Logansport. The route passed through several Miami reserves and villages, bringing hundreds of workers into contact with the Indians. Many of the former were Roman Catholics and thus reinforced small parishes largely composed of French and Indians.[27] Father Stephen Theodore Badin was missionary to these groups from 1829 to 1835, and his pungent observations on the relative habits of his French, German, Irish, and Indian parishioners are well known. He felt the new members were not an uplifting influence upon his Indian neophytes:

> I will not expatiate on the character of our Catholics. It is known that the lower class of the Irish, such as work on canals and is too fond of drinking . . . and that there are very few of the devout sex, and few children among them. . . . The Canadians are light headed, light hearted, light footed and very ignorant, having been without a pastor before I came in the backwoods, and being much inter-mixed with the Indians. . . . The Germans are of much better dispositions, as also the French from Larraine and Alsace . . . . As to the Indians, the greatest number of Christians are on the border of Michigan. . . .[28]

The Black Hawk affair crystallized the attitude that "the Indian must go" from Indiana. The Indian battle frontier was in northern

[26] President Andrew Jackson proposed the removal policy in his annual message to Congress on December 7, 1829; it was enacted in 4 Stat. L., 411. Abel, History of Events, I, 233–454, is the classic presentation of the historical background of the Indian removal policy.

[27] Buley, Old Northwest, I, 452–54; II, 51–52, 261–62. Thomas T. McAvoy, The Catholic Church in Indiana, 1789–1834, 153–78, 189–90.

[28] Quoted from a translation of Father Badin's original letter from Huntington to Reverend Purcell of Cincinnati, September 23, 1834, in the Notre Dame Archives. Badin was the first Roman Catholic priest ordained in the United States (in 1793) and one of the Church's indefatigable missionaries on the frontier. Thomas T. McAvoy, "Father Badin Comes to Notre Dame," Indiana Magazine of History, XXIX (1913), 7–16.

Illinois by 1825, and the perennial raids near the Mississippi River by both whites and Indians were nearly ignored by everyone except William Clark, superintendent of Indian affairs at St. Louis. However, Sauk Chief Black Hawk's return from west of the Mississippi with his band of Sauks, Foxes, Winnebagos, and Potawatomis in 1832 captured the American imagination. The whites of sparsely populated northern Indiana erected forts, while the wary Indians took to the woods to avoid reprisals. The incident convinced many Indians they could never be at ease among the whites and so made emigration more palatable to them.[29]

Even the distant Miamis were collected in their villages by federal agents at the beginning of the Black Hawk alarm. Agent William Marshall at Logansport believed his charges were not safe from attack in their little hunting camps. At the same time, he profited from the occasion to gain information about them by sending a Dr. Decker of Vincennes to vaccinate them against smallpox. Decker reported to Superintendent Lewis Cass that he had vaccinated seventy-nine Miamis. He found those who had no fixed residence at Logansport and proceeded to vaccinate them. Wrote the doctor:

> After which I spent one week at their villages on the Mississinewa, and after explaining the object of the Government all manifested a perfect willingness to submit . . . . The remainder of the nation could be more readily vaccinated at the Payment as they are more scattered, I therefore returned Home on the 4th Instant. . . .
>
> My inquiries respecting the Small Pox was [sic] not as satisfactory as I could have wished, my inquiries were confined to the people I met with including some of the most Intelligent, such as the sons of Rusherville who are Learned intelligent men, all of whom say it had not been amongst them for the last century or longer, but from the fact of its having raged in this place about the first settlement of the Americans

[29] Thomas B. Brown, Lafayette, to John Tipton, May 30, 1832, in *John Tipton Papers*, II, 616–17, is an example of an Indiana citizen's fear of a general Indian uprising. Prucha, *American Indian Policy*, 275–76. The Black Hawk War was only one phase of the endemic clashes on the frontier. See Bert Anson, "Variations of the Indian Conflict: The Effects of the Emigrant Indian Removal Policy, 1830–1854," *Missouri Historical Review*, LVIV, 1 (October, 1964), 64–89.

here some Fifty years since, and at which time many of the Aborigines of the country fell victims to its fury, but it may not have extended to this tribe as they resided at a greater distant then than now. The information on other and the most Prevalent diseases was more satisfactory.

The inflamatory diseases to which they are most subject is the Rheumatism, and their practice the most rational & succesful towit General and Local Bloodletting, with emetics, the bath, etc. Their Practice in Febrile diseases to which they are subject is less successful. In all my inquiries the *Buck eye* was mentioned and as the most frequent emetic they used a variety of Purgatives, and are acquainted with the tonic effect of Myny barks within their reach, but say they are too unpleasant to use. The venerial diseases appear to be general and more destructive than all others. Of simple Gohnorrhea they have a cure but it is not generally known. Of the syphilis which is most common, likely from imperfectly cured Gohnorrhea with faulty habits it is believed they have no certain cure. . . .[30]

Decker's observations seem now to indicate a primitive people whose health habits differed little from those of previous centuries. To the doctor, this was not so. The Miami curatives were interesting, and the only benefit he could add was the vaccination process.

The United States failed in its efforts to secure a Miami treaty in 1833. Three federal commissioners met at the Forks of the Wabash on October 8, but the Indians did not assemble there until October 22. Chapine, or Rivarre, Miami speaker for Richardville, was a match for both Governor George B. Porter of Michigan and the Reverend J. F. Schermerhorn, one of the most active agents in the Bureau of Indian Affairs. Schermerhorn made the government's proposals: assignment to a large area on the Marais des Cygnes River near the Weas and other migrated tribes in the Unorganized Indian Territory west of Missouri, a guarantee of safety, and a perpetual title to their new reservation. Said the Reverend:

[30] Dr. Decker, Vincennes, to Lewis Cass, Detroit, July 10, 1832, in Letters Received by the Office of Indian Affairs, 1824–1881, Microcopy 234, Roll 416 (items will be cited hereafter by roll number).

... Perhaps some of your young men, your warriors and young men are afraid to go to that country for fear the Indians will make war upon you. . . . All the Indians who have moved are at peace among themselves and at peace with the Indians of the country. . . .

His words would have sounded hypocritical to Black Hawk's band, slaughtered by the Sioux as it tried to escape across the Mississippi.

Porter repeatedly urged the Miamis to sell at least a part of their lands and met their refusals by returning to the attack:

... You must not understand me urging you to sell them, nor that we are anxious about the matter. Consult your chiefs and headmen, and give us an answer. We have come here this time upon your request and at your invitation. We have come here from your Great Father, because he supposed it was your wish, and that you had a desire to see his Commissioners. When we were at this place two moons ago, you seemed kind to us, and invited us to return and talk about this matter. We sent the word back in writing, and on paper to your Great Father in Washington. It would grieve us now. It would make our hearts sore if we had to send back such words to our Great Father as would make him ashamed. We had some reason to believe, when you invited us back so kindly, that you would let your Great Father have some portion of your land, if not the whole. But if you have since that time thought better of it, we do not press you now to sell it to us, but we beg of you all, we request all of our red children who are now here, to remember, that if they must get into trouble, it is not the fault of their Great Father. He has been kind to them, and has advised them for their good. . . . Our desire therefore is that young men should authorize their chiefs to get together, and act promptly together. Let us put an end to it. The moment we are done talking about this, you will get your money, and we will separate as good friends. . . .[31]

The Miamis finally ceased to attend the council meetings and the commissioners were unable to secure the treaty.

The delay whetted the appetites of white men eager to secure sites on the almost completed canal and profit by the speculative

[31] "Journal of a Negotiation at the Forks of the Wabash, October and November, 1833, by Messrs. G. B. Porter, J. F. Schermerhorn, and Wm. Marshall," in *ibid.*

land boom of the early 1830's. Constant pressure finally reduced Miami resistance, and a treaty was signed at the Forks of the Wabash on October 23, 1834. Its provisions were not complete. The village reserves of Flat Belly, White Raccoon, at Mud Creek, and on the Salamonie River were reduced by sixty sections. The tribe ceded a portion of the Ten Mile Reserve at the mouth of Aboite River, a strip from the western side of the Big Miami Reserve of 1818, and a 23,000-acre tract from the same reserve at the junction of the Eel and Wabash rivers. Out of these cessions, the federal government bestowed individual Indian titles to nineteen persons. In addition, Richardville, Little Charley, Lavonture's daughter, Francis Lafontaine, Metchinequea (Majenica), and Francis Godfroy received grants in fee simple. Richardville's grant included the sections he had previously held only by Indian title at the Forks.

The immediate financial return to the tribe was $58,000 in cash within six months and $50,000 to pay the Indians' individual debts. They were given $100,000 in ten annual installments of $10,000 each and $1,500 for their stolen horses. The appraised value of the improvements made by the Indians on their newly ceded lands was to be matched by government funds, which were to be expended on new improvements at sites selected by the chiefs. The Miamis made a good bargain, for their remuneration was high in relation to the area of ceded land. More significantly, five village chiefs received fee simple titles to their land, as Richardville had before them, permitting them also to dispose of those lands without interference from the federal government. This cession brought white settlers still closer to their villages, which further restricted their freedom and reduced the area of land which constituted their bargaining position.

The earlier failures of the Bureau of Indian Affairs to secure a Miami treaty in 1832 and 1833 seemed unimportant after this success. However, President Andrew Jackson refused to accept the treaty because it did not provide for emigration of the Miamis. Because they refused to give up their reservations, even though a new commissioner was sent to negotiate with them in 1836, the 1834 treaty was not approved by the United States Senate and promulgated until December 22, 1837.[32]

The treaty of 1834 was received with a storm of criticism in Indiana because it had not evicted the tribe, but it was only a question of time until a new treaty would replace it. Three circumstances reinforced the demands. The Wabash River to Lake Erie canal, nearly completed between Fort Wayne and Logansport, enhanced land values; although the Miamis and Potawatomis had already ceded most of this land, several of the Miami reserves were at the most strategic and valuable sites. The panic of 1837 paralyzed the economic base of the whites and forced traders to see Indian commerce as the obvious escape from bankruptcy. Furthermore, the piecemeal emigration of the Potawatomi bands, which the Miamis witnessed each year, completed their isolation.

Commissioner Abel C. Pepper, the Miami agent, secured a new treaty at the Forks of the Wabash on November 6, 1838. It was a compromise in which neither the Miamis nor the commissioners retreated from their basic positions concerning emigration. However, each gained advances which made the treaty a tentative success.

The Miamis did not promise to emigrate, but they agreed to send a party of six chiefs, at federal expense, to view the lands west of the Missouri River. The Metocina band, now led by the oldest of the chief's ten sons, secured a new reservation. It was granted from the new cessions, as were fifty cessions by Indian title to individual Miamis. Several of the individual grants were to be surveyed after their location was selected by the individual, but most were situated in portions of the former village reserves.

The Miamis ceded a portion of the land south of the Wabash above the Big Miami Reserve, the remainder of the Aboite Reserve, and the reserves below the Forks of the Wabash, at the mouth of Flat Rock Creek, and at Seek's village. The only land retained by the tribe was its winter hunting grounds on the Big Miami Reserve.

[32] Kappler, *Indian Affairs*, II, 315–18. *John Tipton Papers*, III, 78n., 297–98.

There remained also one band reserve and a multitude of individual holdings by Indian patent or fee simple.

The consideration accepted by the Miamis was $335,680, of which $60,000 was to be paid immediately and the remainder, except that used for debt settlements, in ten annual payments of $12,568. Richardville and Francis Godfroy had previously been denied payment for some of their claims against the tribe by the debt commissioners on the grounds that chiefs were not entitled to repayment under the terms of previous treaties. The sums of $6,800 and $2,612 were now ordered paid to the respective chiefs by Article 4, transaction which was undoubtedly a major precondition of the treaty.

The debt-payment provisions were more elaborate than those of earlier treaties. A commissioner was to be appointed immediately to investigate all claims against the tribe by anyone, regardless of white or Indian blood. He was to use $150,000 of the total grant, set aside to pay the claims he certified; to pay Richardville and Godfroy; and to pay any claims still pending from the debt investigation after the 1834 treaty. If the sum designated for these purposes was not sufficient, the tribe's future annuities were to be used. However, in the unlikely event that there was an unclaimed remainder it was to be returned to the tribe.[33]

The Miamis revealed increased sensitivity to changing cultural values and vanishing tribal identity in the second paragraph of Article 6 of the new treaty. They announced that only members could share in the land or annuities of the tribe; individuals who were permitted to live among them or married into the tribe could secure membership only by adoption through the tribal council. They also decided that no Miami could contract individual debts which would have the status of a lien on the tribe's lands or annuities. The last had become a controversial point in Indian treaties. Individual Indians contracted varying amounts of debts, and when

---

[33] Kappler, *Indian Affairs*, II, 384–88. The acres ceded are Tracts 251, 252, 253, 254, 255, on Royce's map of Indiana detail. They originated from the terms of the 1818 treaty.

all were repaid from the sale of tribal lands, the frugal paid for the extravagances of the spendthrifts.

By 1838, whites who had commercial relations with the Wabash tribes had so consistently presented exorbitant accounts that their claims had become notorious, so much so that the commissioner appointed to examine the claims submitted after the treaty of 1834 discovered they had grown in various fashions from an estimated $50,000, for which that treaty had appropriated funds, to more than $200,000. It was evident that charges of fraud would delay payment and many claims would have to be rejected by the commissioner.[34]

The 1838 treaty confused the already complex problem of settling debt claims against the tribe. It permitted the new debt commissioner, Nathaniel West, to review the claims which had been rejected after the 1834 treaty. The effects of the Panic of 1837 can be seen in the desperate expedients used by the traders to secure payment for any and all of their claims.

The Miami chiefs found most of their time for the next two years occupied in claims investigations. Political leaders, too, were sensitive to Miami claim adjudication. The United States senator from Indiana, Oliver H. Smith, presented a resolution asking for a report on the subject from the commissioner of Indian affairs, in response to which Secretary of War Joel R. Poinsett and Commissioner T. Hartley Crawford submitted the report of Nathaniel West, who had spent nearly three months in 1839 as claims commissioner to fulfill the terms of the fifth and sixth articles of the treaty of November 6, 1838. West, who concentrated his investigations at the Forks of the Wabash and the agency at Logansport, made perceptive observations about the Miamis which deserve at least a concise summary.

His method of verifying claims was unusual in that he advertised his presence, purposes, and methods of procedure in the newspapers. Claimants were required to bring their accounts and to itemize and explain them in the presence of the individual debtors

[34] *Senate Document 1,* 25 Cong., 3 sess., I, 447.

and the assembled chiefs. West found that the Indian men readily acknowledged their debts, but seldom knew the amounts unless these concerned money or furs paid to their accounts; in such cases, the men were always accurate. When false claims were made against them, they were adamant in their objections. Only the women could be relied upon for exactness when debt totals were discussed. The chiefs were always given an opportunity to make remarks or enter objections. Through this process, West finally reduced 118 claims for $142,439.25 to 98 claims for $84,010.40, which he approved.

West formed a high opinion of the Miamis' attitudes and intelligence:

> . . . I cannot refrain from bearing witness to the general honesty of this people; indeed, I hardly met with an instance of gross and barefaced denial of a debt, unless the Indian knew he was right; then he was firm and decided and unwavering in his replies.

The commissioner's other observations are significant. None of the bands was prospering except Meshingomesia's, which West said had an intelligent and prudent chief. However, it did not take part in the settlement since it was satisfied with its relationship with the only trader the band patronized. The remaining bands were diminishing rapidly. The chiefs said more than sixty persons had died in the preceding twelve months and most of these had been killed. While West conducted his councils, there were six cases of bloodshed, one fatal, near his cabin, which was Richardville's house at the Forks. West thought this was inevitable since every Indian, man or woman, was armed with knife or gun.

He saw only two possible methods by which the Miamis could escape extinction: immediate emigration to the west or enactment of a federal law which would make the tribe liable for personal debts. The latter approach to the debt problem was contrary to the method approved by the Miamis in the second paragraph of Article 6 in the 1838 treaty. West preferred it because it would permit a federal review of merchants' credit policies, prevent them from imprisoning individual debtors, and force them to collect their claims at the annual payments. The debts were exaggerated, not only by the traders, but also by the Indians' unrealistic tastes. West sent Crawford samples of the cloth the Miamis demanded and lists of the prices they paid for it. He said they were contemptuous of any product except the best and most expensive, which no doubt horrified the meticulous commissioner.

West's integrity can be judged from the accounts he did not approve. Although the numerous Ewing companies, the Hanna companies, Jean Baptiste Richardville, and Francis Godfroy accounts were usually approved, the largest rejected accounts came from these influential merchants. Since Richardville and Godfroy sat in the full reviewing council and approved West's awards, he must indeed have convinced the Miamis of his justice and honesty.[35]

The commissioner's remarks about Indian traders were not explicit, but a more experienced man indicted many of them when John Tipton wrote a letter warning his young son, Spear, of the dangers encountered among traders of the worst type along the Wabash.[36] Nevertheless, these merchants were also the creditors of the white settlers during the worst part of the Panic of 1837, and Indiana residents did not question Miami extravagance or traders' claims against the Indians if the same traders needed those funds in order to absorb their delinquent white accounts.

A treaty of major significance soon followed the tribe's 1838 agreement. The chiefs, who had resisted all attempts to force Miami emigration for twenty years, finally agreed among themselves, for reasons which can only be conjectured, that emigration was now acceptable. Thus they approached Agent Samuel Milroy with a proposal for a new treaty. The tribe's willingness to consider emigration caught Milroy and Subagent Allen Hamilton by surprise. Although they had no commission to negotiate a treaty, the wily Richardville and his adviser, Hamilton, planned to draw up an

---

[35] Nathaniel West's report is in *Senate Document 164*, 26 Cong., 1 sess., IV, 2–10.
[36] John Tipton, Washington, to Spear S. Tipton, January 24, 1833, in *John Tipton Papers*, II, 789–90.

unauthorized treaty to their own specifications; it would be free of the restrictions which the commissioner of Indian affairs always placed upon negotiations with the Indians. The agents realized that any treaty with unreasonable conditions would be a *fait accompli* gaining the approval of the commissioner and the secretary of war if it provided for Miami emigration. Events proved that the agents had calculated correctly.

Richardville, of course, had long been the major obstacle to emigration. Nearly eighty years old and disillusioned by the customs of his sons and other Miamis, he had become increasingly Indian in dress and habit. It was also obvious that he had used the Miami tribal lands and his office to provide for his own family's wealth. His successes in these efforts aroused opposition among the villages whose chiefs, less adept at securing or retaining influence among the whites, were continually suspicious of Richardville. Therefore, the Chief was unable to dictate to the Miami council. In order to gain support from the other chiefs, he had to secure concessions for them. Even though only four chiefs—Richardville, Godfroy, Lafontaine, and Meshingomesia—signed the new treaty completed November 28, 1840, at the Forks of the Wabash, the others gave their tacit consent or it could not have been concluded. Richardville and Godfroy controlled the Wabash villages; the Meshingomesia family was willing to accede, since it had a reserve and was anticipating exemption from emigration; and the smaller groups were persuaded by judicious grants of land with Indian patents or fee simple titles made to their chiefs. Moreover, by 1840, West's debt investigations had been completed and two annuities, part of the 1838 treaty, had been paid. Both extravagant Indians and importunate traders were ready for another round of negotiations.

A study of the treaty reveals that it required the emigration of about half the tribe. Meshingomesia's relatives, most of the chiefs' families, and most of the mixed bloods were exempted, either by the treaty or by congressional action at a later date. However, failure to achieve total emigration was unimportant in view of the fact that nearly all tribal lands were made available to white settlement. This made the treaty acceptable to the people of Indiana.

Under terms of the treaty, the remnant of the Big Miami Reserve was ceded, excluding that portion already reserved for Metocina's ten sons, which was patented in fee simple to the oldest son, Meshingomesia, to be held in trust for the family. The estate of Francis Godfroy received $15,000, payable at Fort Wayne in annuities to his family until the youngest child became twenty-one years old. This necessitated the family's residence in Indiana and was equivalent to exemption from emigration. Richardville was given $25,000 and Indian title to seven additional sections of land, which could be contained in seven or fewer parcels located wherever he wished in the Big Miami Reserve at sites his favored traders selected. His son-in-law, Francis Lafontaine, received one section of land on the same terms. He selected a seven-sided section at the rapids of Wild Cat Creek—at the prompting of Allen Hamilton, who was acting for trader David Foster. After due legal steps were taken, Foster platted the village of Kokomo on the site.[37] Richardville's locations were made with equal care and forethought.

The Miamis agreed to emigrate within five years, for which, and for the final cession of their ancient lands, they received what appeared to be a munificent payment. It was certainly more equitable than those of earlier treaties made with the Miamis or with most other tribes. The major item was $550,000, of which $250,000 was to be paid in twenty equal annual installments. The remaining $300,000 was reserved to pay claims against the tribe. The sum of $250,000 was budgeted to pay debts already contracted by the tribe or its individuals with any Indian or white. The remaining $50,000 was reserved to pay debts the Miamis might contract between the time the treaty was signed, November 28, 1840, and its eventual ratification by the Senate. If any money remained unexpended, it was to be paid to the tribe at the next annuity.[38]

[37] *Stat. L., VII, 582.* Kappler, Indian Affairs, II, 393–94. Royce, *Indian Land Cessions,* Plate CXXVII, Map 20, Indiana Detail.

[38] Allen Hamilton, Fort Wayne, to Commissioner T. Hartley Crawford, July 30, 1843, Roll 417.

Frances Slocum and her daughters. Original painting by George Winter.

*By permission of Cable C. Ball, of Lafayette, Indiana,
and the Tippecanoe County Historical Association*
Indian women. Original painting by George Winter.

A Miami Indian. Original painting by George Winter.

Chakapeah. Wife of Metocina and mother of Meshingomesia. From a
photograph in the William C. Goodpasture Collection.

Courtesy, L. F. Craven, Marion, Indiana
Meshingomesia. From a photograph in the William C. Goodpasture
Collection.

Wahcaconah, who lived on the Mississinewa River ca. 1818–1882. From
a photograph in the William C. Goodpasture Collection.

Courtesy, L. F. Craven, Marion, Indiana
Mrs. Wahcaconah. From a photograph in the William C. Goodpasture
Collection.

Official view of the Mississinewa Battleground. From a photograph in the William C. Goodpasture Collection.

Such terms made it certain that the traders and most of the citizens of Indiana would appeal to their political leaders for ratification of the treaty. While it awaited senatorial confirmation, the Miamis continued to receive their annuity from the previous treaty and were confident any debts they incurred in the interim would be paid. About half the tribe would receive a reservation of 500,000 acres west of the state of Missouri, while the other half could remain in Indiana. All emigration expenses were to be borne by the federal government and the immigrants provided subsistence in the new country for twelve months after their arrival. A delegation of their chiefs had already seen and approved the proposed territorial reservation, which was bounded by Missouri on the east and by the tribal reservations of the Weas, Kaskaskias, Potawatomis, and the Senecas of New York.[39]

Nevertheless, the treaty's terms were inequitable. While the more importunate families, largely the mixed-blood groups of Godfroy and Richardville lineage, were exempted, the less influential members of their villages were required to emigrate. The latter included those tribesmen who had not secured title to reserves and who had copied the extravagant habits of their leaders but had only annuities and tribal property for support. Some chiefs probably felt they would be unable to survive in the Indiana of the 1840's and would no longer be able to cope with a racial situation which was growing more complex. Nathaniel West would have found among the Miamis supporters of his view that segregation offered the only hope for these unfortunate members of the tribe.

The Meshingomesia band's reserve grant, converted to fee simple, is more perplexing. It has been said that Richardville arranged for it to be held in fee simple to placate the band's members because he had secured $70,000 which was properly theirs from the annuity payments. It is difficult to believe that even Richardville could have swindled the wily Metocina or Meshingomesia without imme-

---

[39] Royce, *Indian Land Cessions,* Plate CXXXIV, Map 27. The new Miami reservation was in Tracts 329 and 330 and totaled 324,796.88 acres. *Appeal No. 2–59,* U.S. Court of Claims, decided July 15, 1960.

diate and violent retaliation.[40] Metocina was the highly respected chief who had curbed anti-American sentiment in the Mississinewa villages after Campbell's raid in 1813. Their exemption from emigration with a fee simple reserve may have been a tardy recognition that the destruction of their villages was not justified.

A more reasonable explanation—and a more cynical one—seems to depend upon the cleverness of Milroy and Hamilton. Both knew this group was determined to remain in Indiana and that it might lead other reluctant villages in an adamant refusal to emigrate. Metocina's village had become a center of retreat for many Indians who rejected white contact. Also, on its small reservation, the band could provide a sanctuary for any Miami who failed to adjust to life on his individual reserved section of land.[41] Still another view is equally valid. This reservation on the Mississinewa was far from land needed for internal improvements and settlement, and its Indian occupancy was unimportant to Indiana or its settlers. In other words, since these Miamis posed no threat to white settlements, it was only Indian control of certain areas essential to the whites which brought forth ideas for Indian salvation. Only then was there concern about changes in the Indian way of life. Since the Meshingomesia family's lands were unessential, its way of life became unimportant to its neighbors. Hamilton and Milroy, who understood the Miamis, the white settlers, and the federal government, probably considered all of these ideas and in the end secured the support of all three groups for their treaty of 1840.

Richardville's death on August 13, 1841, brought to a close another era in Miami history. The old chief acted wisely when he decided to make the treaty of 1840 because he probably foresaw that his successor could not secure any council's approval to emigration and that the tribe would be rent beyond repair. The Miamis' reluctance to emigrate is amply demonstrated; the five-year extension provided in the 1840 treaty was not honored, and only the

[40] This is one of the persistent Miami tales and its reception immediately identifies the listener's band allegiance.

[41] This was the event predicted by the commissioner of Indian affairs. T. Hartley Crawford to William Wilkens, January 31, 1845, Roll 417.

threat of force in 1846 and 1847 made the Miamis comply. At the same time, Richardville was ruthless in obtaining property for his own family and the Godfroys, property that was secured at the expense of the whole tribe. He may have believed that his more acculturated and sophisticated relatives could easily blend into the growing white communities, whereas others could not. It is obvious that he had long since discarded the idea of common ownership of Miami land and that he excelled in the business practices of the whites.[42] However, Richardville, like his son-in-law, Francis Lafontaine, may have imbibed a portion of the mystic ideas of the Shawnee Prophet, whom he had rejected in the past, and hoped for a cultural regeneration of his followers when they passed beyond white contact. Allen Hamilton appeared to believe this was the old chief's sentiment.[43] If so, he had little support among the younger chiefs, who still preferred to live in Indiana under any conditions and who had no wish to undertake the hardships of life in the west as neighbors of the Plains Indians.

The Miamis were almost submerged by the influx of settlers into their ceded lands in the quarter-century before 1840. Political unity of a kind was maintained because federal policy required a tribal structure through which it could negotiate and was supported by the frequent assemblages for annuities or treaties. Some aspects of Richardville's authority became greater than that of his predecessors because of Bureau of Indian Affairs support and because of the tribe's dependence upon his manipulation of treaty negotiations.

There were profound changes in Miami culture during these years. The chasm between individuals who tried to adopt white ways and those who maintained Miami habits widened. Only financial benefits united them. To illustrate one aspect of this, three daughters of William Wells received an excellent education in private schools and a son graduated from West Point. The daughters then married a medical doctor, an army captain, and a judge.

---

[42] Hugh McCulloch, *Men and Manners of Half a Century*, 109–10, said the Chief was a man "of whom no one ever got the better in a trade."
[43] Allen Hamilton, Fort Wayne, to Crawford, June 10, 1844, Roll 418.

The Richardville children and grandchildren and many other mixed-blood Miamis also received a fine education and came to be considered important members of their white communities.

Nevertheless, the majority of the Miamis in 1840 re-created the drunken scenes which Volney had described among the Piankeshaws in 1787. They were re-enacted at nearly every treaty session and annuity payment, yet in spite of them, veteran Indian trader William G. Ewing of Fort Wayne, whose investment in an expedition to the California gold fields was lost or squandered by his partners, wrote with deep conviction:

> . . . We have been used to do this on the frontier with the confiding Indians, half-breeds and Frenchmen! And hence our folly much like old Coquillards, on trusting white *Rogues!* . . . But this should be a lesson—Trust no *white man* with our Interest or Money unless well guarded by written agreements. . . . We must redouble our care in Trusting or confiding in White Men.[44]

As the threat of Indian warfare faded from Indiana, its new citizens became aware of their Miami neighbors' individual characteristics. Familiar with the virtues or iniquities of eastern Indians long dead and well aware of Little Turtle's integrity, they now had opportunity to see and recount the exploits of their own "vanishing red men."

One incident evoked a storm of sympathy toward the Indiana Indians. It occurred in 1824 near the falls of the creek which has given its name to the principal tributary of the White River near present-day Pendleton. The members of a mixed encampment of Shawnees and Miamis composed of two men, three women, and five children were murdered by five white settlers who stole their furs and other possessions. The leader escaped, but the others were apprehended, tried, and convicted. Three were hanged and the youngest pardoned. There was wild speculation that the Indians might retaliate, but Agents John Johnston and William Conner reassured the apprehensive white settlers. This rare example of

[44] W. G. Ewing, Fort Wayne, to G. W. Ewing, January 20, 1851, Ewing Papers, Indiana State Library.

white justice on the frontier became a matter of self-congratulation for all the men who enforced it.[45]

Two other incidents of a different kind occurred during the same period. They were captures whose stories can be placed beside the well-known career of William Wells. The least publicized was that of Hannah Thorpe, or Tharp, a young girl captured near Connersville in 1813. When found, she was living in the Mississinewa villages as the wife of Metahkekequah, or Captain Dixon, one of Metocina's ten sons, to whom she bore two children. About 1850, she committed suicide, drowning in the river near Hogback Bluff. She has many descendants among the Miamis.[46]

The most romanticized Miami tale is that of Frances Slocum, or Maconaquah (Little Bear). A five-year-old Quaker girl, she was abducted from the Wyoming Valley of Pennsylvania in 1778 by a Delaware war party. Although negotiations were held to secure the release of all Indian captives, she was not returned to her family. Eventually, she married a Delaware warrior who made his home near Kekionga during the Miami Confederacy era. There she divorced the Delaware and married the Miami warrior named Shapoconah, who succeeded Little Turtle as war chief. When his hearing failed after the War of 1812, they moved to the Mississinewa River, where he was known as Deaf Man. He died about 1833. Her two sons died in infancy, and after Shapoconah's death, she lived with her two daughters, Nancy (Kekenokeshwa), the wife of Captain Jean Baptiste Brouillette, and Jane (Ozahshinquah), whose fifth husband was Peter Bundy (Waupopetah).

Frances first told a part of her story to trader George W. Ewing of Logansport in 1835. His letter to Lancaster, Pennsylvania, reached Joseph Slocum in 1837, and two brothers and a sister hastened to Peru, Indiana. Frances was able to recall some of her early life, and her story became widely circulated. George Winter painted the family in 1839. On March 3, 1845, Congress passed

---

[45] Dunn, *True Indian Stories*, 197–212. Oliver H. Smith, *Early Indiana Trials and Sketches*, 51–53.

[46] Otho Winger, *The Frances Slocum Trail*, 67–69. *John Tipton Papers*, I, 713–14.

a joint resolution exempting twenty-two members of the family from emigration to Kansas. Her sons-in-law both became Protestant ministers, partly because of the influence of her nephew, George Slocum, who moved to the area in order to manage her affairs. She has a large number of descendants through her youngest daughter's union with Peter Bundy. Although she died in 1847, her name has been perpetuated in parks, highways, and books.[47]

[47] Winger, *Lost Sister,* "Journal of a Visit to Deaf Man's Village, 1839," in *The Journal and Indian Paintings of George Winter,* 151–96. John F. Meginness, *Biography of Frances Slocum, the Lost Sister of Wyoming,* is the early account upon which later writers rely.

7
EMIGRATION, 1841-1847

Jean Baptiste Richardville died August 13, 1841, at his home on the St. Mary's River a few miles southeast of Fort Wayne on the tract he had secured in 1818. At a tribal council held later in 1841 at Black Loon's village on the present site of Andrews, Indiana, Francis Lafontaine, or Topeah, was elected principal chief, defeating Meshingomesia of the Mississinewa villages and Jean Baptiste Brouillette, Frances Slocum's son-in-law, from the mouth of the Mississinewa near Peru; neither Richardville's surviving son, Meaquah, nor any of his several grandsons was considered for the office. Such events were usually stormy affairs among the Miamis, and Lafontaine's election followed the usual pattern. Chief Chapine, who had served as Richardville's spokesman in 1834, successfully championed the new chief.[1]

Before the election council met, Logansport trader George W. Ewing wrote to Allen Hamilton concerning the merits of the candidates. Although it is biased, Ewing's letter indicates he was generally well informed:

I am truly sorry to hear of the death of Chief Richardville, and can not

[1] B. F. Bowen, *Biographical Memoirs of Huntington County, Indiana,* 226; Frank Sumner Bash, *History of Huntington County,* I, 36.

but fear some trouble and inconvenience in consequence. I had promised ourselves the aid and friendship of this distinguished and extraordinary man in bringing to an amicable close the vast unsettled business of his people. How this matter will now end I can't say. It may possibly result more favorably than at present I anticipate. The Indians finding themselves left without a Head may the more readily fall into general meaness. I hope they may not be permitted to split up and divide off into different Bands or parties—this would be very injurious and I fear some of the Band and their advisors may aim at this—They should be kept together and their national character sustained, and should be made to do all their business as heretofore, as one Nation, and I hope a good successor may be appointed to the late principal chief. Who that should be is not for me to say. You will best know. I am told Ozandeah is the proper successor, if so he will be a good man, for he is decidedly in favor of paying all the just debts and of removing West at once. Next to him I would suppose Lafountain would be a safe man. Yet he will not consent to move west I presume. Meshingomesea, I am fearful would not be a safe man, as I am told he is not in favor of paying debts, and as all know he is opposed to going west. Poqua Godfroy is a rash man and is very unpopular among the Indians. I do not think he would answer, or that he would be the choice of the Indians. Black Raccoon, if a sober man, would be their first choice I have no doubt, and he may at any rate—In all these things here I look with all confidence to you—your long acquaintance and high standing with these people will bring them to you for council in all these things, and I doubt not you will recommend the best man they have for principal chief. Lafontain would be a safe man. Poqua I fear would not—as he is intemperate and violent in his disposition . . .[2]

New Civil Chief Lafontaine, about thirty-one years old, was described as a "tall, spare, athletic" youth "noted for fleetness of foot," but he became "robust and corpulent" and in his later years weighed about 350 pounds. He was at least half—or perhaps three-quarters—Indian. He usually wore Indian clothing and followed Indian customs,[3] which practices, along with his tendency to avoid contact with the whites, indicate he accepted Richardville's pat-

[2] George W. Ewing, Peru, to Allen Hamilton, Fort Wayne, August 16, 1841, Allen Hamilton Papers, Indiana State Library.

214

tern of cautious and reticent behavior. Between his eighteenth and twenty-first birthdays, he married Richardville's daughter Catherine (Poconaqua). Lafontaine and his family probably stayed at the Forks of the Wabash most of the time, but he may have spent at least part of the 1830's on his reserve opposite the mouth of the Aboite River. After his election as principal chief of the Miamis, he lived at the Forks west of present-day Huntington.

Lafontaine had not received as many sections of land through treaty grants as had some of the other prominent Miamis, but he was later able to acquire other large holdings. He also operated Richardville's old trading post at the Forks, conducting a successful business there. As a family headman and chief, Lafontaine had legal control of the extensive property of his dependents, and as principal chief, he secured, through the courts, the guardianship of Richardville's minor heirs. The old chief had provided well for the security of his family. Under the terms of his will, Lafontaine's wife, Catherine, inherited two sections of land at the confluence of the Mississinewa and Wabash rivers and one section at the Forks of the Wabash. The section at the Forks included her father's houses and store next to the tribal council house. Lafontaine's oldest son, Louis, received a section of land opposite the mouth of the Mississinewa. Each of the old chief's grandchildren and great-grandchildren—including Lafontaine's five younger children—inherited a half-section of land.[4]

Lafontaine's election as principal chief made him the major spokesman for all of the Miamis and the guardian of all the finan-

---

[3] Lasselle, "Old Indian Traders," 4; *John Tipton Papers*, I, 330n.; Bert J. Griswold, *The Pictorial History of Fort Wayne, Indiana*, 74–75, 97n.

[4] Richardville's will specified the locations of the tracts of land bequeathed to his family. Father Julian Benoit of Fort Wayne and Allen Hamilton were made executors of the will, which disposed of a total of twenty-two sections of land. A copy of the will is in the John Roche Papers, as is a copy of Father Benoit's final report to the Huntington County Probate Court, November 20, 1852. Henry Rowe Schoolcraft estimated Richardville's "wealth some years before his death at about $200,000." Brice, *History of Fort Wayne*, 286. Lafontaine's other five children were Thomas, John, Esther, Francis, and Joseph. Another daughter, Archangel, was born after Lafontaine died. Bert Anson, "John Roche—Pioneer Irish Businessman," *Indiana Magazine of History*, LV (March, 1959), 47–58.

cial affairs of the Richardville village. He followed the Miami practice of making the village subchiefs the agents for peaceful settlement of claims for damages committed by Indians against white property. The legal status of the Indians was changed in the first year of Lafontaine's leadership when the Indiana General Assembly passed an act removing the necessity of bail for those accused persons with one-eighth Indian blood or more and prohibiting whites or Negroes from contracting or collecting debts from Indians. While this law may indicate the confidence the local courts placed in the ability of the tribal chiefs to produce any erring member of a village at a court session, it may also reflect the reluctance of communities to furnish jail lodging and provisions for impoverished Miamis during the long periods of court recess. More important, the law required Indian merchants to conduct legal phases of their business through white men—not a new practice, but one which this process made mandatory.[5]

The career of an Indian chief was closely bound to the motives and actions of the white men who cooperated with or influenced him. Fort Wayne banker and merchant Allen Hamilton was probably the most important adviser associated with the Miamis. He had worked closely with Chief Richardville and had participated in the 1840 treaty council. Hamilton became intimately involved in Richardville's commercial affairs, but he could only attempt to influence the old chief, who was astute in the ways of both white and Indian negotiations. At the tribe's request, Hamilton was appointed Miami agent in 1841 before Richardville's death and continued in this post after Lafontaine's election until 1845.[6]

Hamilton and Lafontaine cooperated as emigration time neared. In 1843, Hamilton notified T. Hartley Crawford, commissioner of Indian affairs at Washington, of the final selection of the seven sections of land granted Richardville in the 1840 treaty. There had been no delay in the selection of Lafontaine's reservation, since

[5] General Laws of Indiana, 25 Session of the General Assembly, 134.
[6] Brice, History of Fort Wayne, Appendix, 18–22; John Tipton Papers, III, 222, 238–39.

its location had been specified in the treaty. However, Lafontaine had not yet received the patents for his reserves of 1838, and Hamilton wrote Crawford concerning the need for clear titles. The General Land Office provided thirty-six patents for various Miami individual reservations granted in the 1838 treaty, including Lafontaine's, plus thirteen patents for parcels reserved in the treaty of 1834.[7] In May, 1843, Hamilton told the commissioner that the Indians and Lafontaine were afraid of losing some of their best tracts in the surveys which the state's agents were making to locate the canal lands. He declared, too, that the timid Indians were being annoyed by squatters, who were obstacles to those Indians living on reserves who wanted to sell their lands or who had already sold and wished to give possession to the new owners.[8]

Matters of land ownership and transfer and the disposal of property were the major problems blocking emigration and absorbed most of Lafontaine's time. His duties increased in number and urgency as the time of emigration approached. Earlier, he had been able to conduct his affairs with one secretary-clerk; in 1844, he added a chief clerk, John Roche of Huntington, a young Irishman with experience in Wabash and Erie Canal construction and maintenance. In 1846, Roche was made a partner in Lafontaine's business to circumvent the legal restrictions that harassed the Indian merchants. He also continued Lafontaine's enterprises when the latter traveled to Washington and later to Kansas.[9]

The preparations were timely, for on May 6, 1844, Thomas Dowling of Terre Haute was granted a contract to move the Miamis to their western lands. The document provided $55,000 for the expenses of emigration, including salaries for conductors and physicians, the cost of assembling the tribe, and the expense of one

[7] Allen Hamilton, Fort Wayne, to T. Hartley Crawford, Washington, May 4 and July 30, 1843, Roll 417; John M. Moore, Washington, to T. Hartley Crawford, Washington, August 10 and October 23, 1843, *ibid.* A Lafontaine memorial regarding the patents was enclosed in Allen Hamilton, Fort Wayne, to T. Hartley Crawford, Washington, November 11, 1843, *ibid.*

[8] Allen Hamilton, Fort Wayne, to T. Hartley Crawford, Washington, May 4, 1843, *ibid.*

[9] Anson, "John Roche," 50–52.

year's subsistence for the Miamis in their new location.[10] Dowling immediately traveled to the Wabash country for consultations with Hamilton and Lafontaine; then, on October 6, during a second trip, he met with the tribe and its chiefs. Hamilton's cooperation and understanding of the problems connected with the undertaking impressed the contractor, but the Indians countered Dowling's haste with amiable and frustrating procrastination. They wanted more time to complete the sale of their property but agreed that if additional time were not granted by the federal government, they would empower Lafontaine to dispose of it after their emigration. Dowling reached the conclusion that traders would foster the Indians' efforts to remain in Indiana as long as annual payments were made there.[11]

Since the Miamis had agreed in the treaty of 1840 to emigrate within five years, preparations for the impending event accelerated in 1845. Secretary of War William Wilkins told Crawford there would be no further extensions of time and ordered Hamilton to press the Miamis for a definite commitment to move. There were still sporadic maneuvers to create delays, however. Lafontaine tried to divert the attention of the Bureau of Indian Affairs by suggesting to Hamilton that the Meshingomesia band might be troublesome. He indicated its members feared they might be evacuated from their reservation of ten sections along the Mississinewa, even though the land had been granted as a communal holding under their chief's guardianship until it should be alienated. Lafontaine thought their fear was based partly upon the fact that only the family of Meshingomesia had been specifically exempted from emigration. He suggested that the government try to purchase all of the reserve except a section or two which could be retained for Chief Meshingomesia. Although Commissioner Crawford approved Lafontaine's suggestion, it was not implemented. Hamilton

---

[10] Thomas Dowling, Terre Haute, to T. Hartley Crawford, Washington, May 6, 1844, Roll 418; William Medill, Washington, to John Petit, Washington, April 5, 1848, *ibid.*

[11] Thomas Dowling, Terre Haute, to T. Hartley Crawford, Washington, October 17, 1844, *ibid.*

added that the area was increasing in value. Land valued at $1.10 an acre in 1840 was bringing $3.00 by 1845, and the Richardville family had received as much as $5.00 an acre. While one Miami group had asked for $3.00 an acre, Hamilton thought the tribe would set a price of about $1.25 an acre.[12]

During the summer of 1845, Lafontaine's oldest son, Louis (Wahpahsapanah), and several village chiefs were sent to the proposed Miami reservation on the Marais des Cygnes River (which becomes the Osage River at its confluence with the Little Osage in western Missouri) in what is now eastern Kansas. On their return, they reported their satisfaction with the land's natural features; the valley of the Marais des Cygnes bore a striking resemblance to the Wabash Valley.[13] The Indian courts were petitioned to declare Lafontaine legal guardian of the properties of various individuals who were either minors or who wished to emigrate before they had disposed of all their possessions. The Chief also secured court orders for the sale of several pieces of real estate on which he held mortgages and which he wished to add to his own extensive properties. The Bureau of Indian Affairs authorized Hamilton to pay Lafontaine's accounts with wholesale merchants in New York, since the Chief planned to emigrate with his tribe and remain on the new reservation for at least six months.[14]

The federal government's eagerness for the emigration was evident in the authorization it gave in 1845 for the selection of a commission of three arbiters to review the Miamis' claims and debts to their traders. The Indians were instructed to select two traders, and the claimants named the third man. This unusual agreement was made October 27 and later approved by President James K. Polk. William L. Stuart and Dr. Graham N. Fitch, two residents of Logansport, were chosen by the Indians, and Elias Murray of Hunt-

[12] William Wilkins, Washington, to T. Hartley Crawford, Washington, December 4, 1844, *ibid.;* Allen Hamilton, Fort Wayne, to T. Hartley Crawford, Washington, February 6 and March 7, 1845, Roll 417; T. Hartley Crawford, Washington, to William Wilkins, Washington, January 31, 1846, *ibid.*

[13] George W. Ewing, Osage Subagency, to William Medill, Washington, November 11, 1846, Roll 418.

[14] Anson, "John Roche," 50–51.

ington was named by the traders who had claims against various members of the tribe.[15]

Sometime in 1845, Joseph Sinclair of Fort Wayne was appointed agent to the Miami, replacing Hamilton. Sinclair sent Crawford's successor, William Medill, a petition from Lafontaine requesting reassurance that the Chief's family would be exempt from emigration. "I will remark that Lafontaine married the favorite daughter of the late chief . . . . Lafontaine has relatives and connections to the number of thirty-four," wrote Sinclair, who thought anything which protected the prestige of the Chief would expedite the emigration, since the Miamis gave unusual obedience to their paramount officer and members related to chiefs were extremely proud of that relationship.[16]

In spite of the terms of the treaty of 1840, the Miami emigration did not take place in 1845. Several factors contributed to the delay. Miami debts were not yet liquidated, and the Indians were dispersed among their villages and refused to assemble. In addition, it is doubtful that Dowling had ever intended to attempt the removal, but had instead entered into the contract as a speculative venture. Nevertheless, by 1846, emigration was inevitable, and the events leading to its culmination occurred with increasing frequency as the year began. Using his removal contract as security, Dowling negotiated a loan of $6,000, then sold the contract to Robert Peebles of Pittsburgh. Peebles notified Commissioner Medill of the purchase, acknowledged his legal obligation to conduct the emigration in the name of Dowling, the original contractor, and informed Medill that Allen Hamilton had aided him in securing a conference with Lafontaine at which they had arranged for a council to be held at the Forks of the Wabash in March, 1846.[17]

---

[15] There are many allusions in official correspondence to the unusual nature of this arrangement, but the most revealing reference to it and to President Polk's confirmation of the agreement is in William G. Ewing, Fort Wayne, to William Medill, Washington, November 9, 1846, Roll 416.

[16] Joseph Sinclair, Fort Wayne, to William Medill, Washington, December 29, 1845, Roll 418.

[17] Robert Peebles, Pittsburgh, to William Medill, Washington, February 27, 1846, *ibid.*

Agent Sinclair was appointed superintendent of the emigration in March, 1846. On March 30, Peebles reached the Forks, where Lafontaine approved the new contractor and his appointed physician, Dr. Fitch. Sinclair believed the only remaining obstacle was the final debt accounting, but again the removal contract was sold, this time to a group of four men. The Ewing brothers, William G. and George W., bought one-third of the joint venture; Samuel Edsall of Fort Wayne bought another third; and Alexis Coquillard of South Bend bought the remaining third. Coquillard was designated the "active partner," or actual conductor.[18]

While there is no hint of the circumstances which motivated Peebles' withdrawal, subcontracting was a common practice and the actual removal of Indians was usually performed by experienced men like Coquillard. The contract—it was still the one originally granted to Dowling—contained the customary terms required by the Bureau of Indian Affairs: the contractor was obligated to issue rations to Indians waiting at the place of assembly, to assume the expenses of the actual migration, to provide rations to the tribe for one year after its arrival at the western reservation, and to pay the salaries of all of the conductor's assistants.

Sinclair and the new contractors immediately moved to liquidate Miami financial affairs, using the procedure devised the previous October. Arbiters Stuart, Murray, and Dr. Fitch met the Indians and their debtors on May 4, 1846, and completed the settlement in five days. During the conference, there were rumors that some traders received preferential treatment from the Indians or from the arbiters and that many claims were fraudulent. The arbiters, however, were able to obtain an immediate settlement, leaving individual traders who were dissatisfied to make their charges of corruption to the commissioner of Indian affairs or their congressmen.[19]

Another meeting was held June 1 to make final arrangements

[18] Joseph Sinclair, Fort Wayne, to William Medill, Washington, March 30 and April 23, 1846, *ibid.*

[19] The May 4–8 council is summarized in William Stuart's notarized statement, July 18, 1846, Roll 416.

for the actual emigration. In his letters to Commissioner Medill between June 1 and August 14, Sinclair described the progress being made and the problems he faced. Sinclair and Coquillard discovered the Miamis were still reluctant and evasive; the customary excuses were offered, with the Indians asking for an extension until August to dispose of their remaining "houses, cows and other property." When Sinclair warned them, on his own authority, that no more annuity payments would be made in Indiana, they countered with their fears of moving west in the heat of summer. The clearest commitment Sinclair could get at the June council was Lafontaine's offer to pay half the expenses of a party composed entirely of Indians who were ready to leave immediately with Coquillard, plus the Chief's promise to bring the remainder on August 1. The offer would not fulfill the terms of the removal contract, and Sinclair refused it. He asked Commissioner Medill not to make any more annuity payments in Indiana and not to pay the debts which would be reported by a new commission then at work; these actions, Sinclair insisted, would prod the Miamis toward their new home.[20]

Lafontaine's boldest action came in late June when, uninvited and at his own expense, he went to Washington to appeal to the President for a further delay. He took with him Dr. Fitch, a few subchiefs, and the agency interpreter, George Hunt. Sinclair, who had not authorized Hunt's absence from the agency, later complained that his work had been impeded while the interpreter was away and pointed out that Lafontaine spoke English well and did not need to take an interpreter to Washington. Meanwhile, the Miamis refused to assemble until their chief returned.

When the delegation came home in July, the impatient agent again indicated to Lafontaine that future annuities would be paid only in the west and hinted that force might be used against the tribe. Sinclair, who had probably opposed the Washington trip, wrote Medill: "The chief expected to effect wonders, and he feels alarmed to report, nothing done." Later, when the agent was still

[20] Joseph Sinclair, Fort Wayne, to William Medill, Washington, June, 1846, Roll 418.

trying to collect the tribe "peaceably" at Coquillard's assembly camp near Peru, he charged that "the chief is certainly acting in concert with the traders." Sinclair also accused Dr. Fitch of being an instigator of Lafontaine's procrastination and stated that Lafontaine had been avoiding the councils. The Chief may have been having some difficulty in maintaining his position of leadership because Sinclair reported that Lafontaine had apparently promised some of his village chiefs to secure their exemption from emigration but had failed to gain such authorization, that Lafontaine might have to resign as chief, and that Lafontaine had been threatened by one of the village chiefs who had accompanied the delegation to Washington.[21]

In August, Sinclair's patience evaporated. He asked for a small military force and intimated that the only alternative to force was "starvation"—a seemingly futile gesture when directed toward a tribe whose chiefs still possessed extensive lands. He also reported that a group of traders was promising to secure permission for more Miamis to remain in Indiana if the Indians would sign fraudulent claims in the May awards. The traders countered with charges against Sinclair, claiming he had become their active ally without the knowledge of the Indians or the arbitration commission.[22] These incidents are examples of the traders' varied efforts to keep the Indians in Indiana and thus maintain a valuable source of income. Each charge and countercharge, regardless of its significance, had to be investigated and this caused delay.

The commissioner of Indian affairs was not to be diverted from his primary objective of removing the Miamis from Indiana. On September 7, he instructed Sinclair to demand an immediate council with the Indians and to inform the Miamis and the traders that neither annuities nor debt awards would be paid until the emigration was completed. Lafontaine called the meeting at the Forks after Sinclair assured him the Lafontaine family could make the

[21] Joseph Sinclair, Fort Wayne, to William Medill, Washington, June 1, June 22, July 20, and August 14, 1846, *ibid.*

[22] Joseph Sinclair, Fort Wayne, to William Medill, Washington, July 16, 1846, *ibid.;* Samuel Driver, Notarized Statement, August 1, 1846, Roll 416.

trip west with the tribe and then return to Indiana. The agent received notice on September 21, 1846, that the commanding officer of the army district at Cincinnati had been ordered to send a small group of soldiers to assist him. The force arrived the following day and encamped at Peru.[23]

Lafontaine had apparently been ill, but his recovery and regular attendance at the meetings now permitted the tribe to resume its deliberations. The presence of troops seemed also to convince the Chief that further delay was useless. The Miamis held a council at Coquillard's camp near Peru on October 1 and selected a few chiefs to complete the disposal of their remaining properties. Sinclair reluctantly concluded that Lafontaine was acting in good faith, even though the Chief had not yet succeeded in persuading a single Miami family to move to Coquillard's camp. He finally told Lafontaine that many families must report within the next two days or the troops would begin a search for fugitives. Sinclair had qualms about popular reaction to such an extreme measure, since he had received protests from Hamilton and others against forcible action, which the presence of troops clearly implied.[24]

The emigration finally began at Peru on October 6. Three canalboats were loaded with baggage, Indians, and white officials. Although no military action was necessary—partly because of the Lafontaine family's presence—Sinclair cautioned Medill that it would be expedient to have the semi-annual payment ready for distribution to the Miamis as soon as they reached their western reservation. On the second day, the three boats reached Fort Wayne, where the remainder of the tribe was awaiting the conductors; two more boats were added to accommodate them.[25]

[23] Joseph Sinclair, Fort Wayne, to William Medill, Washington, September 21 and 23, 1846, Roll 418; R. Jones, Washington, to J. Ewing, Cincinnati, September 11, 1846, *ibid.*

[24] Joseph Sinclair, Peru, to William Medill, Washington, October 1, 1846, *ibid.* The colorful Miamis remained a picturesque feature of Fort Wayne's past. One hundred Miamis in full costume were a prominent part of the Wabash and Erie Canal celebration in 1843.

[25] Joseph Sinclair, Peru, to William Medill, Washington, October 5, 1846, *ibid.*

There is no reliable account of the Miamis' departure in 1846. October 1 to 6 must have witnessed veritable madhouse scenes at Coquillard's camp near Peru as families assembled and exempted relatives came to say farewell. Even greater confusion must have reigned on the St. Mary's and Eel rivers while families packed to join the large contingent at Fort Wayne. The curious gathered along the canal to watch "The Indians" leave for the west: relatives, friends, and sensation seekers, the latter hoping to witness violence or grief. Once again the observers reported that which they wanted to see: disorder or dignity, unrestrained grief or stoic behavior. At least it was a ceremonial exodus—more humane, more worthy of both the federal government and the Indians than the herded caravans of the 1830's.

The party followed the Wabash and Erie Canal to its junction with the Miami and Erie Canal in Ohio, then passed through Dayton to Cincinnati, where the entire party was transferred to the steamer *Colorado* on the Ohio River. In a report from Evansville, Indiana, Sinclair wrote that a few Indians had eluded the conductors at Peru but that Coquillard had hired Ezekial French, an experienced trader, to find as many as possible and take them west via a land route. The agent suggested placing these fugitives—some of whom had been involved in murders on the Mississinewa in 1844 and 1845 and thus were also fugitives from their own tribe—on the western reservation of the Potawatomis when they emigrated.[26]

The expedition reached St. Louis on October 20, 1846, transferred to the *Clermont II,* and three days later steamed up the Missouri River. The Indians and baggage were unloaded at Kansas Landing (now Kansas City) on the first of November and reached the Osage subagency reservation eight days later. Meanwhile, Joseph J. Comparet of Fort Wayne, who had contracted with the conductors to deliver the Miamis' horses to the western reservation, arrived there on November 5. He had left Peru one day after the

---

[26] Joseph Sinclair, Evansville, to William Medill, Washington, October 14, 1846, *ibid.* French was sent to collect the Wauwasee band, which had fled to Michigan. William G. Ewing, Fort Wayne, to William Medill, Washington, March 13, 1847, *ibid.*

boat party and had lost only nine of the original herd of ninety-nine animals in crossing Indiana, Illinois, and Missouri.[27]

At the reservation, Indian Agent Alfred J. Vaughan certified the arrival of 323 Miamis. A few were ill when the journey began; during the first part of the trip, there had been six deaths and two births, and the conductors had acquired a few additional Indians on the way. The party included 142 men and 181 women; 51 males and 53 females were under eighteen. Vaughan also prepared lists of the names and relationships of the family or village of each subchief.[28]

The census lists of 1846 and 1847 were less accurate than this cursory examination indicates. A new treaty was made with the Miamis in 1854, and a revised list of 302 "Miamis of Indiana" was accepted. It included individuals who avoided emigration, but was still incomplete. In 1858, the Bureau of Indian Affairs placed 68 more people on a special list of those who received no annuities from 1846 to 1857, then added them to the Indiana list, without the Indiana Miamis' consent. The Miamis in Indiana therefore outnumbered those in Kansas.

However, the actual number of permanent emigrants in Kansas was less than Vaughan's figure of 323. The Lafontaine party, at least, was only temporarily at the agency, since it was included among the 148 individuals who at that time were specifically exempt from emigration. The exemption lists approved in 1846 included 55 members of the Meshingomesia family, 22 from the Slocum family, 28 of the Godfroys, and 43 Richardville-Lafontaine members.[29] Therefore, at first glance, the 1846 emigration apparently placed two-thirds of the tribe in Kansas.

Sinclair began his return journey to Fort Wayne on November

[27] Joseph Sinclair, St. Louis, to William Medill, Washington, October 20, November 1, and November 11, 1846, *ibid.*

[28] Joseph Sinclair, Evansville, to William Medill, Washington, October 14, 1846, *ibid.*; Alfred J. Vaughan, Osage Subagency, to Thomas H. Harvey, St. Louis, November 12, 1846, Roll 416.

[29] Roll 418 gives the names of the Slocum, Godfroy, J. B. Richardville, and Meshingomesia family individuals exempted from emigration.

10, leaving Vaughan and the Indians with the assurance the Miamis would have subsistence for another year under terms of the Dowling contract. After Sinclair's departure, the Miamis called a council at which Lafontaine told Vaughan the Indians wished to apologize for their fractiousness at Peru and said they were pleased with their new home. He praised Coquillard's supervision, accused Sinclair of neglect and inattention during the emigration, and charged Dr. Fitch with drunkenness. Lafontaine spoke of other Miami grievances. The Miamis had been disappointed in the past with the results of training received by some of their children at the Choctaw Academy in Kentucky. The Chief criticized the continued use of tribal school funds at the school, to which they had sent no pupils for about ten years, and indicated that in their new home they now wanted a school operated by the Roman Catholic church.[30]

When Thomas H. Harvey, superintendent of Indian affairs at St. Louis, sent $10,000 for the relief of the new arrivals in December, he ordered that the money be paid to the heads of families. Later, when Harvey accompanied the officials who transported the March, 1847, annuity payment of $33,500 to the Miamis, he found Lafontaine still with the tribe. They refused to accept their money as individuals and voted unanimously for the Chief to direct the distribution. They also voted to pay their remaining debts out of their next two annuity payments.

"Lafontaine's influence on these peoples," Harvey insisted, "is unlimited. He will leave in a few days for Indiana after which I hope they will begin to think and act for themselves. . . . It is due Mr. Lafontaine to say that he expressed himself warmly in favor of ample provision for education of their children. . . . Lafontaine says he will send his own children to school here." Harvey soon changed his opinion of Lafontaine's prestige in the tribe; after the Chief's departure, the western Miamis immediately held a meeting,

[30] Alfred J. Vaughan, Osage Subagency, to Thomas H. Harvey, St. Louis, November 12, 1846, *ibid.*; Thomas H. Harvey, St. Louis, to William Medill, Washington, November 26 and December 13, 1846, *ibid.*

selected a new chief for themselves, and declared they would no longer listen to Lafontaine. Harvey was sure, however, that Lafontaine and the Indian traders would continue to exert a great influence on the tribe, even though the emigrants had declared themselves no longer dependent upon their former leaders.[31]

Although many of the Miamis emigrated in 1846, the tribe remained a factor in the Ewing group's efforts to collect payment on the removal contract and the attempts of opponents to delay final settlement as long as possible. A few Indians had eluded the contractors, notably Wauwasee's and Papakeechi's (Flat Belly's) bands, which had gone to Michigan. Also, four Miami chiefs—Coesse, Meaquah, Rivarre, and White Loon—had returned to Indiana with Lafontaine's family, since they had been designated to remain in Indiana until all the tribe's property was sold. Because the contract specified emigration of every Indian not exempted by treaty, the contractors feared they would be forced to make another collection and another emigration in 1847, to be followed by a full year's extension of the contract as they subsisted the second group of Miamis.[32]

Coquillard felt that the Indians who returned to Indiana after being conducted west were no longer the responsibility of the contractors, but he offered to remove them again for an additional sum if this would expedite fulfillment of the contract. He was informed by Commissioner Medill that all unexempted Miamis were part of the original contract. Accordingly, in the spring of 1847, Coquillard opened a camp in Kosciusko County and collected thirty Indians. Miami, Eel River Miami, and Potawatomi villagers north of the Eel River had intermarried extensively, especially in the village of the old fur trader Francis Aveline. Coquillard offered to include any members of the Potawatomi tribe in a new emigration which would cost the federal government $55 to $65 for each individual,

[31] Thomas H. Harvey, "Miami Camp," to William Medill, Washington, March 18, and May 17, 1847, *ibid.*

[32] Alexis Coquillard, South Bend, to William Medill, Washington, May 18 and June 25, 1847, and William G. Ewing, Fort Wayne, to William Medill, Washington, March 13, 1847, *ibid.*

but Medill finally directed him to collect these Indians at $25 for each one.[33]

Commissioner Medill rejected all claims beyond the original contract terms of $55,000, since the document expressly stated that sum was to cover all expenses, including extensions of time. He described the original contract as extravagant because it was based on an anticipated removal of about 650 Indians when in fact only 384 were finally transported. Medill accused the contractors of causing the delays in the summer of 1846 in order to collect old claims or create new ones. The Treasury Department finally presented documentation that the contract eventually paid about $140 for each Miami removed. While this was certainly not all profit, it was about double the per capita rate paid in similar contracts.[34]

In spite of evidence produced by the Bureau of Indian Affairs and the Treasury Department that the Miami emigration of 1846 had been excessively profitable for the contractors, the federal government paid $4,410.29 for the second emigration in 1847 and permitted the Miamis to pay the contractors $4,215.40 as the Indians' contribution. Thus the total cost to the federal government and the Indians for the 1846 and 1847 expeditions and the required subsistence amounted to $63,625.69. Since this sum was used for the relocation of only 384 Indians, it is not difficult to understand the eagerness of various traders to share in Indian removal contracts.[35]

Meanwhile, Francis Lafontaine died at Lafayette, Indiana, on April 13, 1847. When the news reached Harvey, he wrote Medill that although the Chief had seldom spoken at the western council

---

[33] Alexis Coquillard, South Bend, to William Medill, Washington, May 18 and June 25, 1847, *ibid.* For his second emigration, Coquillard collected 78 people, "which included every thing in the shape of an Indian in the country." As the conductor was ready to leave for the west, some traders protested the removal of several members of Coquillard's party. The case was taken to the Miami County Court, where 17 Indians were declared to be Weas instead of Miamis. Coquillard finally delivered 61 Indians to the western reservation on September 10, 1847. Undated report from Alexis Coquillard, South Bend, to William Medill, Washington. *ibid.*

[34] Copy of report by Hiland Hill, September 8, 1851, *ibid.*

[35] *Ibid.* The report does not explain the Miami payment.

229

sessions, he had been the real leader of the Miamis and, with the help of the white traders, could have controlled the "imbecile and indifferent Indians" of his tribe. Harvey explained that he had reported only what he had seen of the Chief and knew nothing of Lafontaine's background or previous leadership. Although Sinclair had called the chief "faithless," Harvey had no doubts about Lafontaine's anxiety and sincerity when representing his people. Even the fact that he saw enough of Lafontaine to be convinced that the Chief was "avaricious to a fault, a passion which is not uncommon among traders, and especially Indian traders," this did not, in Harvey's judgment, detract from Lafontaine's qualities of leadership and dedication to his tribe.[36]

The Miamis in Indiana waited for their chief's return during the winter of 1846–47. Since they expected him to arrive by May 3, 1847, they refused to accept their spring annuities until he could be present. Such devotion to the prerogatives of the principal chief persisted among the Miamis in spite of the rumored bitterness of some Indians against those families who had secured exemptions from emigration. The gossip was given impetus by the members of Lafontaine's family, who insisted he had been poisoned by rivals remaining in Kansas. Sinclair's statements that "Lafontaine's death will not be regretted by anyone so severely as by the traders" and that "he never was faithful to his tribe" were colored by the agent's failure to receive compensation for cooperating with the contractors in addition to his regular salary as federal superintendent of the removal. But Lafontaine's influence in the emigrant councils on the Marais des Cygnes River, the respect in which his office was held by the Miamis in Indiana, and the skill he had shown in his tribe's behalf as he delayed emigration beyond the original terms of the 1840 treaty indicate that the Chief was devoted to the welfare of his people and that the Miamis recognized his interest. Lafontain's pronounced obesity and the rigors of travel

[36] Thomas H. Harvey, St. Louis, to William Medill, Washington, May 14, 1847, Roll 416.

are more acceptable explanations for his death than the theory of tribal vengeance.[37]

Lafontaine's office as principal chief elected in full council had united the scattered Miami villages when all of the Miamis were still in Indiana; his death severed the political link connecting the emigrated Miamis with those remaining in Indiana. After Coquillard's removal of the small party in 1847, there was only informal contact between the two factions. The problems of such groups as the Meshingomesia and Godfroy villagers or the white administrators of the Lafontaine and Richardville assets in Indiana were different from those of the successive chiefs on the western reservation. Individuals still in Indiana received annuities; the Meshingomesia band remained a vestige and court-appointed administrators of Indian property performed their duties. But as far as the federal government, particularly the Bureau of Indian Affairs, was concerned, the Miami tribe now resided in the Unorganized Indian Territory, not in Indiana.

Owl (Ozandiah), the elderly chief elected by the Kansas group, died after one year in office. His successor was Big Leg, who had escaped hanging by means of a pardon from the governor in 1830 and whose tenure also was short. Big Leg was followed by a succession of chiefs who held office for short terms.[38] Explanations for this departure from tradition seem obvious. No one young man among the emigrated Miamis had been able to build a reputation for leadership before removal from Indiana, for Richardville and Lafontaine had monopolized the financial affairs of the tribe. Or the Miamis may simply have wished to discard the custom of lifetime elections to offices which had been held by related families for at least a century.

Since the emigrations of 1846–47 occurred late in the period of

37 Isaac D. G. Nelson, Fort Wayne, to Office of Indian Affairs, Washington, January 5 and February 18, 1847; Joseph Sinclair, Fort Wayne, to William Medill, Washington, April 26, 1847, *ibid.*; Bash, *History of Huntington County*, I, 37.

38 Thomas H. Harvey, "Miami Camp," to William Medill, Washington, March 18 and May 17, 1847, Roll 416.

general Indian removal, the Miamis encountered little harassment from the displaced tribes of the plains. Thus they were not pressed to combine forces against these tormentors as had earlier emigrant tribes. Their problem lay in the fact that they were close to the Missouri state line, which was dotted by taverns and squatters' cabins in which whisky was dispensed. A few years later, the Miamis were removed to a new Indian Territory where they might merge with related tribes. Nevertheless, the emigrants were more fortunate than the tribesmen who chose to remain in Indiana. The former carried a sense of unity because of their physical exile, which developed pride in their survival. White acculturation of Miami individuals was an uneven process by which the individual often removed himself from Indian society without becoming acceptable to the white community.[39] Even though the Indiana Miamis retained physical residence in their historic homeland, the individual often became conscious of his being neither Indian nor white. It was only on the Meshingomesia Reserve that he could find a cultural union with the past and obliterate his white surroundings for a short time. In time, the reserve became a sanctuary for Indiana Miamis, as did visits to the Osage or Quapaw agencies of the emigrants, and helped to retain a sense of Indian identity. The traditionalists' bitterness toward apostates who adopted white customs and dress and denied their Indian heritage motivated the western council which elected Ozandiah. The same attitude is found in Meshingomesia's deposition of 1855.

The correspondence of those involved in the emigration reveals that Lafontaine had exerted a more profound influence in the event than has generally been credited to him. He was cooperative in dealing with whites, but at the same time he could be evasive and calculating. He understood the privileges and powers of his office in his relations with the subchiefs, the traders, and the Indian agent. He was prepared to bow to the inevitable emigration, but only after

---

[39] T. Hartley Crawford, Washington, to William Wilkens, Washington, January 1, 1845, Roll 417, had predicted the Meshingomesia Reserve would became a Miami refuge. *House Executive Document 23*, 49 Cong., 1 sess. IV, 1–27.

he had discovered it was useless to object further and had secured the best possible terms for himself and his tribe. And he was well aware of the rivalries among the white merchants and the advantages of fostering controversies involving the Indian agents or the Bureau of Indian Affairs. His reliance upon Hamilton and Roche demonstrates that he understood the necessity of cooperating with men whose integrity or self-interest could be used to serve his own interests.

As a trader and businessman, Lafontaine accumulated assets amounting to nearly $40,000, much of it in specie. There is nothing to indicate that he was ever involved in a poor business transaction. There is a great deal of evidence, however, that he could control his tribe and dominate the factions within the Miami tribal-council organization. Although some who had failed to dictate Lafontaine's policies complained that he was a puppet for Roche or Hamilton, the men best acquainted with the Chief testified this was untrue.

Lafontaine's authority as principal chief rested on four bases: personal magnetism, undisputed leadership of his own village and family, his ability to control subchiefs of other villages who were apt to be his rivals for office and influence, and his ability to contend with white traders and the federal government. Lafontaine symbolized a strong union between the Miami groups, a fact which was acknowledged by the federal government as well as the tribe. Had he lived and continued to prosper financially, it is probable that more of the western Miamis would have returned to Indiana to seek his protection. Instead, his illness and death on the return journey widened the gap between the two groups.

The emigration of the Miamis, followed by the death of Chief Lafontaine, brought to a close an extended period in which they had exerted much influence in the development of the Old Northwest. There now began a century of near-obscurity.

8
THE MIAMI TRIBE
OF OKLAHOMA, 1846-1968

The Miamis, led by Coquillard and Lafontaine in 1846 to the Un-organized Indian Territory near the line dividing the eastern wood-land area from the western plains, fared well if we use the tribula-tions of the Shawnee party of The Prophet as a comparison. His group started west from Ohio in 1827 without the assistance which was provided in later federal removal contracts. The band nearly starved before reaching St. Louis, and Superintendent William Clark frantically tried to save them. He appealed to various Indian tribes for supplies, but the Delawares, especially, were reluctant to provide them because of The Prophet's part in the border wars of 1809–1814.[1]

The Miamis were settled at the western edge of an area, believed hospitable, on the periphery of the so-called Great American Des-ert, inhabited only by nomadic Indian tribes. The Great Plains remained virtually unknown and unexploited, although they had been traversed by nameless French and Spanish fur traders and American Mountain Men during the three centuries that had elapsed since the expeditions of Coronado and De Soto had nearly met in Kansas in 1541.

[1] Anson, "Variations of the Indian Conflict," 64–89.

As the Miamis left Missouri, they entered what was in reality a hostile territory. While many Americans sincerely believed the Miamis would benefit by their removal from pernicious white contacts, only a few realized that even the most conservative Miamis had become so acculturated they could scarcely hope to survive on a frontier where Pawnee, Cheyenne, Sioux, and other Plains Indians ruled.

The Unorganized Indian Territory was a vast region where the only federal authority since 1808 had been that of an Indian superintendent residing in St. Louis who had a few agents scattered among the tribes east of the Rocky Mountains. None of the far western tribes had yet consented to treat with the United States, nor had they been convinced they were subordinate and dependent nations and therefore wards of the federal government. Only forty years had passed since Lewis and Clark returned from their Pacific Coast odyssey, twenty-five years since the first Delaware band moved west of the Mississippi River to escape the American settlers, and only sixteen years since the Federal Removal Act was passed.

A study of the manuscripts Bernard DeVoto used while writing *The Year of Decision* reveals the extent to which this region was unknown at the time the Miamis reached the Osage Agency.[2] During the preceding three centuries, there had been vast cultural changes and tribal migrations among Indian tribes from the Rockies to the Mississippi and from Canada to Mexico. Spanish, French, British, and American traders had brought their goods—and some of their vices—to the western Indians as they had done among the Indians east of the Mississippi. However, the western Indian tribes remained comparatively unmolested, while those in the east lived under constant pressure and harassment.

A better perspective of the times can be gained if one studies events which occurred in the ten months of 1846 before the Miamis

[2] Bernard DeVoto, *The Year of Decision*. Ray Allen Billington, *Westward Expansion: A History of the American Frontier*, 564–66. Indian Superintendent Thomas H. Harvey, St. Louis, to Indian Commissioner William Medill, Washington, September 8, 1846, Microcopy K70, Part 8.

arrived at the Osage Agency. War with Mexico had begun in May, and General Stephen W. Kearney marched his Army of the West from Fort Leavenworth across the plains to capture Santa Fé. Since many of Kearney's wagonmen were from the Mormon encampment on the west bank of the Missouri River above Bellevue in what is now Nebraska, Indian Superintendent Harvey worried about the possibility that these Mormons would incite the Indians to make war against the Gentiles, an action which might embroil the Miamis. The Mormons, still gathering when the Miamis arrived, planned to cross the plains on a trek which would take them beyond the reach of persecution. California and Oregon boosters had persuaded less than three hundred immigrants to make that journey in 1845. It was a hazardous journey, and the price of failure was being paid by the Donner party in the Sierra Nevadas even as Agent Vaughan was issuing the first rations to the Miamis in November, 1846.

More than a century has passed since the Miami emigration, and during much of that time, the tribe has appeared to be an obscure little group of less than one hundred people of no real significance to anyone but themselves. Yet the Miamis have maintained a tribal structure with a sense of historical continuity. Explanations for their ability to survive lie in federal Indian policy and in the contributions made by the group in the west, by the dispersed individuals in the west, and by the tribal remnants in Indiana. When all of these factors are considered, Miami survival becomes understandable.

In the eyes of the Bureau of Indian Affairs, the Miami tribe resided at the Osage Agency west of Missouri after 1846 and at the Quapaw Agency after 1873. In order to treat with Indian tribes, the federal government had long recognized them as bodies politic —states within states. Since the Miami communal lands were now in the west, it was the western group which the Bureau of Indian Affairs considered to be the Miami tribe. Therefore, federal legal and administrative contacts with the tribe were necessarily conducted through this group's council, which the government recognized as the tribal council and the spokesman for all members of the tribe, no matter where they resided.

Immediately after Lafontaine set out for Indiana, the western Miamis called a council and elected Ozandiah, the Owl, to replace him. Although the Indiana Miamis protested that it was not a legal council, Ozandiah had been a respected leader and no one could challenge his election after Lafontaine's death. Despite Ozandiah's death after about a year in office, tribal stability was ensured by the undisputed election of Big Leg as his successor.[3]

Fortunately, the Miamis did not suffer from Plains Indian raids as did the tribes who emigrated in the 1830's, and the hysteria about the Mormons was groundless, but they experienced several difficult years. Their first complaint arose when Agent Vaughan employed his son to deliver rations to them. They objected to the expense of his employment, the kinds of rations he supplied, and the frequency of his visits. They then began to criticize the agent's failure to supply the blacksmith and other mechanics who were to help them carve out farms.

The Miamis soon split into two factions over the influence of Baptiste Peoria, or Lanapeshaw, of the Peoria tribe. Peoria worked closely with Superintendent Harvey to consolidate the Miamis with their Illinois relatives. There was a monotonous but familiar round of Miami complaints to Commissioner of Indian Affairs William Medill against Harvey and Vaughan. First Ozandiah, then Big Leg, complained through their interpreter, John B. Bourie, himself part Miami, that a few Peorias and Potawatomis related by marriage to Miamis had been presented to the tribal council and adopted. The adoptions are evidence that Peoria had gained a strong following among the Miamis. Bourie included the charges that Peoria was an agent of the Chouteau Fur Company of St. Louis, which the Miamis thought the largest dispenser of whisky

---

[3] Agent Joseph Sinclair, Fort Wayne, to William Medill, Washington, April 4, 1847, commented on the death of Lafontaine and the election of his successor. Superintendent Harvey, at Osage Agency, to Medill, Washington, May 3, 1848, reported the death of Ozandiah on May 20, 1848. Harvey notified Medill of Big Leg's election. Roll 416.

in the west, and was part Negro—both anathemas to the Miamis. The Miamis also objected to Harvey's plans for mills as useless expenditures, placed at inaccessible locations and of no use to the tribe whatever except to drain their funds.[4]

During these disputes in 1848, most of the Miamis moved a few miles from their original location on Sugar Creek to the east bank of the Marais des Cygnes River in order to be nearer their new Baptist and Roman Catholic missions—and farther from the Missouri border. Alcohol, the worst enemy of the Miamis, was abundant only a few miles to the east in Missouri grog shops.

Vaughan's original list of the emigrants, drawn up in 1846, consisted of 42 families containing 323 individuals. Although one writer states that nearly 1,100 made the original migration and nearly half returned to Indiana, the same writer says only about 250 moved to the new location on the Marais des Cygnes.[5] It is impossible to give accurate numbers, since the population at the agency was never stable; many Miamis spent parts of the year in Indiana, as well as in Kansas. It is possible that some individuals left the reservation to join Indian tribes or white communities in other places in the west. In addition, there may have been more incidents similar to the one in which John B. Bourie led a party of seven Miamis toward the gold fields of California in the early 1860's. The members of the party wrote to their families when they reached Colorado, but were never heard from again.[6]

At first, the Miamis did not accept the situation with their customary flexibility. "The Miamies are a miserable race of beings, and in consequence of their dissipated habits, are fast passing off

---

[4] Thomas H. Harvey, St. Louis, to William Medill, February 24, 1848, Roll 418. Harvey to Medill, June 18, 1848, Roll 416, contains most of the complaints. The first entry of National Council No. 1 in the Miami National Council Book, dated October 29, 1860, asked for the removal of their interpreter, Baptiste Peoria, and his replacement by Thomas F. Richardville. This entry included the election of Nopshingah as chief. From a photostatic copy of the original in the Thomas F. Richardville Papers.

[5] Muriel H. Wright, *A Guide to the Indian Tribes of Oklahoma*, 132–33.

[6] Forest D. Olds, chief of the western Miamis, reports this is still one of the most popular Miami stories. Bourie was the Miami interpreter and signed the Washington treaty of 1854 as a delegated representative of the tribe.

their stage of being. . . . They now number about two hundred and fifty," reported the Osage agent in the fall of 1847.[7] Commissioner George W. Manypenny, who toured the western areas in the 1850's, thought the Miamis had made little progress, despite better reports from their agent.

Manypenny discovered that some of the immigrant tribes, especially those farthest from Fort Leavenworth and the Missouri border, were adjusting to an agrarian culture. The northern immigrant tribes were less well established than the civilized tribes west of Arkansas, partly because the former gave two to six months each year to hunting on the buffalo ranges and neglected their farms. In 1856, Manypenny complimented all of the Indians in Kansas Territory on their behavior during the civil disturbances of 1854. The Miamis managed to avoid the strife in "Bleeding Kansas" in the years that followed, but the influx of white settlers was a constant threat to their reservation. The commissioner believed the western routes of travel and the efforts to create the territories of Kansas and Nebraska were two of the worst menaces to Indian tranquillity. Accordingly, he preferred a separate Indian state, and in order to further his plan, he concluded a series of treaties with the tribes of Indian Territory, of which the treaty signed at Washington on June 5, 1854, was made with the Miamis.[8] The agreement was followed by years of litigation and marked the beginning of a Miami preoccupation with legal cases which continues today.

The treaty's title phraseology was explicit. It specified "the following named delegates representing the Miami tribe of Indians, viz: Nahwelanquah, or Big Legs; Macatachinquah, or Little Doctor; Lanapincha, or Jack Hackley; Sonelangisheah, or John Bourie; and Wanzapoeah; they being duly authorized by said tribe," but none was designated the principal chief. Five Miami "residents of the state of Indiana" also signed the treaty.

The principal purpose of the treaty was to reduce the 324,796-

---

[7] *Senate Document 1*, 31 Cong., 1 sess., II, 1096.
[8] George W. Manypenny, *Our Indian Wards*, 115, 118–26.

acre Miami Reservation to 70,640 acres, about one-seventh of its original area. This, of course, made a larger tract available to white settlers and secured for the Americans that part of the reservation crossed by the upper Santa Fé Trail. The reduced area was to be surveyed and allotments of 200 acres were to be selected for each person. Family heads were directed to select sites containing their own dwellings, if possible, and the chiefs were delegated to select the tracts for individuals who were absent or unable to make their own choices. The chiefs were also directed to select a 640-acre tract on which a school could be placed. All land in excess of that allotted was to be held in a contiguous tract as community property, but might be sold with presidential approval at any time the tribe agreed to alienate it.

An evasion clause was included in Article 2: the allotments were held by Indian patent and were not subject to levy, sale, execution or forfeiture, "provided" that the legislature of a future state within which the land "may be embraced" might later remove these restrictions, with the assent of Congress. Such a clause could have only one meaning in an American frontier state: The Indian lands would be alienated.

The tribe was paid $200,000: $150,000 in twenty annual installments of $7,500 beginning in 1860 and $50,000 in stocks. The interest from the latter was to be used for educational purposes. None of the money was to be paid to any Miamis who were permitted to remain in Indiana by the treaties of 1838 or 1840, or by the resolutions of Congress passed March 3 and May 1, 1845, "or otherwise," which, of course, meant those on the approved list of 302 Miamis in Indiana.

The treaty also provided for dividing between the western and Indiana Miamis installments of the limited annuity of 1840; and western Miamis received $5,636.36 annually. The blacksmith and miller services provided by the 1818 and 1834 treaties were continued. The United States was released from all claims on the permanent annuity of $25,000 provided by Article 4 in the 1826 treaty, as well as the other provisions of that treaty, and from all other claims for depredations and wrongful acts. It is impossible to conceive inducements which could have made the delegates agree to abandon this permanent annuity; nevertheless, in its place they agreed to accept $190,434.68 in six annual installments beginning in 1854. They also received $30,000 for various other losses, including the expenses of their removal from Sugar Creek, and compensation for white depredations.

Although the treaty piously admonished the Indians against the use of whisky and warned them of contracting individual debts, an unusual provision was made in Article 13 by which $6,500 from each of the four annual payments to the western Miamis was to be "applied as far as it may be necessary, to the settlement of their affairs." This could only be a new phrase for the old term *debts*.

A new and important departure was made in Article 10. The Miamis acknowledged the federal right of eminent domain when any road or railroad right-of-way was needed through Indian lands.

More than a century later, the United States Court of Claims ruled that the western Miamis actually received only 38 per cent of the true value of the land ceded and 78 per cent of the value of their permanent annuities in the commutation. The court described the transaction:

> Commissioner Manypenny stated that the Government wanted to "blot out" the old annuities by making several large payments. One of the Miami delegates answered that his party did not want it that way, but wished the annuities to run on. We find no evidence that the Miami wanted the annuities commuted. Under such circumstances, we can think of no reason for their having taken less than the value of their annuities other than that they were less than completely aware of the meaning and methods of commutation, and were incapable of determining for themselves the value of the annuity.[9]

The western Miamis dealt with their allotments in a generous fashion. When the first, consisting of 200 acres each, were made

[9] Kappler, *Indian Affairs,* II, 478–83. *Stat. L., X, 1082.* The Miamis had received a tract of 324,796 acres rather than 500,000 acres. *Appeal No. 2–59.* U.S. Court of Claims.

in 1857, 162 individuals received tracts. In 1858, the tribal council decided 43 people had been missed and proposed to provide for them also.[10]

Meanwhile, white settlers had moved onto the Miami Reservation. Troops sent to drive them away in 1856 arrived in midwinter. Because the Indians had no wish to dispossess the squatters at such a time, the troops were withdrawn when the intruders promised to leave in the spring, which, of course, they failed to do.

The tribe planned to sell the undivided residue of their reserve in 1859 but soon decided against it. Chief Nopshingah explained:

> But as ther is some amongst us who have no land such as children of Bowrie, since the original allotments were made and some that have come amongst us from Indiana with the intention of residing here with us permanently. It was necessary therefore to retain the communal lands.[11]

This familiar encroachment continued, and the Miamis convened a conference, which they called a "National Council Meeting," on October 10, 1860, to prepare more petitions to the Bureau of Indian Affairs. The council elected Nopshingah principal chief and Gotecopwa, Onezopeah (George Hunt), and Louis Lafontaine subchiefs. Thomas F. Richardville was made interpreter to replace Baptiste Peoria.[12]

The white intruder problem assumed a new form in 1861. The Civil War began, Kansas Territory became a state, and warfare— organized as well as guerrilla—engulfed eastern Kansas. While the larger tribes of Indian Territory played important roles in the war, the Miamis and most other Kansas tribes did not permit themselves

---

[10] "Miami Reserve Matters: Statement of John Roubidoux, head Chief of the Miami Indians of Kansas, Paoli, Kansas, 1871," from a photostatic copy of the original in the Miami Reserve Papers.

[11] Nopshingah, Chief, Miami Village, to A. B. Greenwood, Council of Indian Affairs, November 18, 1860. From a photostatic copy of the Miami National Council Book, National Council No. 2, Thomas F. Richardville Papers. The minutes of the Council Book contain lists of reservation allottees, including new arrivals from Indiana, complaints against various Miami agents, and the arguments for instituting a suit against the federal government for violation of the 1854 treaty.

[12] Ibid.

to become a part of the conflict. Agent Colton made an ingratiating offer to Miamis who would join the Union cause, but Nopshingah returned a diplomatic refusal:

> I speak for my People. We are few there is But a handful of Miami now and though we love the Great White Father and would wish to help him in his great trouble and time of need we are not able to do so as our numbers are so small[.] the year last past has been hard upon the Miamis and it will require all our exertions to care for our families. But we sincerely sympathize with our Great Father and hope he will punish his rebelious children. . . .[13]

In 1867, the Bureau of Indian Affairs returned to its plans to remove the Kansas tribes to areas more isolated from white settlers and from the transportation routes to the west, a program forecast in 1863 when Congress had authorized President Abraham Lincoln to make such transfers.[14] At the same time, the Bureau proposed to combine or terminate small tribal entities for the sake of efficient administration. There was continuous pressure from the Bureau to consolidate the Miamis with the remnants of their relatives. While some small tribes sought to unite in order to gain strength— and various small bands often tried to obtain the same end by joining the Cherokees or other strong tribes—most of the Miamis objected to either course. Their sense of national identity was strong, and the plans for a merger threatened to cause a schism.

At the persistent urging of the Bureau of Indian Affairs, part of the tribe finally agreed to leave Kansas. On February 23, 1867, a new treaty was made with fractions of several tribes in order to locate them on new reserves of land ceded by the Quapaws in the northeast corner of Indian Territory south of Kansas. The treaty stated that the Miamis could join the Peoria confederation "if they so desired"; it was signed by Thomas F. Richardville and Metocin-

---

[13] National Council Meeting No. 12, at the House of Onezopeah, March 12, 1862, in the Miami National Council Book. The agent informed the Miamis at the next council meeting that Indian volunteers were no longer needed. Annie Heloise Abel, *The American Indian As a Participant in the Civil War*, 76–77.

[14] *12 Stat. L., 793*. Schmeckebier, *Office of Indian Affairs*, 107.

yah [Metocina], or Thomas Miller. The document established a reservation of 50,000 acres for the Peorias and Miamis, if the latter acceded, at the new Quapaw Agency. Allotments totaling 30,455 acres were surveyed for 153 Peorias, while 65 Miamis who decided to emigrate from Kansas received 12,878 acres.

Another provision of the treaty was a condition that those Miamis who refused to move to the new reservation should receive fee simple title to their Kansas lands, plus American citizenship. They retained their interest in the Miami suit then before the Bureau of Indian Affairs and soon sent to the federal courts, even though they withdrew, of their own volition, from membership in the tribe. Thus they became ineligible to receive future Bureau services and funds. Even more importantly, they accepted exclusion from the tribal rolls, councils, and identity with their past. This proved to be a more drastic cleavage than that of 1846, but it did not infringe upon the right of a Miami to choose separation from the tribe. At the time, constriction of the tribe appeared to pave the way for confederation at the Quapaw Agency, but its most obvious value was that it avoided the embarrassment of creating the nucleus of a third Miami group.[15]

While individual Miamis debated the proposed move to the new reservation in 1869, they made additional allotments from the Kansas reservation to forty-three individuals whom they had formerly neglected and to twenty-two young children, in addition to some recent immigrants from Indiana, even though some of the Indiana immigrants were never placed on the western Miami roll. By the time the tribe moved to Indian Territory in 1873, less than 10,000 acres remained unsold or divided from the original Kansas reservation of 70,000 acres.[16]

In 1869, the Kansas Legislature petitioned Congress in the man-

[15] The Quapaw Agency was established by *15 Stat. L., 513*. The 1867 treaty is in Kappler, *Indian Affairs*, II, 740–48. Eventually located at this agency were the Quapaw, Miami, Ottawa, Shawnee, Seneca, Wyandot, Peoria, and Modoc tribes.

[16] The basic act disposing of the Miamis' Kansas land was *Stat. L., X, 1082*. This was followed by a series of acts, beginning with *Stat. L., XVII, 631*, in 1863 and finally concluding with *Stat. L., XXII, 116*.

ner made familiar by older eastern states as they tried to hasten Miami departure:

> . . . Whereas the value of these lands have been greatly enhanced by the energy, enterprise and institutions of the white people settled among them, the benefit of whose laws and institutions these Indians enjoy exempt from taxation or any of the burdens of civilization, a condition of things inconsistent with the rights of the State and unjust to the people thereof; . . . .[17]

There was an uneasy truce with the squatters until 1870, when violence seemed inevitable. The Miamis again appealed for troops and the government sent them in December. Again the Miamis proposed that the intruders should stay until spring, but Chief John B. Roubidoux made a restrained but eloquent complaint:

> What rights have the settlers upon our lands? The answer is plain—none in justice or equity. But politically they have voted, and in this they are stronger than we. Our claims and rights are nothing, and the promised protection of the Government idle words. It is claimed that those settlers were encouraged to settle our lands by ourselves. This is not the fact, as the records of the Indian Office will show. Time after time have we made application to the Department to have them removed. In 1856 Maj. McCaslin was ordered to remove them. Troops were sent him for that purpose. It was in winter; snow was on the ground, after repeated promise from these said settlers, that they would leave in the spring they were permitted to remain for the time. But the settlers did not keep their promise. They remained, for the troops were gone, and they had no cause of fear. Time and time again were they warned to leave the Reservation. At last, after we had been threatened by violence should we dare to come upon or take possession of the lands patented to us by the United States, we appealed to the Government, asking that troops be sent to remove the trespassers. We made the application ourselves, through our Agent, James Stanley, in last June or July. We again petitioned the Department in October last, and in December last the troops were ordered here. When informed that the troops were about to remove these intruders, we of our own accord,

[17] "Resolutions of the Legislature of Kansas, February 17, 1869," *Senate Miscellaneous Document 56*, 40 Cong., 3 sess., I.

requested Mr. Stanley to delay matters until spring, only stipulating that the troops remain until that time. Had no one interfered in the behalf of those men, Indians as we are, we would not have the untold hardship of removal in mid-winter fall upon women and children, who have been guiltless of harm to us. While we want quiet and undisputed possession of our own, we do not wish to be unnecessarily harsh.

It is true there are farms and orchards upon those lands. Does that give them rights? Does the continued evil doer for that reason, in time, have full liberty to transgress the law without fear of punishment? How were these improvements made? Has not our timber made them? Have not our timber lands been encroached upon, and the thousands of dollars' worth of the most valuable timber cut off and sold by these very men, and proceeds gone into their pockets? Many of them have resided on our lands for ten and twelve years. Have they paid rent to any one? Have they paid a cent of real tax in all these years? What part of the treaty of 1854 gave them any hope of ever securing these lands at Government rates? Have not their own actions shown that they never had any such hopes? Have they not always been holding meetings and employing agents to work for them to obtain these lands? Would they have done so, did they believe for a moment they could obtain them without a special effort?

They claim to have been soldiers, and suffered for their country. Would that give them any privilege to rob us of our inheritance? We think not. How many were soldiers? Eighteen, according to their own list. And good soldiers they were, too, for all but one or two have either bought their land or moved off. Those remaining have been trying to buy. How many settlers are there upon our Reserve? Between three and four hundred men, women and children, all told. Will the Government undertake to say that we must give up our lands for a song, when we know their value, and desire to keep them as the last hope for our children?[18]

After the United States had negotiated 370 treaties with Indian tribes, it finally ended this policy in 1871, but those treaties still in force were not abrogated. Tribal sovereignty had by that time become a legal fiction as well as an anachronism. Thereafter, Indian affairs were conducted by agreements, usually placed in congres-

[18] "Statement of John Roubidoux."

sional appropriation acts, and by executive orders administered by the Bureau of Indian Affairs. There was no change in the agency Indian's legal status: he was still neither alien nor citizen, but a ward of the federal government, a status not established by the U.S. Constitution and inconsistent with the terms of the Fourteenth Amendment, as well as those of the First, Second, Fifth, Tenth, and Thirteenth amendments.[19]

Only a few western Miamis left Kansas and then only after one chief resigned and another was impeached and removed. They authorized the sale of the unallotted lands, as well as their individual tracts. Those who refused to emigrate received fee simple patents to their allotments and their shares from the tribal funds. On October 14, 1871, the *La Cygne* (Kansas) *Journal* began publishing the "headrights" issued to the Miamis, with descriptions of the individual parcels. The list was alphabetized, but nearly half the group of 262 people still used only their Indian names. It included four of Francis Lafontaine's children and a few Richardvilles who had been exempted from emigration a generation earlier but later moved to the Osage Agency.[20]

A few items from the La Cygne newspaper indicate the Miamis were still newsworthy after nearly thirty years in Kansas. Dr. J. B. Harris married a daughter of Chief Roubidoux in 1871. Harris became a notable doctor in Montana, whence he bombarded the Chief and the Quapaw agent with letters questioning the guardianship services Roubidoux performed for Harris' child. Brief personal items record the pranks of two Miamis and a white man who celebrated a Saturday night in town. The Indians were finally arrested, but the white man escaped. That same year, Miami Peter Cabbage died, leaving an estate of about fifteen hundred acres of Kansas land, while in the following year a confirmed Miami toper did not die from a rattlesnake bite.[21]

---

[19] Schmeckebier, *Office of Indian Affairs*, 58, 65. Harmon, *Sixty Years*, 323.

[20] *La Cygne* (Kansas) *Journal*, October 14, 1871. Schmeckebier, *Office of Indian Affairs*, 91.

[21] *La Cygne Journal*, May 10, 1871; January 6, 1872; December 7, 1872; August 2, 1873. From a photostatic copy furnished by Forest D. Olds.

An example of Miami acumen worth noting occurred at the time of the move to the Quapaw Agency. Young Joel Trinkle, son of Henry Trinkle, the tribe's blacksmith, and Peter Bundy's daughter Mahzehqueh, alienated himself from the tribe, took United States citizenship, and received a cash settlement. He then followed the tribe to the agency, took a Miami wife, used his money to build a house on her allotment, and watched his family and descendents maintain their place on the western Miami roll.

The sixty-five Miamis at the Quapaw Agency were now considered by the Bureau of Indian Affairs to be the Miami tribe. The immigrants adjusted well to their new home; they were accustomed to reservation life after a generation in Kansas, and their dual allotments, located on the Neosho River and the near-by prairie, differed little from their Kansas farms along the Marais des Cygnes. At the Quapaw Agency, they could escape increasing white aggression in Kansas and live near familiar tribes in the Indian Territory. The payment for their share of the Kansas tribal lands was added to their consolidated fund, a part of which was then transferred to a fund held jointly with the Peorias, while the remainder was distributed to individuals. Their contribution to the fund of the pending confederacy amounted to $24,952.[22]

Despite the Bureau's turnover in personnel and subsequent policy changes, it remained determined to consolidate the tribes. With the death of Baptiste Peoria in 1873, however, the faction which favored confederation lost its most important leader. Quapaw Agency officials recognized the Miamis as separate from the confederation tribes. The tribe continued to operate under the Miami National Council and its own chiefs. While some Miami individuals may have joined the "United Peorias and Miamis" authorized by an act of March 3, 1873, the union was never completed. In 1889, the Bureau recognized its failure to complete the organization which had agitated the tribe for years.[23]

22 Letter from the Commissioner of Indian Affairs, Washington, to H. W. Jones, Quapaw Agency, May 15, 1875; William Nicholson, Superintendent, to Agent Hiram W. Jones, Quapaw Agency, May 15, 1875, Miami Papers, Quapaw Agency Collection.
23 "An Act to Abolish the Miami Tribal Relations, March 3, 1873" is in *Stat. L.*,

Miami tribal continuity was attested in 1899 by Thad Butler, Huntington, Indiana, editor and historian, who visited Thomas F. Richardville at the Quapaw Agency to verify the names of the western Miami chiefs who had continued to lead the tribe. After Ozandiah, Big Leg served as chief until 1857, followed by John Ozandiah until 1860. Nopshingah was named chief in 1860 by National Council Number I, and his election was recorded in the Miami National Council Book. John Big Leg, or Wanzoppeah, succeeded him in 1867. The latter's term was short, and Lumkekumwah was elected the same year but was impeached and removed by the tribe. Their successor in 1867 was John B. Roubidoux, or Acheponquah, who was deposed in 1871.[24] The chiefs during the critical period from the treaty of 1867 until the tribe's migration to the Quapaw Agency in 1873 were obviously unable to unify the tribe or even to hold their office. The Miamis were unable to reconcile themselves to a new emigration or to the possible loss of their tribal identity, as they confessed to Quapaw Agent Hiram W. Jones in 1874:

> ... our people are all agreed to continue their chiefs Tho Miller Head Chief and David geboe Second Chief. and thay have also appointed Two councilmens John Lum Ke Com wah and Peter La falier for the term of good behavior. and also our people have Impowered us to signe any papers for them in there behalf. and our People wish to continue there chiefs after the consolidation with the Peorias and to hold the same Privlage as the Peorias. as our Bill dose not make any disstinction. but the two tribes shall be called the United Peorias and Miamies. . . .[25]

XVII, 631. A. C. Tanner, Acting Commissioner of Indian Affairs, to Thomas F. Richardville, Miami, Indian Territory, May 31, 1899, Miami Papers, Quapaw Agency Collection, explains the Miamis had never consummated the confederation, even though joint land allotments had been made. The act failed to secure the required consent of three-fourths of the adult males of each tribe. As proof of their separate existence, Tanner said the Peoria in 1899 were U.S. citizens while the Miamis were not. Sixty-seven Eel River Miamis shared in the 1889 annuity payroll, while seventy-three Miamis shared their annuity two years later. Both rolls were prepared by Quapaw Indian Agent F. J. Moore. Copies of the originals in the National Archives were made by Mrs. Forest D. Olds.

[24] *Huntington* (Indiana) *Herald,* August 7, 1928.

[25] Ely Geboe *et al,* Neosho River, to Quapaw Agent Hiram W. Jones, November

The following years were more peaceful. Thomas Miller served as principal chief until 1886, David Geboe until 1888, and Charles S. Walsh the two following years.

There were numerous federal acts dealing with the little Miami tribe at the agency, of importance at the time but insignificant now. An exception was a lawsuit culminated by a decision of the U.S. Court of Claims in 1889. When the Indiana Miamis' charges against the federal government for violating the terms of the treaty of 1854 were ignored by the Bureau of Indian Affairs, the western Miamis filed suit on behalf of all Miamis. The violations had occurred when some Miamis in Indiana had evaded emigration, although not exempted, and therefore found themselves on no annuity roll. The Indiana Miamis objected vociferously when the Bureau paid annuities to first sixty-eight and finally seventy-three of these people from the Indiana Miami funds. The western Miamis brought suit when they discovered that part of their own funds and their Kansas reservation land were also being used.

The western Miamis won a favorable decision from the commissioner of Indian Affairs in 1885. After deciding the Bureau had acted charitably but injudiciously in placing these persons on any Miami membership roll without tribal consent, he clearly stated the Bureau's intent to support the Miami organization in the west:

> ... In various parts of the treaty the Miami Indians, in what is now Kansas, are recognized as the Miami tribe, and it is clearly inferable, from certain sections of the treaty, that the Indians remaining in Indiana were not regarded as members of the tribe proper. ... It seems to me manifest that a clear distinction is made by this treaty between the Miami tribe and certain Indians who had failed to accompany the tribe west of the Missouri, and continued to reside elsewhere, and that none are included as members of the tribe except those who had accompanied the chiefs of the tribe west of the Missouri, and that the benefits to be derived from the reservation of 70,000 acres for their future homes, and the annuity or annuities granted by the third article of the

22, 1874, Miami Papers, Quapaw Agency Collection. This letter was signed by both men and women.

treaty, were accrued to the members of the tribe of Miamis, as herein defined and explained. . . .[26]

In 1889, the Court of Claims handed down its decision in the case. It recognized both the sole right of the authorized members of the Indiana Miami tribe to add people to their roll and the financial losses of this group, of the western Miamis, and of the Miamis who had recently renounced their membership to remain in Kansas but had been members of the tribe when the violations occurred. In 1891, the western Miamis received $18,370 for the Bureau's violations of the treaty of 1854 and $43,600 for the Bureau's illegal disposal of 14,533 acres of their Kansas reservation.[27]

The last quarter of the nineteenth century saw little change in the condition of the Miami group at the Quapaw Agency. The reports of its agents essentially agree and can be summarized briefly to show the effects of forty years' residence in the west on these Miamis.

The Miamis, Wyandots, Peorias, and Ottawas at the agency were "practically white people"; in 1886, their farms were as good as those of white settlers across the borders in Arkansas and Kansas. By 1891, 75 Miamis had received their land allotments, and the number increased to 85 in 1894. They were described as better farmers than stockmen, with 17,803 acres under cultivation.[28] They might have preferred raising cattle, for their lands were well suited to that purpose, but their initial herds were nearly

[26] "Report of the Commissioner of Indian Affairs," *House Executive Document 23*, 49 Cong., 1 sess., IV, 1–27, contains the affidavits of the Miamis, the Bureau's several actions, and the commissioner's final decision. The evidence and court's decision are also given in *Senate Miscellaneous Document 1*, 53 Cong., 3 sess., I.

[27] The western Miami appropriation was made by act of March 3, 1891, *26 Stat. L., 1000. House Executive Document 23*, 49 Cong., 1 sess., largely concerning the Indiana Miamis, is the complete report of Commissioner of Indian Affairs William P. Dole on the Miami suits and their conclusions. It is one of the most informative of all federal documents concerning the Miamis and is quoted extensively in Chapter 9. The congressional appropriation act for the Indiana award is *28 Stat. L. 909*.

[28] "Report of the Secretary of the Interior," *House Executive Document 1*, 50 Cong., 2 sess., I, 172–76; II, 108–10. "Report of the Secretary of the Interior," *House Executive Documents*, 52 Cong., 1 sess., II, 234–40.

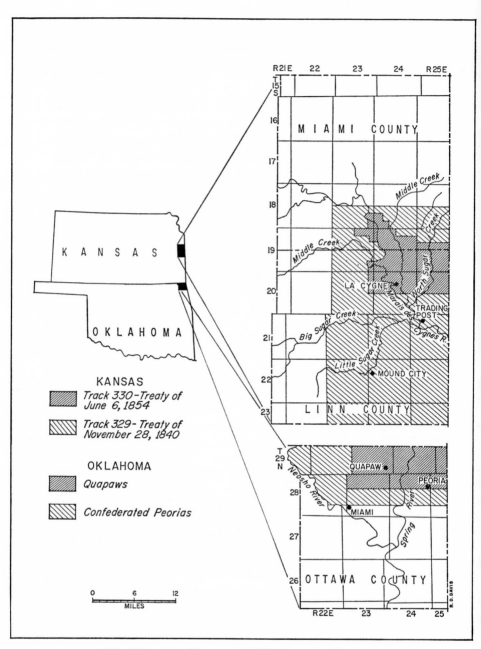

The Miamis in Kansas and Oklahoma, 1846–1969.

destroyed by Texas fever, carried by cattle driven from Texas to Sedalia, Missouri, on the eastern branch of the Shawnee Cattle Trail. The trail passed north of Muskogee along the divide between the Verdigris and Neosho (or Grand) rivers, turned northeast through the Quapaw Agency, and continued to Neosho, Missouri, or to Sedalia. The Texas herds infected the Indians' cattle in the 1870's, and it was years before they learned how to control the disease or could rebuild their herds.[29]

In 1887, 65 Miamis wore white dress, 50 spoke and read English, and the day school (which was the only school among them) was an excellent institution. In 1894, they had boarding schools because the day-school system had been abandoned.[30]

Indians of the Quapaw Agency tribes comprised the police force: a captain and six privates. Indian behavior was so good that the police acted in only one civil case and no criminal cases in 1886. In 1891, the agent declared the only crimes still prevalent were those connected with the use of alcohol; he considered the Miamis highly moral, especially in their respect for marriage customs. The Court of Indian Offenses, established in the Indian Territory in 1889, was also pertinent to Miami life. This system of petty tribunals, purposely given a vague definition of its jurisdiction, worked well. Three elderly Indian judges, open court sessions, and a particularly reliable police force did much to create mutual respect between the tribes and the federal government.[31]

By 1891, the Miamis had increased from 65 to 75 members, of whom 14 were children under sixteen years of age. The little group recorded one marriage, six births, and five deaths that year. The agent called them self-supporting and capable, and three judges

---

[29] *House Executive Document 1*, 50 Cong., 2 sess., I, 172–76; II, 108–10. "Report of the Secretary of the Interior," *House Executive Documents*, 53 Cong., 5 sess., II, 134–40.

[30] William T. Hagan, *Indian Police and Judges*, 104–25, discusses the Indian courts. He uses the Quapaw Agency force for illustrative purposes, 51–52. *House Executive Documents*, 52 Cong., 1 sess., II, 234–40.

[31] *House Executive Documents*, 53 Cong., 5 sess., II, 134–40.

served with distinction in the agency's Indian court. Methodist, Quaker, and Baptist missions were located at the agency, but most of the Miamis were Roman Catholics, and there were no longer medicine men among them.[32]

The agents' reports support opinions of federal Indian policies voiced by Superintendent William Clark in 1826 when he said:

> The largest annuity which we pay affords—but a few dollars per head when divided among a tribe, and constitute nothing of much importance to the amount of their property, and it is *property* alone which can keep up the pride of an Indian and make him ashamed of drunkenness, begging, lying and stealing. It is *property* which has raised the character of the Southern Tribes. Roads and Travellors through their country, large annuities and large sums [page 11] for lands from the United States, and large payment to Chiefs, have enabled them to acquire *Slaves, Cattle;* hogs, horses and these have enabled them to live independently, and to cultivate their minds and keep up their pride, while those even of the Southern Indians who have no *property* as I am informed, are in the lowest state of moral and mental degradations. An Indian will not work while in his uncultivated State; that is considered a disgrace; The period of danger to him is that in which he ceases to be a hunter, from the extinction of game, and before he gets the means of living, from the produce of Flock and Agriculture: In this transit from the *hunter* to the *Farming State,* he degenerates from a proud and independent Savage to the condition of a beggar, drunkard and thief; neglecting his family, suffering for food and clothes, and living the life of a mere animal. To counteract the dangers of this transit, *property* in *Cattle,* hogs, and horses is indispensable, and to furnish these, [page 12] the permanent annuities should be commuted into a group sum payable in equal annual payments for a moderate term of years; and the women and children, upon whom the labour of cultivating the ground devolves, should be assisted in making fences, to which their own means and strength are inadequate, also in planting orchards and instructed in raising cotton, and in spinning and weaving it into cloth, and making it up into garments. Small mills should be built and a miller provided to save the woman from the labour of pounding the corn—useful (mechanics)

[32] *Ibid. House Executive Documents,* 52 Cong., 1 sess., II, 234–40.

254

employed to make their ploughs, carts, wheels, hoes, axes etc. and for the purpose of teaching the young Indians how to use and make them. Most of these provisions I have found incorporated in your letter to the committee, and contained in the bill which has been reported and the adoption of others herein suggested I now recommend; and if enacted into a law I anticipate the commencement of a people, who have strong [p. 13] claims upon the justice and generosity of this government.[33]

Commissioner Francis E. Leup later recognized, with some misgivings, the changes Clark had predicted. He was concerned with the possibility that the reservation tribes might become "poor white men rather than good Indians." The reports of the Quapaw agents indicated they believed their charges were both good Indians and good white men.[34]

A major change in federal Indian policy came with the passage of the Dawes (or Allotment in Severalty) Act of 1887. Nearly every piece of Indian legislation since that time has been an amendment, supplement, or revision of the Dawes Act. Through an oversight, it did not apply to the Quapaw Agency tribes or to a few others at first, but by 1893, the Miami allotments were completed under its provisions, most of them having been made before its passage.[35]

Meanwhile, the Eel River group presented the kind of confusion which the Miami had learned to exploit. No Quapaw Agency official could untangle Miami and Eel River group membership, but the latter band agreed to accept the final settlement of all of its claims in 1889 and combine with the western Miamis. A census was prepared, and the payment that year to sixty-seven Miamis ended the basis for preserving a separate entity which long had been artificial.[36]

[33] William Clark, St. Louis, to Secretary of War James Barbour, Washington, March 1, 1826, Microcopy K70, Part I.

[34] Francis E. Leup, *The Indian and His Problem*, 48.

[35] *24 Stat. L., 388. Schmeckebier, Office of Indian Affairs*, 79–81.

[36] A congressional act of June 29, 1888, for the Bureau of Indian Affairs the following year appropriated $24,000 to settle in full their demands on the United States under treaties made in 1795, 1805, and 1809.

In 1890, the Quapaw Agency had a population of nearly 1,300, of whom only 57 were white settlers. It was overshadowed by the more populous southern region, where the Five Civilized Tribes had lived since 1830. In the same year, the latter area had 50,000 Indian, 110,000 white, and 19,000 Negro inhabitants. Four years later, nearly 2,500 whites lived at the Quapaw Agency by invitation of the eight tribes there, with no indications of any discord. Much of the white influx was due to increasing white-Indian marriages.[37] And Miami marriages into other tribes at the agency were, of course, inevitable. It is indeed surprising that these Woodland Amerindian tribes, coming from a common region and with centuries of contact in the past, were able to maintain separate identities. Tribal intermixtures have been only matters of family pride and tradition in most circumstances, while tribal enrollment and identification have remained primary. An outstanding example is the Miamis' pride in their connection to the Peoria chief Guy Froman, a great-grandson of Kilsoquah, or Angelique Rivarre, the granddaughter of Little Turtle.

Indian Territory, which lay south of Kansas and west of Arkansas, was divided in 1867. The eastern portion was retained by the Indian immigrants from the southern states, who had been among the earliest to move west of the Mississippi River and who now gave up possession of the western part of their lands in order that new reservations might be created for the western tribes. In 1890, the western district was organized as Oklahoma Territory. The Quapaw Agency, the lands of the Five Civilized Tribes, the Cherokee Outlet, and the Public Land Strip remained as Unorganized Indian Territory. The first two areas named remained so until 1907.[38]

Former Commissioner Leup called Indian Territory an experiment—a confederation outside United States law and a refuge for white outlaws after its separation from Oklahoma Territory. A

---

[37] Schmeckebier, *Office of Indian Affairs,* 127. "Report of the Quapaw Agency, August 27, 1894," *House Report 2503,* 82 Cong., 2 sess., 452. "Report of the Secretary of the Interior," *House Executive Documents,* 53 Cong., 3 sess., II, 134–40.

[38] Schmeckebier, *Office of Indian Affairs,* 91, 124–27.

federal movement was begun in 1893 to combine both territories into a state in order to deal with the settler problem. Leup believed that the resident traders among the Indians were their best friends and thought the "squaw-men" and "half-breeds" were "fine citizens," a compliment he did not bestow upon the white settlers. His judgment was vindicated in 1901 when citizenship was granted to all Indians of Indian Territory—before it was given to tribesmen in Oklahoma Territory.[39]

The Oklahoma Enabling Act of 1906, followed by statehood in 1907, was a great event in western Miami history. The Indians first opposed statehood but were finally mollified when the Enabling Act promised United States citizenship to all Indians who had not yet received it. Leup was sure the Oklahoma Territory tribes were ready for statehood but thought the Indian Territory tribes were not.[40]

Citizenship did not terminate Miami association with the Bureau of Indian affairs as it had for the Miamis of Kansas. Property management and assistance had created complex procedures with regard to heirs, estates, wills, leases, and depredations. Finally, the Omnibus Indian Act of 1910 tried to bring more order into federal administrative confusion created by the many legal categories developed by the government.[41]

The Miamis' relationship with the Bureau was simple when compared to that of other tribes. At the Quapaw Agency, they had received allotted lands, annuities, claims awards, and their share of proceeds from the sale of lands in Kansas and at the Quapaw Agency. They had been under the Bureau's supervision, subject

<hr>

[39] Leup, *The Indian and his Problem*, 328, 335, 344. *31 Stat. L., 1447*, gave these Indians citizenship but did not end the Indian Service's control of their property. The list of applicants registered for membership by the Miami Tribe of Oklahoma Council on September 1, 1959, includes the children of thirty-two Miami mixed marriages in which sixteen male parents were "white" and an equal number of female parents were "white."

[40] The Oklahoma Enabling Act is *34 Stat. L.; 267*. Leup, *The Indian and His Problem*, 206, referred to the exclusion of the Indian Territory tribes from the Burke Act. *Ibid.*, 342.

[41] *36 Stat. L., 855.*

to the Court of Indian Offenses and to their tribal laws. They had had nothing to do with state laws for forty years.

Some Miamis had abandoned this life of little change. It could be done by leaving the reservation for the "habits of civilized life." A more common method, after the Dawes Act provisions were extended to include them, was to file a federal relationship form certifying that the individual was of one-half or more white ancestry and therefore qualified to sell his allotted land without restriction. The certification removed Bureau supervision of the Indian's own control of his property. It also compounded genealogical and Bureau roll confusion, and we find brothers, children of the same two parents, who certified different degrees of Indian blood so that one could be classified as white and the other as Indian.

The western Miamis evidently had some degree of that "feverish activity" toward claims against the federal government which Leup deplored. After the payment of their claim award in 1891 and the Indiana payment in 1895, the western Miamis filed a new claim for interest due on those awards. To prosecute this claim, the Bureau of Indian Affairs in 1899 approved a contract in which the tribe engaged Thomas F. Richardville's "professional services." The contract expired in 1902, and Richardville and an attorney presented a new contract to continue the suit. The second agreement increased the legal fee and Secretary of the Interior Richard A. Ballinger refused to approve it.[42]

By 1890, Richardville had become the leader, but not the chief, of the western Miamis. The son of John B. Richardville, he was a worthy successor to the old chief, his grandfather, Jean Baptiste Richardville. He attended Notre Dame, at that time an academy and college, and worked as a clerk in the Lafontaine store at the

[42] "Miami Indians," a report to accompany S. 3795, March 10, 1910, in "Report No. 380," Senate Calendar, 61 Cong., 2 sess., includes Secretary Ballinger's report of February 21, 1910. From a photostatic copy in the possession of Forest D. Olds, August 7, 1929. Approval of Richardville's election is requested in Nopshingah, Miami Village, to A. B. Greenwood, November 13, 1869, in Miami Council No. 2, Miami National Council Book.

258

Forks of Wabash. After the 1846 emigration of the tribe, he soon moved to Kansas, where the western Miamis eventually tried to adopt him so he could serve as chief. Since Richardville refused to sever his ties with the Miamis in Indiana, the Bureau of Indian Affairs did not permit him to hold the office. However, he remained the most important leader in the tribe until his death in 1913.[43]

Not all of the western Miamis approved Richardville's leadership, nor could they forget their grievances against his grandfather. Simeon F. Geboe was happy to report that Richardville had been discovered collecting annuities from both the Eel River and the Indiana Miami funds, while Thomas Miller had received annuities from the western Miamis and the Peorias. Both had been ordered to make restitution, and Geboe wrote his sister:

> Mr. T. F. Richardville has been compelled to pay back the Miamis the money that he drew for his children, the decision having come from Washington that he could not draw in two places. Tom did not like it, and Miller sided in with him but then they could not help it. My impression is that Mr. Miller (Head Man) will either have to refund back to the Miamis or Peories the money that has been drawing for his boy. And you can bet he will if it lays in my power.[44]

Richardville's importance to the tribe cannot be minimized. His "Business Record Book, 1865–1892" and his "Marriage Records, 1866-1902" attest to his active career, and his records of guardianships, contracts, and other business papers are testimonials of his importance to the Miamis.[45]

The liberalization policies of the Bureau's Competency Commission of 1917–21 did not directly affect the Miamis. And the Citizenship Act of 1924 merely gave to other tribes of Indians a status which the Miamis had already achieved. The Quapaw Agency

[43] Information supplied by Forest D. Olds. *Huntington Herald,* August 7, 1928.

[44] Simeon F. Geboe, Miami Reservation, to Mary B. Geboe, July 11, 1881, from a photostatic copy of the original in the possession of Forest D. Olds.

[45] Various Richardville papers comprise a large portion of the Miami Papers, Quapaw Agency Collection, in the Oklahoma Historical Society Library. Commissioner Price, Washington, to Thomas F. Richardville, Indian Territory, June 28, 1881, presents the Bureau's charges of Richardville's multiple annuity collections. Other Richardville papers are at the Gilcrease Institute in Tulsa.

report of 1926 reveals that the Miamis no longer had a reservation, agency rations, tribal funds, government reservation schools, or a medical division, although health services have recently been restored to the tribe. The Miamis were the only one of the agency tribes to achieve this degree of emancipation from Bureau services by 1926.[46]

The Indian Reorganization Act of 1934 (Wheeler-Howard Act), represents the federal policies which govern the Indians' situation today.[47] The legislation was influenced by the findings of the Institute for Government Research, whose Meriam Survey, begun in 1927, reached thirty-six volumes by 1939 and became a turning point in Indian affairs policy. The information assembled during the survey influenced the terms of the 1934 law, which attempted to regenerate Indian tribal consciousness and culture through tribal governments organized as business corporations.

The Oklahoma Welfare Act of 1936 (Thomas-Rogers Act) supplemented the federal act, permitting tribes to form federal corporations with constitutions and bylaws.[48] The Quapaw Agency Miamis were well prepared to take this step. Their chief, Harley T. Palmer, who served in that office a total of fifty years before his retirement in the 1960's, was ably assisted by several other leaders. They prepared a tribal roll in 1937, with supplemental corrections in 1938 and 1939. In 1939, the "Miami Tribe of Oklahoma" submitted its constitution. The tribe ratified the constitution on October 10, 1939, and received its corporate charter April 15, 1940.

Such Indian charters have a common purpose: they create a business corporation which can sue or be sued, negotiate in financial matters or with governments, and protect the interests of members of the tribe. They also provide for review, by the secretary of the interior, of certain actions of the group.

The Miami charter of 1940 required approval by 30 per cent

---

[46] Schmeckebier, *Office of Indian Affairs,* 300–309.
[47] 48 *Stat. L., 984,* is usually called the Wheeler-Howard Act.
[48] The Oklahoma Welfare Act is *49 Stat. L., 1967.*

of the tribe's eligible voters, and a new roll was prepared. Harley T. Palmer, who served as chief from 1910 to 1963, signed the document, as did Marie Lucas Downing, secretary-treasurer of the tribe. Both also signed the certification of the Miami Tribal Business Committee. The Bureau of Indian Affairs area office once again requested a final roll, which was compiled in compliance with the new constitution. Membership requirements of the corporation, called the Miami Tribe of Oklahoma, are governed by Article II, Sections 1 and 2, of the tribe's constitution and bylaws:

> Section 1. The membership of the Miami Tribe of Oklahoma shall consist of the following persons:
>
> (a) All persons of Indian blood whose names appear on the official census roll of the Tribe as of January 1, 1938.
>
> (b) All children born since the date of this said roll, both of whose parents are members of the Tribe.
>
> (c) Any child born of a marriage between a member of the Miami Tribe and a member of any other Indian tribe who chooses to affiliate with the Miami Tribe.
>
> (d) Any child born of a marriage between a member of the Miami Tribe and any person, if such child is admitted to membership by the Council of the Miami Tribe.
>
> Section 2. The Council shall have power to prescribe rules and regulations, subject to the approval of the Secretary of the Interior, covering future membership including adoptions and the loss of membership.[49]

Considerable correspondence between the Miamis of Oklahoma and the Muskogee Area Office indicates that members of the tribe were of the opinion that they had "closed" their rolls variously on January 1, 1938; May 1, 1954; September 3, 1955; September 4, 1956; and September 1, 1959, by tribal action; however, as of this date, there have been no amendments to the constitution, and the provisions on membership are still in force, making the Miami corporation membership roll an "open" one.

The same federal policy which produced the Indian Reorgani-

[49] "Constitution and By-laws of the Miami Tribe of Oklahoma" also appears in *House Report 2503*, 82 Cong., 2 sess., 453.

zation Act of 1934 was responsible for the Indian Claims Commission Act of 1946, which created an agency to reassess the Indian treaties of the past. It accepts suits filed against the United States, investigates their charges, and presents its findings before the U.S. Court of Claims. It has opened to adjudication, hopefully for the last time, various charges by Indians that they have been exploited by the United States over the past century and a half.[50]

The Miami Tribal Business Committee presented the tribe's claims for damages suffered under terms of the treaty signed October 6, 1818, at St. Mary's, Ohio. The suit was accepted as a valid claim, given the title "Docket 67," and filed July 5, 1950. The Miami Indians of Indiana, apprehensive lest they not be included in the petitioner's term "all the members of the Miami Tribe," presented their claims against the terms of the same treaty; their suit was accepted as Docket 124. In 1954, Docket 67 Consolidated was created to include previous Dockets 67, 124, 314, and 337 in order to consider and resolve parallel claims by the Weas and Delawares as well as the Miamis.[51]

In 1954, the Indian Claims Commission announced its preliminary findings of fact for Docket 67 Consolidated in order to determine the Miamis' title to Royce's Tract 99, which could be separated from conflicting claims by the Weas, Potawatomis, Eel River Miamis, Kickapoos, and Six Nations. The supplemental findings of 1956 concluded that the Miamis had held undisputed title to 4,291,500 acres of Tract 99, not to the entire 7,036,000 acres of the cession, and the original payment of 6.4¢ an acre which they had received was unconscionably low. The Commission then decided the Miamis should have been paid a fair price of 75¢ per acre and an additional award of $5,277,000 should be paid to them.[52]

[50] *60 Stat. 1049.* Congress created a temporary three-member claims commission in 1952. Frank B. Horne and Margaret F. Hurley (comps.) *Federal Indian Law,* 356–57.

[51] The original petition as amended was filed August 9, 1951, as Docket 67, *Before the Indian Claims Commission: Amended Petition Relating to Treaty of October 6, 1818.* The official file is the record of appeal filed March 21, 1958, and cannot be circulated. Copies of these petitions and dockets were furnished to me through the courtesy of the Bureau of Indian Affairs and by the clerk of the U.S. Court of Claims.

The supplemental findings were based on prodigious research and most of the facts were not disputed, but the Miamis refused to accept the conclusion that 75¢ per acre was a fair evaluation of central Indiana land in 1818. They appealed the Commission's decision, and on July 13, 1959, the Court of Claims upheld their appeal and remanded Docket 67 Consolidated to the Commission for reconsideration. On June 30, 1960, the Commission re-evaluated the Miami lands in Tract 99 at $1.15 per acre and concluded the judgment against the United States should be $4,647,467.67 for 4,291,500 acres of land ceded in 1818. Congress passed the appropriation act May 17, 1963.[53]

The Miamis also sued for redress from the terms of the treaty of 1854. In Docket 251, the Miami Tribe of Oklahoma charged it had received only 324,796 acres in Kansas instead of 500,000, that it was paid an unfairly low price for those parts sold to the federal government, that the commutation of annuities arranged by the treaty of 1854 had been inequitable, and that the tribe had not been paid interest on the funds repaid it in 1891. In Docket 124A, the Miamis of Indiana made parallel claims against the commutation of annuities in the same treaty and also asserted they had claims to share in the sum paid for the sale of the Kansas reservation lands.

The Indian Claims Commission returned its findings of fact for both claims on July 14, 1958.[54] The Miamis again appealed the Commission's decisions and on July 15, 1960, the Court of Claims delivered its final opinion on these dockets. It awarded the Miami Tribe of Oklahoma $195,723.70 to reach a fair price for the sale of the Kansas lands, $53,397.70 for its losses by the commutation of annuities in 1854, and $100,072.19 for interest unpaid on the 1891 award. The court denied the Miamis of Indiana any right

[52] *Before the Indian Claims Commission,* decided September 17, 1956, Vol. 4, Ind. Cls. Comm., pp. 12–13, supplements the previous *Findings of Fact,* March 26, 1954, by the Indian Claims Commission, Vol. 2, Ind. Cls. Comm., pp. 617–34.

[53] *Appeal No. 2–58,* U.S. Court of Claims, decided July 13, 1959. *Before the Indian Claims Commission: Amended and Additional Findings of Fact, 9 Ind. Cls. Comm. 1,* June 30, 1960. The congressional appropriation act was *77 Stat. 43.*

[54] *Before the Indian Claims Commission: Findings of Fact,* decided July 14, 1958.

to share in the sale of the Kansas reservation lands, since they made no claims to these in 1854 when the subject "was before the Indiana Miami Council." However, the court awarded them $64,738.80 for their losses from the commutation of annuities in 1854.[55] Funds were appropriated to pay judgment in Dockets 251 and 124A on September 30, 1961.[56]

Funds for payment of the awards made for Dockets 67 and 124 were appropriated May 17, 1963, but the payment was delayed when it proved difficult to compose a satisfactory formula to determine the eligibility of Miami claimants not on the membership roll of the Miami Tribe of Oklahoma. Finally, on October 14, 1966, Congress passed an act which included a formula and the other conditions for making payment on these judgments. Briefly stated, the formula provided that the funds appropriated in 1961 and 1963 be awarded to the Miami Tribe of Oklahoma according to the plans adopted by its governing body and approved by the secretary of the interior, by which all persons enrolled as members of the tribe shall be entitled to equal shares in a per capita distribution.[57]

The Miami Tribe of Oklahoma distributed the funds awarded for Docket 251 in December, 1966. Its "open-end" roll of 816 members made this prompt distribution possible. The Miami Tribal Business Committee had failed to find and pay two individuals but was still searching for them. During the summer of 1967, nine Miami children were born and were immediately added to the corporation's roll. In 1969, the final payments on the claims in Docket 67 were paid to 1,231 western Miamis. Each individual received $1,217.69.[58]

The western, or Oklahoma, Miami tribe's unity has been preserved in a flourishing condition by its persistent demands that

[55] *Appeal No. 2–59*, U.S. Court of Claims, decided July 15, 1960.

[56] *75 Stat. 747.*

[57] *80 Stat. 909 (Public Law 89–659, 89th Congress, H.R. 7466, October 14, 1966).*

[58] Information supplied by Forest D. Olds, chairman of the Oklahoma Miami Tribal Business Committee. Also, Arthur C. Harker, attorney, Marion, Indiana, to William F. Hale, Eaton, Indiana, August 4, 1969. Copy of letter in author's possession.

the Bureau of Indian Affairs and the United States government fulfill the terms of past and existing contracts and treaties. The Miamis have maintained an active tribal organization, held frequent councils, and occasionally reaped the rewards of successful litigation. Meanwhile, their individual lives have been lived with constantly diminishing agency supervision or interference. The Indian Reorganization Act of 1934 and the Oklahoma Welfare Act of 1936, followed by tribal incorporation in 1940, were met quietly by a tribe well trained in self-government. Incorporation gave the Miamis an efficient business committee which could utilize the Indian Claims Commission Act of 1946; it could also cooperate efficiently with the Miamis of Indiana in claims cases. The major point of emphasis, however, is the advantageous legal position which the Oklahoma Miamis occupy.

9
THE MIAMIS IN INDIANA, 1846-1968

The Miami emigration in 1846 and 1847 removed the last "Indian menace" from Indiana. Removal had been a contrived issue and more than half the tribe remained, to become the basis for romantic legend and the source of local pride.

Except for those on Meshingomesia's reservation, most of the Indiana Miamis were already "white" in culture, since the majority were offspring of mixed marriages. Successful Indian farmers, such as Brouillette, Frances Slocum's son-in-law, were at no social or economic disadvantage in their communities. Annuity payments continued to bring federal money into the state, and the Richardville and Godfroy descendants were wealthy by Indiana standards. Extensive intermarriage with their white neighbors continued, and since northern Indiana settlers lived near the last great fur-producing region east of the Rocky Mountains, an Indian partner was an asset in many forms of business enterprise and a liability in none.

The older Indians had many white friends. They received respect and counsel from the first generation of Indiana settlers and traders, who still formed the economic aristocracy of the Wabash Valley. Alexis Coquillard, L. M. Taylor, George W. Ewing, Allen

Hamilton, and hundreds of other men knew and respected the older Miamis.

Marriage was the chief problem of the young Indian. Prohibitions against closely related unions within the tribe were strict, which helps to explain the visits of western and Indiana Miamis to each other's homes as they searched for eligible marriage partners. But ponder this example of intertribal marriage by an Indiana Miami. A part-Delaware named John Newman from Maryland or Virginia visited the Meshingomesia reserve. He soon married Jane Bundy, a widow. Their many children, farther removed from Miami taboos on incest, married freely with Miamis on the reserve.[1]

As the number of available Indian partners decreased, most Indian marriages were with white men or women. Two things made this acceptable in the small Indiana towns. First, most of the marriages were with recent Irish or German settlers, who were usually Roman Catholic members of churches attended by Miamis. Such marriages aroused little attention in the Protestant community. The second aspect of interracial marriages is more conjectural and subtle. The Indian boys and girls became less different from their white contemporaries in dress, speech habits, and appearance. The parochial schools, the Choctaw Academy, and White's Indiana Manual Labor Institute were partially responsible for the integration. More important, Indiana was no cultural oasis; it had recently held the dubious title of having the highest rate of illiteracy of any state north of the Ohio River, and the farm child visiting the local village could scarcely be distinguished from the Indian children.

The Miamis often preferred to send their children away to school rather than use the local or district elementary schools. Isaac McCoy's mission school was operated successfully at Fort Wayne in the early 1820's, though not without some hair-raising incidents. The Sisters of Providence School at Fort Wayne was attended by many Miami children in the 1840's and 1850's. After the Miami emigration, Josiah White, a Philadelphia Quaker,

---

[1] Winger, *The Frances Slocum Trail*, 64–65.

founded White's Indiana Manual Labor Institute in 1852 on the edge of the Meshingomesia Reserve. It was for "poor children, white, colored and Indian" and many of the nearby Miami children attended it. They were joined in 1885 by twenty-seven children from the Quapaw and Sac and Fox agencies who were assigned to the school under a contract with the Society of Friends. With financial aid from neighboring Miamis and under Quaker sponsorship, the Institute had a steady growth.[2]

On the reserve, a small elementary school, built close to the Indian Village Baptist Church, sheltered several generations of Miami children. Otho Winger taught there from 1895 to 1898 and began his long interest in the Miamis. The building still stood in 1969, but on Tawataw's old farmstead near that Meshingomesia grandson's beautiful brick house.

In time, a few Indians who refused acculturation and maintained an uncompromising adherence to Miami ways became sources of local pride. The state of Indiana carved Richardville County from a part of the Big Miami Reserve to perpetuate the chief's name.[3] Although the county's name was soon changed to Howard, hundreds of Miami place names are still to be found in Indiana as well as in other states. In bygone days, county fairs, town parades, and Independence Day festivities were complete only when local Indian residents took part in the ceremonies.

One phase of Miami life during the last half of the nineteenth century can be understood only in relation to its legal and social status. This was the Miamis' failure to take part in the Civil War. Although a large number had become "white" and were even excluded from the tribe by the council, a search of the records of military units from Cass, Miami, Wabash, Grant, Huntington, and Allen counties fails to reveal even one Miami name. Nearly

[2] Richard G. Boone, *A History of Education in Indiana*, 226–28. It is probable that Meshingomesia donated the land on which White built his school. The Sisters of Providence School was attended by the children of most of the Miami chiefs. Anson, "John Roche," 51. McCoy, *History of the Baptist Missions*, 67, 73, 125, 164.

[3] George Pence and Nellie C. Armstrong, *Indiana Boundaries: Territory, State and County*, 442–45. Richardville County was organized May 1, 1844, but the name was changed to Howard County on December 28, 1846.

every able-bodied white in these counties saw some military service during the war, and the Miamis' failure to take part indicates apathy toward appeals for their participation and a radical departure from their warlike past. The Miamis had often "observed" before they took an active part in warfare, but their noninvolvement at this time was a sure sign of their rejection of any citizenship responsibility during the war to either the federal government or the state of Indiana.[4]

Individualism, whatever its cause, produces "characters." Indiana has seen its share of these interesting personalities, and some of them were Indians. Nevertheless, the Indian's devotion to the culture of his tribe tended to draw the largest concentration of Miamis in the state to the Meshingomesia Reserve, where they constituted a group of Indian conformists, leaving the whites in communities surrounding the reserve in the minority.[5]

Another problem for the Miamis of Indiana was the changing legal status of Indians. The Indiana Miamis had little direct interest in the federal administrative change which placed the Bureau of Indian Affairs in the newly created Department of the Interior in 1849.[6] However, federal Indian policy changes were needed as Oregon Territory and the Mexican Cession were acquired and migration to the Pacific Coast passed through lands held by tribes not one of whom had treated with the United States. Many new Indian treaties were negotiated, and the treaty made at Washington on June 5, 1854, although primarily concerned with the western Miamis, included provisions dealing with the Indiana group.

Commissioner George W. Manypenny evaded the problem of the tribe's division by recognizing the Kansas emigrants as the tribe and the Indiana residents, with all their contending factions, as "absent members." He referred to the western leaders as the "dele-

---

[4] W. H. H. Terrell, *Report of the Adjutant General of the State of Indiana.*

[5] In 1845, Indian Superintendent Crawford had foreseen the possibility that the Meshingomesia Reserve would become a refuge which would attract Indians of all tribes, as well as interfere with Miami emigration. T. Hartley Crawford, Washington, to William Wilkins, Secretary of War, January 31, 1845, Roll 417.

[6] *9 Stat. 395.*

269

gates representing the Miami Tribe of Indians" and to "Meshing-omesia, Pocongeah, Pimyiohtemah, Woppoppetah, or Bondy, and Keahoctwah, or Buffalo, Miami Indians, residents of the State of Indiana, being present." He thus clearly stated the Bureau's position that the tribe was in Kansas but that the Indiana Miamis were still members of the tribe, were legally involved in the conditions of the treaty, and merited recognition in its terms.[7]

The principal objects of the treaty were to secure the cession of a large portion of the Miami reservation in Kansas Territory and to consolidate the various Miami annuities. The first article dealt with the Kansas land cession and stipulated the Indiana Miamis should receive none of the purchase price. The treaty of 1826 consolidated the "permanent, perpetual, and forever" annuities of earlier treaties into a "permanent annuity" of $25,000 which by 1854 had grown to $26,400. This amounted to the annual interest from a sinking fund of $530,800. Manypenny wanted to convert the permanent annuity by making several large payments.

The chiefs and the Commissioner agreed in Articles 4 and 5 to the commutation of the old annuity for the sum of $421,438.68, of which the Miamis of Indiana were to receive $231,004. The Miami chiefs opposed the commutation but finally acquiesced because "they were less than completely aware of the meaning and methods of commutation, and were incapable of determining for themselves the value of an annuity." A permanent annuity of $26,400, if still being paid when this book was published, would have returned a sum many times the face value of the sinking fund, but even that was discounted. The time and methods of payment to which the Miamis agreed were such that they actually received only about 78 per cent of the face value of the original sinking fund which the treaty acknowledged was rightfully theirs.[8]

In Article 4, the Indiana Miamis and the Commissioner agreed on the names of 302 Miamis who thenceforth were eligible to draw annuities. The list included not only those originally exempted from

[7] 10 Stat. 1093.
[8] Appeal No. 2–59, U.S. Court of Claims, decided July 15, 1960.

Martha Newman (1873–1887), daughter of John and Jane Newman. Her Indian name was Lanonnokizurnquali. From a photograph in the William C. Goodpasture Collection.

George Bundy, son of Coon and Jane Bundy. His Indian name was Shapenemaw. He died at Upland, Indiana, about 1920. From a photograph in the William C. Goodpasture Collection.

Western Miami chiefs. *Front row (from left)*: David Geboe, Peter Lafalia, John B. Roubidoux, Thomas Miller, Louis Lafontaine. *Back row*:
unidentified government agent, Thomas F. Richardville, McKinsey,
unidentified government agent.

The home of Thomas F. Richardville northwest of Commerce and Miami, Oklahoma. From a newspaper photograph made by Craig Studio, Miami, Oklahoma.

Thomas F. Richardville about 1910.

Courtesy Harold Moore, Muncie, Indiana
Indiana Miami Chief William F. Hale, (*left*) and
Oklahoma Miami Chief Forest D. Olds in 1966.

Tribal chiefs at the Quapaw Agency, 1966. *Front row (from left)*: Clarence King, Ottawas; Forest D. Olds, Miamis; Guy Froman, Peorias. *Second row*: Bob Whitebird, Quapaws; Leonard Cotter, Wyandots; Julian Bluejacket, Shawnees. *Third row*: John Belindo, Kiowas and Navahos; Vernon Crow, Senecas and Cayugas.

Courtesy Forest D. Olds, Miami, Oklahoma

A Miami chief in 1968. Forest D. Olds with his grain combine machine.

emigration in 1838, 1840, and the congressional resolutions of 1845, but also nearly 150 Miamis who had eluded emigration ten years earlier. Additions to the "Indiana roll" could be made only by the "consent of the said Miami Indians of Indiana, obtained in council, according to the custom of the Miami Tribe of Indians." In effect, this phrase gave Bureau approval to a tribal council for the Miamis of Indiana and has been a source of confusion and recrimination since that time.[9]

The Washington treaty became the cause of a legal struggle which lasted thirty years in its first stage, and further litigation has continued for more than a century. A number of Miamis, many of mixed blood, did not emigrate to Kansas, although they had not received permission to remain in Indiana. Therefore, they were not placed on the Osage Agency Miami roll, and when a new annuity roll of the Indiana Miamis was compiled, the chiefs approved only about 150 names to add to the list of those permitted to remain in the state. This excluded 68 persons who had drawn annuities in Indiana before the emigration, and these 68 collected evidence to prove they were members of the tribe. Those excluded were restored to the roll in 1851 by the Bureau of Indian Affairs, against the wishes of the Indiana Miami council, and collected annuities that year and in the following one before being removed from the roll once more. They were omitted from the roll authorized by the treaty of 1854, with the Miami delegates' approval, but the Bureau then placed their names on a special annuity roll in 1858 so they could receive past annuities. The following year, they were added to the Indiana roll once more in spite of the disapproval of the Indiana Miami council. By 1867, these claimants, now numbering 73, had drawn $32,899.11 from the Miami fund.[10]

[9] Kappler, *Indian Affairs*, II, 478–83.
[10] Special Agent John A. Graham's annuity payment report of 1860 to the Miamis "east of the Mississippi" details payments to family heads, including persons whose payment was contested, guardians, and trusted agents. As representatives of the latter two categories, James T. Miller received most of the money paid the Mississinewa group and John Roche received much of the money destined for the Richardville and Lafontaine groups. Copy of Graham's report supplied by Forest D. Olds.

The payments were challenged by the 302 Miamis authorized to share these funds. The group collected evidence supporting its objections, and in 1868 the attorney general of the United States ordered the additions removed from the Indiana roll until a final decision could be reached in a suit brought in the same case by the western Miamis.

The repudiated Miamis were mostly of mixed descent and nearly half were descended from Josetta Beaubien Roubidoux, daughter of Maria Louisa Richardville by her second marriage to Fort Wayne trader Charles Beaubien. Josetta was therefore Jean Baptiste Richardville's half-sister. Her descendants were included in the Minnie, Roubidoux, Lafalia, Harris, and other mixed-blood families. Others disqualified were from the villages of Papakeechi and his brother Wauwasee, who had dispersed among the Potawatomis of Michigan in 1846. These villagers had long been allied with the Potawatomis and were seldom seen on the Wabash except at payment time.

Former Miami Agents Allen Hamilton and Joseph Sinclair testified that the seventy-three people or their families had drawn annuities before the emigration to Kansas and had been considered members of the tribe until 1846. However, Hamilton admitted that several chiefs had protested when the names were first placed on the Indiana roll in 1851.

The long-smoldering grievances of the Mississinewa villages colored the testimony gathered in that area. Some of the emotion probably originated as early as the Pickawillany incident in 1752 and had been nourished by tribal elections and, especially, through the treaty period by the favoritism Meshingomesia felt had been shown the Godfroy and Richardville families. Meshingomesia now said Richardville had been elected chief only because he spoke both English and French and could conduct the tribe's business in those languages. He repudiated the importance of Le Gris and Pacanne, claiming that Kahkowichkowah was the civil chief who preceded Richardville and that the former followed Tawataw, grandfather of Metocina, who in turn had succeeded his father.

272

Meshingomesia insisted Richardville had no brothers or sisters, thus excluding the claims of Josetta's family, and accused him of concealing from the tribe all treaty terms which could benefit the old chief and his friends.

The most important trader to the Mississinewa villages was Samuel McClure. He testified that Metchinequea (Majenica) forced Richardville to omit payment to mixed-blood families of the Miamis in 1834. A Dr. William McKinsey, who had visited the village at Forks of Wabash a half-century earlier when White Loon was chief, testified that Richardville was but an impoverished member of the group who was ignored because of his white ancestry.

Commissioner of Indian affairs finally sent all of the collected evidence to Congress in 1885 with his final conclusions in the case. He defended the Bureau's actions, but because of stipulations in the treaty of 1854, he conceded that the funds of both the Indiana and western Miamis had been illegally used. The treaty declared that any additions to the roll of 302 Indiana Miamis must be made with the consent of the recognized Indiana council. He ordered the seventy-three disputed names stricken from the Indiana roll and the dispersed funds restored by the federal government. He also declared that most of the rejected group had been required to emigrate to the west in 1846 but had refused to go, which had little weight since in 1854 the Bureau had approved a large number of additions of people who had done the same because it was agreeable to the Indiana Miami council.

Meshingomesia had often opposed the Wabash villages, especially their mixed-blood chiefs, but his primary purpose in the case was to defend the council prerogative, both in Indiana and the west, and his success strengthened the chiefs' authority, even though the tribe's membership was reduced and it now had two councils.

The commissioner of Indian affairs made it clear that the Bureau now considered that the Miami tribe consisted only of those who had migrated to the west and then moved to the Quapaw Agency, even while he conceded that the Indiana Miamis must be reimbursed for the federal government's previous error and recognized the existence of an Indiana council.[11]

The legal status of Indians in Indiana involved the rights of individuals rather than those of tribal entities. Such rights were developed from precedents established during the half-century before 1847, and a brief review of them is helpful. The Indian was a ward of the federal government, an alien, when he stepped on land under the jurisdiction of the state of Indiana, and since he was not a white male, of course he could not vote.[12] His subordinate place was emphasized in Article VII, Section 1, of Indiana's first constitution, which prohibited Indians, Negroes, and mulattoes from serving in the state militia.

The emotional and political climate of the frontier fostered change, and when two men, three women, and five children, Miami and Shawnee Indians, were murdered near Pendleton in 1824, three of the white men were tried and hanged. The trial was conducted as if the victims were white people, and the judge's summation included the statement that law knew no color of skin.[13] This was the first Indiana trial and execution of white men for the murder of Indians.

The first official request for Indian removal was made by the Indiana General Assembly in a memorial to Congress in 1829. It petitioned for Miami removal from the state for the Indians' protection and to expedite the development of internal improvements.[14] The General Assembly of 1831 proposed a constitutional amendment which would have given citizenship to Indians in the state. It was defeated, but the same legislators then enacted a law making the sale of spirits to Indians a state offense.[15]

An important change was embodied in an Indiana act of Febru-

---

11 The lengthy correspondence, testimony, and decisions in this case are in *House Executive Document 23*, 49 Cong., 1 sess., IV, 1–27.
12 *2 Stat. L., 139*, the Intercourse Act of 1802, was the basic act for Indian affairs until 1834.
13 Smith, *Early Indiana Trials and Sketches*, 55–57.
14 *Laws of the State of Indiana, 13 Session of the General Assembly*, 155–56.
15 *Laws of the State of Indiana, 16 Session of the General Assembly*, 268–69.

ary 3, 1841. It repealed the use of writs of capias ad respondendum against Indians, which exempted them from the legal requirement in certain actions at law in which a sheriff is required to take and keep a defendant so that he may be presented in a court on a certain day. The new law also abolished the requirement for bail for those one-eighth Indian or more and denied the right of Negroes or whites to collect debts from Indians. It provided only for the use of a common fieri facias against Indians who lost suits at law, which in effect directed sheriffs to levy and secure from the property of an Indian the amount of money required when the Indian lost a suit at law. These provisions prevented Indiana courts from imprisoning Indians for debt or for failure to make bail and may have originated from a respect for the Indians' willingness to appear voluntarily in court and also from Indiana courts' reluctance to house Indians in jail for long periods of time.[16]

Huntington County court records reveal the practice of greater local latitude, or citizenship rights if we interpret freely, than that granted by the state. There were many civil suits with Indians as both parties. There were also a few cases in which Indians sued white men.[17]

The right to control land transactions was as important as citizenship qualifications. On December 5, 1848, the general assembly granted the right of land conveyance to Indians upon petition to the Allen County Probate Court. The sales had to be made through a bonded agent, and Father Julian Benoit was appointed to that position. His selection was due to Miami trust in the Fort Wayne priest, who was already the administrator of the extensive Richardville and Lafontaine estates. Father Benoit had no control over land held in fee simple title by adults of those families, but many of the Miamis who had not emigrated also had fee simple titles, as well as Indian patent lands, and the new law restricted conveyance.

[16] *General Laws of Indiana, 25 Session of the General Assembly,* XXV, 134.

[17] Most of these cases were brought in the name of Lewis Berthelette, Richardville's chief clerk. *State of Indiana* vs. *Swawcocimuah* on a charge of murder was entered in the Order Book, but final disposition of the case was not recorded. *Huntington County Circuit Court Order Book, A-1,* 319–20, 325–26, 328–29, 350, 352–53.

The law was a clear limitation upon the right of the individual Indian to convey land.[18]

In 1861, a new property conveyance law was enacted. It granted to citizens, aliens who were bona fide residents of the state, Indians, Negroes, and others of mixed blood the right to convey property.[19] By placing the Indian in a special category, the law gave him a special status, though with lessened restrictions.

The 1861 law did not prove satisfactory, and a new act in 1863 declared an Indian could devise a valid will conveying property as a resident alien. As such, he could also acquire property and could enjoy the protection of the law and the services of the courts.[20]

Until 1851, Article II, Section 2, of the first state constitution included the word "white" in its definition of voter qualifications, and Miamis who voted did so as white men. The second state constitution made the same provision until 1881. It also permitted only white males to enroll in the militia.

The Miamis in Indiana who had not yet secured citizenship by 1881 achieved it in that year. The federal act of June 1, 1872, which ordered the division of the Meshingomesia Reserve provided for citizenship for its individual allotees after 1881.[21] By inference, all Indiana Miamis not included in this group already possessed state and federal citizenship. The sixty-three individuals who received allotments on the reserve thus became the last large group of Miamis in Indiana to receive federal and, by the terms of the state constitution, state citizenship. By this time, it was difficult to differentiate any Indian from other Indiana residents, and even those most obviously of Indian descent were almost unnoticed in the populous state.

Federal Indian policies were still important to some people in Indiana. A federal act of 1871 abolished traditional but outmoded

18 *General Laws of Indiana, 33 Session of the General Assembly*, XXXIII, 71–73.
19 Burns, *Annotated Indiana Statutes*, XI, 2, is the amendment to *I.R.S., 1852*, Ch. 23, p. 232.
20 *West's Indiana Law Encyclopedia*, XXIX, 440.
21 *United States Statutes at Large*, Vol. VII, pp. 569–70, is the Meshingomesia Reserve Allotment Act.

concepts of "domestic but dependent nations." It recognized the validity of all former treaties with Indian tribes, but abolished the treaty system in favor of one of executive authority exerted through the Bureau of Indian Affairs.[22] This authority was used to order the partition of the Meshingomesia Reserve into allotments held in fee simple and granted citizenship to members of the Meshingomesia family. Their allotment act received mixed response along the Mississinewa. It also provided a lengthy document which includes the names of those individuals accepted by the group and those who claimed membership but were rejected. Three federal commissioners were appointed to make the allotments. They advertised in the Peru, Marion, and Wabash newspapers so that their purpose would reach all interested parties. They also sent copies of the notices to the Miamis of Kansas and to those at the Quapaw Agency, since Indiana Miamis were constantly visiting there.

The commissioners' first meeting was held in the reserve schoolhouse on May 14, 1873. It was originally scheduled for the Miami Union Missionary Baptist Church located near by. Even though the church building was on the reserve and was largely built with Miami funds, its congregation was white and the trustees refused to permit its use by the Indians.

Meshingomesia appeared first and presented a list of persons he believed were entitled to allotments. The commissioners then began to compile testimony from all of the claimants. Both the Chief and his opponents had the aid of legal counsel. The commissioners spent weeks arriving at their decisions, which can be summarized briefly. The Meshingomesia family in 1840 had 56 members, of whom 14 were still living in 1873. In 1873, 43 persons were direct descendants of the original 56. There were also 6 women from other tribes or families who had married into the group and were equally entitled with the preceding members to full allotments. The commissioners compiled lists of persons in each group and decided that only 63 people were eligible for allotments. They also filed a list of 55 persons who claimed membership in the family but whose

[22] 16 Stat. L., 566.

claims were disallowed. Forty-six of these were also found liable for the costs of their unsuccessful negotiations, a good indication that the commissioners were unsympathetic toward unsupported claims. The reservation was divided into 63 parcels, including the residence of each individual in the parcel granted to him.

Nine lists, or exhibits, were prepared by the commissioners. Meshingomesia listed members of his family by their Indian names, with some Anglicized first names. The other lists gave both Indian and "white" names, and the final list of sixty-three successful claimants gave family relationships. The lists of rejected claimants included many who had been residents of the reservation for years. Richardville, Lafontaine, and Bundy or Slocum descendants are found in this list. They admittedly gave allegiance to the Indiana Miami council and lived on the reserve, but Meshingomesia made a distinction between welcome guests or refugees and members of his own family. It is equally clear the family had increased in size very little since 1840. In Meshingomesia's eyes, it had actually decreased, but the reservation had become the refuge of other Miamis for a variety of reasons.[23]

Another valuable census was compiled for all of the Miamis "residing in Indiana or elsewhere" in 1881 in order that final payment could be made in accordance with the amended Article 4 of the 1854 Washington treaty. Since the principal sum was now $221,257.86, Special Indian Agent Thad Butler worked meticulously to compile Indian and white names, as well as relationships and ages. All Miami families were represented, and scattered individuals who usually paid little attention to their Indian ancestry made every effort to gain enrollment on the list. There were 321 names, numbered consecutively but also including the numbers by which the appropriate individuals were designated on the 1854 census and on the 1880 annuity lists. The place of residence was also given.

---

23 "Report of Commission Appointed by the Secretary of the Interior to Make Partition of the Reserve to Meshingomesia and His Band Under Provisions of the Act of Congress, Approved, June 1, 1872." The report to Commissioner of Indian Affairs E. P. Smith is dated July 12, 1873. From a photostatic copy in my possession.

A superficial survey shows that although most of these Indiana Miamis lived "near Fort Wayne," "near Peru," "near Reserve," "near Lafontaine," "at Huntington," and so on, a significant number had gone to Kansas or to the Quapaw Agency since 1854. One example shows that residence information was not always reliable or permanent: Kilsoquah, granddaughter of Little Turtle and widow of Rivarre, spent most of her life near Roanoke, but at this time she was living at the Quapaw Agency.[24]

A subsequent census was required in 1895 to distribute the sum of $48,528.38 finally appropriated by Congress because of the 1868 intervention of the attorney general and the 1889 decision of the United States Court of Claims. Special Agent M. D. Shelby listed 439 Miami names, arranged alphabetically, but a few of the last were young children. The new numbering system was supplemented by adding the numbers assigned by Butler to the same individuals in 1881. Shelby did not enter the names of those who had died since 1881 but, at the proper alphabetical space, placed the census number given by Butler with the notation "dead." Shelby also included a few Miamis who had not been on earlier rolls, but there now seemed to be no opposition to expanding the membership.

Shelby used Anglicized surnames whenever possible, followed by the term "alias" and the Miami name. He also included age, sex, and children of the family; the alphabetical arrangement simplified the latter information. Shelby's census became increasingly important to the Miamis when it was made the basic Indiana roll used in Court of Claims decisions after 1954. Another significant point was the inclusion of five Miami signatures testifying to Shelby's list: Gabriel and Peter Godfroy, Judson and Peter Bundy, and Anthony Walker. Gabriel Godfroy signed as chief—the first time since Lafontaine's death in 1847 that the federal government gave tacit recognition to the office in Indiana—in addition to the

---

[24] "Census List of the Miami Indians in Indiana and Elsewhere, Prepared by Thad Butler, September 10th, 1881." From a photostatic copy of the census book in my possession.

chief of the Miami tribe formally recognized by the Bureau of Indian Affairs as residing at the Quapaw Agency.[25]

The legal maneuvers and investigations for compiling tribal rolls in the 1880's and 1890's helped to maintain the common historical heritage of the scattered Miamis. "Miami Day" at Lafontaine, Indiana, in 1909 was well documented with photographs of individuals, families, and a group picture of nearly two hundred people. Such gatherings were primarily social and "family," but they also perpetuated the group's knowledge of federal Indian policies. Miami leaders used the occasions to maintain a semblance of unity.[26]

Most federal policies did not affect the Indiana Miamis. The Dawes Act of 1887 did not apply to them; the Burke Act of 1906 merely duplicated their own experience when partitioning the Meshingomesia Reserve; and the Omnibus Indian Act of 1910 generalized legal processes already in practice in Indiana. The so-called liberal policy of the Bureau of Indian Affairs from 1917 to 1921 was unimportant to the Miamis of Indiana, except that an act of June 30, 1919, gave the secretary of interior the authority to prepare final tribal rolls. Even the Naturalization Act of June 2, 1924, cannot be considered important to Indiana Miamis except for its removal of the "alien" stigma from their Amerindian relatives.[27]

Federal policies during the 1920's were designed to terminate tribal organizations by accelerating cultural, economic, and politi-

[25] "Roll of Miami Indians of Indiana, June 22, 1895, Prepared by M. D. Shelby." From a photostatic copy of the Annuity Pay-Roll Book in my possession. The attorney general's decision is in *12 Atty-Genl., Op.,* p. 236. The Court of Claims final summaries are in *Ct. Cls., Congressional Case No. 1843; Pet. Ex. 207, Docket 251.* The 1891 western Miami payment was authorized in *26 Stat. L., 1000,* while *28 Stat. L., 903* authorized the 1895 Indiana Miami payment.

[26] *Paul* vs. *Chilsoque, 1895 (70F. 401),* by which it was declared an Indian, though unnaturalized, was not an alien, was the kind of subject discussed at these meetings. The photographs reveal that social display was the primary concern of the young Miami.

[27] *24 Stat. L., 388* is the Dawes Act; *34 Stat. L., 182* is the Burke Act; *43 Stat. L., 253* is the Naturalization Act of 1824. Schmeckebier, *Office of Indian Affairs,* 87–90, briefly summarizes this period.

cal absorption into the American way of life. The process was partially reversed in 1934 by the Indian Reorganization Act,[28] which was designed to revitalize vanishing Indian cultural ways.

In the same decade, numerous northern Indiana celebrations commemorated the centennials of counties and communities. In these gala affairs, Indians and longtime white residents occupied honored places. It gave meaning on the local level to federal sponsorship for the preservation of Indian culture. Newsmen and amateur historians scanned older historical accounts of 1876, 1887, or 1916, which contained scraps of Indian history they found fascinating. The writings of Miami Clarence Godfroy and Potawatomi Leopold Pokagon were not overlooked.[29] As a result of all this activity, nearly every county in northern Indiana seemed to have at least one Indian historian who broadcast his findings.

John B. Dillon had once been the only reputable historian of Indiana's past, and his writings on the Indian period were in great demand. Otho Winger, at first a teacher at the school on the Meshingomesia Reserve and later president of Manchester College, was the most popular writer of Miami Indian tales. The works of Bert I. Griswold and Wallace A. Brice of Fort Wayne, Sanford C. Cox of Logansport, and the county histories compiled by Thomas B. Helm of Roanoke and Frank Sumner Bash of Huntington were studied with renewed respect.

As part of the increased interest in the past, the most popular feature in the scattered Indiana museums was usually the Indian collection, while such youth organizations as the Cub and Boy Scouts perpetuated Indian crafts. Fortunately, the science of archaeology came of age in the 1930's to give some guidance to the antiquarians of Indiana's past. And public schools, colleges, historical societies, professional journals, and publishing houses sought to discover and preserve Indian cultural anthropology and history. Indiana's acceptance of the Indian contributions to its

[28] The Wheeler-Howard Act is *48 Stat. L., 984.*

[29] Martha Una McClurg (ed.), *Miami Indian Stories Told by Chief Clarence Godfroy (Kapehpuah)*, contains many of the tales which made Godfroy a popular speaker.

past was paralleled by the dawning awareness that the descendants of the Indians were still an important segment of the state's population.

Indiana was not alone in its interest in Indian matters. Four federally sponsored general field investigations produced a mass of information. The House of Representatives Committee on Indian Affairs compiled reports in 1920 and 1944. In 1927, the Institute for Government Research published its *Service Monograph No. 48,* which was used in preparing the terms of the Wheeler-Thomas Act of 1934. In 1943, the Senate Committee on Indian Affairs published a forty-one part report of its fifteen-year study. The voluminous material on the Amerindian even required numerous "guides" to manuscript and printed material. The most recent governmental report is the comprehensive volume produced for the House of Representatives in 1953.[30]

Sometime before this federal government–inspired interest in the Indians, the Indiana Miamis attempted to form an organization in connection with their annual gatherings. In 1934, they met at Wabash, with C. Z. Bundy as the presiding officer, and completed their plans. The group then petitioned Congress for approximately one million dollars, which they believed was due them from funds still held by the federal government. Meanwhile, on September 30, 1937, they filed articles of incorporation for the "Miami Nation of Indians of the State of Indiana" in an attempt to utilize the terms of the Indian Reorganization Act of 1934. Their petition was rejected by Congress.[31]

The Indiana Miami organization was repeatedly refused recognition by the Bureau of Indian Affairs. The Miami Tribe of Oklahoma received a federal charter in 1940, and the Indiana Miamis

---

[30] Edward E. Hill (comp.), *Preliminary Inventories of the National Archives of the United States, Records of the Bureau of Indian Affairs, Number 163;* Philip M. Hamer (ed.), *A Guide to Archives and Manuscripts in the United States;* and John E. Freeman and Murphy D. Smith (comps.), *A Guide to Manuscripts Relating to the American Indian in the Library of the American Philosophical Society,* are scholarly aids to the subject area. Horne and Hurley, *Federal Indian Law,* are the current authorities in this field.

[31] Information supplied by William F. Hale.

appeared to lose their last chance to gain legality in the Bureau's eyes. They again tried to gain recognition when the Indian Claims Commission Act of 1946 created an agency to reassess the Indian treaties. Ira Sylvester Godfroy and William A. Godfroy of Peru and John A. Owens of Huntington, their authorized representatives, employed a Washington, D.C., law firm to prepare and prosecute their claims. In 1949, they petitioned for redress of the terms of the St. Mary's treaty of 1818, but their petition was rejected. However, an amended contract with their legal firm empowering it to prosecute their claims was approved by the Bureau in 1951, primarily because it complied with the Bureau's requirements in such cases. This became tacit recognition that the interests of the Miamis of Indiana in the treaty of 1818 could neither be ignored nor equitably investigated through claims originated only by the western Miamis.[32]

The Miami Tribe of Oklahoma petitioned the Indian Claims Commission on July 5, 1950 (amended August 9, 1951), in a similar action under terms of Section 2 of the Indian Claims Commission Act. It claimed damages of $13,400,000 in Docket 67, which became the basic document for Miami legal maneuvers after 1953.[33]

Limited recognition of the Indiana Miami petition came on June 7, 1951. The Indian Claims Commission recognized the Indiana Miamis' separate but parallel existence in Docket 124.[34] While Docket 67 was entitled "The Miami Tribe of Oklahoma, also known as the Miami Tribe, and Harley T. Palmer, Frank C. Pooler and David Leonard as representatives of the Miami Tribe and of all the members thereof, Petitioners vs. the United States of America, Defendant," the titles of the petitions, appeals, and findings slowly changed to give status to the Indiana Miamis.

[32] Exhibit A and Exhibit B, photocopies in my possession. The claim was filed under Land-Claims 4391. The contract is No. I-1-ind. 42496 in the Bureau's *Miscellaneous Records*, XVIII, 37.

[33] Docket 67, *Before the Indian Claims Commission: Amended Petition Relating to Treaty of October 6, 1818,* Filed August 9, 1951, p. 2.

[34] D. S. Myers, Commissioner, July 9, 1851, In Re: Miami Indians of Indiana Contract. Copy in my possession. *Before the Indian Claims Commission: Opinion of the Commission,* decided March 26, 1954, 2–636.

It soon became evident that Dockets 67 and 124 involved conflicting claims made by other tribes. Therefore, on March 26, 1954, the Indian Claims Commission ordered the two dockets consolidated with the related claims so that it could determine whether a Wea claim in Docket 413 or a Delaware claim in Docket 337 conflicted with the Miami claims. Later that year, the Commission also permitted the Potawatomi petitioners in Dockets 15D, 29D, and 311; the Six Nations in Docket 89; and the Kickapoos in Docket 315 to intervene in Docket 67 Consolidated for the "limited purpose of asserting on behalf of the respective petitioners . . . title or interest in or to Area 99 or any part thereof."[35]

In 1956, the Commission found the price of 6.4¢ per acre paid to the Miamis for 4,291,500 acres of land in 1818 was unconscionably low. It said the tribe should receive $5,277,000 in order to bring the original purchase price to 75¢ per acre.[36]

The supplemental findings issued by the Indian Claims Commission on September 17, 1956, represented an exhaustive study of the types and values of land purchased from the Miamis in 1818. The appraisers included contemporary accounts, tables of values of the public lands, amounts and prices for land sales during the period, and tables of the kinds of lands included in the cession. They gave the amounts and values of the lands sold from Tract 99 for the two decades after the Miami treaty. The successive federal land laws and policies were summarized and U.S. economic fluctuations evaluated. The result was a model of research conducted in order to ensure a land valuation which would be fair to both seller and buyer.[37]

The Indian Claims Commission finally gave the Indiana Miamis the recognition they had long demanded. In 1958, its findings of fact in Docket 251 and Docket 124A, dealing with the treaty of 1854, said of the Miamis: "The two petitioners constitute and

[35] *Ibid.,* 2–644.
[36] *Before the Indian Claims Commission: Opinion of the Commission,* decided September 17, 1956, 4–399–405.
[37] *Before the Indian Claims Commission: Supplemental Findings,* decided September 17, 1956, 4–346–97.

represent all descendants of members of the Miami tribe of American Indians (Miami Tribe *vs.* United States, Dkts. 253, 131; 5 I.C.C. 181) and are organized entities having the capacity to present claims under the Indian Claims Commission Act of 1946. (Def. Ex. 16, p. 3, Dkt. 251)." They were no longer dependent upon western Miami initiation for their petitions.[38]

About 400 Indiana Miamis met at Peru and voted to accept the award of 75¢ per acre,[39] but they were finally persuaded that they should appeal their case to the U.S. Court of Claims. The United States government filed a cross appeal, and the court returned a new judgment on July 18, 1959, remanding the case to the Indian Claims Commission on the issue of the value of the land and vacating the Commission's 1956 findings of value. The Commission reevaluated its findings and on June 30, 1960, revised its award to $1.15 per acre, the total award to all claimants amounting to $8,091,400. This sum was reached because the land involved had been finally determined at 7,036,000 acres, of which the Miamis were considered the original owners of 4,291,500 acres.[40]

These changes required a great deal of consultation and restraint on the part of the Indians and their attorneys, but on July 13, 1959, the Court of Claims made its final decision in the case of Dockets 67 and 124.[41] The following month, the Court of Claims found in favor of the Miamis in two related suits, Docket 251 and Docket 124A. The Indiana Miamis were awarded $64,738.80 additional compensation for annuities commuted in 1854 in the court's decision on Docket 124A.

---

[38] *Before the Indian Claims Commission: Opinion of the Commission,* decided July 14, 1958, 6–513–51.

[39] *Huntington* (Indiana) *Herald-Press,* January 8, 1957.

[40] *Before the Indian Claims Commission,* decided September 17, 1956, Vol. 4, Ind. Cls. Comm., pp. 346–97, supplements the previous *Findings of Fact,* March 26, 1954, by the Indian Claims Commission, Vol. 2, Ind. Cls. Comm., pp. 617–34. The final revision by the Commission is in *9 Ind. Cls. Comm. 1,* pp. 12–13.

[41] *75 Stat. 747,* enacted September 3, 1961, was the congressional appropriation for the award for Docket 124A. A congressional appropriation for the award for Docket 124 was enacted May 17, 1963 *(77 Stat. 43). Public Law 89–659, 89th Congress, H.R. 7466 (80 Stat. 909),* October 14, 1966, contains the formulas used to determine eligibility to share in both Indiana awards.

The title used in the decision was lengthy: "The Miami Tribe of Oklahoma, also known as the Miami Tribe, and Harley T. Palmer, Frank C. Pooler and David Leonard, as Representatives of the Miami Tribe, and all the Members thereof, Appellants; Ira Sylvester Godfroy, *et al.*, on Relation of the Miami Indian Tribe and Miami Tribe of Indiana, and each on behalf of others similarly situated and on behalf of the Miami Indian Tribe and various Bands and Groups of Each of them, comprising the Miami Tribe and Nation, Appellants *v.* The United States, appellee."[42] Although they were members of the tribe and possessors of a council, the non-emigrants occupied the position of exiles in the eyes of the Bureau of Indian Affairs. The Mississinewa council insisted that it was the true nucleus, if not of *the* Miami tribe then at least of *a* Miami tribe. The court's use of the term "Miami Tribe of Indiana" gave legal status to the Indiana Miamis.

The problems of Indian claims against the federal government are complex. Fortunately, competent law firms specialize in this area, and the Indian Claims Commission produces models of legal and historical research in its opinions. The claims procedures now work more rapidly than they did before the turn of the century. Nevertheless, the Miamis and other tribes, whether operating through business committees or tribal councils, use democratic processes which require informed members. Bureau officials, tribal operation officers, attorneys, and chiefs encounter the age-old Indian prerogative of individual dissent. Common interest in the awards may bind together the members of a tribe; it also may serve to drive members apart. Most disagreements concern the formulas which should be used to determine eligibility for sharing claims awards.

After the Court of Claims ruled in the Miami cases, it was still necessary to secure congressional appropriations for the payments. The Miamis were fortunate to gain support from Indiana and Oklahoma congressmen. Their appropriations were authorized

[42] *Appeal No. 2–59*, U.S. Court of Claims, decided July 15, 1960.

October 14, 1966, and the Tribal Operations Office of the Bureau of Indian Affairs was placed in charge of securing and validating individual Miami claims. The "Rolls of Miami Indians of Indiana," compiled by M. D. Shelby in 1895, was to determine eligibility. An office was immediately established in Marion, Indiana, to serve the Miamis in that area. There, claimants could secure "obligation" forms and obtain help in establishing their eligibility according to the provisions of Title 25, Code of Federal Regulations, Part 41.[43]

Meanwhile, the Indiana Miamis petitioned the Indian Claims Commission in Docket 131 for permission to institute a suit for damages incurred from the treaty negotiated at Fort Wayne on September 3, 1809. Dockets 124C, 124D, 124E, and 124F concerned minor adjustments in the major suits.[44]

The descendants of Francis Godfroy were moving forces among the Indiana Miamis for years as the older generations slowly passed away. An important step was taken in 1961 when William F. Hale, great-grandson of Metocina and a veteran of World War I (he served as a noncommissioned officer in the campaign against Pancho Villa) and World War II, was elected tribal chief and council chairman of the Miami Tribe of Indiana. The meeting at which this was done designated itself as the tribal council, thus giving substance to terminology already used by the Court of Claims. Eleven other men were then elected councilmen—and also clan chiefs to recognize a cultural memory. The Richardville, Godfroy, Meshingomesia, and smaller family groups were represented at the meeting, and a measure of Indiana Miami unity was finally achieved. The council also became affiliated with the Long House League of North American Indians, an organization incorporated under the laws of Kansas.[45]

Hale and the tribal council have been guided by the 1895 roll. The Indiana Miamis' 1965 roll of membership, compiled by the

[43] *Appeal No. 2–59*, U.S. Court of Claims, decided July 13, 1959.
[44] Information supplied by William F. Hale.
[45] The Miamis of Indiana were hosts to the annual Grand Council of North American Indians at Fort Wayne in 1965 and 1966 and at Gary, Indiana, in 1967.

council, first contained 317 names but was subject to change. Many persons no doubt were unaware of the fact that their claim to Miami tribal membership needed to be substantiated; others preferred to sever all ties with Indian ancestry, even at a financial loss, but the council expected a flood of valid and invalid claims at the time of harvest.[46]

Enrollment applications were made at the Muskogee Tribal Operations Office, and a special office was opened at Marion, Indiana. The application period ended June 30, 1967, after hundreds of people filed their forms at the latter place. The Tribal Operations Office then began its check of the validity of the claims, and to the great surprise of the Indiana leaders, 3,066 people were declared eligible for membership on the Indiana Miami roll, and each received $1,237.69 in 1969. It appears that the large increase has not been caused by adding descendants of the two groups removed from the rolls during the last century, but is due to a natural increase in population.[47]

The larger membership roll adds to the prestige of the Miamis. It will also cause them to re-examine their old problems of cohesion, alliance between the two groups, and the degree of activity which the tribe will maintain after the awards are made.

It is well that the Indiana Miamis are securing a definitive tribal roll, for it becomes more difficult each year to clarify their genealogies and sizable areas of their homeland are disappearing rapidly. Federal watershed control and conservation projects have already inundated the Salamonie Valley and will soon cover the Wabash Valley for miles east of Huntington. A federal bypass highway will obliterate much of the Forks of the Wabash and the remnants of the treaty and payment grounds. A Mississinewa Valley flood control project is contemplated. The Salamonie River project has already caused the removal of five Indian cemeteries and has erased

[46] Information supplied by William F. Hale.
[47] Clyde Busey, Tribal Operations Officer, Muskogee, Oklahoma, to Martin E. Hale, South Bend, Indiana, March 8, 1968. Copy in author's possession. Also, Arthur C. Harker, attorney, Marion, Indiana, To William F. Hale, Eaton, Indiana, August 4, 1969. Copy of letter in author's possession.

many historic sites and small villages. However, the question of burying such "white" people as Frances Slocum in Indian cemeteries has been a troublesome one, and it is on such things that the old Miami band and racial antipathies still thrive.

10
THE MODERN MIAMIS

Membership in any Indian tribe has always had varying requirements. In past centuries, the Miami phratry, clan, and band systems, reinforced by council-fire decisions, enforced acceptable standards of membership. However, even then the various kinship systems created some variations, and not even the customary tribal ceremonies could eliminate every conflict concerning adoption. The Miamis recognized the system of adoption into the tribe, as well as that of voluntary withdrawal of groups or individuals. This did not, and does not today, clarify the position of the individual of undoubted Miami ancestry who by some circumstance is not considered a member of the tribe. However, such a person's dilemma can be understood if one accepts in their entirety both the Miami system and the position of the United States government.

The individual who seeks to prove his name belongs on a Miami tribal roll today faces a task at least as old as recorded history. The rules and requirements have changed, but the need to supply proof of membership has often been difficult.

A tribe is not only a social group; it is also a body politic whose right of self-rule in local matters the white man has recognized since the country began. Except as limited by federal law, a tribe has govern-

290

ing powers similar to those of a state or municipality. . . . Indian tribes are not States. They have a status higher than that of States. They are subordinate and dependent nations possessed of all powers as such only to the extent that they have been expressly required to surrender them to the superior sovereign, the United States. . . .[1]

Miami membership problems probably originated during prehistoric tribal schisms and are most clearly marked at the time of Wea and Piankeshaw separation. The Miamis' membership customs explain and justify the ejection of seventy-three people of undoubted Miami ancestry from the Indiana Miami roll in 1885 and the lack of dissension when the western Miamis added to their roll some of these same individuals who moved to the Indian Territory.

After the 1846 emigration, the Bureau of Indian Affairs in effect created two Miami councils and two Miami rolls; at the same time, it tried to consolidate all Miami transactions within one tribal organization, first in the Indian Territory, then at the Quapaw Agency, and finally in the federally chartered Miami Tribe of Oklahoma. Bureau policy was never completed because of Miami legal actions, which invariably reverted to earlier treaties involving Miami members who had not emigrated, and because of the Bureau's admission that membership in either part of the tribe could not be dictated by the Bureau, but only through each part of the tribe.

The Bureau's efforts were complicated by the reaction of the Miamis of Indiana to its efforts to add to their roll after that document had been approved by the Indiana leaders and the commissioner of Indian affairs in 1854. The Indiana Miamis were not in favor of two tribal organizations; nevertheless, they demanded a council of their own which might in some fashion serve the same functions and possess equal prestige with the council in the west. The Indiana Miamis remain in this dilemma; individuals have been adopted into the Oklahoma group, but the Indiana Miamis are unwilling to give up their identity and at times have contem-

---

[1] William A. Brophy and Sophie D. Aberle, M.D. (comps.), *The Indian: America's Unfinished Business*, 24, 33.

plated efforts to secure for themselves a federal charter. It seems doubtful that they can qualify for one, and they do not wish to place a barrier between themselves and their Oklahoma relatives, but a new and Bureau-approved roll compiled in 1968 may make the project more attractive.

The position of the Miamis who accepted the terms of the 1873 "Act to Abolish the Miami Tribe" and elected to leave the tribe is a controversial one. They shared in the sale of the Kansas reservation, and their names were then omitted from the Eel River Miami roll of 1889 and the western Miami roll of 1891. Their descendants have received no recognition in suits before the Indian Claims Commission since 1951 to adjudicate treaties made while their ancestors were members of the Miami tribe. The same situation exists for the descendants of the seventy-three persons removed from the Indiana roll in 1885; they will not share in the awards made to rectify the treaties of 1818 and 1854.

Although the Oklahoma Miamis have had full and equal U.S. and state citizenship for years, they still retain important legal affiliations with the federal government. As a tribe of the Quapaw Agency and a federally chartered entity, they can receive group or individual help and advice from the Bureau of Indian Affairs. The Indiana organization receives fewer services than the western Miamis, but even these are important when the Indians seek relief in the courts.

The western Miami council and the Miami Tribal Business Committee meet at the Quapaw Agency. Members of both organizations must be residents of Oklahoma, according to the tribe's constitution. Its corporate charter contains numerous provisions which end with the phrase "except with the express approval of the Secretary of the Interior." Leases, grazing permits, timber sales on tribal lands, the fixing of attorney fees, approval of contracts, distribution of corporate income, and even amendments to the constitution itself go to the Bureau of Indian Affairs for advice and approval.

"Review of corporate acts" and "supervisory powers" by the

Bureau were made mandatory for ten years. After that time, the secretary of the interior could propose an extension of these provisions, but the Miami council retained the power to terminate some federal services, even though the Bureau wished to retain such authority.[2]

The Quapaw Agency program report of 1944 described conditions there:

> . . . the Peorias and Miamis have no restricted trust lands, as their restrictions expired at the end of the 25 year trust period and were not renewed. . . . any program involving these two tribes of Indians would have to be based upon the acquisition of land. In view of the fact that these two tribes of Indians have been out from under Government supervision for the past 29 years, it does not seem fitting that a land-buying program should be undertaken for the group as a whole.
>
> These two tribes of Indians present no more of an Indian problem than the other tribes of the jurisdiction, and their living standards are just as high on an average as those of the other tribes. . . . we have assisted some members to get on the State Old Age Pension rolls, and we have rendered relief in a few individual cases. . . .[3]

The report included the Miamis among the agency tribes which had not secured quorums for any council meetings since the adoption of their constitutions. The situation undoubtedly changed when the Miamis filed their suits under the Indian Claims Commission Act, and the Indiana Miami meeting of March 30, 1968, was attended by hundreds of people.

Miami children attend the Ottawa County public schools unless, for various reasons, they are unable to do so. In these few cases, they are educated at the government boarding school at Wyandotte, Oklahoma.

> Indians [of the Agency] participate in general activities of the areas in which they live; attend public schools, are members of school boards,

[2] "Corporate Charter of the Miami Tribe of Oklahoma," a six-page pamphlet published by the Bureau of Indian Affairs.

[3] Program, Quapaw Indian Agency, Oklahoma," 31-page pamphlet issued by the Quapaw Indian Agency in March, 1944, p. 11.

participate in public elections, hold office, and their economic status runs from very low to very high.[4]

The degree of Indian blood has no significance to the question of whether or not the Quapaw Agency Indian is a ward of the agency.[5] The Miami tribe is the authority which determines its own membership. Most assistance given to individuals by the Bureau of Indian Affairs is similar to that rendered by state or federal agencies to non-Indians in other states. This is the case when Oklahoma Miamis live in other states, outside Quapaw Agency jurisdiction.[6]

The Indiana Miami organization, which is affiliated with the Long House League of North American Indians, receives much less federal assistance. The Indian Claims Commission, of course, has included them under its supervision of claims and attorney fees. The federal government has helped them to secure new cemetery sites and to move bodies located in old Indian burial grounds which will soon be inundated by water conservation projects on the Wabash Valley tributaries. The Tribal Operations Office at the Muskogee Area Office of the Bureau of Indian Affairs has been in charge of collecting and verifying the genealogical information required for participation in the 1966 Miami appropriations. This roll is designed to supply irrefutable proof of Miami descent for this group.

The Miamis were so reduced in number at the time of the 1846 emigration that they were virtually one family with divergent branches. This made the task of preserving oral genealogy records an easy one, and as in many families, it also made easier the preservation of family grudges, each branch preserving its stories of past injuries, scandals, failures, and successes. Claims litigation and land allotment cases continued to focus Miami attention on the past, and these legal actions became the vehicles for stories, true or false, of Miami events.

As one would expect, the Miami family (or national entity) has

[4] *Ibid.,* 19. [5] *Ibid.,* 23.
[6] *Ibid.,* Section 4, "Services Supplied by the Government," 15–17.

often produced its own critics. Individual Miamis point with wry pride to their ancestors' excesses and foibles. Their criticism of some attitudes of contemporary members contains less charitable viewpoints, especially when tribal membership formulas are at issue.

The last well-documented collection of Miami history, related by members of the tribe who remembered the period immediately after the War of 1812, the vicissitudes of the treaty years, and the emigration, first to the Osage Agency and then to the Quapaw Agency, was made between 1898 and 1900. Mrs. Mitchell (Allonzetah) died in 1898, and her estate was settled only after testimony was collected from many older Miamis in Indiana and at the agency. Once again, the confusing Miami kinship system became important, as did the multiple marriage unions, which were due in part to the high Miami mortality rate. Copies of these depositions must have been widely circulated, for they seem to be the sources of some of the most familiar Miami stories of today, including the return of the Thorntown Miamis to the Eel River villages, Miami concern for widows and orphans, the extended "visits," and especially the murder of Wapshingah, Mrs. Mitchell's uncle, by Majenica, "The Big Miami." The attorneys who collected the depositions necessarily were dependent upon the memories of the older Godfroys and of Kilsoquah, then nearly ninety, but after this time, such oral history could no longer be secured from contemporary accounts of old Miamis.[7]

The Miamis' attitude toward their national history seems securely fixed. It is one of pride in their place in past Indian history, combined with determination that their tribal existence must continue. Although the latter runs counter to the federal policy of gradual termination of tribal groups, the Miamis will probably be able to continue a tribal or corporate structure and seem in no danger of losing their pride in their past.

---

[7] Eleven pages of depositions collected by attorneys and supplied by D. W. Talbot, attorney, to Elmer S. Morris, attorney, Miami, Indian Territory, January 27, 1900. Copy of the original in the National Archives in the possession of Forest D. Olds.

One still hears tales of both the days of Miami greatness and the days of degradation, of past periods of discrimination against the Miamis' Indian origin, adopted religion, or cultural progress. Surprisingly, there are few complaints or protests about the laws which endowed them with U.S. citizenship. There seems to exist a combination of American national pride coupled with defensive responses which result from the long period of exploitation. The latter attitude is usually concerned with social, not economic, exploitation and is therefore more commonly encountered among the Indiana Miamis than among those in the west.

The Miamis who did not emigrate remained in territory they had once ruled. As expected, their Indiana past has survived in their oral history more tenaciously than in that of the western group. While constant visiting and individual emigrations have preserved its continuity with its Indiana history, the western group has had problems of survival which reinvigorated its tribal bonds. After 1867, the Quapaw Agency Miamis were again able to combine their own way of life with elements of white culture which they chose to assimilate—and at the leisurely pace so essential to Indian custom. They were reduced to less than one hundred individuals, but they were surrounded by other tribes in similar circumstances. Changes were made slowly. The agency became a refuge for Indiana Miamis who finally chose to live on the distant reservation rather than become part of a peculiar minority in the Wabash Valley. By 1942, the Quapaw Agency census showed a total of 305 western Miamis, but only 143 resided at the agency. They very sensibly placed in their charter the requirement that their officers should live in the agency in order to conduct the tribe's business with efficiency.[8]

The other seven Quapaw tribes, like the Miamis, obviously did not object to intermarriage with white people. By 1894, more than 2,500 whites lived on the reservation at the tribes' invitation. In the same year, no Negroes lived at the agency, although there were nearly 19,000 Negroes in the remainder of Indian Territory, oc-

[8] "Program, Quapaw Indian Agency, Oklahoma," p. 4.

cupied by the Five Civilized Tribes.[9] In 1940, only three western Miamis were considered fullblood Indians, while 254 were of less than one-quarter Indian blood.[10]

The Miamis at the agency were wealthy by Indian or white standards of the time, and at least five eastern Indiana Miami families made wisely calculated use of their funds with the connivance of the Quapaw tribe. They were adopted by the latter, which enabled them to buy desirable land from their new tribe without agency interference. It was on the tract purchased by the family of Mrs. Emma Gordon McBee of Miami, Oklahoma, that the first lead and zinc deposits were discovered in 1912. Some of the other tracts were also rich in minerals.

A sequel to these adoptions and purchases came later. When the Quapaw claims against the federal government were settled, the adopted members were excluded. However, their self-imposed alienation has been terminated and they have now been restored to their proper Indiana Miami roll and will share in subsequent claims awards.

Acquisition of marriage partners was a major problem for Indiana Miamis. As expected, Miami girls encountered the least difficulty in securing white or Indian mates. An Indian wife was more socially acceptable than an Indian husband in rural Indiana. A white husband also might be a more secure financial and conjugal partner than a young Miami man, whose virtues, while many, sometimes failed to include sobriety and industry.

Intermarriages produced children who were accepted by some Indiana communities but not by others. The children of white intermarriages with the first generation of offspring from Miami-white marriages usually bore only slight resemblances to their Indian relatives, and many ignored this heritage. In a fluid society, this could be further accomplished by changing places of residence. However, by the end of the first quarter of the twentieth century, a degree of Indian ancestry was esteemed in many Indiana com-

9 Schmeckebier, *Office of Indian Affairs,* 127.
10 "Program, Quapaw Indian Agency, Oklahoma," p. 4.

munities. At the same time, European national minorities were often established in small enclaves in Indiana, and to an increasing extent, Indian ancestry became a badge of distinction denoting the true "first Americans."

The extent of Miami-white intermarriage is illustrated by the list of people whose 1959 applications for Oklahoma Miami tribal membership were rejected. Of these thirty-two families, half the Miami men had white wives, while the same number of Miami women had white husbands. Applications made at this time were probably repetitions of previous attempts to gain enrollment, and they again failed to meet the constitutional requirements.[11]

The rebirth of pride in ancestry fostered a re-examination of Miami virtues. Long used as an excuse for failures or personal peculiarities, the expression "that is from my Indian heritage" is now used to explain interesting attitudes, personal accomplishments, and, above all, moderation or objectivity in reaching decisions. This interesting change of viewpoint reflects the passing of the "drunken Indian" stereotype from the Indiana experience. Even though caricatures of these pitiful products of the annuity payment and treaty days sometimes reappear in various fields of entertainment, the representations no longer touch upon tender consciences in Indiana. No present-day observer can be aroused by the righteous indignation which stirred John B. Dillon to mourn the Miamis in the 1840's, or by the sympathy and curiosity which placed Englishman George Winter on the Wabash to paint the remnants of its tribes. Otho Winger and other Indiana historians later preserved one chapter of Indian history as it unrolled before them, but they were eyewitnesses.

No modern historian can duplicate these feats. The Miamis in Indiana and other states have a peculiar heritage, as do all ethnic groups in America today. Indian history is better preserved through census rolls, government documents, and frequent special-feature

[11] "List of Applicants Submitted to the Miami Tribe of Oklahoma . . . Duly Voted on by the Miami Council at a Legal Meeting Held on 1 September 1959 and Were Rejected." Photostatic copy of the original supplied by Forest D. Olds.

articles in newspapers than is the history of most American ethnic groups. However, the dances, oral accounts of ancient religious practices and social customs, and genealogical labyrinths are of less interest to most Miamis of today than recollections of the part played by their tribe in the long struggle to preserve Amerindian sovereignty south of the Great Lakes.

While the latest census roll of the Indiana Miami is definitive— until another is compiled—certification on that document is only partial testimony that an individual is a Miami Indian, since it merely indicates his genealogical connection with the tribe. To me, tribal membership has seemed to be a state of mind, a confession of faith or act of public union, and certainly a declaration of pride in membership. Many Miamis have little genetic inheritance from their progenitors, but they are nevertheless Miamis. Even some individuals whose ancestors were removed from the tribe's census rolls in the nineteenth century try to maintain their Miami contacts and heritage, not to secure a share in financial gains, but from pride in their ethnic past.

The preservers of the Miamis' peculiar past seem anachronistic to some Americans. There is a flavor of pathos in an Indian council. However, a cynic may see the same pathetic picture duplicated by other groups. "Britannia Rules the Waves" and countless other examples can be cited to illustrate the futility of trying to recall an era that is gone forever. Many individuals whose ancestry is largely Indian have the same response toward efforts to preserve any aspect of their forebears' culture. To these people, a Cub Scout display of so-called Indian decorations and dances is not only pathetic, but seems insulting, a parody of a past or a racial distinction which should be forgotten.

When Forest D. Olds introduced himself at a Seneca ceremonial meeting in the 1960's, his status was assured: he was accepted and respected as a ranking member of a tribe of peers. William F. Hale assumed the role of host as an equal in a Long House League of North American Indians meeting at which delegations from the Creek, Cherokee, Sioux, and other far larger tribes were present.

The Miamis have long needed a new tribal hero, a man of unique qualities to place beside the ever present Little Turtle. Both white men and Indians agree this war chief was a dangerous enemy, a wise and eloquent diplomat and a loyal ally. He deserves to rank as one of the greatest Indians of historic times. The Miamis have seldom given deserved recognition to other men of nearly equal ability. In time, their oral traditions became copies of written reports by white men and reflect their opponents' values. Surviving legends extol the diplomatic venture of Little Turtle's father, Aquenackquah, who led his party out of the flat Indiana forests and over the wild Appalachian ranges to the Lancaster treaty council in 1748. All Miamis can repeat many stories of Jean Baptiste Richardville or Francis Godfroy, and the stories will either acclaim or criticize these chiefs, depending on the band allegiance of the speaker. Meshingomesia is also admired because he was able to avoid emigration, even though his father, Metocina, probably merited more praise. However, Little Turtle remains the Miamis' sole representative of national stature.

La Demoiselle deserves, but has not gained, the recognition from the Miamis which he has already received from historians. His influence on the French-English imperial struggle in the Ohio Valley continued after his death. If he had been able to maintain his village, the English might have driven a wedge between Louisiana and New France to the Mississippi River in the 1750's. Miamis today know little of this once important Piankeshaw chief. Other chiefs who seldom appear in their oral histories are Le Pied Froid, Little Face, and the two named Le Gris. The Le Gris called Dappled Fawn, Little Turtle's contemporary, was considered more important than the war chief by Henry Hay, and his personal qualities made him one of the powerful leaders of the Miami Confederacy.

Pacanne succeeded Le Gris after years of leadership in Indian frontier diplomacy and for a time was considered of national importance to the military leaders on the frontier. Chapine was the tribe's orator while Richardville was chief. Metocina's village became a rallying point for bands of many tribes which left the

Wabash-Maumee frontier, and his sons' reservation was granted as a reward or an apology for United States injuries to the old chief. All of these men were of at least statewide significance.

Although the Miamis have not produced individuals of national stature during the past century, the tribe has not suffered from a lack of national publicity, and individuals have become well known as Miami representatives in their own states or regions. The isolated little group at the Quapaw Agency and the dispersed fragments of the tribe seem to have adopted the ideals of thrift, industry, and *good citizenship* which the Bureau of Indian Affairs long tried to impose. This seems to be an extension of the philosophic virtues of common sense, pragmatic materialism, and courteous behavior which was often noted by so many white observers of the tribe.

Such virtues seldom accompany newsworthy individuals in literature, the arts, or political activities. They are ingredients of the solid citizen who occupies a place of respect and some honor in the community. The post-emigration period has produced many such persons, especially among the leaders or chiefs, who have persistently pressed the tribe's claims against the federal government. One of these, Forest D. Olds, can serve to illustrate or establish these generalizations.

The Yield, a Farmers Union Cooperative Marketing Association monthly magazine published in Kansas City, Missouri, in 1965 devoted a feature article to Olds's farm operations. The Chief operates a 900-acre farm a few miles from Miami, Oklahoma, where he raises soybeans, milo, wheat, corn, and oats. He also has a large hog and beef operation. He has been active in 4-H Club work, serves on various watershed and school boards, the board of directors of the Miami Co-op Association and the Farm Bureau, and the Metropolitan Planning Committee. He served from 1956 as second chief of the Miamis under Harley T. Palmer until he was first elected to a constitutional term of three years as chief in 1963. Before he became a farmer, Olds was a professional guitarist for seven years. These activities have not interfered with his constant and successful prosecution of Miami suits in the Court of Claims.[12]

Mention of Indian claims awards has ignited varied and violent emotional responses from Indiana audiences which I have addressed. On whatever grounds the opponents of such payments may base their objections or approval, they fail to comprehend that the federal government, like the British and French before it, has always been concerned with the welfare of the Indians, although its performance has never equaled its intent and its policies have seldom been the right ones.

Federal philanthropy in Amerindian affairs is not a recent political policy. The Confederation Ordinance of 1786 for the Regulation of Indian Affairs; Washington's Indian policies of 1791; the Indian superintendency system, followed by the Bureau of Indian Affairs; and innumerable statutes and executive orders have been more than lip service to the Indians' welfare. No one can discredit the sincerity or good will with which such men as George Washington or John C. Calhoun sought a proper Indian policy. In fact, there was probably no equitable policy which could effectively operate in the conquest of the Americas. The Indian treaties and annuity payments were given in the name of justice but are less defensible. Emigration was even less admirable, and the benefits it has brought to the Indians seem bought at a high price.

The financial appropriations now being made to various tribes at first seem futile, since they are given to rectify unjust acts which U.S. courts admit were committed a century or more in the past against people long dead.

It was probably impossible to negotiate equitable treaties from 1778 to 1870. In spite of official federal benevolence, no Senate would have ratified a treaty that penalized the federal government for the benefit of Indian tribes. At the same time, every Indian treaty penalized the political and cultural structure of the Indian party. However, there remains the legal fact that the treaties were

[12] *The Yield,* I, 4 (July, 1965), 50. Other Miami musicians were Simeon Geboe and Peter Lafalia, who toured Europe as members of the Barnum and Bailey Band.

made with tribes or political bodies, not with individual Indians, and the Indian Claims Commission findings seek to rectify injustices, no matter how far in the past, to tribes which still exist. Therefore, individual award recipients correctly feel no guilt or regrets at accepting such payments, since they are the present components of a continuing entity.

Among the Miamis, there is occasionally heard the suggestion that their bonds will loosen after the claims awards are completed. While this may well occur, other unifying forces appear able to replace this financial incentive. National Indian associations, Indian-orientated publications and periodicals, more frequent and colorful powwows, an increasing number of Indian employees in governmental fields, not just in the Bureau of Indian Affairs, and leaders in the fine arts develop an extratribal sense of pride in accomplishment. The sense of a common Indian heritage, as well as a Miami heritage, has emerged as a strong emotional bond.

Bibliography

FEDERAL GOVERNMENT DOCUMENTS

American State Papers: Documents, Legislative and Executive, of the Congress of the United States. 36 vols. Washington, 1832–61. Class II, *Indian Affairs.* 2 vols. 1832–34. Class V, *Military Affairs.* 7 vols. 1832–61.

Appeal No. 2–58. U.S. Court of Claims. Decided July 13, 1959.

Appeal No. 2–59. U.S. Court of Claims. Decided July 13, 1959.

Appeal No. 2–59. U.S. Court of Claims. Decided July 15, 1960.

Before the Indian Claims Commission. Decided September 17, 1956. Vol. 4, Ind. Cls. Comm.

Before the Indian Claims Commission: Amended and Additional Findings of Fact, 9 Ind. Cls. Comm. 1. June 30, 1960.

Before the Indian Claims Commission: Amended Petition Relating to Treaty of October 6, 1818. Docket 67. Filed August 9, 1951.

Before the Indian Claims Commission: Findings of Fact. March 26, 1954. Vol. 2, Ind. Cls. Comm.

Before the Indian Claims Commission: Findings of Fact. Decided March 26, 1954. In Docket 67 *et al.* 2-626-28.

Before the Indian Claims Commission: Findings of Fact. Decided July 14, 1958.

Before the Indian Claims Commission: Opinion of the Commission. Decided March 26, 1954. 2-636.

Before the Indian Claims Commission: Opinion of the Commission. Decided September 17, 1956. 4-399-405.

Before the Indian Claims Commission: Opinion of the Commission. Decided July 14, 1958. 6-513-51.

Before the Indian Claims Commission: Proposed Findings of Fact and Brief of Petitioners in Docket No. 67. December 14, 1952.

Before the Indian Claims Commission: Supplemental Findings. Decided September 17, 1956. 4-346-97.

"Constitution and By-Laws of the Miami Tribe of Oklahoma." Washington, Bureau of Indian Affairs, 1940.

"Corporate Charter of the Miami Tribe of Oklahoma." Washington, Bureau of Indian Affairs, 1940.

Ct. Cls., Congressional Case No. 1843; Pet. Ex. 207, Docket 251.

Ford, W. C., *et al.* (eds.). *Journals of the Continental Congress, 1774–1789.* 34 vols. Washington, 1904–37.

House Report 2503, 82 Cong., 2 sess. Washington, 1953.

Kappler, Charles J. (ed.). *Indian Affairs: Laws and Treaties.* 2 vols. Washington, Government Printing Office, 1904.

"Letter From the Secretary of the Interior." *House Executive Document 23*, 49 Cong., 1 sess. 12 vols. Washington, 1886.

Paul vs. *Chilsoque, 1895 (70F. 401).* St. Paul, West Publishing Company, 1960.

"Report of the Commissioner of Indian Affairs." *House Executive Document 23*, 49 Cong., 1 sess. Washington, 1886.

"Report of the Commissioner of Indian Affairs Made November 25, 1838." *Senate Document 1*, 25 Cong., 3 sess. 5 vols. Serial Nos. 338–342.

"Report of the Secretary of the Interior," in 5 vols. Vol II, Serial No. 3305–3307. *House Executive Documents*, 53 Cong., 3 sess. 35 vols.

"Report of the Secretary of the Interior." *House Executive Documents*, 50 Cong., 2 sess. 6 vols. Serial Nos. 2636–2641. Washington, 1886.

"Report of the Secretary of the Interior," in 5 vols., Serial Nos. 2933–2937. *House Executive Documents*, 52 Cong., 1 sess. 38 vols. Washington, 1892.

"Report of the Secretary of the Interior," in 5 vols., Serial Nos. 3305–3309. *House Executive Documents*, 53 Cong., 3 sess. 35 vols.

"Report of the Secretary of War." *Senate Document 164*, 26 Cong., 1 sess. 8 vols. Serial Nos. 354–361.

"Resolutions of the Legislature of Kansas, February 17, 1869." *Senate Miscellaneous Document 56,* 40 Cong., 3 sess. 2 vols.

Senate Document 1, 31 Cong., 1 sess. 14 vols. Serial Nos. 549–562. Washington, 1850.

Senate Miscellaneous Document 1, 53 Cong., 3 sess. 7 vols.

U.S. Bureau of Indian Affairs. Letters Received, 1824–1881, St. Louis Superintendency. National Archives. Microcopy K70, Ball State University Library.

————. *Miscellaneous Records.* Vol. XVIII.

————. Letters Received by the Office of Indian Affairs, 1824–1881. National Archives. Microcopy 234, Roll 416, contains "Miami Agency, 1824–1841, 1846–1850" and "Journal of a Negotiation at the Forks of the Wabash, October and November, 1833, by Messrs. G. B. Porter, J. F. Schermerhorn, and Wm. Marshall." Roll 417 contains "Miami Agency Reserves, 1838–1850." Roll 418 contains "Miami Agency Emigration, 1842–1853." Microfilm in Ball State University Library.

U.S. Statutes at Large. Stat. L., II, 139; Stat. L., VII, 74; Stat. L., VII, 209; Stat. L., VII, 307; Stat. L., VII, 582; Stat. L., IX, 395; Stat. L., X, 1082; Stat. L., X, 1093; Stat. L., XII, 793; Stat. L., XV, 513; Stat. L., XVI, 566; Stat. L., XVII, 631; Stat. L., XXII, 116; 2 Stat. L., 139; 4 Stat. L., 411; 12 Stat. L., 793; 15 Stat. L., 513; 16 Stat. L., 566; 24 Stat. L., 388; 26 Stat. L., 1000; 28 Stat. L., 903; 28 Stat. L., 909; 31 Stat., L., 344; 31 Stat. L., 1447; 34 Stat. L., 182; 34 Stat. L., 267; 36 Stat. L., 855; 43 Stat. L., 253; 48 Stat. L., 984; 49 Stat. L., 1967; 60 Stat. L., 1049; 9 Stat. 395; 10 Stat. 1093; 75 Stat. 747; 77 Stat. 43; 80 Stat. 909 (Public Law 89–659, 89th Congress, H.R. 7466, October 14, 1966).

STATE GOVERNMENT DOCUMENTS

Burns. *Annotated Indiana Statutes.* 12 vols. Indianapolis, Bobbs-Merrill Company, 1961.

Huntington County Circuit Court Order Book A-1. Huntington County Court House, March 1, 1835–March 25, 1843.

General Laws of Indiana, 25 Session of the General Assembly. Indianapolis, 1841.

General Laws of Indiana, 33 Session of the General Assembly. Indianapolis, 1849.

Bibliography

Laws of the State of Indiana, 13 Session of the General Assembly. Indianapolis, 1829.

Laws of the State of Indiana, 16 Session of the General Assembly. Indianapolis, 1832.

Terrell, W. H. H. *Report of the Adjutant General of Indiana.* 8 vols. Indianapolis, A. H. Connor, 1865–69.

West's Indiana Law Encyclopedia. Vol. XXIX. St. Paul, West Publishing Company, 1957.

Wollen, William Wesley, *et al.* (eds.) "Executive Journal of Indiana Territory, 1800–1816," *Indiana Historical Society Publications,* III (1900), No. 3.

Document Collections

Allen Hamilton Papers. Indiana State Library, Indianapolis.

Elmer S. Morris Papers. Miami County (Indiana) Museum. Deposition papers compiled by Elmer S. Morris in the Mitchell inheritance suit.

Ewing Papers. Indiana State Library, Indianapolis.

John Roche Papers. In possession of Bert Anson.

Miami Indian Papers. In possession of William F. Hale, Eaton, Indiana.

Miami Papers. Quapaw Agency Collection. Oklahoma Historical Society Library, Oklahoma City.

Miami Reserve Papers. College of Emporia Library, Emporia, Kansas.

Miami Tribe of Oklahoma Papers. In possession of Forest D. Olds, Miami, Oklahoma.

Thomas F. Richardville Papers. Miami Collection. Thomas Gilcrease Institute of American History and Art, Tulsa, Oklahoma.

Newspapers

Huntington Herald, Huntington, Indiana.

Huntington Herald-Press, Huntington, Indiana.

Indiana Centinel and Public Advertiser, Vincennes, Indiana, 1819–21.

La Cygne Journal, La Cygne, Kansas.

Dissertations and Theses

Anson, Bert. "The Fur Traders of Northern Indiana, 1796–1850." Unpublished Ph.D. dissertation, Indiana University, 1953.

307

Burford, Dora Eddie. "A History of the Indians Under the Quapaw Agency." Unpublished M.A. thesis, University of Oklahoma, 1932.

Smith, Dwight L. "Indian Land Cessions in the Old Northwest, 1795–1809." Unpublished Ph.D. dissertation, Indiana University, 1948.

Unger, Robert W. "Lewis Cass: Indian Superintendent of the Michigan Territory, 1813–1831." Unpublished Ph.D. dissertation, Ball State University, 1967.

Wehr, Paul W. "Treaty of Fort Finney, 1786: Prelude to the Indian Wars." Unpublished M.A. thesis, Miami University, Oxford, Ohio, 1958.

MISCELLANEOUS

Holiday, Murray. "The Battle of Mississinewa, 1812." Pamphlet of the Grant County (Indiana) Historical Society, 1964.

"Program, Quapaw Indian Agency, Oklahoma." Pamphlet issued by the Quapaw Indian Agency, March, 1944.

Prucha, Francis Paul. "Lewis Cass and American Indian Policy." Wayne State University Publication for the Detroit Historical Society, 1967.

"Thomas Morris' Diary," with Introduction by Howard H. Peckham, *The Old Fort News*, I (February, 1941). Publication of the Allen County-Fort Wayne Historical Society, Fort Wayne, Indiana.

The Yield, I, 4 (July, 1965).

BOOKS

Abel, Annie Heloise. *The American Indian As Participant in the Civil War*. Cleveland, The Arthur H. Clark Company, 1918.

———. *The History of Events Resulting in Indian Consolidation West of the Mississippi River. In Annual Report of the American Historical Association for the Year 1906*. 2 vols. Washington, 1908.

Alvord, Clarence Walworth. *The Illinois Country, 1673–1818*. Vol. I in *Illinois Historical Society Collections*. Chicago, A. C. McClurg & Co., 1920.

———. *Kaskaskia Records, 1778–1790*. Vol. V in *Collections of the Illinois State Historical Library*. Springfield. 1909.

———. *The Mississippi Valley in British Politics*. 2 vols. Cleveland, The Arthur H. Clark Company, 1917.

Alvord, Clarence Walworth, and Clarence Edwin Carter (eds.). *The Criti-

cal Period, 1763–1765. Vol. X in *Collections of the Illinois State Historical Library.* Springfield, 1915.

———. *The New Regime, 1765–1767.* Vol. XI in *Collections of the Illinois State Historical Library.* Springfield, 1916.

———. *Trade and Politics, 1767–1769.* Vol. XVI in *Collections of the Illinois State Historical Library.* Springfield, 1921.

Bailey, Kenneth P. *The Ohio Company of Virginia and the Westward Movement, 1748–1792.* Glendale, Calif., The Arthur H. Clark Company, 1939.

Barnhart, John D. *Valley of Democracy: The Frontier Versus the Plantation in the Ohio Valley, 1775–1818.* Bloomington, Indiana University Press, 1953.

——— (ed.) *Henry Hamilton and George Rogers Clark in the American Revolution, With the Unpublished Journal of Lieut. Gov. Henry Hamilton.* Crawfordsville, Indiana, R. E. Banta, 1951.

Bash, Frank Sumner. *History of Huntington County, Indiana,* 2 vols. Chicago, Lewis Publishing Company, 1914.

Billington, Ray Allen. *Westward Expansion: A History of the American Frontier,* New York, The Macmillan Company, 1967.

Blair, Emma Helen (ed.). *The Indian Tribes of the Upper Mississippi Valley and Region of the Great Lakes.* 2 vols. Cleveland, The Arthur H. Clark Company, 1911.

Boone, Richard G. *A History of Education in Indiana.* New York, D. A. Appleton and Company, 1892.

Bowen, B. F. *Biographical Memoirs of Huntington County, Indiana.* Chicago, B. F. Bowen Company, 1901.

Brice, Wallace A. *History of Fort Wayne from the Earliest Known Accounts of This Point to the Present Period.* Fort Wayne, Ind., D. W. Jones and Sons, 1868.

Brophy, William A., and Sophie D. Aberle, M.D. (comps.). *The Indian: America's Unfinished Business.* Norman, University of Oklahoma Press, 1966.

Buley, R. Carlyle. *The Old Northwest: Pioneer Period, 1815–1840.* 2 vols. Indianapolis, Indiana Historical Society, 1950.

Burnett, Jacob. *Notes on the Early Settlement of the Northwestern Territory.* Cincinnati, 1847.

Cass, Lewis. *Inquiries Respecting the History, Traditions, Languages,*

Manners, Customs, Religion, etc., of the Indians Living Within the United States. Detroit, 1823.

Charlevoix, Pierre François Xavier de. *History and General Description of New France.* Translated by John Gilmory Shea. 6 vols. New York, Francis P. Harper, 1900.

———. *Letters to the Dutchess of Lesdiguieres; Giving an Account of a Voyage to Canada.* London, R. Goadby, 1763.

Cist, Charles. *The Cincinnati Miscellany; or, Antiquities of the West, Compiled From the Western Advertiser.* 2 vols. Cincinnati, 1846.

Colden, Cadwallader. *The History of the Five Indian Nations of Canada.* 2 vols. New York, Allerton Book Company, 1922.

Crane, Verner W. *The Southern Frontier, 1670–1732.* Ann Arbor, University of Michigan Press, 1956.

De Vorsey, Louis, Jr. *The Indian Boundary in the Southern Colonies, 1763–1775.* Chapel Hill, University of North Carolina Press, 1966.

DeVoto, Bernard. *Across the Wide Missouri.* Boston, Houghton Mifflin Company, 1947.

———. *The Course of Empire.* Boston, Houghton Mifflin Company, 1952.

———. *The Year of Decision.* Boston, Little, Brown and Company, 1943.

Dillon, John B. *A History of Indiana From Its Earliest Exploration by Europeans to the Close of the Territorial Government in 1816.* Vol. II. Indianapolis, Bingham and Doughty, 1859.

Downes, Randolph C. *Council Fires on the Upper Ohio.* Pittsburgh, University of Pittsburgh Press, 1940.

Driver, Harold E. *Indians of North America.* Chicago, University of Chicago Press, 1961.

Dunn, Jacob Piatt. *True Indian Stories, With Glossary of Indiana Indian Names.* Indianapolis, Sentinel Printing Company, 1909.

Eavenson, Howard W. *Map Maker and Indian Traders: An Account of John Patten, Trader, Arctic Explorer, and Map Maker; Charles Swaine, Author, Trader, Public Official, and Arctic Explorer; Theodore Swaine Drage, Clerk, Trader and Anglican Priest.* Pittsburgh, University of Pittsburgh Press, 1949.

Esarey, Logan (ed.). *Messages and Letters of William Henry Harrison.* Vols. VII and IX in *Indiana Historical Collections.* Indianapolis, Indiana Historical Bureau, 1922.

Freeman, John E., and Murphy D. Smith (comps.). *A Guide to Manuscripts Relating to the American Indian in the Library of the American Philosophical Society.* Philadelphia, 1966.

Gipson, Lawrence Henry. *The British Empire Before the American Revolution.* 13 vols. New York, Alfred A. Knopf, 1956.

Griswold, Bert J. *The Pictorial History of Fort Wayne, Indiana.* 2 vols. Chicago, 1917.

―――― (ed.). *Fort Wayne, Gateway of the West, 1802–1813.* Vol. XV in *Indiana Historical Collections.* Indianapolis, Indiana Historical Bureau, 1927.

Hagan, William T. *Indian Police and Judges: Experiments in Acculturation and Control.* New Haven, Yale University Press, 1966.

Hamer, Philip M. (ed.). *A Guide to Archives and Manuscripts in the United States.* New Haven, Yale University Press, 1961.

Hanna, Charles A. *The Wilderness Trail; or, The Ventures and Adventures of the Pennsylvania Traders on the Allegheny Path.* 2 vols. New York, The Knickerbocker Press, 1911.

Harmon, George Dewey. *Sixty Years of Indian Affairs.* Chapel Hill, University of North Carolina Press, 1941.

Hill, Edward E. (comp.). *Preliminary Inventories of the National Archives of the United States, Records of the Bureau of Indian Affairs, Number 163.* 2 vols. Washington, General Services Administration, 1965.

Hill, Leonard U. *John Johnston and the Indians in the Land of the Three Miamis.* Columbus, Ohio, 1957.

Hodge, Frederick Webb (ed.). *Handbook of American Indians North of Mexico.* Bureau of American Ethnology *Bulletin 30.* 2 vols. Washington, Rowman and Littlefield, 1965.

Horne, Frank B., and Margaret F. Hurley (comps.). *Federal Indian Law.* Washington, Government Printing Office, 1958.

Horsman, Reginald. *The Causes of the War of 1812.* Philadelphia, University of Pennsylvania Press, 1962.

Hultkrantz, Ake. *Conceptions of the Soul Among North American Indians.* Stockholm, Caslon Press, 1953.

Hurlbert, Archer Butler, and William Nathaniel Schwarze (eds.). *David Zeisberger's History of the North American Indians.* Columbus, Ohio State Archaeological and Historical Society, 1910.

Hurlbut, Henry H. *Chicago Antiquities: Comprising Original Items and*

Relations, Letters, Extracts, and Notes Pertaining to Early Chicago. Chicago, 1881.

Hutchins, Thomas. *The Papers of Sir William Johnson.* Vol. X. Albany, 1951.

Hyde, George E. *Indians of the Woodlands: From Prehistoric Times to 1725.* Norman, University of Oklahoma Press, 1962.

James, James Alton. *The Life of George Rogers Clark.* Chicago, University of Chicago Press, 1928.

Journal and Indian Paintings of George Winter, 1837–1839, The. Chicago, The Lakeside Press, 1948. Special publication of the Indiana Historical Society.

Kaler, S. F., and R. H. Maring. *History of Whitley County, Indiana.* Chicago, B. F. Bowen and Company, 1907.

Kellogg, Louise Phelps. *The British Regime in Wisconsin and the Old Northwest.* Vol. II in *Publications of the State Historical Society of Wisconsin, Wisconsin History Series,* Madison, 1935.

———. *Early Narratives of the Northwest, 1634–1699.* New York, Charles Scribner's Sons, 1917. In J. Franklin Jameson (ed.), *Original Narratives of Early American History.* 19 vols. New York, 1906–1917. Reprinted New York, 1952.

———. *The French Regime in Wisconsin and the Northwest.* Madison, State Historical Society, 1925.

———. *Frontier Advance on the Upper Ohio, 1778–1779.* Madison, State Historical Society of Wisconsin, 1916.

——— (ed.). *Frontier Retreat on the Upper Ohio, 1779–1781.* Madison, State Historical Society of Wisconsin, 1917.

Kinietz, W. Vernon. *The Indians of the Western Great Lakes, 1615–1760.* Ann Arbor, University of Michigan Press, 1940.

——— (ed.). *Meearmeear Traditions, by C. C. Trowbridge.* Ann Arbor, University of Michigan Press, 1938.

Leup, Francis E. *The Indian and His Problem.* New York, Charles Scribner's Sons, 1910.

Lindley, Harlow. *Indiana As Seen by Early Travelers.* Vol. III in *Indiana Historical Collections.* Indianapolis, Indiana Historical Bureau, 1916.

Lossing, Benson J. *The Pictorial Field-Book of the War of 1812.* New York, Harper and Brothers, 1868.

McAfee, Robert B. *History of the Late War in the Western Country.* Bowling Green, Ohio, Historical Publications Company, 1919.

McAvoy, Thomas T. *The Catholic Church in Indiana, 1789–1834.* New York, Columbia University Press, 1940.

McClurg, Martha Una (ed.). *Miami Indian Stories Told by Chief Clarence Godfroy (Kapehpuah),* Winona Lake, Ind., Light and Life Press, 1961.

McCoy, Isaac. *History of the Baptist Indian Missions: Embracing Remarks on the Former and Present Condition of the Aboriginal Tribes, Their Settlement Within the Indian Territory and the Future Prospects.* Washington, 1840.

McCulloch, Hugh. *Men and Manners of Half a Century.* New York, 1888.

Manypenny, George W. *Our Indian Wards.* Cincinnati, Robert Clarke and Company, 1880.

Meginness, John F. *Biography of Frances Slocum, the Lost Sister of Wyoming.* Williamsport, Pa., Heller Bros. Printing House, 1891.

Michigan Pioneer and Historical Collections. 39 Vols. Lansing, 1874–1915.

Mohr, Walter H. *Federal Indian Relations, 1774–1788.* Philadelphia, University of Pennsylvania, 1933.

Mulkearn, Lois (ed.). *George Mercer Papers Relating to the Ohio Company of Virginia.* Pittsburgh, University of Pittsburgh Press, 1954.

O'Callaghan, E. B. (ed.). *Documents Relative to the Colonial History of the State of New York.* Albany, Weed, Parson and Company, 1855.

Parkman, Francis. *Count Frontenac and New France Under Louis XIV.* Vol. VIII in *France and England in North America.* 17 vols. Boston, Little, Brown and Company, 1907.

Peake, Ora Brooks. *A History of the United States Indian Factory System, 1795–1822.* Denver, Sage Books, 1954.

Pease, Theodore C., and Raymond C. Werner (eds.). *Collections of the Illinois State Historical Library,* 23, French Series, I (1934).

Peckham, Howard H. *Pontiac and the Indian Uprising.* Princeton, N. J., Princeton University Press, 1947.

—— (ed.). *George Croghan's Journal of His Trip to Detroit in 1767.* Ann Arbor, University of Michigan Press, 1939.

Pence, George, and Nellie C. Armstrong. *Indiana Boundaries: Territory, State and County.* Vol. XIX in *Indiana Historical Collections.* Indianapolis, Indiana Historical Society, 1933.

Philbrick, Francis S. *The Rise of the West, 1754–1830.* New York, Harper and Row, 1965.

Porter, Kenneth Wiggins. *John Jacob Astor*. 2 vols. Cambridge, Mass., Harvard University Press, 1931.

Prucha, Francis Paul. *American Indian Policy in the Formative Years: The Indian Trade and Intercourse Acts, 1770–1834*. Cambridge, Mass., Harvard University Press, 1962.

Quaife, Milo M. *Chicago and the Old Northwest, 1676–1835: A Study of the Evolution of the Northwestern Frontier, Together With a History of Fort Dearborn*. Chicago, University of Chicago Press, 1913.

———. *The Western Country in the 17th Century: The Memoirs of Antoine de La Mothe Cadillac and Pierre Liette*. New York, The Citadel Press, 1962.

Quimby, George Irving. *Indian Life in the Upper Great Lakes, 11,000 B.C. to A.D. 1800*. Chicago, University of Chicago Press, 1960.

Roosevelt, Theodore. *The Winning of the West: An Account of the Exploration and Settlement of Our Country From the Alleghanies to the Pacific*. 6 vols. New York, G. P. Putnam's Sons, 1889–96. New Library Edition, 6 vols. in 3. New York, 1889–1896.

Royce, Charles C. (comp.). *Indian Land Cessions in the United States: The Eighteenth Annual Report of the Bureau of American Ethnology, 1896–97*. Part II. Washington, 1899.

Schmeckebier, Lawrence F. *The Office of Indian Affairs: Its History, Activities and Organization*. No. 48 in *Service Monographs of the United States Government*. Baltimore, The Johns Hopkins Press, 1927.

Schmitt, Edmond J. P. *Records of the American Catholic Historical Society of Philadelphia*. Vol. XII. Philadelphia, 1901.

Schoolcraft, Henry Rowe. *Historical and Statistical Information Respecting the History, Condition, and Prospects of the Indian Tribes of the United States*. 6 parts. Philadelphia, Lippincott, Grambo and Company, 1851.

———. *Personal Memoirs of a Residence of Thirty Years With the Indian Tribes on the American Frontiers; With Brief Notices of Passing Events, Facts and Opinions, A.D. 1812 to A.D. 1842*. Philadelphia, Lippincott, Grambo and Company, 1851.

Slocum, Charles Elihu. *History of the Maumee River Basin: From the Earliest Account to Its Organization Into Counties*. Defiance, Ohio, Slocum, 1905.

Smith, Oliver H. *Early Indiana Trials and Sketches*. Cincinnati, More, Wilstach, Keys and Company, 1858.

Smith, William Henry. *Historical Account of Bouquet's Expedition Against the Ohio Indians in 1764.* Cincinnati, Robert Clarke and Company, 1907.

———. *The St. Clair Papers: The Life and Services of Arthur St. Clair.* 2 vols. Cincinnati, Robert Clarke and Company, 1882.

Sullivan, James, *et al.* (comps.). *The Papers of Sir William Johnson.* 13 vols. Albany, The University of the State of New York, 1921–62.

Swanton, John R. *The Indian Tribes of North America.* Bureau of American Ethnology *Bulletin 145.* Washington, Government Printing Office, 1953.

Thompson, Charles N. *Sons of the Wilderness: John and William Conner.* Vol. XII in *Indiana Historical Society Publications.* Indianapolis, Indiana Historical Society, 1937.

Thornbrough, Emma Lou. *The Negro in Indiana Before 1900.* Vol. XXXVII in *Indiana Historical Collections.* Indianapolis, Indiana Historical Bureau, 1958.

Thornbrough, Gayle (ed.). *Letterbook of the Indian Agency at Fort Wayne, 1809–1815.* Vol. XXI in *Indiana Historical Society Publications.* Indianapolis, Indiana Historical Society, 1961.

———. *Outpost on the Wabash, 1781–1791.* Vol. XIX in *Indiana Historical Society Publications.* Indianapolis, 1957.

Thwaites, Reuben Gold (ed.). *Early Western Travels, 1748–1846.* 32 vols. Cleveland, The Arthur H. Clark Company, 1904–1907.

———. *The French Regime in Wisconsin, 1634–1727.* Vols. XVI–XVIII in *Collections of the State Historical Society of Wisconsin.* Madison, 1902–1908.

———. *The Jesuit Relations and Allied Documents.* 73 vols. Cleveland, Burrows Brothers Company, 1896–1901.

Thwaites, Reuben Gold, and Louise Phelps Kellogg (eds.). *Documentary History of Dunmore's War, 1774.* Madison, Wisconsin Historical Society, 1905.

———. *Frontier Defense on the Upper Ohio.* Madison, Wisconsin Historical Society, 1912.

———. *The Revolution on the Upper Ohio, 1775–1777.* Madison, Wisconsin Historical Society, 1908.

Volney, Constantin F. S. *A View of the Soil and Climate of the United States of America; With Supplementary Remarks upon Florida; on the French Colonies on the Mississippi and Ohio, and in Canada; and on the Aboriginal Tribes of America.* Philadelphia, J. Conrad and Co., 1804.

Volweiler, Albert T. *George Croghan and the Westward Movement.* Cleveland, The Arthur H. Clark Company, 1926.

Walum Olum or Red Score: The Migration Legend of the Lenni Lenape or Delaware Indians. Chicago, The Lakeside Press, 1954. Special publication of the Indiana Historical Society.

Washburn, Wilcomb E. (ed.). *The Indian and the White Man.* New York University Press, 1964.

Wauchope, Robert. *Lost Tribes and Sunken Continents: Myth and Method in the Study of American Indians.* Chicago, University of Chicago Press, 1962.

Winger, Otho. *The Frances Slocum Trail.* North Manchester, Ind., *The News-Journal,* 1966.

———. *The Lost Sister Among the Miamis.* Elgin, Ill., The Elgin Press, 1936.

Wright, Muriel H. *A Guide to the Indian Tribes of Oklahoma.* Norman, University of Oklahoma Press, 1951.

Young, Calvin M. *Little Turtle (Meshekinnoquah), the Great Chief of the Miami Indian Nation.* Greenville, Ohio, 1917.

ARTICLES

Anson, Bert. "John Roche—Pioneer Irish Businessman," *Indiana Magazine of History,* LV (March, 1959), 47–58.

———. "Variations of the Indian Conflict: The Effects of the Emigrant Indian Removal Policy, 1830–1854," *Missouri Historical Review,* LVIV, 1 (October, 1964), 64–89.

Bald, F. Clever. "Colonel John Francis Hamtramck," *Indiana Magazine of History,* XLIV, 4 (December, 1948), 355–56.

Bushnell, David I. (ed.). "Journal of Samuel Montgomery," *Mississippi Valley Historical Review,* II (1915), 261–73.

Dean, John Candee (ed.). "The Journal of Thomas Dean," *Indiana Historical Society Publications,* VI (1918), 2, 273–345.

Dillon, John B. "The National Decline of the Miami Indians," *Indiana Historical Society Publications,* I (1897), 4, 121–43.

Dunn, Caroline, and Eleanor Dunn (transs.). "Indiana's First War," *Indiana Historical Society Publications,* VIII (1924), 2, 74–143.

"The Expeditions of Major-General Samuel Hopkins up the Wabash, 1812: The Letters of Captain Robert Hamilton," *Indiana Magazine of History,* XLIII, 4 (December, 1947), 393–402.

Helderman, Leonard C. "Danger on the Wabash: Vincennes Letters of 1786," *Indiana Magazine of History,* XXXIV, 4 (December, 1938), 455–67.

Horsman, Reginald. "Western War Aims, 1811–1812," *Indiana Magazine of History,* LIII, 1 (March, 1957), 1–18.

Jacobs, Wilbur R. "Presents to Indians Along the Frontiers in the Old Northwest, 1748–63," *Indiana Magazine of History,* XLIV (September, 1948), 245–56.

Krauskopf, Frances (ed.). "Ouiatanon Documents," *Indiana Historical Society Publications,* XVIII (1955), 2, 139–58.

Lasselle, Charles B. "The Old Indian Traders in Indiana," *Indiana Magazine of History,* II (1906), 1–13.

McAvoy, Thomas T. "Father Badin Comes to Notre Dame," *Indiana Magazine of History,* XXIX (1913), 7–16.

McGrene, Reginald C. (ed.). "William Clark's Journal of General Wayne's Campaign," *Mississippi Valley Historical Review,* I (1914), 418–44.

Parsons, Joseph A., Jr. "Civilizing the Indians in the Old Northwest," *Indiana Magazine of History,* LVI, 3 (September, 1960), 195–216.

Pease, Theodore C., and Ernestine Jenison (eds.). "Illinois on the Eve of the Seven Years War, 1747–1755," *Collections of the Illinois State Historical Library,* XXIX (1940), 23–31.

Phillips, Paul C. "Vincennes in Its Relation to French Colonial Policy," *Indiana Magazine of History,* XVII (1921), 311–37.

Quaife, Milo M. "Fort Wayne in 1790," *Indiana Historical Society Publications,* VII (1921), 7, 293–361.

Robertson, Nellie A. "John Hays and the Fort Wayne Indian Agency," *Indiana Magazine of History,* XXXIX, 3 (September, 1933), 221–36.

Rouse, Shelley D. "Colonel Dick Johnson's Choctaw Academy: A Forgotten Educational Experiment," *Ohio Archaeological and Historical Publications,* XXV (1916), 88–117.

Roy, Pierre-Georges. "Sieur de Vincennes Identified," *Indiana Historical Society Publications,* VII (1911), 1–130.

Setzler, Frank M. "Archeological Perspectives in the Northern Mississippi Valley," in *Essays in Historical Anthropology of North America,*

Published in Honor of John R. Swanton, in *Smithsonian Miscellaneous Collections,* Vol. 100, pp. 253–90. Washington, Smithsonian Institution, 1940.

Smith, Dwight L. (ed.). "From Greene Ville to Fallen Timbers: A Journal of the Wayne Campaign," *Indiana Historical Society Publications,* XVI (1952), 3.

————. "William Wells and the Indian Council of 1793," *Indiana Magazine of History,* LVI (1960), 3, 215–26.

Whickcar, J. W. "General Charles Scott and His March to Ouiatanon," *Indiana Magazine of History,* XXI, 1 (March, 1925), 90–99.

Index

319

326

The paper on which this book is printed bears the watermark of the University of Oklahoma Press and has an effective life of at least three hundred years.